THE COMPLETE

ILLUSTRATED GUIDE

TO

FISH

JACK POLLARD

All the varieties anglers are likely to encounter
Fully illustrated, including over 200 original paintings by Walter Stackpool

BANTAM BOOKS
SYDNEY • AUCKLAND • TORONTO • NEW YORK • LONDON

THE COMPLETE ILLUSTRATED GUIDE TO FISH
A BANTAM BOOK

First published in Australia and New Zealand in 1991 by Bantam

National Library of Australia

Cataloguing-in-Publication Entry

Pollard, Jack, 1926-
The complete illustrated guide to fish

Includes index.
ISBN 0 947189 86 6.

1. Fishing—Australia. 2. Fishes—Australia. I. Title.
II. Title: Fish directory.

799.10994

Bantam Books are published by

Transworld Publishers (Aust.) Pty Limited
15-25 Helles Avenue, Moorebank, NSW 2170

Transworld Publishers (NZ) Limited
Cnr Moselle and Waipareira Avenues, Henderson, Auckland

Transworld Publishers (UK) Limited
61-63 Uxbridge Road, Ealing London W5 5SA

Bantam Doubleday Dell Publishing Group Inc.
666 Fifth Avenue, New York New York 10103

Text and cover designed by Trevor Hood

Typeset by Midland Typesetters, Maryborough, Victoria
Printed by Dai Nippon Printing Company, Hong Kong

Cover photographs supplied by
International Photographic Library, North Sydney, NSW

CONTENTS

FOREWORD

Australia is indeed the lucky country in regard to the number of different fishes available to the fisherman. With more than 3600 separate species in over 300 families recorded from Australian waters, it is not surprising that such a variety of fishes end up in the fisherman's basket and on the dinner plate. Various families of fishes have different habits, living in different places and feeding on different kinds of animals and even plants. **The Complete Illustrated Guide to Fish** is about those two aspects of Australian fishes, how to fish for the various kinds of fishes based on their habits, and how to distinguish the most common species of Australian fishes.

The study of Australian fish taxonomy, the distinguishing, describing and naming of species, is more active now than at any time in the past. The number of fish species known from Australian waters has increased some 50% in the last 25 years. This increase is due in part to the recent exploration of unknown areas, deep sea fishing to 1500 metres in the search for commercial species like the orange roughy, and the use of scuba gear in deeper water and the northern portions of the Great Barrier Reef.

As well, there are more ichthyologists working in Australia than at any time in the past. Each state museum has at least one scientist working on fish taxonomy, the museums of Western Australia and the Northern Territory have two and the Australian Museum in Sydney has three, as well as taxonomists in some universities and CSIRO.

This increased activity has one aspect that some find frustrating or even irritating—the changing of scientific names and sometimes common names. For instance, recent studies have shown that a number of species found on both east and west coasts actually represent two separate species, one on each coast, often with an area somewhere on the south coast where neither species occurs. Such species pairs are now known to include the eastern and western wirrahs, the eastern and western blue gropers and the eastern and western foxfishes. Obviously one of each pair will require a new scientific name and in these cases two new common names, from common wirrah to eastern and western wirrahs.

Other name changes may result from studying relationships and finding two species are so closely related they should belong in the same genus (the first name of the two-part species name), or that two species thought distinct are really one, and the oldest name is the one that should be used. Name changes are frustrating, but they are necessary and indicative that study is advancing. One year, certainly beyond my time, we may have it all sorted out and no more name changes will occur. It will, however, be a longer time before all of Australia's fishes are discovered. The Australian Fishing Zone, defined by the 200-mile law of the sea convention, includes depths of more than 4000 metres, and many shallower areas have yet to be systematically surveyed.

Jack Pollard has distilled a large amount of material, in both original scientific papers and numerous more popular books on Australian fishes, in his attempt to prepare an up-to-date volume. His efforts are commendable. I believe he has been successful and **The Complete Illustrated Guide to Fish** will become a favourite of many fishermen as other Pollard fishing books have done.

Dr John Paxton, Curator of Fishes, Australian Museum, Sydney

INTRODUCTION

Australian fishermen are the luckiest in the world. They have a climate that allows them to go out on most days of the year, three of the world's largest oceans wash their shores, huge coral reefs and a network of inland and coastal rivers and big estuaries provide ideal fish breeding conditions, and there are thousands of kilometres of cliffs and beaches for specialists.

Periodically catches decline in some of these places. Pollution, the Japanese and Korean long-line fleets, subtle changes in water temperatures and currents, and other factors cause fishing hotspots to decline. But there is such a diversity of places to choose from sportsmen can usually find satisfying replacement spots. This is why fishing attracts all age groups, all religions, and both sexes, with adherents spread through every State who appreciate that there are no social barriers here, as there are in countries where land-holders inherit the exclusive right to fish large rivers and lakes. Australian anglers are judged by the fish they catch, not by the cost of their gear or by their financial status.

The notion that fishing is a sport for everybody is sustained by the remarkable variety of fish Australians can catch. More than 3,650 species have so far been identified in our waters. This book deals with the 650 that may appear in the average angler's lifetime. The remainder are deepwater varieties or fish so isolated in their habitat and lifestyle they are unlikely to be encountered by sportsmen.

Many of our best fishermen started when they were boys, learning the fundamentals from their fathers or grandparents. But it is never too late to start and a growing number of accomplished anglers are men and women who did not have time to take the sport seriously until they finished working. They appreciate the benefits of escaping from business pressures, enjoying the fresh air, and if they are lucky, topping off an outing with an appetising catch.

The wisest way to begin is to invest modestly in a handline attached to a spool or cork, a few hooks and sinkers, and a modest landing net, and then after you have learned how to keep the bait on the hook and the need for differing line strengths and hook sizes to graduate to a rod and reel.

By then you will have picked the form of fishing you find most rewarding and can start to look at special floats, sinkers, swivels, berley nets, and even boats.

LINES AND HANDCASTERS

The majority of lines, rods, sinkers and reels are still sold in Australia in imperial measures. This is because metrication has had less success in fishing than in any other sport, with anglers failing to accept the term "newton" when referring to their line strength. A newton is defined as "the force needed to accelerate a mass of one kilogram to one metre per second squared." The Metric Conversion Board told fishermen when the newton became law that 1 lb breaking strain equalled 4.44 newtons and 1 kg b/s equalled 9.80 N. But newtons proved unacceptable in tackle shops and to their customers. The lines came in from overseas in imperial measures and tackle shop managers complied with the law by attaching stickers to them converting the line breaking strengths to newtons which were quickly washed away or peeled off and completely failed to educate anglers.

LINE WINDERS AND CASTERS

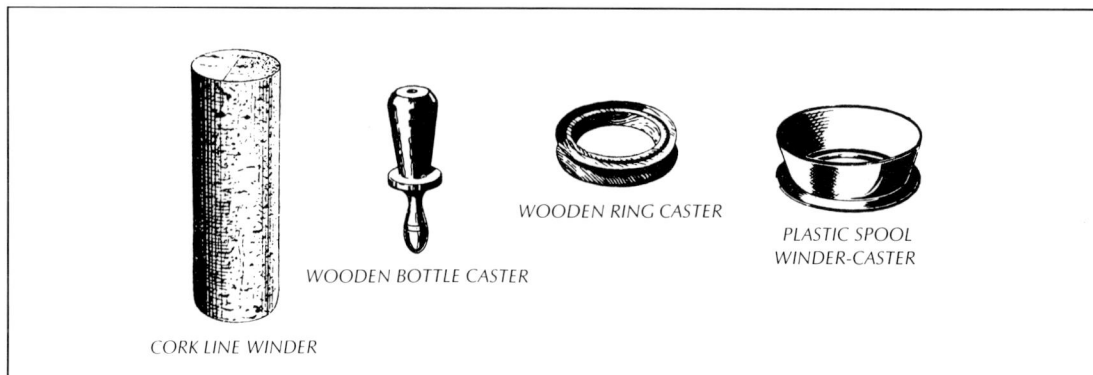

CORK LINE WINDER

WOODEN BOTTLE CASTER

WOODEN RING CASTER

PLASTIC SPOOL WINDER-CASTER

The Australian Sport Fishing Association has tried to overcome the problem by assessing national records in kilogram line strengths, but the majority of our fishermen still find it simpler to ask for lines in the tackle shops using pounds, not newtons.

Lines are less likely to kink or tangle if they are kept on a large plastic or wooden spool rather than on the traditional cork. The casters usually have a casting lip on them that allows the line to flow smoothly from the spool and improves casting accuracy both from the beach or from a boat. If you are casting regularly from a spool it is advisable to insert a small swivel a few metres from the hook to prevent a build-up of line twist.

Line winders have become increasingly popular over the past decade on deep-sea boats and are standard fittings on Barrier Reef charter boats. They are simply large reels, fitted to the gunwales of the boats, which provide easy handling and stowage, and at the same time eliminate any need for long lengths of line to be stretched out on the deck. If the line is held in the hand, a big fish can cause over-heating and burns to the angler's hands, a risk eliminated with fitted line-winders. When fishing with line attached to a cork or hand-held spool, heavy lines have to be used for big fish, whereas lighter lines and lighter sinkers can be used on line winders.

SINKERS IN COMMON USE

Sinkers should never be dismissed as merely a means of keeping lines and bait below the surface. A little care in their selection will take the hook to the intended spot, a task the bait alone cannot be relied on to achieve. A lot of amateur anglers make their own sinkers, seeking the shape and weight they want for various feats with their own moulds, filling old socks with their backyard products. The most popular sinkers in use in Australia are:

• *Ball* or *ball shot*: Small spherical sinkers with holes through the centre or split into halves that are pinched on to the line. Their disadvantage is that they damage or weaken the line at the spot where they are pressed into position and many experienced anglers prefer to wind small pieces of lead around the line.

• *Bean* and *barrel sinkers*: These are running sinkers ideal for estuary fishing, often used with pieces of matches to position them where needed.

• *Pyramid sinkers*: A pear-shaped model with a ring at one end, usually used to keep rigs involving more than one hook on or near the bottom.

• *Snapper lead*: The most popular sinker for deep-sea fishing or fishing from reefs, favoured by anglers seeking distance with their casts.

• *Channel lead*: A running sinker used to overcome running tides or currents, also known as "Picker's Doom". The bait is dropped or cast from the boat and allowed to drift to the required position. The sinker is then

SINKERS

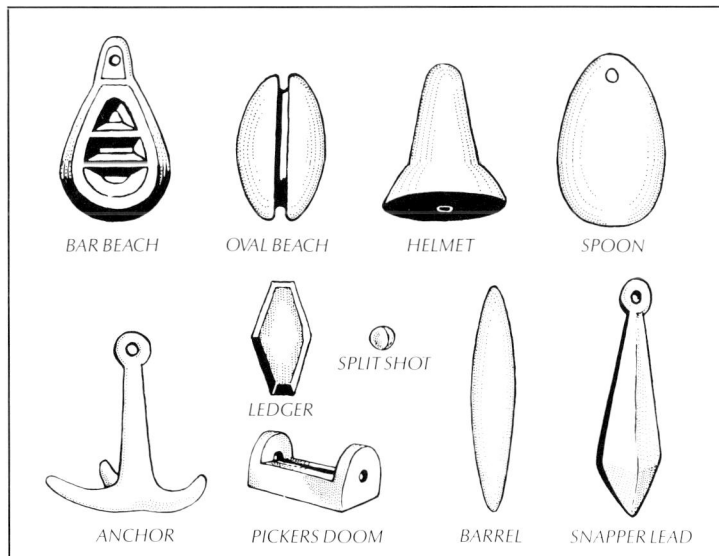

BAR BEACH   OVAL BEACH   HELMET   SPOON

LEDGER   SPLIT SHOT

ANCHOR   PICKERS DOOM   BARREL   SNAPPER LEAD

lowered into the water and runs down the line. This keeps the line deep, often with a long leader moving gently in the current. When the bait is taken the line is free to run through the sinker.

POPULAR HOOKS AND THEIR ROLE

PARTS OF A HOOK

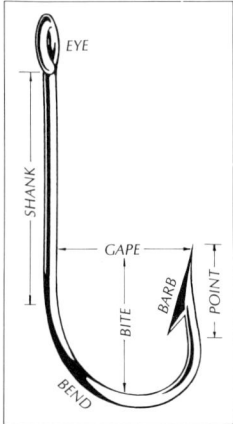

The skill with which anglers select their hooks for various types of fishing, from the hundreds of available hooks and hook patterns, has an important influence on success or failure. They should consider the size of the fish they are seeking, its feeding habits, the shape of its mouth and teeth, the bait being used, the water being fished, and the ability of the target fish to make a run when hooked. The parts of the hook such as the point, barb, bend, shank, eye, gape and bite all have a bearing on the final choice.

HOOK CHART

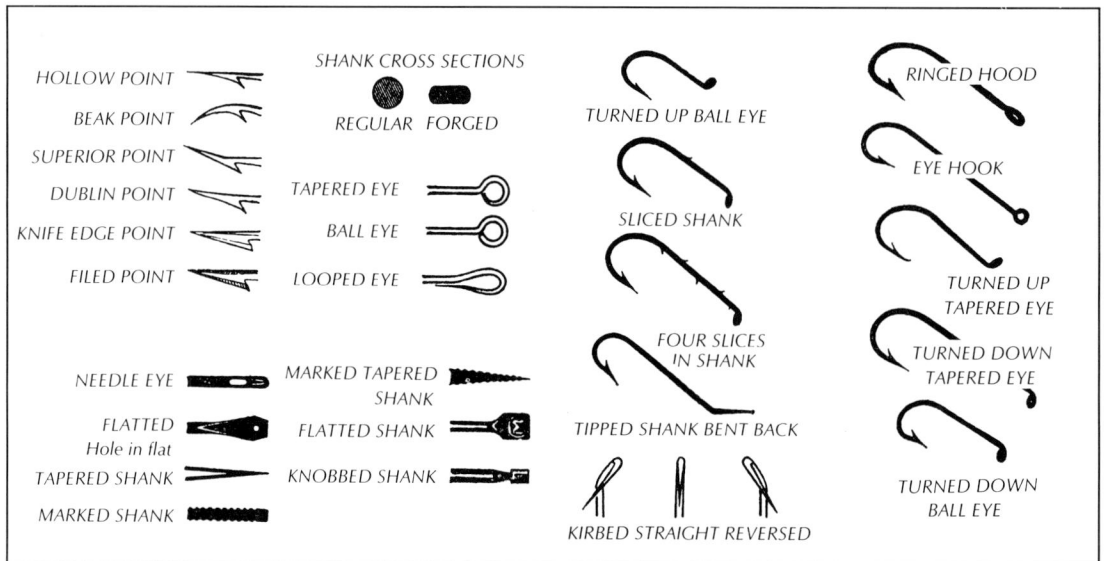

Before World War II much of the development in fish hooks centred around the little English town of Redditch, from which brand names like Millward, Allcock, Sealey and James emerged. Redditch was heavily bombed during the war, often taking bombs intended for nearby Coventry, so for almost 30 years after the war English hooks were seldom seen in Australia. In this period, the Norwegian company, Mustad & Son, based in Oslo, became the world's leading producer of fish hooks, offering more than 6,000 patterns to a world market. No wholesaler or dealer could carry Mustad's entire range but they were able to build an enormous business stocking the types of hooks popular in major fishing towns. Mustad's lead has now been challenged by English hooks, such as the Shakespeare-Allcock brand of stainless steel hooks, and a range from Sealey. The result is that Australians now enjoy a range of hooks superior to any in the world.

A few minutes spent studying hook charts will pay big dividends, and it pays to ask questions of salesmen about the performance of the hooks you propose to buy. There are around a dozen popular types to familiarise yourself with: Kirby, Kendal Kirby, French, Viking, Beak, Snecked, Suicide, Carlisle, Limerick, O'Shaughnessy, Tuna and Sea hooks. These will satisfy your needs for most saltwater and inland fishing, bearing in mind that special hooks are needed for game fish, trout and sharks.

SELECTING RODS AND REELS

Australia's sportsfishermen have seen a big swing recently towards tackle that exploits graphite and other types of material originally invented for space flight. Graphite rods or a mixture of graphite and plastic have proved lighter and stronger than fibreglass and tackle shops have simply followed the trend evident with tennis rackets and switched to graphite. Threadline reels with corrosion-free graphite spools are popular, and most of the fly rods sold today are made of graphite, which offers more accurate casting and greater strength in the rods themselves, notably in the rod tips.

As a general rule, novices should avoid telescopic rods, which feature sections that slide into one another. Their ease of storage and transportation is obvious but they continually break down and completely lack the touch or feel that needs to be encouraged when you are mastering basic skills. The only justification for them is that they sometimes allow their owners to fish in exotic locations that can only be reached carrying haversacks.

ROD HANDLES

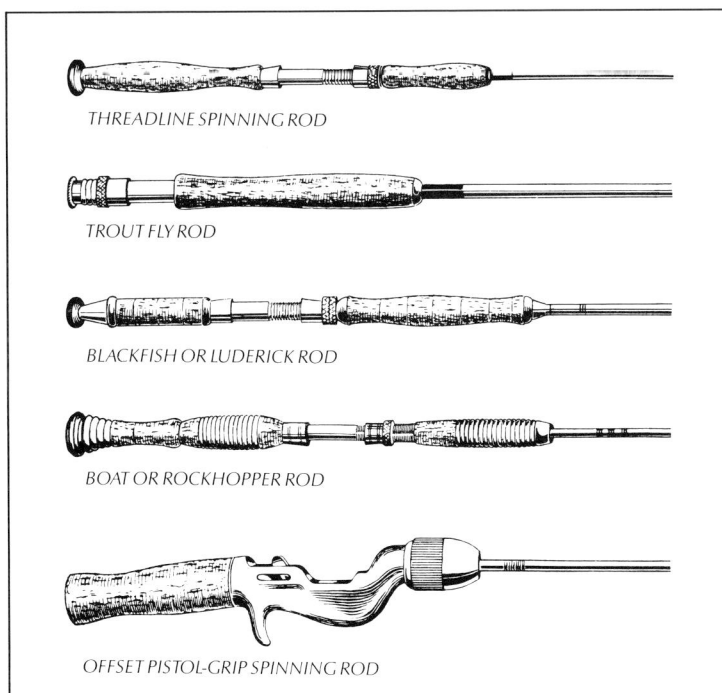

THREADLINE SPINNING ROD

TROUT FLY ROD

BLACKFISH OR LUDERICK ROD

BOAT OR ROCKHOPPER ROD

OFFSET PISTOL-GRIP SPINNING ROD

The angler's first priority should be to buy a rod that will endure frequent use. Over the past decade cane rods have given way to fibreglass, solid and hollow, to graphite and carbon fibre, and more recently to Boron and Kevlar, and to composites of all of these. The next decade undoubtedly will produce a similar flourish of new materials accompanied by extravagant claims about their performance. The wise course is to stay with proven products until the new rods prove themselves.

Sticking with a proven material, select a rod that suits the particular style of fishing you have in mind. Rods made to use with baitcaster and closed-faced reels, for example, usually are fitted with special trigger-grip handles, which do not function well with other styles of reel. There is no such thing as an all-purpose rod. The way in which the rod bends under the weight of a good fish and the shape of its curve when bent is called the rod's "action", which is determined by factors such as the rod's thickness and the spacing and number of runners. For beginners, a rod with "medium" taper and "medium" action is suggested.

The most popular Australian reels are the centrepin reel, the sidecast reel, the threadline or fixed-spool reel, the closed-face or push-button reel, the baitcasting reel and its big brother, the multiplying surf reel. Reels for trout fishing are in a specialised category of their own.

For novices, the threadline reel is by far the best choice. It is always mounted on the rod and performs several tasks simultaneously. Before casting, the angler holds the rod with the index finger holding the line against the rod. He then moves the bail-arm across the face of the spool until it locks in the open position. To cast, the rod is raised above the shoulder, with the free-running line trapped against the foregrip by the index finger. Bring the rod forward sharply with a jerking, snapping motion and at the ten o'clock

POPULAR OLD AND NEW REELS

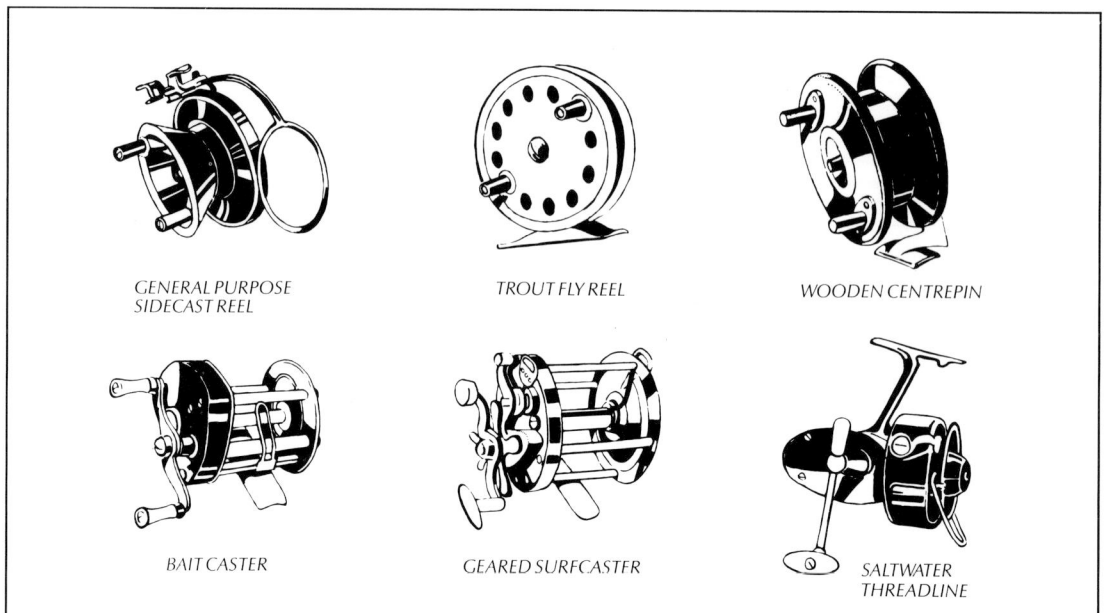

GENERAL PURPOSE SIDECAST REEL

TROUT FLY REEL

WOODEN CENTREPIN

BAIT CASTER

GEARED SURFCASTER

SALTWATER THREADLINE

position release the line held by the index finger. To retrieve, simply wind the reel handle in an anti-clockwise direction. The handle in turn rotates a main gear in mesh with a pinion gear and as the rotating head revolves, it carries the line pick-up assembly with it, traps the line, and winds it round the spool, automatically cross-laying the line on the spool.

The closed-face reel is fitted on top of the rod and many consider it easier to operate than the threadline reel. The spool and the mechanism are totally enclosed, with a small circular hole in the centre of the cone covering the spool through which the line passes. By using a pistol grip, the push button on the closed-face reel drops to just the right height for the thumb. When the thumb holds the button down, pins on the pick-up head trap the line against the lip of the winding cup until the angler wants it released. When the cast is finished, the fisherman turns the handle to re-engage or extend the pick-up pins which then trap and hold the line. The pins must be examined regularly if used continually.

Since World War II sidecast reels have made dramatic advances in popularity largely because of the activities of the Alvey company. Queensland anglers favour the sidecast reel almost to a man and there is no doubting these reels' efficiency, used with matching rods, in casting baits precisely to the target area. The sidecast reel on which the spool can be rotated or turned through 90 degrees offers the direct drive and sensitivity of a centrepin

CASTING WITH A THREADLINE REEL

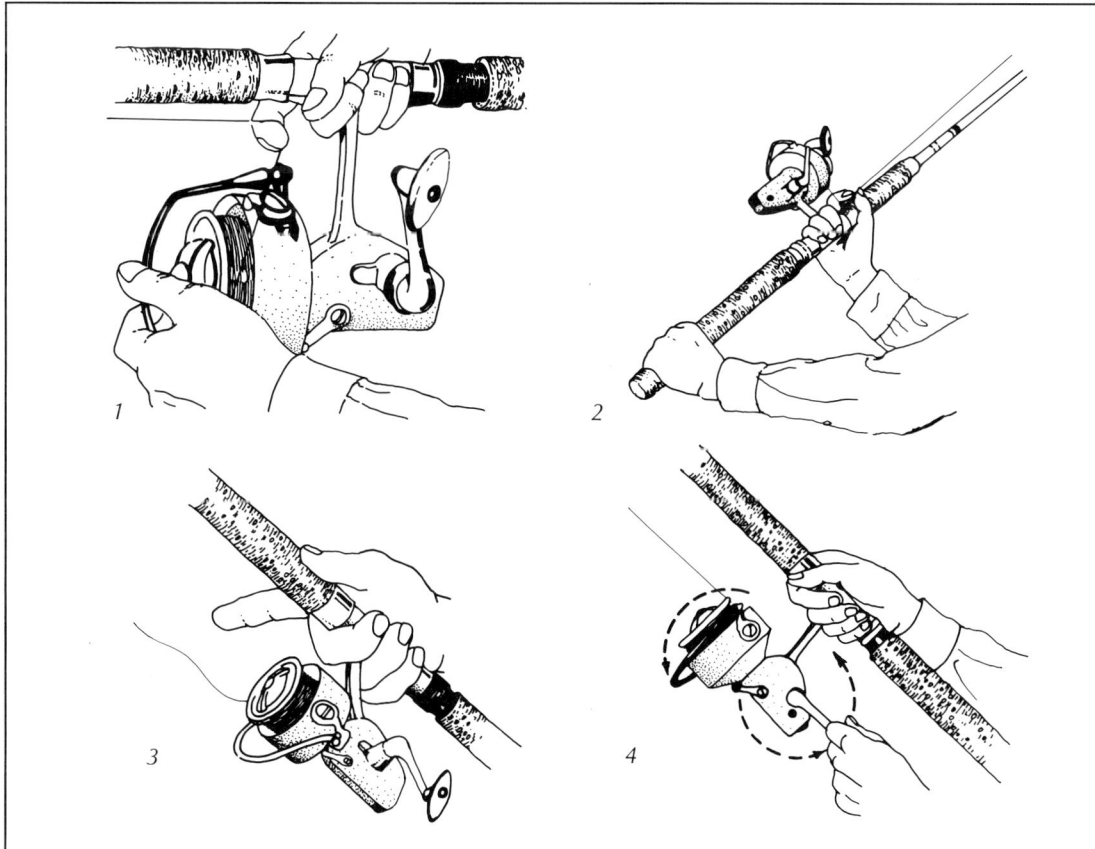

CASTING WITH A CLOSED-FACE REEL

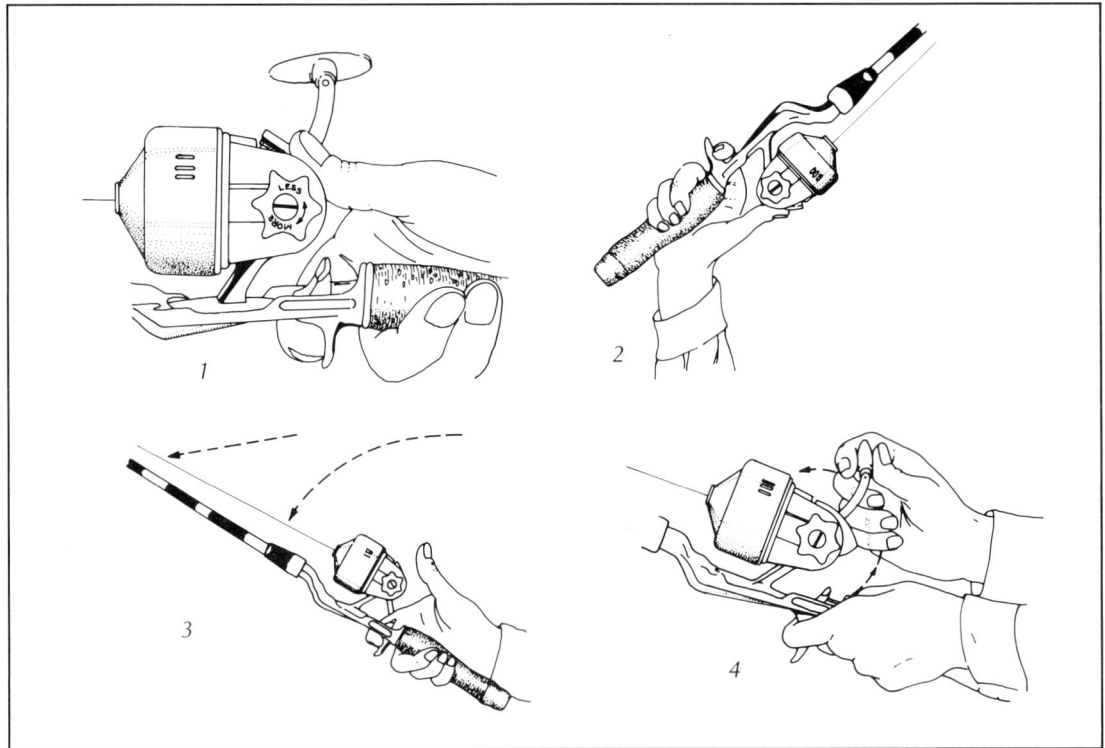

reel plus the easy casting capabilities of a threadline reel. But they have a relatively slow retrieval speed and can cause unwanted line twist when the spool is rotated and re-aligned. This is why Alvey offer them with gears. Queenslanders overcome twist problems by using small swivels on all their rigs.

Considering all the facts involved, the aspiring sportsfisherman probably is wisest to learn on a threadline or centrepin reel before moving to sidecast or surf-casting and bait-casting reels.

KNOTS FOR SPORTSFISHERMEN

Nylon is a peculiar material, difficult to tie securely, on which incorrect knots have a tendency to creep and curl back on themselves and cause frequent breakages. Newcomers should concentrate on mastering the knots that take care of the basic tasks, such as joining or mending a line, and attaching hooks, rings or swivels. Books of more than 1000 pages showing how to tie specialist knots are available in our libraries if the beginners want to further their knowledge of knots.

Joining Lines: The blood knot stands supreme for this purpose, but a fine line with a breaking strain under 6 kg should be tied with four turns on each side. Heavier lines must be tied with three turns on each side. The turns should be carefully laid, with the ends pulled up evenly until the knot

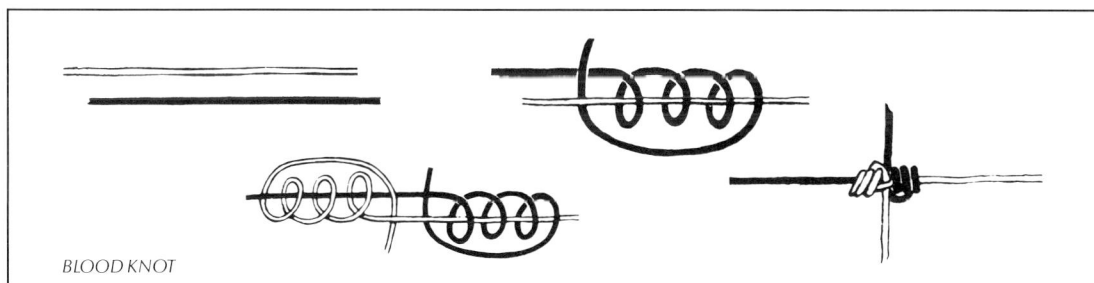

BLOOD KNOT

is firmly tied. The ends can then be cut off flush with the knot without risk of them slipping through. The three half-turn blood knot is clearly the best for attaching nylon line to a wire ring.

The most effective method of attaching line to a hook is to use the snood knot, the traditional technique. Snooding a hook to a line or cast is a simple procedure, and many fine-line breaming buffs are capable of executing it again and again in the dark without error. But it is tedious to explain and many novices do not have the patience to stay with it until they master the snood.

To tie this knot, start by laying the end of the line along the shank of the hook and then forming a large loop in front of it as shown by figure 1 in our diagram. Near the flat or eye of the hook, double a portion of the back of this loop, as at figure 2, to provide a compact grip for the thumb and finger. The hook and the three strands of line are then firmly gripped by the thumb and forefinger of the left hand as shown in figure 3. Now roll the bottom strand around the shank of the hook and the other two strands. This is achieved by placing the forefinger of the right hand in the end of the loop. Next swing the end of the loop up above the hook and turn the wrist so that the ball of the finger comes uppermost. This puts a half twist in the two strands of the loop and causes them to cross near the point of the thumb. Then lower the finger so that the bend and barb of the hook passes through the loop. Finally rotate the finger so that the ball is turned downwards, thus introducing another half twist and crossing the strands over. This completes the first turn and additional turns are added by repeating the process. Four, five or six more turns may be wound on in this manner, depending on whether the line is coarse or fine.

As each turn is added, the second finger of the left hand (the holding hand) clamps down on it to prevent it springing, as the right hand pulls it in underneath. When the required number of turns are made, the snood is closed as in figure 5 by first pulling back the standing line to take up the loop. Some twist should be seen being carried back through the knot as the loop closes. Care must be taken to ensure that in the final stage the loop does not slip in under the free end of the line, to get between it and the shank. Before the snood is finally pulled quite tight, it should be worked back into its proper position against the flat on the shank as in figure 6. Where a turned-up or turned-down eye is involved, the snood should be turned until the line is pulling directly through it.

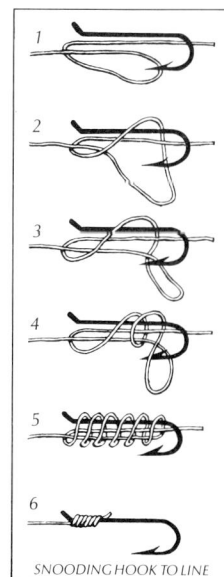

SNOODING HOOK TO LINE

Rings, Swivels and Floats

Anglers basically use two types of rings, split rings and brass rings and both are usually sold in a range of sizes in packets of a dozen or more. Split rings are mainly used for hanging hooks to lures and are made of brass, stainless steel or chromed steel. Solid brass rings are essential in some rigs.

Swivels are used primarily to reduce line twist and generally are over-rated by novices. The secret is to use the smallest swivel size suited to the line to ensure they spin or swivel as intended. But the angler must be sure the small swivel will be equal to the strain. Generally speaking, box swivels are stronger than barrel types of similar size.

Floats have the job of suspending the bait at a predetermined depth below the surface and to provide an immediate sign of a bite, but it is remarkable how often these basic requirements are forgotten when novices confront the huge array of floats in our tackle shops. One English fishing writer commented that floats catch more anglers than fish, for there is little doubt that many fishermen become "float happy". The basic rule in selecting floats should be that its weight is consistent with the distance it has to be cast and that it should not lessen the chances of the fish taking the bait.

POPULAR FLOATS

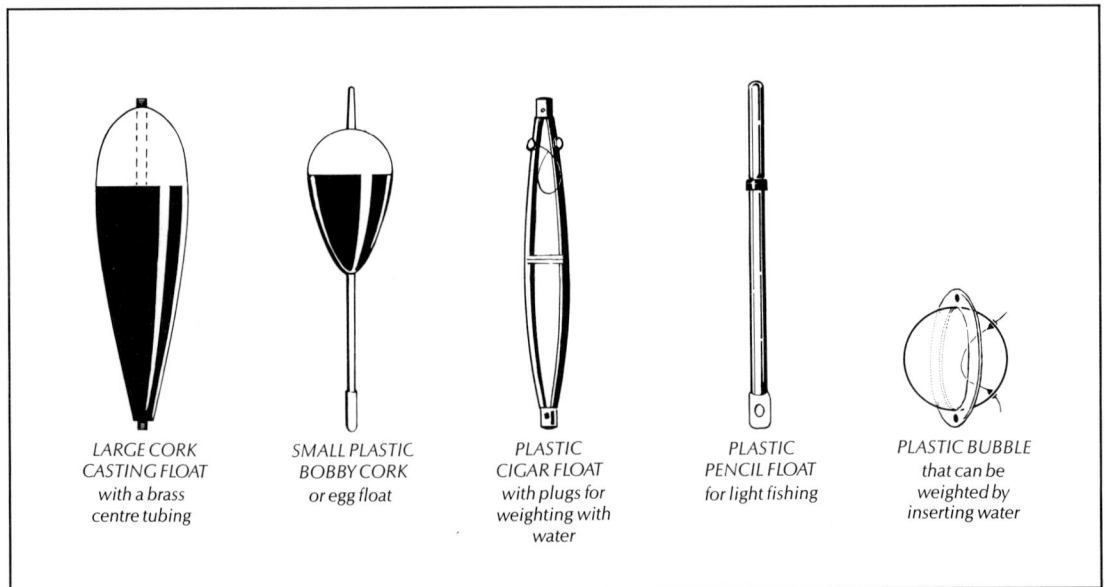

LARGE CORK CASTING FLOAT with a brass centre tubing

SMALL PLASTIC BOBBY CORK or egg float

PLASTIC CIGAR FLOAT with plugs for weighting with water

PLASTIC PENCIL FLOAT for light fishing

PLASTIC BUBBLE that can be weighted by inserting water

SWIVELS

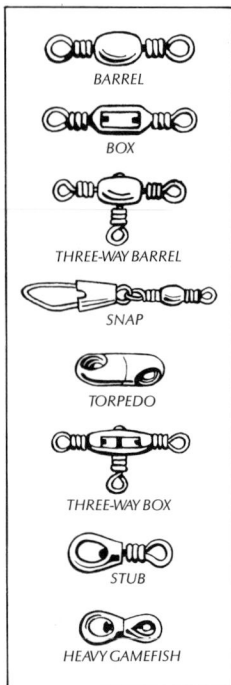

BARREL

BOX

THREE-WAY BARREL

SNAP

TORPEDO

THREE-WAY BOX

STUB

HEAVY GAMEFISH

The most popular floats are the quill or pencil type which are used fishing from boats in estuaries, and are considered ideal for bream, small garfish, luderick and yellowtail; weighted casting floats for rough conditions and strong winds, streamlined to offer the least possible drag in the water when the bait is taken; bobby corks, which are really stemless floats, and effectively cope with live baits or in casting up to 60 metres from the rocks with geared sidecast reels; plastic bubble floats, which can be weighted by inserting water; and cigar floats for use with plugs that can be weighted with water.

LANDING NETS AND GAFFS

A suitable landing net is essential for most forms of successful fishing. The idea is to select a net that will suit its workplace. A long-handled net, for example, is required for fishing from ocean rocks or when working seawalls or jetties, whereas rounded, short-handled nets are better for boat fishing for bream or luderick. Fishing for snapper it is always advisable to use a net to lift out larger fish and this means a net handle about a metre and a half long.

Only fish that cannot conveniently be retrieved in a net should be gaffed. Home-made light gaff hooks attached to a broomstick are useful for small fish. For heavier, more active fish that require deeper penetration, most tackle shops offer a wide range of strong gaffs. A long-handled gaff is essential for fishing in northern Australian waters, where large groper, sawfish and sharks cannot be landed without it.

SELECTING THE RIGHT BAIT

The essential factor in presenting a bait that will work to the fish is to ensure that it is fresh. Some fish are highly selective and will only approach one or two baits. They prefer bait that is as fresh as they can get it, and often will be tempted by live bait but scorn fillets and fish pieces. Thus it is a prime requirement to carry bait in an ice box or refrigerator, tightly sealed in a polythene bag so that it will not contaminate food.

Most beginners buy their bait from fish shops but as their skill improves they accept the challenge by collecting their own bait. This not only reduces the cost of a fishing outing but guarantees that the bait will be fresh. Bait buckets that can be worn on a belt or carried in a boat are handy, and aerators operated by batteries that keep the bait fish alive are becoming increasingly popular. Live bait anglers usually prefer to use a bait tank on their boats rather than a bucket as the bait fish live longer in the tanks, particularly if they are fed with submerged pumps.

Prawns—By far the most popular of all fishing baits, relished by most saltwater fish, but very difficult to keep fresh. It's far better to chop up stale prawns for berley than to try and rejuvenate them. They should be snap-frozen while still fresh or they will become spongy and discolored. Live prawns are a deadly bait for many fish, and it pays to collect them before the fishing outing and keep them alive in a tin of saltwater or in a bag of wet weed. The prawn looks more lifelike to the fish if the hook is passed through the tip of the tail from above and brought through the butt from beneath so that it lies straight along the shank.

Weed and Cabagge—Although weed can be bought at baitshops it is best collected fresh from the rocks where it grows. The trick is to drape the weed over the hook so that it fluffs out in the water but stays on. Use four or five strands a few centimetres long. Hold a couple of centimetres of it along the hook shank, with the hook vertical. Twist the other end of it around

METHODS OF BAITING

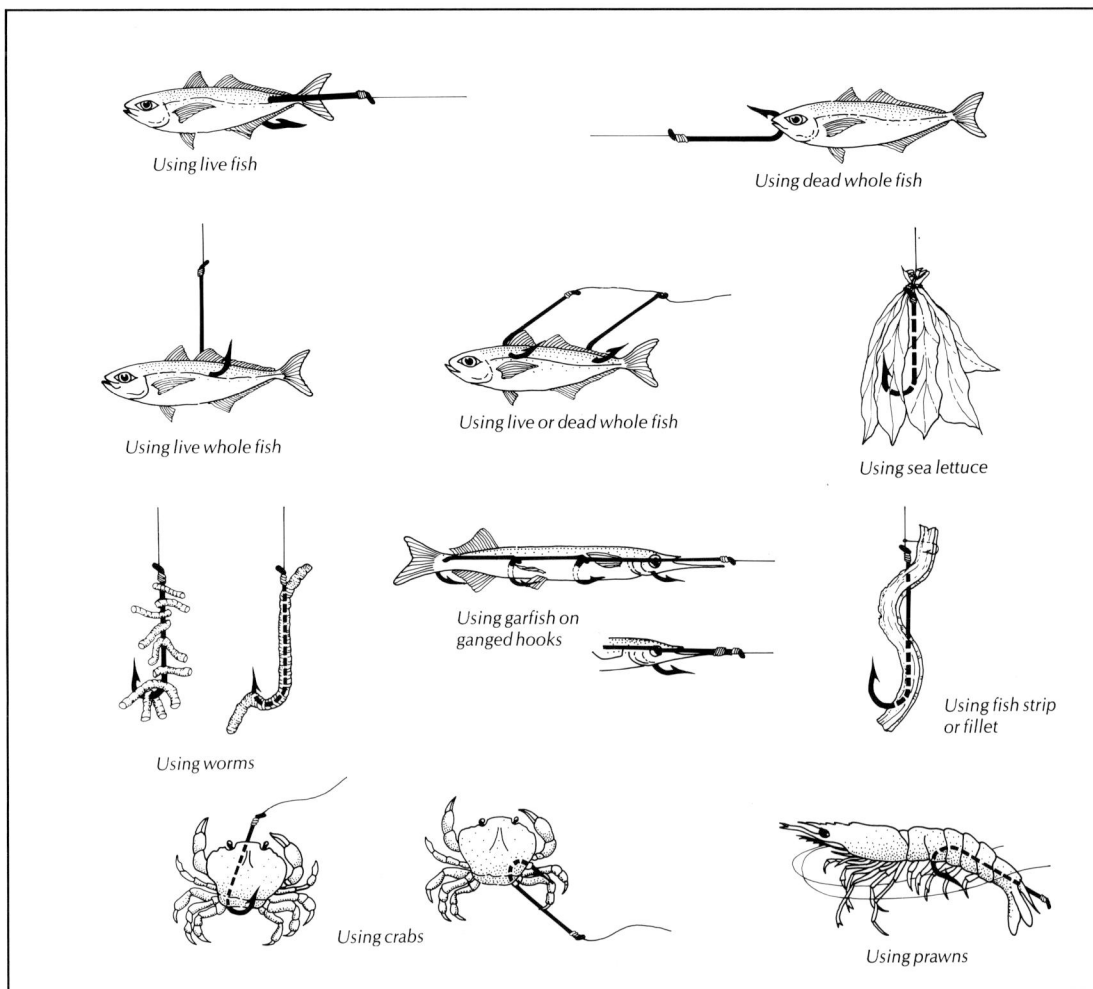

Using live fish

Using dead whole fish

Using live whole fish

Using live or dead whole fish

Using sea lettuce

Using worms

Using garfish on ganged hooks

Using fish strip or fillet

Using crabs

Using prawns

the line three or four times above the eye or the flat of the hook and continue twisting it down the shank of the hook to the bend. Finally, nip off the trailing ends after passing them over the point of the hook.

Pipis—Bivalve molluscs that occur in large quantities in the sand under the surf on most Australian beaches. They are easily gathered by digging with the feet in the sand until a large shell is felt, but often they are exposed by receding waves. Cracked out of their shells they make an appealing bait for whiting, salmon, bream, flathead, and in bobby-corking from ocean rocks are attractive to trevally, red bream, parrot fish, and dart.

Cunje and *crabs*—Cunjevoi are large, leathery molluscs that grow on ocean rocks between high and low tide levels. When disturbed, they squirt out streams of water. They are gathered by tearing them from the rocks with cunje hooks or simply by knocking them off with a tomahawk. They are bait par excellence and the only really reliable bait for silver drummer or rock blackfish. Most of the crabs found along the Australian coastline, in rivers and waterholes, provide good bait. Ghost crabs, sand crabs, soldier crabs and hermit crabs are at their best as bait if they are found with soft shells after moulting.

Yabbies, nippers and *worms*—Yabbies can be collected by sucking them out of the sand with a yabby pump. They are kept alive in a can of saltwater and are an excellent bait. The freshwater variety are crayfish that inhabit waterholes, dams and bore drains and are easily taken by a length of prawn netting or by using a yabby rake. They can even be coaxed out with hunks of meat on a string.

Nippers are the small, green members of the prawn family, with one big claw, that live in the mud under weeds on tidal flats. They are collected by puddling the mud with feet or rakes and are kept alive as they come to the surface on bags of wet weed. Like yabbies, they have great appeal to bream, whiting, flounder and flathead.

Beach worms are located in the shallow wash at low tide in the surf with a "stink bait". This comprises an ancient fish or a putrid piece of meat. The worms raise their heads to bite on the bait and are taken with special pliers or bare fingers. They should be kept fresh by rolling them in sand to remove the slime and then placed in a tin or bag with cool sand. Like many fishing tricks, worming is an art that is best learnt by watching skilled anglers.

PREPARATION FOR COOKING

Successful anglers have a big advantage over those who buy their fish in the shops, both in the wide variety of species they can sample and in the freshness of the catch. Their fish are bright and lustrous in colour, the eyes bright and bulging, not sunken, and the flesh is firm and exudes a pleasant sea smell. Their fillets are shiny and firm, not dull, soft and oozing water when touched. Many of the fish they eat are never seen in the markets. But there are still a few basic procedures to follow to achieve the most appetising meals from what they catch.

Cleaning the catch—Lay the fish on its side and with a sharp knife cut in front and behind the gills, then down the belly to the vent. Slit open the gills and remove the entrails. Wash briskly in water, rubbing off any of the black lining. A nail brush and salt is needed for blackfish.

Skinning—Place the cleaned fish on a flat surface and hold it firmly, using a little salt on the fingers to prevent them slipping. Using a sharp knife, make an incision around the neck and remove the pectoral fin. Slide the knife between the skin and the flesh to separate them slightly, then grasp the skin in the fingers and draw it back. Cut the skin at the tail and repeat the process on the other side. Often it is easier to cut the fish into fillets before skinning. Mirror dory fillets, for example, should be skinned just before cooking. For flatfish, such as sole or flounder, make a cut in the tail, and pull the skin firmly towards the head.

Filleting—Lay the cleaned fish on a flat surface and with a sharp knife cut down to the bone around the neck and along the middle of the back. Starting at the neck, slice the upper side of the flesh cleanly from the backbone,

PREPARATION OF THE CATCH

Scaling, Cleaning and Filleting Sea Bream

NOTE: Steps require that you hold the fish firmly—keep the fingers salted so they don't slip.

Use a fish knife or scaler and scrape from the tail (held firmly) towards the head, lifting the fish slightly to ensure the scales fly. The task is best achieved out of doors or in a sink.

It is essential to use a sharp knife as you slit the scaled fish along the belly from tail to head. The insides will come out with a little help. Thoroughly rinse the fish, inside and out, in cold running water.

Hold the fish by the head, cut just behind the gills until you are halfway through the body, work from head to belly.

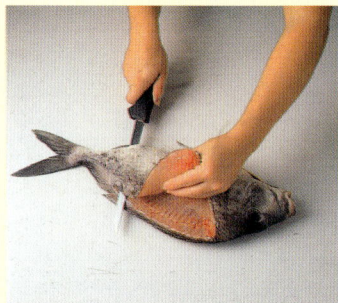

Lay the fish on a clean surface and slice down its length with a sharp knife, removing the top flesh to reveal the backbone. Trim and repeat on the other side. The trick is to keep the knife as close as possible to the backbone. Remove any remaining small bones separately.

To skin the fillet, place it skinside down on a board. Working from the tail, run the knife between the flesh and the skin, pushing firmly down but lifting the flesh as you go.

Filleting and Skinning John Dory

Start at the tail, make a sharp cut around the belly to the head, ensure that the knife gets through to the bone on one side only. Then continue the cut right round the edge of the fish.

Position the knife along the backbone, lift the fillet until the backbone is exposed and can be lifted free. Most chefs prefer to cook the fillets without removing the skin.

Turn and remove the head from the other side, leaving you to cook two splendid fillets. John Dory have firm, white flesh, and are among our outstanding table fish.

Pilchard Tricks

Pilchards provide a surprisingly appetising meal if well prepared. Start by making a cut behind the head and gill fin, ease out the guts as the head is removed and cut open the belly, rinse thoroughly.

Cut the fish open, clear away any small bones. Take the bone at the tail and remove by lifting towards the head.

Both sides of the pilchard can now be opened like butterfly wings and cooked in one piece, entirely free of the head, guts and bones.

Boning Snapper

Scale and clean the fish, usually leaving the head on. Slit the flesh from belly to tail, making short strokes with a sharp knife and

lifting the flesh from the middle of the backbone. Try not to pierce the skin. Turn over and repeat.

Using scissors or a long knife, cut out the entire backbone, trimming off the rib bones on each side.

The result is a well-boned snapper, with head and tail remaining and a delectable steak. The other side can also provide a fine steak, and the head can be used for fishing stock, or even angling berley.

Kingfish Steaks

Scale, remove the fins and gut as with sea bream. Hold the fish firmly, make a series of sharp cuts, breaking through the bone by pressing hard down on the knife handle. Some prefer to use a knife with a saw edge. The fish cuts up ideally into steaks about $2\frac{1}{2}$ cm (an inch) wide.

Cook the cutlets in turn, working from the tail. Some cooks may wish to retain the head for fish stock.

keeping the knife close to the bone. Turn the fish over and repeat the process on the other side. Remove the small bones along the sides separately. To improve flathead fillets, remove the bony "wing" by cutting through the thickest part of the fillet with a sharp knife. Similarly, you can remove the centre bones in blackfish by cutting the flesh on either side of that bone, leaving fillets on either side.

TIPS FOR COOKING, STORAGE

To pan-fry, grill or barbecue fillets, cook for two or three minutes on each side, depending on the thickness of the fillet. Use moderate heat. Turn once. To bake whole fish, cut the flesh on either side (scoring) to allow for even cooking. Cook for approximately 20 minutes per kilogram. For frying fish, coat it lightly with flour, using a small amount of polyunsaturated oil or non-stick spray. For grilling fish, cover the grill tray with foil before cooking and keep the fish moist by basting with a marinade. For microwave cooking, cover all seafood loosely with a plastic wrap or loose lid when cooking. Arrange the fish with the thickest section towards the edge of the dish. Avoid stacking the fish to ensure uniform cooking. Turn the dish at intervals if there is no carousel.

The most effective method of storage is to place cleaned whole fish or fillets on a clean plate, cover, and refrigerate for up to three days. For longer periods, place the fish in freezer bags, seal, label and date. The fish will keep for months like this but should be defrosted for a day before cooking.

ANATOMY OF A BONY FISH

A composite fish showing the technical terms used in describing and identifying the fish in this book. No one fish has all these features. Care has been taken to illustrate Australian fishes rather than copy figures of overseas specimens.

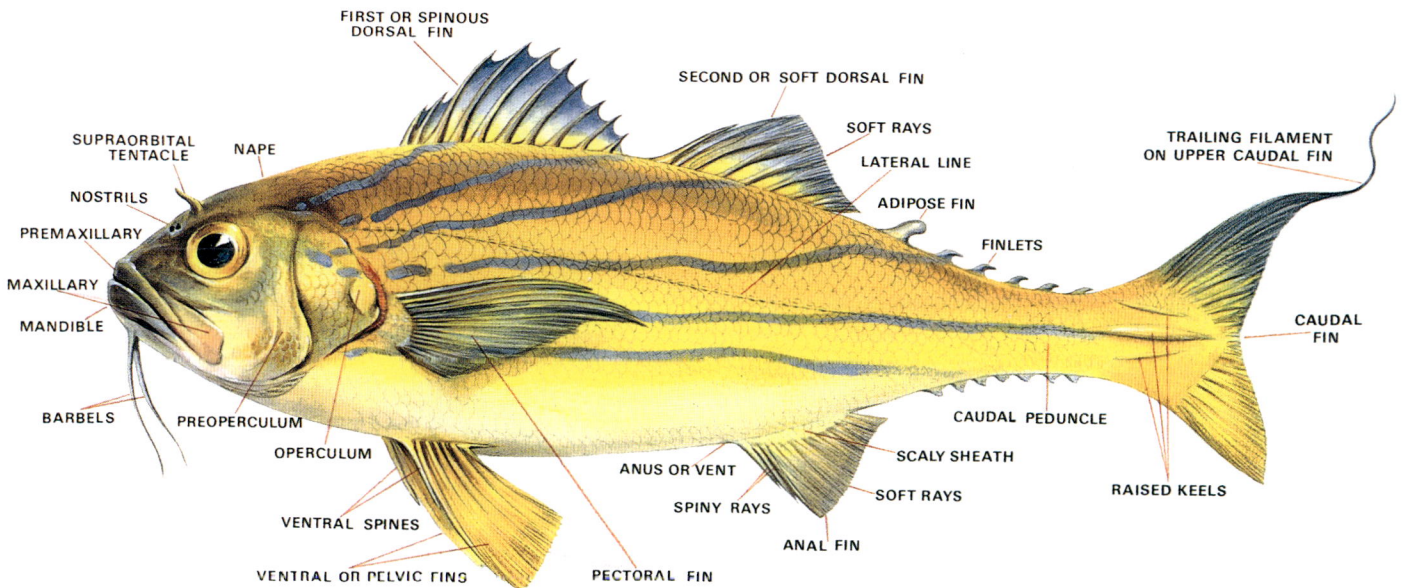

The bony fishes illustrated in this book all have skeletons comprising true bone, whereas the sharks, rays and sawfish shown have cartilaginous skeletons. The formation and shape of a fish's bones depend on factors like water pressure, the action of the muscles which deposit calcium and thus confirm a fish's shape. Most of the fish found in Australian waters are covered with scales that grow with the fish and show rings that indicate age. Australia is liberally supplied with many of the 30,000 kinds of freshwater and saltwater fishes found in the world, but only 30 per cent of Australian fishes are found in New Zealand, where there are fewer varieties. Around 400 species have so far been identified in New Zealand compared with 3,000-odd in Australia.

DIRECTORY

Minimum Legal Lengths

NAME OF FISH	LENGTH MILLIMETRES					
	NSW	VIC	SA	WA	QLD	TAS
Australian salmon	—	210	210	241	—	—
Barramundi (giant perch)	—	—	—	—	500	—
Bass (freshwater)	—	250	—	—	250	—
Black rock cod	330	—	—	—	350	—
Bream, black & yellow fin	254	240	250	241	230	—
Blackfish (freshwater)	—	250	—	—	—	220
Blue & red groper	—	—	460	305	350	—
Butter fish	—	230	—	—	—	—
Callop (yellowbelly)	—	330	260	—	—	—
Catfish (freshwater)	——	—	260	—	—	—
Coral trout	—	—	—	—	350	—
Crabs	—	—	—	127	150	—
Crayfish (NSW full length)	254	110	98.5	760	760	130
Emperor (red)	—	—	—	—	350	—
Emperor (sweetlip and red-finned)	—	—	—	—	300	—
Flathead (dusky)	356	250	260	279	300	—
Flathead (sand and tiger)	330	250	260	279	300	—
Flounder	—	230	230	229	—	230
Garfish	—	200	210	229	—	—
Gurnard (red rock cod in WA)	—	—	210	229	—	—
Javelin fish	—	—	—	—	300	—
Leatherjacket	—	—	—	229	—	—
Luderick	254	220	—	—	210	—
Mackerel (common or blue)	—	—	—	152	—	—
Mackerel (Spanish and school)	—	—	—	381	450	—
Morwong (jackass)	279	—	—	305	—	—
Mullet, fan-tail & sand	229	220	210	229	—	—
Mullet, yellow-eye and silver	229	240	210	229	—	—
Mullet, sea	318	250	460	241	300	—
Mulloway	—	—	460	330	300	—
Murray cod	—	530	460	381	500	—
NW snapper (pigfaced bream)	—	—	—	229	—	—
Nannygar	—	—	280	229	—	—
Pearl perch and WA jewfish	—	—	—	330	—	—
Perch (freshwater)	—	250	—	—	300	—
Pike, long-finned or longtom	—	360	—	330	—	—
Quinnat salmon	—	380	—	—	—	—
Red mullet	—	—	210	—	—	—
Rock cod	—	220	—	229	350	—
Rock blackfish (black drummer)	229	—	—	—	—	—
Salmon (threadfin)	—	—	—	—	400	—
Saratoga (true barramundi)	—	—	—	—	350	—
Sergeant baker	—	—	—	305	—	—
Shark, gummy	—	610	—	—	—	—
Snapper (red bream, squire)	279	270	280	279	250	—
School (snapper) shark	914	910	910	—	—	—
Snook	—	360	360	279	—	—
Sole, black and other	203	200	230	203	—	—
Samson fish (sea kingfish)	—	—	—	381	—	—
Sweep	—	—	150	203	—	—
Tailor	—	230	—	229	—	—
Tarwine	203	—	—	203	230	—
Teraglin	381	—	—	—	300	—
Tommy ruff (sea herring)	—	—	150	178	—	—
Trevally, silver	—	200	210	203	—	—
Trout, brown & rainbow	254	250	280	305	—	220
Whiting, trumpeter	203	230	—	178	—	—
Whiting, sand	267	—	180	216	230	—
Whiting, spotted/King George	241	270	280	254	—	—
Yellowtail kingfish	—	—	400	381	—	—

(Note: 1 inch equals 25.4 millimetres)

ALBACORE *Scombridae*

Albacore, *Thunnus alalunga*

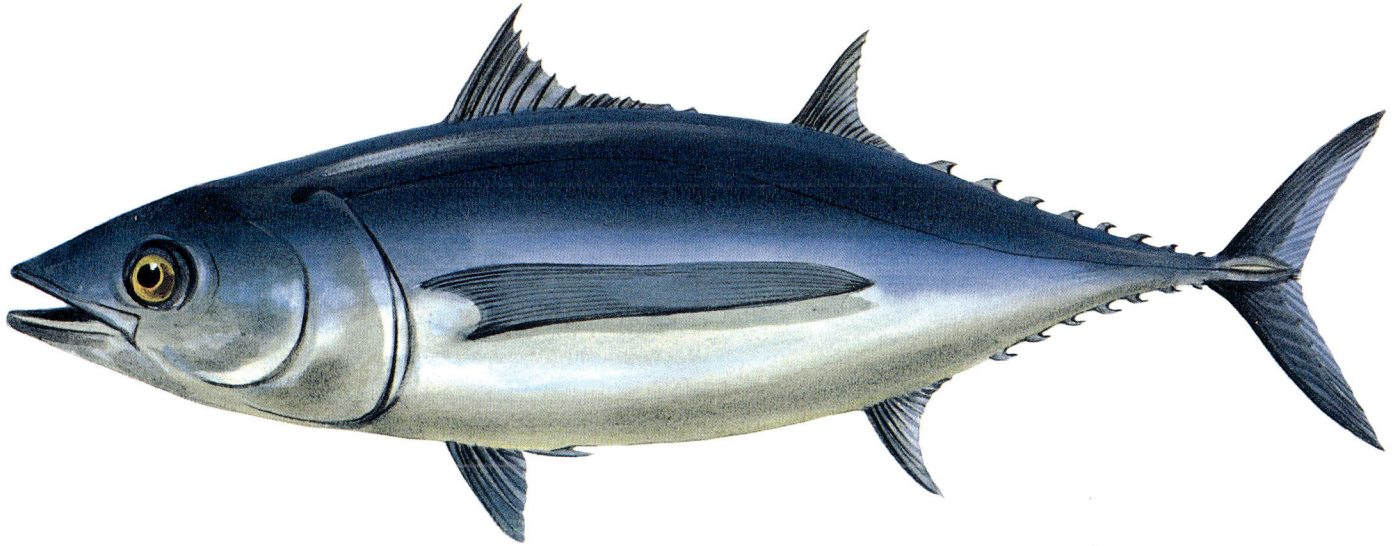

An important member of the tuna family and probably the best table fish in the group. Albacore flesh is white, whereas in other tunas it is red and oily. All the tunas are important commercial fishes, caught by trolling, mostly in the open sea. They are beautifully streamlined, have finlets and well-forked tails for speed and stability. Some have been timed to swim at around 70 km/h. Albacore are very similar in colour to the southern bluefin tuna, which is mainly silvery white, with the body marked by longitudinal streaks that merge into each other. Albacore, *Thunnus alalunga*, can be easily identified by their extremely long pectoral fins that extend back beyond the level of the anal fins. They are sometimes referred to as long-fin tuna.

FEATURES: Albacore and yellowfin tuna form a major sport-fishery off Port Stephens in New South Wales and further south off Bermagui. They are mostly just over a metre in length. They are usually irridescent blue along the top, silvery below. Fins usually are blue, while related species have yellow white, spotted or plain fins. The current Australian Anglers' Association record for

albacore is 21.60 kg for a fish caught at Narooma, New South Wales, by David Green in March, 1981.

FISHING TECHNIQUE: Albacore, like all tunas, will take whole fish or cut fish, but are mostly caught on light game-fishing gear by spinning or trolling with artificial lures. Generally they are taken from game boats but a few are landed from the shore by fishermen using spinning rods. A wire trace is recommended. Experienced game anglers always have a wide selection of small lures on board, changing quickly to the one that appears to be in favour with the albacore on a particular day. Solitary albacore sometimes appear but the exciting action comes when they are encountered in a large school.

DISTRIBUTION: The south-eastern coast of Australia from Coff's Harbour to Phillip Island and on both coasts of Tasmania. They are taken on the south coast of Western Australia and off South Australia, and north of Cook Strait, New Zealand, in summer.

AMBERJACK *Carangidae*

A close relative of the kingfish and often confused with it by anglers and commercial fishermen. Sometimes classified as *Seriola purpurascens* and commonly known as yellow-banded amberjack. Grant lists *Seriola dumerili* as the greater amberjack and also *Seriola rivoliana*, as the highfin amberjack, a rare fish unknown in Australian waters until one was caught off Cape Moreton in 1985. Highfin amberjack have subsequently been identified in Western Australian waters. Although amberjack are sold in southern Queensland as "samson", they are not highly regarded as table fish. The younger fish are good table fare, but should be bled and chilled as soon as possible after capture. The larger specimens are dry and coarse.

FEATURES: The differences between amberjack and yellowtail kingfish are best shown when they are displayed together. The amberjack is purplish-brown on the upper body and the kingfish purplish-blue with a green tinge on the head. The broad lateral stripe along the side of the amberjack is a dull, smudged yellow colour, but in the kingfish it is bright yellow. The amberjack's belly is creamy-white, the kingfish's silvery-white. On the amberjack the fins are olive-blue to dark blue, the anal fin is edged in white, and tail fins show flashes of yellow. The first dorsal fin on the amberjack is markedly higher than on the kingfish, and the amberjack's ventral fins are slightly longer than those of the kingfish.

FISHING TECHNIQUE: Both kingfish and amberjack are taken on the surface and around the bottom of offshore reefs. They will take a wide variety of baits and lures, particularly whole crabs and trolled live fish. They have also been caught on feathered lures, drone spoons and kona-heads. As a last resort, they sometimes head for kelp or coral on the bottom when hooked. The Australian Anglers' Association record for amberjack is 39.46 kg taken by John Dennis in the Albrolhos Islands, Western Australia, in September 1984. The world record is 70.59 kg for a specimen taken in Bermuda in 1981.

DISTRIBUTION: Amberjack are distributed through the warmer waters of the world, including the Indo-Pacific, Atlantic and Mediterranean. Their Australian distribution extends from southern New South Wales right up the Queensland coast to the Northern Territory. They have only recently been identified in Western Australia but clearly were confused with other fish there in earlier times.

Amberjack, *Seriola purpurascens*

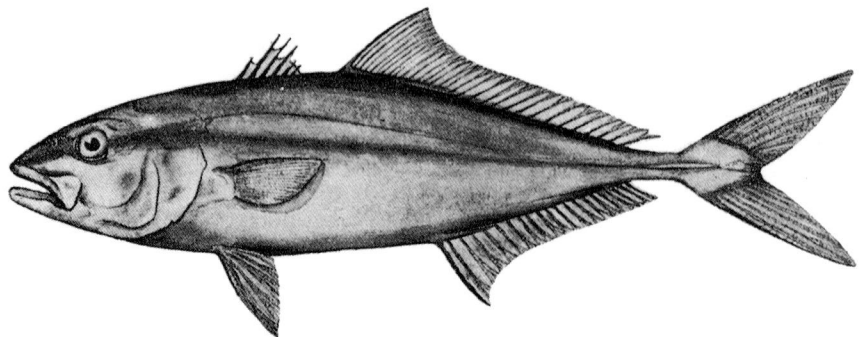

ANCHOVY *Engraulididae*

A family of small fish that moves in huge packs and is found all round the Australian coast. They are mainly taken by anglers for bait, although there is a small commercial sale for them as fish paste. A local demand for canned anchovies is expected to develop as Australians' fondness for savouries increases. Australian anchovies, *Engraulis austral*, have a large body of supporters who argue that they are more flavoursome than imported counterparts.

FEATURES: Anchovies are generally transparent or translucent and should not be confused with sprats or pilchards. Their undershot mouths, which extend to the rear edge of the gill covers, has a very large gape. They abound in large estuaries, big inlets and other sheltered waters rather than in the open sea. They shoal offshore in winter and in summer return to the big inlets to spawn. Young anchovies remain in the upper reaches of large bays until they are around two years old and reach about 8 cm in length before they head for the open sea. In northern Australian waters they spawn earlier than in the south and do so frequently in the open sea.

The Australian anchovy, *Engraulis austral*, inhabits coastal waters south of the Tropic of Capricorn and grows to 15 cm. The smaller specimens are translucent, the mature fish greenish-silver to purplish-green on the back and silver along the belly. They are often found in rock pools or stranded on beaches after being pursued by tailor. Most of our 19 species of anchovy are from Queensland and northern Australian waters. Hamilton's anchovy, *Thryssa hamiltoni*, which grows to 20 cm is probably the most plentiful of these. It inhabits estuaries along most of the Queensland coast. The estuary anchovy, *Thryssina aestuaria*, is mainly found in southern Queensland. De Vis's anchovy, *Stolephorus devisi*, is abundant in northern Australian waters, especially in the Gulf of Carpentaria. The gulf anchovy, *Stolephorus carpentariae*, is a smaller variety that grows to 5 cm. The whiskered anchovy, *Thryssa setirostris*, is a rare variety which grows to 20 cm and is easily identified by the barbel-like ray that projects from both sides of the rear of their upper jaws.

FISHING TECHNIQUE: Anglers seeking bait take small numbers of anchovy in ring nets, enticing the anchovy into the nets with berley. Commercial fishermen take bigger quantities by shining powerful lights onto the water after dark to lure them into big lampa nets.

DISTRIBUTION: Anchovies congregate in huge numbers off the far south coast of New South Wales, Lakes Entrance, Western Port Bay, and Port Phillip Bay in Victoria, in St. Vincent and Spencer Gulfs in South Australia, and at a number of spots on the Western Australian coast. They are taken in numbers at St. Helen's and Devonport in Tasmania. Sportsfishermen mainly use them as bait for tuna.

Anchovy, *Engraulis austral*

23

ANEMONEFISH   *Pomacentridae*

A group of small, vividly-coloured fishes that includes the clownfish. They enjoy a unique association with sea anemone, which provides a home or shelter for the fish. Anemonefish are exempt from the stinging cells with which anemone paralyses and then eats ordinary small marine creatures. Anemonefish obtain pieces of food left over by their hosts and sometimes even nibble the tentacles. This eating of the poison cells is believed to immunise the anemonefish or clownfish against death. The fish in turn freshen up the water and even bring bits of food for their guardian, the anemone, deepening the hole for it to settle in, and defending it against predators such as butterfly fishes. The anemone is believed to sense the presence of its attendant fish by chemical stimulus, whereas the fish recognise their host by smell.

Orange anemonefish, Amphiprion percula

FEATURES: All of the 11 species of anemonefish in Australian waters are easily identified by their spectacular colouring in depths below five metres. Although they live among large sea anemones, they survive without ill-effect if removed from the anemone. Among the most striking are the two-banded anemonefish, *Amphiprion akindynos*, the black anemonefish, *Amphiprion melanopus*, the wide-banded anemonefish, *Amphiprion latezonatus*, and the illustrated orange anemonefish or clownfish, *Amphiprion percula*, which has three distinctive white bars across the bright orange body. *A. percula* has a characteristic habit of pushing its tongue forward of the midline and all its bars have black edging. The tip of the tail also has a prominent black edge. They grow to 75 mm.

DISTRIBUTION: Common right along the Barrier Reef and south into New South Wales. Northwards they range from Torres Straight right across the Pacific and Indian Oceans and as far afield as the southern islands of Japan.

ANGELFISH *Pomacanthidae*

Australia has 23 recognised species of angelfish, a group Whitley said surpassed in colouring and beauty both birds and butterflies. They are certainly a spectacular lot, offering a notable assortment of designs that even overshadow the vivid colours of their close relatives, the butterfly fish and the coralfish. Angelfish must be carefully handled because of the presence of a sharp spine on the lower edge of the preoperculum, which they use in battle. Among Australia's angelfish, the most photographed is the illustrated blue angelfish, *Pomacanthus semicirculatus*, which matures from a juvenile with concentric blue rings on the sides to a glittery green fish with a blue snout. Its entire profile is rimmed in blue. The regal angelfish, *Pygoplites diacanthus*, changes from a gold

bodied juvenile with white vertical bars on the back to a deep golden adult with light blue edging on the white stripes running from gill cover to tail, with barred cheeks. The scribbled angelfish, *Chaetodontoplus duboulayi*, is prized as an aquarium fish because its deep purple body is scribbled with a tracery of deep blue lines extending to the dorsal and anal fins. The eye bar that covers the eye and cheek is speckled in juveniles but solid purple in adults. Behind this bar a golden band stretches from top to bottom. The blue-ringed angelfish, *Pomacanthus annularis*, found mainly in the Indo-Pacific region, is another strikingly beautiful form, with deep-bodied juveniles a bright blue, covered by alternating crescentic streaks of white and blue. On the other hand, adult blue-ringed angelfish

Blue angelfish (adult with juvenile), *Pomacanthus semicirculatus* are a vivid golden-brown colour on the body and throat, with a perfect bright blue circle high on the shoulders.

FEATURES: Apart from the sharp preopercular spine, angelfish are further protected by small, rough scales and about 14 dorsal spines. The fins are pointed in some species, rounded in others. All the angelfish are carnivorous and prefer to run for shelter rather than be photographed.

They are generally less than 30 cm long.

FISHING TECHNIQUE: All adult angelfish will protect their territory but like their juveniles they are of interest to keepers of aquariums rather than anglers.

DISTRIBUTION: Mainly in tropical seas around rocky bottoms of coastal reefs. A few stragglers enter New South Wales.

Two-spined angelfish, *Centropyge bispinosus*

RECORD CATCHES: Australia has two respected authorities which assess and record outstanding catches: the Australian Anglers' Association, and the Game Fishing Association of Australia. The AAA restricts its activities to freshwater, beach, estuary, lakes, harbours and cliff-top catches, leaving deep-sea species like marlin and sailfish to the GFAA. Both associations require clear photographs of the catch, signed statements from witnesses, and clear undertakings that the angler who made the catch, did so without outside help or by the illegal use of tackle. Game fishermen, for example, must play the fish by themselves without any outside help, although they are allowed drinks and can be showered with water. The fish must be cleanly hooked and not "foul-hooked" through an eye, and although assistance from a man with a gaff is allowed, the fish must be brought alongside the game boat by the angler.

ANGLERFISH   *Antennariidae*

The 23 Australian representatives of this family, have pronounced fleshy filaments over the mouth resembling fishing rods. The fish entice their prey within reach by waving flaps of skin like a bait. The anglerfish pounce as curiosity gets the better of their targets, often fish bigger than the angler, and thrust the prey explosively into an upwardly directed mouth. Anglerfish have developed a powerful slow-motion gallop or walk on their hand-like ventral fins that allows them to move over the bottom of the sea by clasping seaweeds and rocks. Anglerfish are notable for having forsaken speed of movement for guile to thwart enemies and take prey.

FEATURES: Head fringed with flaps of skin, mouth large, terminal. Body compressed, wider than high. Gill openings behind the pectoral fins. All the best known anglerfish in Australian waters have developed variable colour patterns. They vary in length from 50 mm to 250 mm and in captivity have to be prevented from death by over-feeding. The biggest anglerfish so far taken by sportsfishermen was the 0.15 kg specimen taken by Colin Wilbrow at Toowoon Bay, NSW, in 1983. Upper surface lilaceous brown, filaments and tentacles darker. Lower body white. Tongue white with black network in front.

DISTRIBUTION: The ocellated angler, *Antennarius nummifer*, is a warm water variety that ranges through the tropical waters of Western Australia eastwards to the Northern Territory and Torres Strait and down to the Great Barrier Reef with occasional specimens reaching Jervis Bay, NSW. The prickly angler, *Echinophryne crassispina*, is found in the colder waters of Victoria, Tasmania, and eastern South Australia. They are most plentiful around the inshore weed beds of South Australia. The striped angler, *Antennarius striatus*, a form streaked with dense bars and black patches, has a mainly yellow body and is usually caught by anglers netting for prawns in coastal waters from Wollongong, NSW, to Queensland.

Striped angler,
Antennarius striatus

ARCHER FISH *Toxotidae*

Small, deep-bodied fish of Australia's tropical waters, widely known for their ability to shoot down insects with a jet of water. The water spurts from a grooved palate and a split in the tongue and the barrage can be repeated quickly several times until the fish downs its prey. The alignment of the archer fish's snout along the nape forms a straight line that enables the fish to line up targets with the precision of a crack rifleman and explains why the species is also called rifle fish. The jet of water is accurate to a distance of about two metres. There are at least four species of archer fish in Australian waters, the common archer fish, *Toxotes chatareus*, which ranges from saltwater up into the backwaters of major freshwater streams and in swampy patches in the wet season, the western archer fish, *Toxotes eligolepis*, which occurs in the Kimberley district, and the gulf archer fish, *Toxotes jaculator*, which is found in New Guinea and the Gulf of Carpentaria, and the primitive archer fish, *Toxotes lorentzi*, from the rivers of the Timor Sea area.

Common archer fish,
Toxotes chatareus

FEATURES: All three Australian archer fish have between four and seven highly distinctive black blotches on the upper body. *Toxotes chatareus* is bright silver in colour with a light brown tint on the sides. Their dark blotches fade with age. The biggest specimens reach 40 cm and weigh around half a kilogram. They are much sought after by aquariums and can be taught to shoot objects from the hands of aquarium staff. Grant also describes another popular trick. "It apparently mistakes the human eye for an insect and is apt to spit in the eye of attendants." They are found around dead logs and over-hanging branches and in reedy waters where insects and bugs are likely to be found. Archer fish cannot survive in southern waters unless the water is heated. In their tropical habitat these captivating conical-headed fish swim in small shoals, just below the surface, ammunition ready. They are classified by fin and scale counts and colour patterns.

FISHING TECHNIQUE: Archer fish are surprisingly pugnacious for their size and will give a better account of themselves when hooked than bass or bream of the same weight. A sprinkling of bread crumbs usually will entice them to the surface where they will jump at small flies and insect bait. Light spinning gear or a fly rod are recommended but they are taken on handlines when the bait is offered just below the surface. They will bite at quite large plugs, and are appetising panfish.

DISTRIBUTION: Tropical rivers and coastal waters, Indo-Malayan and south-eastern Asian waters. Plentiful in the Kimberley region of Western Australia.

BERLEY RIG

Airtight tin

Strong string

Tin of bread, cheese, etc

60-90 cm

Tin of fish, prawns, etc

30-60 cm

Tin filled with concrete

A home-made berley rig which also acts as a marker buoy. Water movement releases the berley from the tins.

BERLEY RECIPES: Any number of ingredients for what Americans call "chum" have been used to attract fish in Australian waters. These include old meat, bread, bran, pollard, fish offal, stale prawns, pilchards, whale oil, fowl pellets, seaweed, cornflakes, blood and bone, boiled wheat, fish gut, potato, cheese, and dead horses. Experts have evolved a pie combining sand and bread crumbs and some of the above items, but success stems from using some device that keeps the berley confined to the area being fished. Dispersal varies from throwing berley in by hand, to injecting berley into floats, cans, or paper bags, but every experienced angler swears by some form of berleying.

SCIENTIFICALLY SPEAKING: Three basic forms of fish have survived centuries of evolution: cartilaginous fish, comprising mainly sharks and rays, cyclosomes or jawless fish, represented by hagfish and lampreys, and the teleosts, which are the fish with bony skeletons. Teleosts comprise by far the biggest number of the world's 30,000 species. Less than 600 species are cartilaginous. Jellyfish, crayfish, cuttlefish, and starfish are not fish at all, but belong to sea-dwelling families such as molluscs, crustaceans, coelenterates and echinoderms.

ATLANTIC SALMON *Salmonidae*

Landlocked salmon,
Salmo salar

A prized sporting fish introduced into Australia in 1963, Atlantic salmon is now bred in cages off Tasmania and has strong claims to being the finest of all Australian table fish. Their firm pink flesh justifies the high prices paid in Australian restaurants, for in whatever form they are prepared they provide a culinary experience of the highest order. They were brought into Australia originally from Nova Scotia in an attempt to improve inland fishing that was in decline. The completion of irrigation schemes had dramatically changed water temperatures and conditions for native species. For three years, more than 100,000 salmon eggs were despatched annually by the Canadian Department of Fisheries to New South Wales government hatcheries. They were introduced as fingerlings into selected streams but failed to prosper, leaving authorities with a brood stock of fish that would not reproduce in the wild. At this point an imaginative commercial venture began in Tasmania, where conditions were ideal for the salmon. Using stock from New South Wales hatcheries, a highly promising business has been built up, the main problem coming from seals that attack the cages in which the salmon mature.

FEATURES: Atlantic or landlocked salmon are more silvery than trout, with a lot of irregular dark spots, some x-shaped. They have a longer, more slender caudal peduncle than trout and their tails are more deeply forked. There are no spots on the tail nor any evidence of red colour. They reach 38 kg in Europe, but Australia's land-locked variety are seldom more than 3 kg.

FISHING TECHNIQUE: Atlantic salmon strike trout flies in a conditioned reflex rather than through a desire to eat. They do not have to be stalked by anglers who remain out of sight, as is required for trout. They mouth the fly and splash at it before taking it with a heavy, dull pull. With trout, their interest declines with each cast, whereas Atlantic salmon become more interested with each cast until they are finally enticed to bite. They will strike at bright spoons, wobblers, plugs and live baits, but are at their best as sporting fish when offered wet and dry flies. The Australian variety do not leap two metres out of the water in attempts to free themselves as their American and European relatives do.

DISTRIBUTION: No sea-run population in Australia. Stocks liberated in Tasmania between 1864 and 1870, in the 1960s in Burrinjuck Dam, New South Wales, and in the 1960s in Lake Jindabyne.

Australian Salmon *Arripidae*

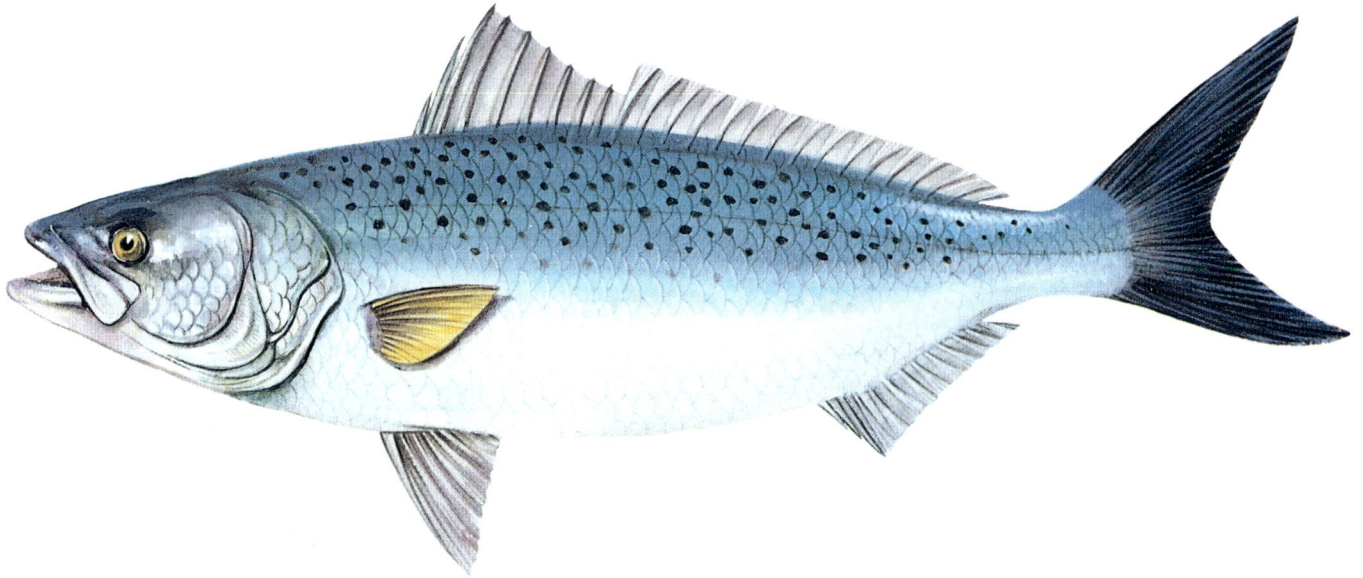

Notable Australian sporting fishes which are not true members of the Salmonidae family, but belong to the perch family Arripidae. There are now two recognised varieties in Australian waters, the western Australian salmon, *Arripis truttaceus*, a rounded, elongate fish olive-green on top and silvery below, with the flanks and upper sides studded by black dots, and the eastern Australian salmon, *Arripis trutta*, also known as kahawai, which has a higher number of gill-rakers than its western relative. Western Australian salmon feed largely on pilchards and other small fish, whereas the eastern Australian salmon mainly eats plankton, using the gill-rakers to sieve out the krill that is common in cold water. Western Australian salmon grow to a weight of 9.4 kg or 20 lb, eastern Australian salmon to 7.4 kg. Ideal for canning, salmon are poor pan fish.

FEATURES: Both species of Australian salmon undertake long migratory journeys and are such legendary sporting fish amateur fishermen eagerly seek news of where the big schools are travelling. In Western Australia, juvenile salmon schools gather on the south coast before migrating right across the bottom of Australia to Victorian and Tasmanian ocean beaches, returning to the west as adults. The eastern variety is smaller but like its western counterpart becomes an extremely dour fighter when hooked.

FISHING TECHNIQUE: Few fish take baits as readily as Australian salmon, who bite in fumbling style quite unlike the slashing chop of tailor. They become exciting acrobats when hooked, either by spinning in the surf or trolling from boats. In Western Australia blue pilchards (or mulies) are the favoured bait. In the east, fresh beach worms, mackerel, pipis and squid are preferred. They sometimes cut through fine nylon casts so linked carlisle hooks are used. This means the top hook holds the bait away from the lower barb so that the point is not hidden and the salmon cannot remove the bait without becoming hooked.

DISTRIBUTION: Most abundant along the southern parts of the east and west coasts. They migrate in huge schools from Western Australia to Tasmania where they are fished for in tidal rivers. They are the most popular of all sporting fish off South Australia. The eastern population migrates north up the coast, starting in February, travelling past Sydney to Coff's Harbour in huge shoals that have become the target for canneries. Sydney anglers lately have been forced to go as far south as Narooma for their salmon.

Eastern Australian salmon, *Arripis trutta*

BARRACOUTA *Gempylidae*

An outstanding sporting fish that will slash at bright or shiny baits and lures and has been known to leap into boats seeking its prey. They are long, narrow in shape, built for speed pelagics that travel in large shoals which have reached 30 km in length. They were misnamed by early settlers, for they are not true barracudas, which are known in Australia as sea pike or dingofish, but are of the gemfish family. At one time the barracouta dominated the commercial fishing industry with thousands of tonnes marketed annually but their hold on the market has been lost because of the inferior milky fish trawlermen have sent to market, emaciated fish said to be full of worms known as 'axe handles'. Barracouta remain an exciting fish for anglers, however, providing plenty of action and excitement because of their voracious appetite. They will pursue small live fish baits for hundreds of metres, and even when they are boated force anglers to take extreme care for fear of damage from their teeth. It is customary to crack them on the head with a heavy club or pick handle to ensure they are dead before unhooking them.

Barracouta, *Thyrsites atun*

FEATURES: Large teeth in the upper jaw. Glittery steel-blue above, silvery white below. The soft dorsal fin and the tail lobes are black-edged. The long first dorsal fin is black through the membrane with the spines thrusting out as white bars.

FISHING TECHNIQUE: Barracouta offer splendid sport by trolling with light gear, but a growing number are caught by anglers with spinning gear from jetties and rocks. One successful ploy is to use big conical floats which have a thin brass tube running through them. This is fixed on a running rig so that when it is cast out, the light sinker pulls the bait down about two metres below it. Best baits are pilchards, herring, small yellowtail, king prawns, squid, salmon or bonito.

DISTRIBUTION: Southern half of Australia. Huge shoals have been sighted in Bass Strait, smaller schools as far north as Moreton Bay. Plentiful off south-eastern South Australia, less abundant in lower Western Australia to Shark Bay.

BARRACUDA *Sphyraenidae*

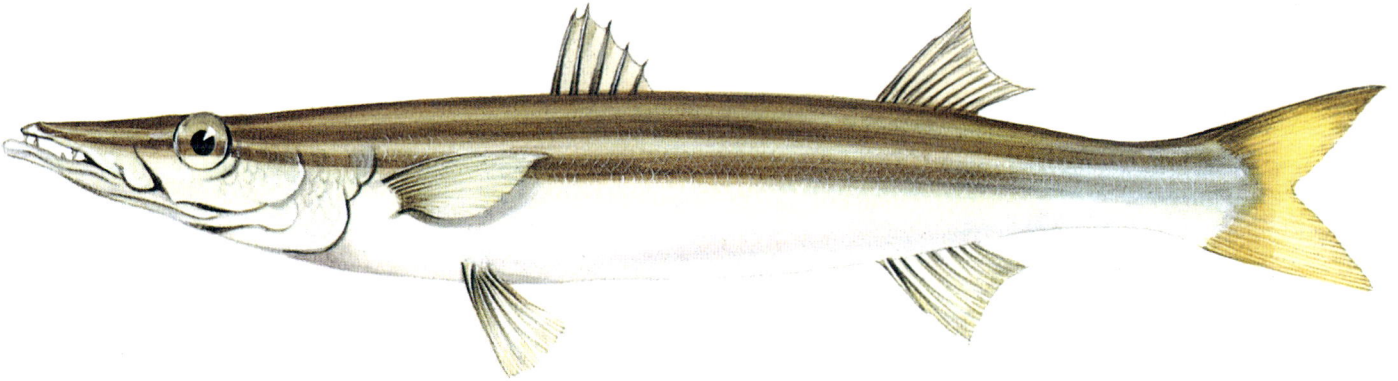

Voracious, slender fish with sharp, slashing fangs, pointed heads and a habit of attacking small fishes savagely. Overseas there are authentic cases of them attacking humans and causing death, but there is no record of them behaving like this in Australian waters. There are six varieties of *Sphyraena* in Australian waters. They are also known as dingofish, sea pike, and snook. These include the illustrated striped sea pike or barracuda, *Sphyraena obtusata*, a fish of great speed that leaps high when hooked; short-finned barracuda, *Sphyraena novaehollandia*, called snook in South Australia where it is an important market fish; the giant barracuda, *Sphyraena barracuda*, which grows to a length of 2.4 metres and a weight of more than 25 kg; the big-eye sea pike, *Sphyraena forsteri*, a greenish-grey fish completely lacking the bands, blotches and stripes seen in other barracuda; the pickhandle barracuda, *Sphyraena jello*, or jello's barracuda, which reaches 2 metres in length and 25 kg: and the long-finned sea pike, *Dinolestes lewini*, a light-brown fish on top with a forked golden tail now placed in a separate family. Some barracuda are known to cause ciguatera poisoning.

FEATURES: Elongate, cylindrical fishes with two widely separated dorsal fins, the first with five spines. Large mouth with fang-like teeth. All members of the family are fast and powerful swimmers and willingly snap at moving objects. In the striped sea pike, the slender snout terminates in a wide-gaping mouth fitted with an impressive array of dog-like teeth. All *Sphyraena* have powerful, forked tails.

FISHING TECHNIQUE: Satisfying sport on light gear as they will repeatedly leap from the sea. When they are schooling, good anglers can catch one a minute, substituting strips of white tape when they run out of bait, but angling for them is a practised skill. Using a whippy rod, flick the bait through the water in jerky movements. As the sea pike takes the bait, time the strike to set the hook before it slashes the bait to pieces. Sea pike and strips of barracuda make ideal bait when trolling for large game fish.

DISTRIBUTION: Barracuda are taken all round the Australian coast, but are abundant in northern tropical waters. Sea pike or snook are mostly taken in Bass Strait or in the Great Australian Bight.

Striped sea pike or barracuda, *Sphyraena obtusata*

BARRAMUNDI *Centropomidae*

Barramundi, *Lates calcarifer*

One of the outstanding fishes of Australian waters, these giant perches can smash the most sophisticated tackle and rank among our finest food fish. They have been flown to the fish shops of southern states for many years and a closed season exists in the spawning season of their native waters of Queensland and the Northern Territory, which is designed to protect this lucrative trade. The evidence over whether barramundi are in decline is confusing, but now that brood stock has been established by breeding them in captivity, their future appears secure as this stock can be used to replenish depleted streams. The all States committee that deliberated for years on uniform names for Australian fishes preferred the name giant perch for *Lates calcarifer* and wanted barramundi to apply only to the Dawson River saratoga, *Scleropages leichhardti*. Barramundi were marketed for more than five years as giant perch to conform with this decree. But neither commercial or amateur fishermen

would accept these findings and the Queensland government was forced to go back to the name barramundi. Conservationists argued in the 1970s and early 1980s that over-fishing, pollution from sugar mills, damming of rivers, and netting had depleted their numbers, but it is now thought that the wrong gear was used, bringing fewer catches and creating the notion that barramundi were scarce.

FEATURES: Barramundi are basically greenish-grey on top, white or yellow along the belly. Each scale has up to three bright red or orange spots on it and the eyes glow like coals. The upward sloping lower jaw has the look of a genuine predator. They will leap from the water when hooked, bodies twisting, gills flared.

FISHING TECHNIQUE: Roughley fixed their maximum size in Australia at 52.17 kg or 120 lb and said one had been caught in the Bay of Bengal that weighed 252.17 kg or 580 lb. Australian sportsmen trying for fish as big as that appear to have used tackle that was far too heavy for fish that average under 8.6 kg. For years, big catches by southern anglers using metal lures convinced the fishing fraternity that this was the way to go with barramundi, but the latest evidence is that they will bite just as well on large prawns, garfish and mullet. They strike with dramatic force at these baits fished below floats.

The technique required is similar to that for bass, but the tackle should include firm action rods and strong reels and at least 140 metres of line up to 9.07 kg breaking strain. For clearly sighting barramundi polaroid glasses are advised as are rigs with split rings and triple hooks. A wide variety of artificial lures have been used successfully, including aeroplane spinners, bellbrook and killer lures and (riggle) rigglejigs. They have the advantage of eliminating bait-collection sessions in regions where natural baits are quickly affected by the heat.

Barramundi move downstream to spawn around river mouths in late summer and the fertilised eggs are quickly carried away into freshwater. They move upstream during floods and often become stranded in billabongs, but have a high tolerance to heat and survive in the most isolated waters. But the table quality of landlocked freshwater barramundi is far inferior to barramundi taken from the ocean. Aborigines used to wrap the fish in leaves of wild ginger plant and bake it in hot ashes. For the white man in his kitchen 2.5 cm barramundi steaks fried in oil until they are golden and served with a simple butter and lemon juice sauce provides a gourmet meal.

Recent research has disclosed some engrossing evidence that barramundi are hermaphrodites. Fish less than five years of age are almost all males and those older than that are females. Scientists are still undecided about whether all males make this change. A bigger problem would arrive if the Queensland government goes ahead with plans to introduce Nile perch into basically barramundi waters. Apart from trout, the 11 fish species so far introduced into Australian freshwater have proved of little benefit either for sport or commercial purposes. An overwhelming majority of our experienced ichthyologists believe the importation of Nile perch would be an ecological disaster.

DAYTIME SURVEYS PAY: Night-time fishing for species such as bass often produces big catches. On warm nights, when the air is heavy with insects, well-presented lures can provide dramatic results. Casting in the dark has special problems and it pays to row in by day and try to make a mental picture of the area to be fished. Distances for casts designed to get in near heavy bushes and the likely habitat of fish can then be noted.

OVERCOMING REEL BACKLASH: Backlash is the result of too much line running out when a cast is made and leaves the angler with a tangle of excess line caused by his failure to stop the spool spinning. It is usually the outcome of unbalanced tackle; this occurs when a rod is fitted with a lure or sinker of the wrong weight. Veteran anglers avoid the problem with skillful use of the thumb. Novices should consult a good tackle shop that can advise on a change of reel. Modern plug-casters restrict the tendency to tangle by laying the line evenly on the spool, and applying sophisticated casting breaks. The vital factor to remember is that the rod, reel, line and lure should all be weight compatible.

BASS *Perchichthyidae*

Bass, *Macquaria novemaculeatus*

Sand bass, *Psammoperca waigiensis*

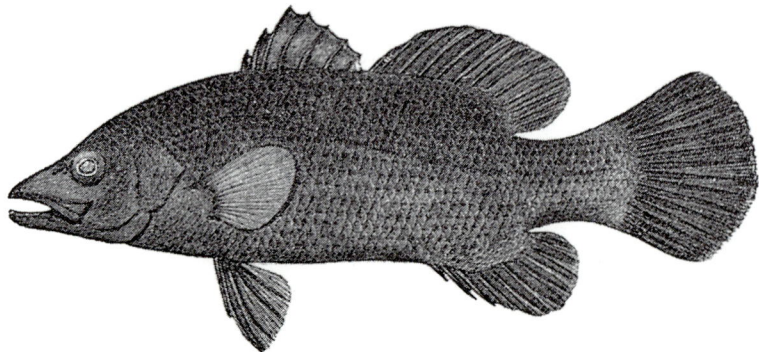

Outstanding sporting fish of high edible quality that are frequently too smart for anglers trying to catch them. Few fish can match the fighting abilities of bass, which appear to handle freshwater and saltwater equally well. Bass catches have markedly improved since the introduction of sophisticated baitcaster and threadline reel outfits, but they remain fish that demand painstaking attention to technique. They grow to 4.5 kg but mostly are caught in the 1 to 1.5 kg size. Some bass experts claim they will bite on anything that moves. They take bait, spinners or flies. Australian bass are among the few sporting fish that cannot be sold commercially. They are related to estuary perch, freshwater perch or Australian perch, *Macquaria colonorum*, and should not be confused with red bass, *Lutjanus bohar*, which cause ciguatera poisoning, sand bass, *Psammoperca waigiensis*, a relative of barramundi, or deep sea bass, *Polyprion moeone*, a variety known by some anglers as bass groper.

FEATURES: Bass live in brackish water from the mouths of rivers to the upper reaches. They are found at all depths but move into shallower water in summer. They vary widely in colour, but mostly their fins are yellowish-green, and their body colour yellowish-brown to olive green, with pale undersides. They spend most of their lives in freshwater, migrating to areas of tidal influence to spawn in midwinter. Experiments by the Queensland scientist Hamar Midgely showed male bass are smaller and are outnumbered three to one by females.

FISHING TECHNIQUE: Bass inhabit sheltered areas of streams where snags abound. They cling to the banks among bushes, logs and tree roots. Novices to bass fishing complain they have to pick their way through thick bush to get at the fish. The most successful technique is to paddle or drift a boat up the centre of bass streams and cast to the banks with a trout spinning rod. They prefer bright-coloured lures and flies and live baits have notably more success on bass than dead baits. Early settlers caught a large number of bass on frogs, cicadas, shrimps, green grasshoppers, spiders and worms and these remain the best baits. They fight with exceptional power and the sight of a bass hitting a surface lure is not quickly forgotten. Bank fishermen without a suitable boat should select a spot where logs or trees overhang the water and prevent the bass spotting them. Wear inconspicuous clothes as bass

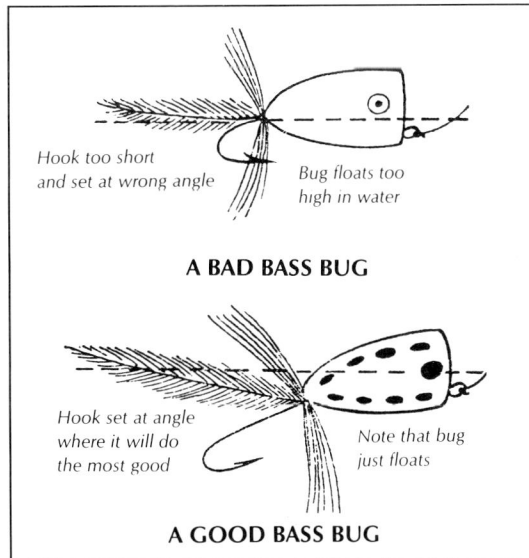

Hook too short and set at wrong angle

Bug floats too high in water

A BAD BASS BUG

Hook set at angle where it will do the most good

Note that bug just floats

A GOOD BASS BUG

have splendid eyesight. A light float is useful in carrying the lure or bait away from where the bass can spot the anglers.

DISTRIBUTION: From southern Queensland down the east coast to South Australia. Typical bass streams are the Maroochy and Noosa Rivers, Richmond, Macleay, Clarence, Shoalhaven, Clyde, Glenelg and The Snowy. Many of the small, lesser known streams in New South Wales and East Gippsland offer exciting bass fishing. Bass should be chilled immediately on capture to prevent the flesh becoming pulpy.

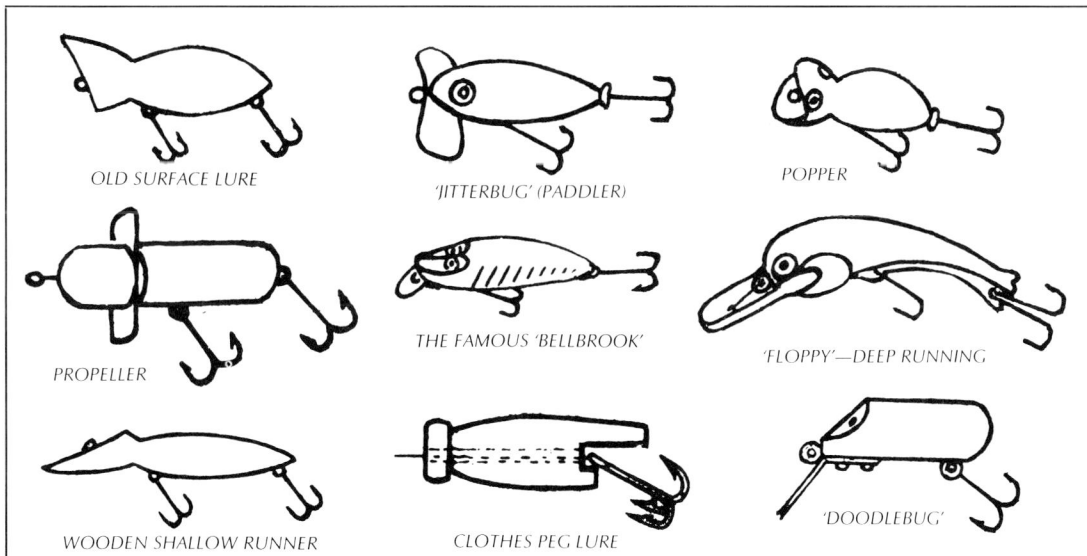

OLD SURFACE LURE · 'JITTERBUG' (PADDLER) · POPPER · PROPELLER · THE FAMOUS 'BELLBROOK' · 'FLOPPY'—DEEP RUNNING · WOODEN SHALLOW RUNNER · CLOTHES PEG LURE · 'DOODLEBUG'

All of the lures shown here have caught good sized bass, including the model fashioned from an old clothes peg. But obviously the modern lures that have resulted from long research will work best.

BATFISH *Ephippididae*

Long-finned batfish,
Platax pinnatus

An odd-shaped fish which floats among leaves and debris when young, camouflaged by its form and colour; a slow swimmer, it becomes crescentic in outline and then rounder and deeper as it reaches full size, which takes about nine years. At first glance mature batfish are completely unrecognisable from the young. Their slow swimming speed and deep bodies make them an easy target for spearfishermen. A foul feeder, its flesh is inferior, and it has an odour like iodine.

FEATURES: All members of the family have brown vertical bands across their eyes which fade with age. The juveniles have three prominent dark bands across the body while they live in estuaries and rivers. The bands fade when the older batfish moves out to offshore reefs. They are much prized by aquariums because of the dramatic colour changes that occur as they mature. The hump-headed batfish, *Platax batavianus*, frequently are confused with Maori wrasse because of the humps that develop on their heads with age. Fully grown hump-headed batfish reach 5.8 kg and in mature fish their depth matches their length. The unrelated but similar silver batfish, *Monodactylus argenteus*, also known as butterfish and butter bream, leave saltwater for freshwater and resemble the Moorish idol. The illustrated long-finned batfish, *Platax pinnatus*, have fins like clipped bird's wings, unusually small mouths, and extended anterior dorsals. Short-finned batfish, *Zabidius novemaculatus*, have a brilliant silvery sheen over most of the body and chocolate-brown fins.

FISHING TECHNIQUE: Few batfish are caught by sportsfishermen. They will take baits of prawn and cut fish, but most are not worth preparing for the table. They are caught on handlines with light sinkers and 2/0 hooks.

DISTRIBUTION: Around tropical coasts, with the narrow-banded batfish also found across the top of Australia. Whitley notes that they are plentiful in the Red Sea and off Japan.

BEACH SALMON *Leptobramidae*

A popular angling fish in Australian temperate waters, respected for the tough fight they put up despite their small size. They grow to 37.5 cm in length and only 900 grams, or 2 lb, but provide plenty of action on light gear. Despite their name they are not true salmon and have been known by a variety of names, including steel-back, flat or silver salmon, slender bream and Moreton Bay tailor. Whitley preferred slender brama in accordance with their scientific name, *Leptobrama mulleri*. Grant believes steel-back is appropriate because of the vivid steel-blue coloration on the back. They are quickly identified by the deep setting of the single dorsal fin, which is a plain silver in females and black-tipped in males. They have small eyes with fatty lids and roam about estuaries and the lower reaches of coastal rivers. These fish have been known to leap into boats, as well as turning up off beaches to attack hardy-heads, herrings and pilchards. Their flesh is soft and they are better suited to smoking than as panfish.

FEATURES: They are heavily arched on top, with steely-grey, slab-sided bodies. The anal lobe is sickle-shaped, beginning well before the level of origin of the dorsal fin. They are unlike any other fish.

FISHING TECHNIQUE: Beach fishermen reach beach salmon with light gear, using pipis, molluscs, squid, worms, prawns, and cut fish. They require small hooks but the sinker must be heavy enough to take the bait out to where they are feeding. On first contact they surprise the angler with their sustained determination.

DISTRIBUTION: From tropical Western Australia, across the Northern Territory into northern and central Queensland, but never in cold water.

Beach salmon,
Leptobrama mulleri

READING A BEACH: Wave action on beaches causes gutters, sandbanks, channels and deep holes, all harbouring some species of fish at various times in the tidal cycle. The most productive section is the channel or gutter, which are of two types, low or high tide gutters, both of them easy to fish. A gutter is a deep body of water and most big beaches provide multiple gutter systems. The waves break some distance from the shore with blue water between the waves and the beach. This channel of blue water usually is the most rewarding for anglers.

BELLOWSFISH *Macroramphosidae*

Crested bellowsfish,
Notopogon lilliei

Strange little fish whose profiles resemble an old fashioned bellows for blowing the fire. Their long dorsal spine and the tail suggest the handles and the tubular snout represents the spout of the bellows. They are trawled in vast numbers in continental shelf waters and are eaten by flathead, snapper and other commercial fishes. There are at least seven species in Australian waters, including the banded bellowsfish, *Centriscops obliquus*, a coldwater variety that grows to 250 mm in length and are common at depths between 450 and 750 metres with five or more reddish, brown stripes slashed across their silvery-white bodies; the common bellowsfish, *Macrorhamphosus scolopax*, which have a long, tapering third dorsal spine, are red or pink on the upper half of the body and silver below; the crested bellowsfish, *Notopogon lilliei*, which have a crest of fine, bristle-like spines over the nape or dorsal surface and are studded in large silvery spots; and the Hawaiian

bellowsfish, *Macrorhamphosus velitaris*, which have tapering snouts, five or six spines on the first dorsal fin, silvery ventral surface and bluish-black heads and bodies.

FEATURES: The bodies of all bellowsfish are very deep and strongly compressed and they are covered in small spiny scales. There are two rows of bony plates embedded on the shoulder in the skin. The dorsal fin has a soft portion made up of rays and an anterior spiny portion carrying a long serrated spine. They resemble pipefishes and seahorses because their mouths are at the end of a bony, tube-like snout. They are seldom seen by anglers and are rated trash fish by trawlermen.

DISTRIBUTION: Deep waters off southern and south-eastern Australia, with varieties in Tasmania. Also off South Africa, South America and New Zealand.

HANDLING THE CATCH: To return captured fish safely to the water, wet the hands. Bare hands remove the slime or scales, natural protection, from the fish's body. If you cannot remove the hook quickly, cut the nylon as close to the hook as possible. The hook will dissolve in the fish's intestinal juices.

BILLFISH   *Istiophoridae*

Billfish is the internationally agreed name for the group comprising swordfish, spearfish, sailfish and marlin. All members of the group are good food fish, all provide outstanding sport, and all are noted for their remarkable speed and fighting prowess. Fishermen recognise members of the group immediately from their upper jaws, which are prolonged into a spear or bill. One member of the group, the broadbill swordfish, has been timed at speeds of 80 kph or 50 mph, which makes it the fastest fish in the sea. A swordfish that attacked a wooden boat penetrated to a depth of 67.5 cm. The piece of pierced planking is in the British Museum of Natural History.

Scientists recognised more than a century ago that billfish use their dorsal fins as a vane or rudder in the water to assist their swimming speed and keep them on a straight course to their targets. They can erect or depress the dorsal fin according to their needs. The sword-like spears attached to their upper jaws are used to slash through shoals of anchovy, pilchards, herrings and whatever else they prey on.

Australia is one of the world's leaders in the tagging of billfish. Under guidance of Dr. Julian Pepperell of the New South Wales State Fisheries Department our game fishermen have come to accept that they should only kill billfish if they are of record size. They happily tag the rest and restore them to the sea. Each spring around 1000 billfish are tagged on the east coast with fishermen using tagging kits supplied by Dr. Pepperell. Some of the tags have turned up off New Guinea, the Solomon Islands, New Zealand, the Marshall Islands and one even appeared 7200 km from eastern Australia, north of Tahiti. A small black marlin weighing only 35 kg was tagged off Cairns and turned up 800 km to the south 14 days later.

At an international symposium on billfish in 1972 in Hawaii Dr. Izumi Nakamura's revision of the world's billfish was accepted. This recognised 11 species of billfish, the swordfish, the Atlantic sailfish, the Pacific sailfish, three species of spearfish, the white marlin of the Atlantic, the striped marlin of the Indo-Pacific, two blue marlin, and the black marlin. Some scientists reduced this list to nine species by only recognising one sailfish and one species of marlin.

Since game fishing began in Australia around 1930 the striped marlin and the Indo-Pacific black marlin have been generally recognised. But the presence in our waters of a third marlin was not recognised until around 1937. Various attempts were made to press the claims for fish named D'Ombrain's marlin and Howard's marlin on the grounds that their colouring differed from the known species but it was not until 1968 that the first authenticated capture of the third species, blue marlin, was made off Sydney Heads by radio and TV identity Bob Dyer. Dyer was able to confirm that his catch matched in every detail blue marlin he had seen taken in Hawaii.

It's likely that many blue marlin were caught off the Australian coast before 1968 but colour had proved such an unreliable guide to identification that game fishing experts were not prepared to accept their presence until Dyer provided additional proof. Marlin often go through dramatic colour changes, perhaps because of the excitement of the fight for freedom. Marlin brought quickly into the cockpit of a boat will run through changes from a beautiful shimmering dark blue to coppery-green, to pale blue and silver, before fading away to a drab greyish-black. In the water the refraction of the light and the angle the fish is swimming against the sun can have diverse effects on colouring. Stripes and spots are more reliable, as are the position and shape of fins and the jaw shape. Here is a rundown on Australian billfish:

Black marlin, *Makaira indica*: Found mainly in the Indian and Pacific Oceans and widely accepted as the most prized game fish in Australian waters. The combination of the black marlin's fighting qualities and their great size makes them an awesome proposition for any sportsman and the thought of so many of them being slaughtered by Japanese and Korean long-line fishermen is saddening. Black marlin have short, thick and sometimes upturned bills and a heavy, powerful body that is deep and rather humped at the shoulders in the larger fish. It is this shoulder hump that helps distinguish it from blue marlin. The black marlin has no marks or colour

Black marlin, *Makaira indica*

FAR RIGHT:
This method of baiting blue pilchards for marlin on a single hook is most effective for snapper and other fish that take their prey head first.

bands on the body after death and the main identification is the pectoral fin, which is rigidly erect and cannot be set down along the body. The name black marlin is unfortunate as this magnificent fish is a striking slate blue on top, changing to a lighter blue around the centre of the body and silvery underneath. Often pale blue stripes appear when black marlin are active but these disappear after death. The Japanese refer to them as white marlin because of their white under-belly and the Chinese refer to them as white skin. The straplike pelvic fins are shorter than in other marlin. The flesh is always light pink. The Australian record of 654.08 kg, by Michael Magrath off Cairns in 1973, was 53.53 short of the world record of 707.61 kg.

FISHING TECHNIQUE: Small marlin will take lures such as plastic squid and knuckleheads but big marlin will only bite on large baits. Baitfish of 3 to 5 kg are used on the marlin grounds 56 km out of Cairns, with the baitfish trolled slowly to give it a natural swimming appearance. The big black prefer to fight deep down, often not broaching when first hooked or for sometime afterwards. They have great endurance and unless hooked deep in the stomach will prolong the fight by surfacing and thrashing about in an attempt to disgorge the hook. Normally a speed of four to six knots is ideal for trolling but the weather and roughness of the sea influence the boat's speed.

DISTRIBUTION: Black marlin are distributed right down the Australian east coast from Cape York to Mallacouta, and are found off all the islands north of Australia and across the Indian and Pacific Oceans. A migratory stock of small fish worked its way down the east coast, appearing off Port Stephens, Sydney and Bermagui around the end of December, but Cairns and the water off Ribbon Reef near Cooktown remain the major black marlin grounds and among experienced game fishermen there is conjecture about how long this will last. All over the world exciting marlin habitats have appeared only to be fished out by anglers ready to pay small fortunes to try for the big fish. This may not apply to Cairns as the Barrier Reef offers plenty of food and Japanese long-liners have been barred from fishing near the reef since 1981.

Blue marlin, *Makaira nigricans*: Dr. Pepperell calculates that blue marlin require water with a minimum temperature of 22 degrees Celsius, and their preference for warm conditions is probably the reason blues are not seen as often as black and striped marlin in Australian waters. The blue's dorsal fin is higher than on the black but not as high as on striped marlin. The pectorals fold in alongside the body and this is the main factor in identification. The blue marlin's spear is longer and more rounded in section than on striped marlin, but not as heavy as on the black. Blue marlin do not have the depth of shoulder and body, black marlin have but are thick and heavy on the sides. The lower jaws are not as long as those of striped marlin and fit close to the underside of the upper jaws.

FISHING TECHNIQUE: The customary method of fishing for blue marlin is to set the hook into the baitfish pointing to the tail, with the trace brought back along the fish and lightly tied with a hitch at the nose or front of the bait. When the blue marlin take the bait and swallow it the ties will come loose and the fish must be hooked, though they sometimes get the hook into their throat or gills, which spoils the fight. The blue marlin's stripes fade quickly after death.

Striped marlin, *Tetrapturus audax*: Smallest of the marlins, averaging between 90 and 135 kg. They are known to reach 440 kg but the Australian record is 169 kg for a blue taken off Bondi in 1985 by Bill Wotton. They take their name from the 14 prominent lavender coloured stripes that extend well across the body and are easily distinguished from black marlin by their more slender shape. Their bill is long and narrow whereas it is short and stout in the black, and the pectoral fin can be folded into the body. Striped marlin are a beautiful cobalt blue along the top, turning to silvery-white along the belly. The high, pointed dorsal fin extends right along the back to the second dorsal fin and is dark blue, often with spots at its base. The dorsal fin is so high it is often as tall as the body is deep and is the major feature in distinguishing the species.

FISHING TECHNIQUE: Striped marlin are more spectacular than other billfish when hooked, often racing across the sea making 20 or 30 immense leaps from the instant the hook is set. In amongst the foam and the spray, striped marlin shake their entire body and flap their pectorals before crashing back again in another gush of foam and spray. Then they turn on a show of greyhound leaps, their heads bowed and

Blue marlin, *Makaira nigricans*

Striped marlin,
Tetrapturus audax

Sailfish, *Istiophorus platypterus*

that long spear pointing downwards, finally diving deep to carry on the fight, first on one side of the boat and then on the other. They will take fish or even dead shark baits, but are much more easily caught on white, red or green feathered lures. They often swim in pairs and when one is hooked the other will follow it around and even swim up to the boat before the captured fish is gaffed. At other times they swim in large schools and one year off Port Stephens, New South Wales, 52 were counted in a calm sea. March is the best month for striped marlin in New Zealand but in Australia they do not turn up until late May.

Sailfish, *Istiophorus platypterus*: Sailfish are easily distinguished from marlin by the extraordinary sail-like dorsal fin that gives it its name. They are far smaller fish than marlin, lacking the great depth of shoulder and body. Their slender bodies and long thin bills make them look like toys by comparison. They are fish that remain in one area for extended periods, brilliant blue in colour from the sail down to the mid-line of the body, where they turn silver and white. The big dorsal fin is liberally flecked in blue or black spots and there are broken lines of greyish-blue across the body from behind the gill cover to the tail. The biggest sailfish taken in Australian waters on a rod and line weighed 79.83 kg and most of those taken in Australia are under 45 kg. Whatever the breaking strain of your line, check with the Game Fishing Association of Australia if you catch one over 55 kg.

FISHING TECHNIQUE: Sailfish are light-tackle fish despite the magnificent fight they put on when hooked. Sailfish specialists along the Barrier Reef, at Cape Moreton in southern Queensland and off Exmouth, Western Australia, do not gaff them, but take hold of their beaks with a gloved fist, tag them, and immediately release them. They take fish-strip baits and the same small live fish as the marlins but in far smaller sizes. They also bite readily at feathered lures. Sailfish are often attracted by schools of pilchards and will circle the school to force them into a tighter circle before they take it in turns to swim through the school, slashing vigorously with their bills to kill or stun their prey. They usually only erect their dorsal fins to scare food into tighter groups and mostly leave only the upper lobe of the tail showing above water. Lines with 10 to 15 kg breaking strain are ample for sailfish, and sometimes lines as light as 2 kg are used.

DISTRIBUTION: Sailfish of world standard have been taken off Western Australia, New Guinea and Queensland and smaller specimens from New South Wales. They are often found among the islands north of Australia but many are seen around Cairns, south to Gladstone.

Pacific short-billed spearfish, *Tetrapturus augustirostris*: Although very restricted in numbers, these spearfish have been taken from Port Stephens to Ulladulla, New South Wales. The biggest so far recorded weighed 30.5 kg. They are greyish-blue on top, silvery-white beneath with about 20 stripes down the back, extending to about a third of the fish. The first dorsal fin is dark, not spotted. When they first appeared in Australian waters spearfish were thought to be young marlin but this has been discredited and the species has been recognised as a separate identity.

FISHING TECHNIQUE: Spearfish will take trolled baits and lures similar to those used for marlin and tuna. They appear in northern Australia in August up to early October and in New South Wales in December, February and April, apparently riding currents.

DISTRIBUTION: Specimens now at the Australian Museum in Sydney came from north-western Australia, northern Australia, and New South Wales.

Broadbill swordfish, *Xiphias gladius*: A much prized commercial food fish and a challenging sportfish. They have been sighted regularly in Australian waters since 1939 and have been washed up on our beaches, but they have only rarely been caught by Australian game fishermen. They have usually been smaller than the breaking strain used and the prized large swordfish has yet to be caught in Australia. Most of the recorded strandings have been on surf beaches and there have been a sprinkling of reports of professional fishermen catching specimens under 10 kg. Dr. Pepperell records that a good many broadbill swordfish were taken by Japanese longline boats operating off the Queensland and New South Wales coasts,

Pacific short-billed spearfish, *Tetrapturus augustirostris*

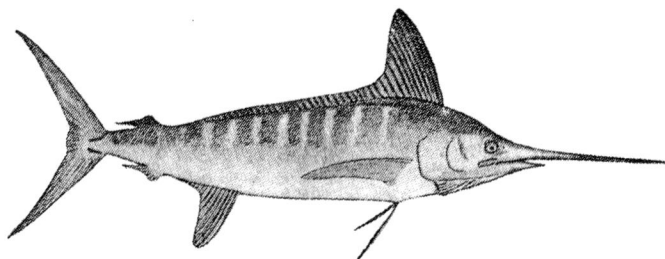

45

Broadbill swordfish, *Xiphias gladius*, the only member of the family *Xiphiidae*

and adds that one of those caught was 4.5 metres long.

FISHING TECHNIQUE: Broadbill swordfish are extremely wary, suspicious fish and must be sought with a completely different technique to that used for marlin. According to master angler Zane Grey, they have very soft mouths and hooks pull out more easily. On a 54-day experiment for the University off northern Chile in 1954 a team, led by Lou Marron from the specially designed launch *Explorer*, sighted 93 broadbill swordfish. Baits were presented to 56 and 27 strikes were made. Of these, 17 fish were hooked but only 11 were landed. One method used successfully against them on other outings was to cut open a baitfish such as a mackerel or small tuna and set two hooks inside. The bait was then sewn up. Bait for swordfish is not trolled as it is for marlin, but is kept ready until the broadbill is seen swimming on the surface. The baitfish is then lowered and the trick is to present the bait across its path, moving it slowly without any jerking movements. Another method is to fish for them at night in deep water, using squid baits suspended under "cyalume" light sticks.

DISTRIBUTION: Despite their wariness, broadbill swordfish have been caught in Japan, Formosa, Hawaii, New Zealand, California, Peru, Scandinavia, Portugal, Iceland, off the Straits of Gibraltar, inside the Mediterranean, off Africa and the Cape and around to Madagascar and Reunion Island. The world record was caught by Lou Marron, a fish that weighed 536 kg or 1,182 lb, off Chile in May, 1953, on a 60 kg breaking strain line.

DISPUTED CATCH: In 1933, a magazine called *Angling And Gun Sport* published an account of Roy Smith catching Australia's first marlin. This was accepted as the first capture of a game fish by an Australian for many years. In fact, the first marlin landed in Australasia was caught by Dr. Mark Lidwill at Port Stephens in April, 1914, when he landed a 52.17 kg (120 lb) black marlin on a 21-thread line.

Blackfish (River)   *Gadopsidae*

Unique freshwater fishes found nowhere in the world except Tasmania and the Murray-Darling River system. They are also known as slippery and slimy. They have been favourites with inland anglers since the early days of Australian settlement. Thousands of them have been caught by anglers fishing for trout using beetles, caddis, larvae, crustaceans and small shrimps. Two species are recognised, *Gadopsis marmoratus*, and the recently described *Gadopsis bispinosus*, known only from central Victoria. Both varieties are notable for the large amount of slime on their bodies. Even experienced anglers find it hard to remove hooks from their mouths. River blackfish are believed to have evolved thousands of years ago when Tasmania was part of the mainland. Their flesh is much lighter than trout flesh and they weigh-in well below trout weight. The poet C. J. Dennis was among those who rated river blackfish a sweet and toothsome dish.

FEATURES: They vary in colour from shades of brown or blue to greenish brown. The scales are very small. They avoid sunlight and apparently only reach their optimum in shadowy, overgrown waters where they can cling to stream debris and submerged tree roots. They have been recorded at weights up to 5.5 kg but generally are much smaller and 62.5 cm in length. Although they take their name from the dark blotches along their sides, they are yellow below.

FISHING TECHNIQUE: Let the line run freely to set the hook when you have a blackfish on. Use a light trout rod, No. 4 to 6 hook, with a little lead a metre above it. The best baits are wood grubs, earthworms, yabbies and mudeyes. Best time to fish for blackfish is between dusk and sundown. If the water is running fast enough to require a sinker, let the line run freely through it. Split-shot on the line a metre above the hook will prevent the sinker slipping down onto the hook.

DISTRIBUTION: Mostly in the streams of eastern Victoria south of the Great Dividing Range. They have also been caught in the Condamine River in central Queensland, in South Australian backwaters and in northern Tasmania. They were introduced into southern Tasmania and the Snowy River.

River blackfish, *Gadopsis marmoratus*

BLENNIES   *Blenniidae*

Little, shoreline fishes found in all Australian States. They shelter among weeds, rocky crevices, stands of cunjevoi, and coral outcrops. They are extremely well camouflaged and more common than anglers realise, usually clinging so closely to their chosen refuge even the most powerful waves cannot dislodge them. They feed on algae, but the largest of the family can produce sharp, painful bites although they grow to only 75 cm. They are also known as saltlickers or grasshopper fishes and are far too small to be considered for the table or even for bait.

FEATURES: They are usually without scales, with the spinous and soft portions of the dorsal fin about equal in length. Snake blennies such as the black-backed snake blenny, *Ophiclinus gracilis*, in the related family *Clinidae*, have unusually long anal and dorsal fins which continue along the body to the tail. The narrow body is eel-like, brown above and yellow below. Reef blennies such as the rippled blenny *Istiblennius edentulus* differ from other blennies in having gill-membranes free from the isthmus and slender, moveable comb-like teeth. Some have the dorsal membrane distinctly notched between spines and rays. The sabretoothed blenny, of the genus *Petroscirtes*, has well developed teeth that protrude from the corners of the lower jaw often shocking anglers. The illustrated oyster blenny, *Omobranchus anolius*, has sabre-like teeth and a flattened helmet or crest above the eyes which provide it with an imposing appearance as it guards the eggs laid by the female amid empty oyster shells. The head and cheeks are boldly patterned with vertical blue-white lines. The rearward rays to the soft dorsal fin become delicate, slender filaments in mature males. Most blennies show up occasionally in amateur fishermen's bait nets but are seldom used for angling.

DISTRIBUTION: Blennies are spread through coastal waters of all States and some such as Tasmanian blenny, *Pictiblennius tasmanianus* are confined to certain regions.

Lined blenny, *Salarias fasciatus*

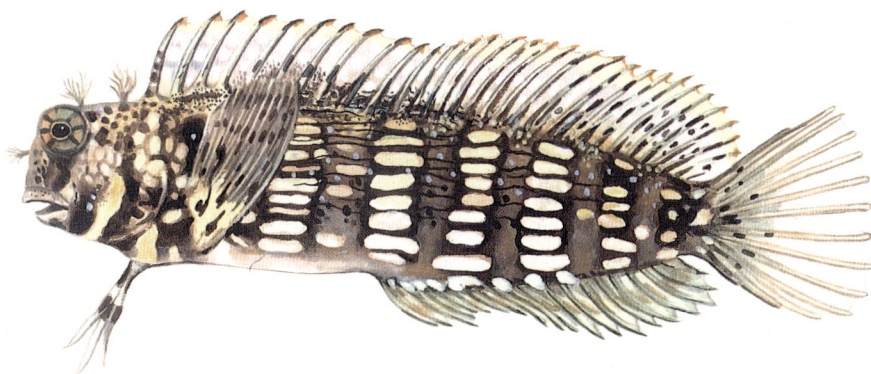

Oyster blenny,
Omobranchus anolius

BLUEFISH   *Girellinae*

Bluefish, *Girella cyanea*

An attractive member of the luderick family. Capture of a bluefish is now rare in Australian waters but it is fairly common in New Zealand and some Pacific islands and Australian holidaymakers at Norfolk Island and Lord Howe Island catch them regularly. They are table fish of outstanding quality. Freshly caught they are among the most beautiful fish in the sea but their colour fades quickly after capture. They are carnivorous, feeding mainly on crustaceans, shellfish and small fish. Bluefish are very similar in shape to the stark rock blackfish but can be identified immediately by their brilliant colouring. They are known in New Zealand by the Maori name korokoropounamu, and are much sought as subjects for underwater photographers. They were once often sighted off the New South Wales coast but are now seldom seen.

FEATURES: Bluefish are a dazzling violet-blue along the back and sides and on the caudal fin. Their golden spots are extremely small. They are deep-bodied fish with small heads and mouths and teeth with three points on each. Mature specimens are yellowy beneath. They have long dorsal fins without notches between the spinous and soft portions, spines and rays about equal in height. They grow to 75 cm and to 4.5 kg.

FISHING TECHNIQUE: Bluefish are caught on medium tackle, with larger hooks than luderick—up to 4/0 is a good size. They respond well to berleying and can be brought right to the surface. They school in large numbers on kelp banks. Experts recommend a sinker on a bottom rig, similar to those used for snapper fishing. Best baits are molluscs and small fish.

DISTRIBUTION: Rocky coastal waters and offshore reefs, but rarely in estuaries. They prefer waters around headlands and islands and seldom venture into colder waters.

BOARFISH *Pentacerotidae*

Spiny-finned, deep-bodied, bottom-dwelling fish with their heads encased in rough, bony plates. They are plentiful in several species in Australia but at depths that mostly put them beyond the reach of sports fishermen. They are a major part of trawling catches, however, competing with nannygai, trevally, snapper and jackass fish because of their splendid eating qualities. Their mouths are at the end of a pronounced snout, and the dorsal, ventral and anal fins carry heavy, robust spines. Some of the family have venomous spines that can inflict painful wounds that call for immediate treatment. The big-spined boarfish, *Undecimus hendecacanthus*, is a fleshy-lipped, deeply-compressed variety taken in the Great Australian Bight, which has its entire body covered in scales; the giant boarfish, *Paristiopterus labiousus*, is an aptly named specimen mostly caught at weights above 12 kg in depths around 100 fathoms, which loses the bold dark markings of its youth once it matures; the brown-spotted boarfish, *Paristiopterus gallipavo*, has an elongated body unusual in the family, but the same large mouth and firm, tasty flesh; black-spotted boarfish, *Zanclistius elevatus*, is a silver-grey variety with broad dark vertical bands across the short, deep body.

FEATURES: The shape of the boarfish's head and the length of the fins change with age, but the nasty long dorsal rays are common at every age. At times they look almost as deep as they are long.

FISHING TECHNIQUE: Boarfish are only taken accidentally by anglers when the fish make rare appearances in shallow coastal waters. They are more generally trawled in depths of 260 metres.

DISTRIBUTION: Western Australia, South Australia, Victoria, Tasmania, and New South Wales.

Giant boarfish,
Paristiopterus labiousus

BOMBAY DUCK *Harpadontidae*

A delicious eating fish when used in Chinese dishes like chop-suey, in fish cakes or in Indian curries but looked on with suspicion when served as orthodox table fish. They are flabby-bodied fish with almost translucent torsos and are probably regarded with suspicion as table fare because of their soft flesh. They are closely related to suaries and grinners. The most widely known varieties are the Indian Bombay duck, *Harpadon nehereus*, which Whitley says was a great favourite of King George V, who developed a taste for it in India, and the illustrated glassy Bombay duck, *Harpadon translucens*, which is also known as ghost grinner. They seldom grow beyond 1.5 kg in weight and average around 25 cm in length.

FEATURES: Bombay duck are easily identified by their milky-white colour and the absence of scales when taken in nets. The scales peel away if they are handled. The tips of the dorsal and tail fins are blackish, and the eyes and viscera are bluish. The mouth has an unusually wide gape and some of the tiny barbed teeth lie outside the lip. The tail is forked, but three-lobed, with the central portion an extension of the body. Bombay duck have little interest for anglers except as trolled bait for large mackerel or cobia.

DISTRIBUTION: From Queensland estuaries, rivers and coastal waters through the Northern Territory into north-western Australia, but seldom in southern Queensland.

Bombay duck, *Harpadon translucens*, the only species known from Australia

THE DUN'S LIFESTYLE: Mayflies are known as nymphs during their life in the water. They then become duns, during which period they do not eat because their mouths atrophy. They live only for a brief time in this form but take on a dull colouring easily recognised by anglers and fish. The duns leave the water and make their way to bushes and trees along the banks of rivers and pools, where they enter their final, "spinner" stage, shedding their skin and mating on the wing in what is known as the "nuptial flight". The most common artificial fly used to imitate the dun is the Australian March brown or Turkey brown.

BONEFISH *Albulidae*

Bonefish, *Albula neoguinaica*

Fast, wary fishes of tropical shallows regarded as one of the most exciting of all the species Australian anglers can catch. Ernest Hemingway, Zane Grey and Ring Lardner ranked the bonefish the fastest in the sea, and there are many authentic accounts of bonefish taking out 350 metres of line on their first run. The world record for a bonefish stands at 8.6 kg but the Australian record is 4.66 kg. The extent of Australia's bonefish population is unknown. They are frequently confused with sand whiting despite the obvious difference in their dorsal fins.

FEATURES: The bonefish has only one dorsal fin, the whiting two. The mouth of the bonefish is underslung, while that of the whiting is terminal, located near the snout tip, which is always tipped in black. Bonefish are bright green to blue above, with brilliantly silver sides and faint longitudinal lines.

FISHING TECHNIQUE: Overseas experts advise the lightest possible gear, but at least 400 metres of line is essential. A two-metre spinning rod, fitted with a good breaking system is recommended as the fish will make several runs after the first strike and it is necessary to reduce the length of each run. Sharpen your hooks and wear polaroid glasses to help pick out the bonefish in clear water. They react badly to the noise of outboard motors so experts use pole boats that can move about the shallows without disturbing them. Strike on the first nibble as bonefish habitually crush their baits and discard them. Examination of the stomach contents of bonefish has shown them partial to squid, surf worms, ghost crabs and pilchards.

DISTRIBUTION: The weedy shallows of north-western Australia, the Northern Territory, most of Queensland, and isolated sections of the New South Wales coast. Tropical north-western Australian anglers have also experienced the silver flash that distinguishes a hooked bonefish from whiting or mullet.

BONITO   *Scombridae*

Fast, durable little tuna that offer good sport on light game tackle. They are much sought as baitfish, and bonito strips are used in catching sharks, marlin, sailfish and the larger tuna. They have a habit of breaking the surface when feeding on shoals of anchovies, pilchards, and hardyheads, and are also known as skipjacks, skippers and horse mackerel. The Game Fishing Association of Australia's record for bonito is 7.5 kg by Bill Jenkins at Bermagui in 1978. Australian bonito, *Sarda australis*, can be identified immediately it comes into view by the pattern of ten or more straight dark stripes that run along the sides, with those towards the belly tending to break into wider bars. The closely related oriental bonito, *Sarda orientalis*, which lacks stripes on the belly; leaping bonito, *Cybiosarda elegans*, a smaller sub-tropical variety also known as Watson's bonito, differs from the common bonito by having a combination of spots and broken bars above the lateral line and continuous longitudinal lines below; striped bonito, *Katsuwonis pelamis*, a New Zealand species also known as striped or skipjack tuna, that sometimes strays into Australian waters, has only five stripes below the lateral line.

Australian bonito, *Sarda australis*

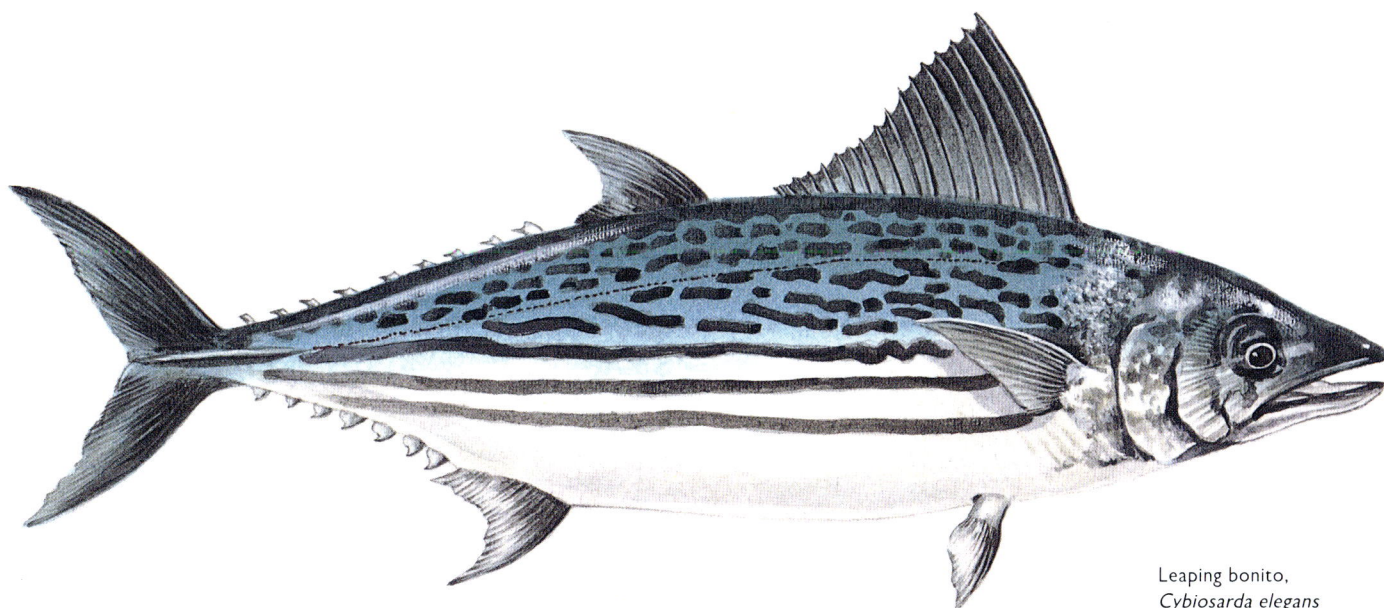

Leaping bonito, *Cybiosarda elegans*

FEATURES: Apart from the body stripes, bonito differ from mackerel because of the keel on each side of their tails. They are beautifully streamlined, with finlets and a well-forked tail, and can really motor through the water. They can be an annoying fish, refusing to take baits while they are frolicking about the surface, but at other times they will strike viciously at any bait or lure offered.

FISHING TECHNIQUE: Bonito are mostly caught trolling behind boats, taking baits of fish, squid, octopus, and feathered and metal lures in the wake. Game fishermen eager to get a few aboard for bait before they try larger game fish often put out half a dozen lines at a time, and when they get into a school of bonito, all eager to bite, the action is fast and eventful. As they feed near the surface in deep water, bonito are proving suckers for the growing practice of fishing in saltwater with flies.

DISTRIBUTION: Both the Australian bonito and the leaping bonito, *Cybiosarda elegans*, are abundant on the east coast and occasionally are taken in Victorian waters. They have not been recorded in Western Australia or South Australia, however. The oriental bonito is known only from Western Australia. A variety with fewer stripes has been caught in northern New Zealand in summer.

USEFUL COMPANION: The legendary Zane Grey made a fortune from his novels on America's wild west and he enjoyed spending it on trips to catch game fish. He has rightly been credited with pioneering the quest for marlin and other billfish in Australia and New Zealand. On all his trips he was accompanied by Captain Laurie Mitchell, whom Grey regarded as a master of the fishing art. On a single day, fishing off New Zealand in 1926, Mitchell caught 10 striped marlin. The photograph showing this catch has faded, but the weights remain clear: 255, 268, 254, 236, 258, 236, 246, 272, 206 and 224 lb. On that same trip to New Zealand Captain Mitchell landed the largest black marlin caught on a rod and reel to that time; a 976-pounder that remained the biggest black marlin taken anywhere in the world for 27 years.

FISH ATTRACTORS THAT WORK: Several States have successfully developed fish attractors for amateur fishermen and skindivers by anchoring small, coloured sections of netting in deep, offshore waters. The netting looks like a road-mender's barrier and is held in place by a buoy with a train wheel or similar heavy object tied to the netting on the bottom. The netting, held about six metres from the surface, is no danger to shipping as the buoy sinks temporarily if hit by a passing ship. Films have proved that fish not only congregate in front of the netting but drive small food fish into it.

Tiger sharks are the trashcans of our oceans, and will eat anything they can swallow. Their stomachs have revealed lumps of coal, dogs, cats, entire sea birds, pieces of cars, a woman's handbag, a watch that was still ticking, half a porpoise, as well as human remains such as legs and shoulders. The celebrated "Shark Arm Case" began at the Coogee Aquarium in New South Wales when a tiger shark disgorged an arm with a piece of rope tied to the wrist.

BONY BREAM *Clupeidae*

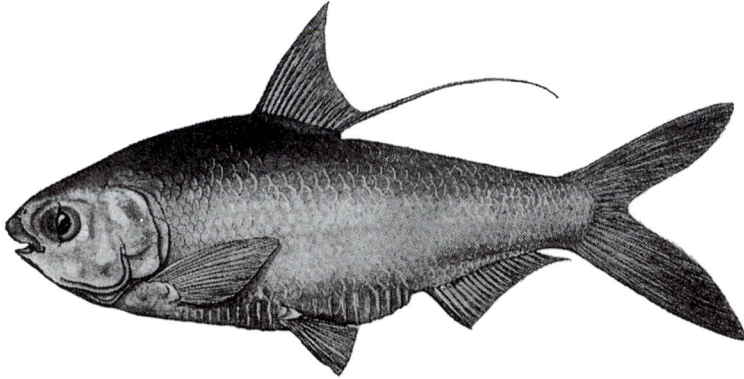

Freshwater bony bream, Nematalosa erebi

Small, silvery, partly iridescent fishes found in both saltwater and freshwater in Australia, and also known as hair-back herrings. They have toothless mouths which are used like vacuum cleaners to transfer mud and vegetation containing small aquatic insects down to their stomach, where a gizzard-like apparatus grinds up the food. They are virtually inedible to humans but during the war Australian servicemen had to endure eating them from cans labelled "Goldfish", fighting their way through a multiplicity of small bones. Oceanic bony bream will swim deep upstream in coastal rivers. The freshwater variety often is carried downstream in floods and lives without inconvenience in marine waters. The bony bream is known in South Australia as pyberry or tukari, *Nematalosa erebi*, has a silvery body with the head and pectoral fins tinged with yellow. The head is scaleless. They are common in the Murray River where they withstand salty conditions. Marine bony bream, *Nematalosa come*, are ideal bait for snapper and mangrove jack and have sharp belly scales, silvery-brown fish with a fleshy snout taken mostly by net fishermen. The freshwater bony bream, *Nematalosa erebi*, has a long trailing filament on the dorsal fin.

FEATURES: None of Australia's bony bream can be handled without losing scales and they usually die rapidly. They die in their thousands in mid-winter, apparently from temperature shock or a reduction of oxygen in the water. They are distinguished by their fin counts; the oceanic bony bream grow to 300 mm, the freshwater variety to 400 mm. Both species have a muddy taste that makes them suitable only as baitfish.

DISTRIBUTION: Widely distributed in Australian rivers by flooding, the bony bream is abundant in Lake Alexandrina and Lake Albert in South Australia, throughout the Murray-Darling system, and in inland rivers of tropical Western Australia and the Northern Territory.

THERMOCLINE: A narrow zone of water which begins at the limit of the sun's penetration. The warmer water on top expands and becomes less dense than the water below it. The thermocline is the area of gradation between the colder and warmer water and presents the most favourable oxygen conditions for trout in large expanses of water such as Lake Eucumbene.

BOXFISH *Ostraciidae*

Yellow boxfish,
Ostracion cubicus

Heavily armoured fish represented by one family in Australian waters. Their flesh is poisonous and should never be eaten but such is the toughness of the armour-plate in which their bodies are encased it is unlikely any sportsfisherman would ever attempt to skin and fillet them. They are wrongly known as stonefish in Western Australia. Boxfish can bend their tails forward so that the tail lies alongside the body. The best known Australian boxfish are the illustrated *Ostracion cubicus* or yellow boxfish, common on the Barrier Reef; the ornate boxfish, *Ostracion meleagris*, which have bright blue bodies covered with black-edged orange spots; the white-barred boxfish, *Anoplocapros lenticularis*, which have broad white bars over their red bodies; *Strophiurichthys robustus* or robust boxfish, found in seas off southern Australia. Boxfish are closely related to cowfish, trunkfish and coffinfish, all notable for their hexagonal bony plates that fuse together. Some of the family can discharge a toxic chemical into surrounding seawater which can kill other fish. Despite their exotic appearance they are not good aquarium fish because of this ability to kill off other fish.

FEATURES: Most boxfish are very stiff in their swimming action and seem incapable of avoiding danger, but they are capable of short, fast dashes. They average between 15 cm and 45 cm in length and reach around 1 kg in weight. They all have bulging eyes. When danger threatens the fanlike tail is expanded and brought into play.

FISHING TECHNIQUE: Boxfish are mostly taken in the nets of prawn trawlers, who regard them as a nuisance, but they will take a hook. They have very little value for sportsmen except as curios when their amazing bodies dry out.

DISTRIBUTION: The yellow boxfish are black-spotted over the snout, cheeks and body when young but as they mature their spots turn blue. They range westward from the Barrier Reef into coastal waters of the Northern Territory and tropical western Australia. The robust boxfish is found in the inshore waters of southern Queensland and New South Wales to eastern Victoria. Their relatives, the coffinfish, turretfish and trunkfish are more drab in colour and are found in the tropical waters of the Indian and Pacific oceans.

BREAM   *Sparidae*

Crafty, wary fish that provide regular tests of angling skill all around Australia and are among our best table fish. They are peculiar to Australia's creeks, harbours, estuaries and ocean waters and have no relationship to the European bream, a carp of the family *Cyprinidae*. They are known by a profusion of local names, including black, bluenose, bony, cockney, emperor, freshwater, pikey, red, sea, hump-headed, government, silver, southern, silver, Cape Moreton, coral, slater, thick-lip and butterfly bream. Biologists have designated only four species in Australian waters, however, the important black or southern bream and tarwhine, and the lesser pikey, yellowfin and Ray's bream. Years of research conducted by New South Wales Fisheries Department biologist Stuart Rowland, which concluded in 1980, showed there were two common angling and commercial species, black bream, *Acanthopagrus butcheri*, and yellowfin bream, *Acanthopagrus australis*. Some of the other varieties in our waters are hybrids resulting from the overlapping of the distribution of these two species.

All bream become extremely cunning as they mature. They have fine teeth which can rip and tear at food and habitually approach baits suspiciously, trying to assess if there is danger near. Tests have shown that they will rip into a loose handful of prawns but as soon as hooks are put into the prawns they will swim away. Even when hungry they try to shake bait clear of the hook without swallowing it. The angler's best chances of catching bream come at night when they are less wary of the baits. They prefer the dark and seldom bite well in moonlight. They are very edgy about noise and a dropped oar or a foot dislodging stones from a river bank will scare them off.

Bream generally are olive and silvery in colour with darker bands running from head to tail. The sea-run variety are lighter

Black bream,
Acanthopagrus butcheri

Yellowfin bream,
Acanthopagrus australis

Tarwhine, *Rhabdosargus
sarba*

in colour than those from shaded waters. They mature at 15 to 20 cm in two to three years, mostly spawning in river mouths in winter. The Australian record for yellowfin bream is 4.44 kg by Horace Sedgley in 1984, for a fish taken from the Camden Haven River, New South Wales, and the record for a black bream was set at 3.45 kg by Jack Netting at Troubridge Point, South Australia, in 1969.

FEATURES: Black bream have a sharp dip in the lateral line near the front which gives them a flatter snout than yellowfin bream. Their ventral fins are always dark, whereas they are yellowish in yellowfin bream, which has greenish tints on the back and sides. Yellowfin bream have deeper bodies than black bream which tend to be more torpedo-shaped. Black bream prefer saline water, yellowfin bream do well in fresh-water.

FISHING TECHNIQUE: Splendid black bream fishing is to be had at night during winter. They feed at almost any stage of the tide, but bite best from half-flood through the first part of the ebb. They keep to deep holes by day but at night move into the shallows where they can often be taken in water only a metre or two deep. Yellowfin do not venture out of estuaries and are not caught in the surf or at sea. Yellowfin bream are caught on most of the best baits for black bream such as shrimps, yabbies, sand worms, soft shell clams, small fish, and cut crabs.

DISTRIBUTION: Black bream range from Shark Bay in Western Australia to the Myall Lakes in New South Wales and are the common species caught in the Gippsland Lakes in Victoria. They are common in South Australia, particularly in the Onkaparinga River and the rivers of Kangaroo Island, where November and January are the best months. Yellowfin bream range from Townsville in the north to Victoria's Gippsland Lakes.

Hybrid bream: Black bream and yellowfin bream sometimes become trapped in a lake or estuary closed to the sea, which makes hybrid bream possible through inter-breeding. Distribution of black bream and yellowfin bream overlaps between the Gippsland Lakes and the Myall Lakes and Stuart Rowland's tests showed populations of both in places like Wallaga Lake, Wongonga River and the Bermagui River. There was a large population of black bream in Myall Lake but their numbers declined in proportion to yellowfin bream as one proceeded up the coast. Specimens taken on the New South Wales coast around Narooma and Bermagui turned out to be hybrids.

Pikey bream, *Acanthopagrus berda*: An important member of the bream family, which takes its name from the conspicuous second spine of the anal fin. They are a tropical variety, usually dark grey to black in colour with a tinge of purple to brass. Some taken from mangrove-lined creeks

Pikey bream,
Acanthopagrus berda

are almost black. The black marks at the base of the pectoral fin usually found on other bream are completely absent in pikey bream. They grow to around 40 cm in Australian waters but have been recorded at twice that length in Indian Ocean waters. They are popular with night time anglers in South Africa.

FISHING TECHNIQUE: Taken in north Queensland by handlining close to jetty piles or from creek banks by anglers using small sinkers and cut baits of mullet, garfish and other small fish. Generally the same tackle and methods used for other bream apply to this species, which is delicious eating.

DISTRIBUTION: From Darwin to the Burdekin River in Queensland and the dominant bream in northern Australia.

Tarwhine, *Rhabdosargus sarba*: A semi-tropical fish of excellent edible quality, often confused with the black bream from which it can be readily distinguished by the shape of its head and the golden streaks along the back and sides. The tarwhine's head is more convex and has a more rounded appearance than the head of black bream. The centre of each scale is golden and this forms those longitudinal golden bands. The dorsal fin on the head is golden brown. Australian tarwhine grow to 52 cm and 2.7 kg but in South Africa they have been recorded up to 11 kg.

FISHING TECHNIQUE: For its size, tarwhine fights strongly, especially in the surf. The same tackle and bait can be used as for black bream and yellowfin bream. May, June and July are the best months. Tarwhine usually take the bait with two or three sharp tugs instead of in the pick-up-and-run style of other bream.

Ray's bream, *Brama brama*: A deepwater variety only occasionally found inshore, also known as pomfret, from the separate family *Bramidae*. They have an entry on page 213, Ray's Bream.

ONION AND GINGER TOPPED FISH

INGREDIENTS

4-8 fillets (according to size)
50 g margarine
1 dessertspoon oil
Juice ½ lemon
2 medium onions, finely chopped
2 cloves garlic, finely chopped
4 cm piece ginger, peeled and grated
1 teaspoon coriander
4 sprigs parsley, chopped

METHOD

Use mullet, red fish, bream or just choose whatever is freshest that day.

Set oven at 180°C. Line a baking dish with foil and place fish in it dotted with half the margarine and all the lemon juice. Bake uncovered for about 15 minutes or until cooked.

While this is happening gently fry the onions and garlic in a frying pan in the oil and margarine mixture until the onions start to turn a pale brown (5-10 minutes). Add the grated ginger, parsley, coriander and cook for one minute longer.

Remove from heat and add the topping to the fish as you serve it.

Serves 4

Reprinted with permission, Carolyn Dunne, *The Semi-Vegetarian Cookbook*, Bantam, 1989

BULLFISH *Chaetodontidae*

Close relatives of the butterflyfishes and coralfishes, which take their name from their conspicuous bony heads and the bony horns above the eyes, and vary in shape and number according to the maturity of the fish. They are in high demand as aquarium fish. The best known varieties are the illustrated feather-fin bullfish, *Heniochus acuminatus*, and the three-banded bullfish, *Heniochus chrysostomus*, which are also known as bannerfish because of the flag-like extension to the fourth dorsal ray. The feather-fin bullfish has two broad black bands across the body, whereas the three-banded bullfish has three. Both have feathery filaments attached to their dorsal fins. In the feather-fin this tapers to a point; in three-banded, the filament straggles about like uncut hair.

FEATURES: Bullfish are frequently seen among staghorn corals on the Great Barrier Reef. The feather-fin is silvery-white with their first black bars at the rear of the gill covers and the second stretching back from the dorsal fin to the end of the anal fin. A short black bar crosses the eyes. The mouth is small and pointed and in mature fish a bump appears between the eyes. The dorsal "feather" is clear white.

DISTRIBUTION: All Australian warm waters from northern Western Australia through the Northern Territory into Queensland and Barrier Reef coastal waters, with a restricted number entering New South Wales.

Feather-fin bullfish, *Heniochus acuminatus*

PICKLING COCKLES: To pickle cockles, cover the cockles with saltwater and leave overnight. Next day drain away the water and dip the cockles into boiling water until they open (about five minutes). Then place the cockles in cold water, remove their shells, and put them in a pickling solution in airtight jars.

BULLSEYE *Pempherididae*

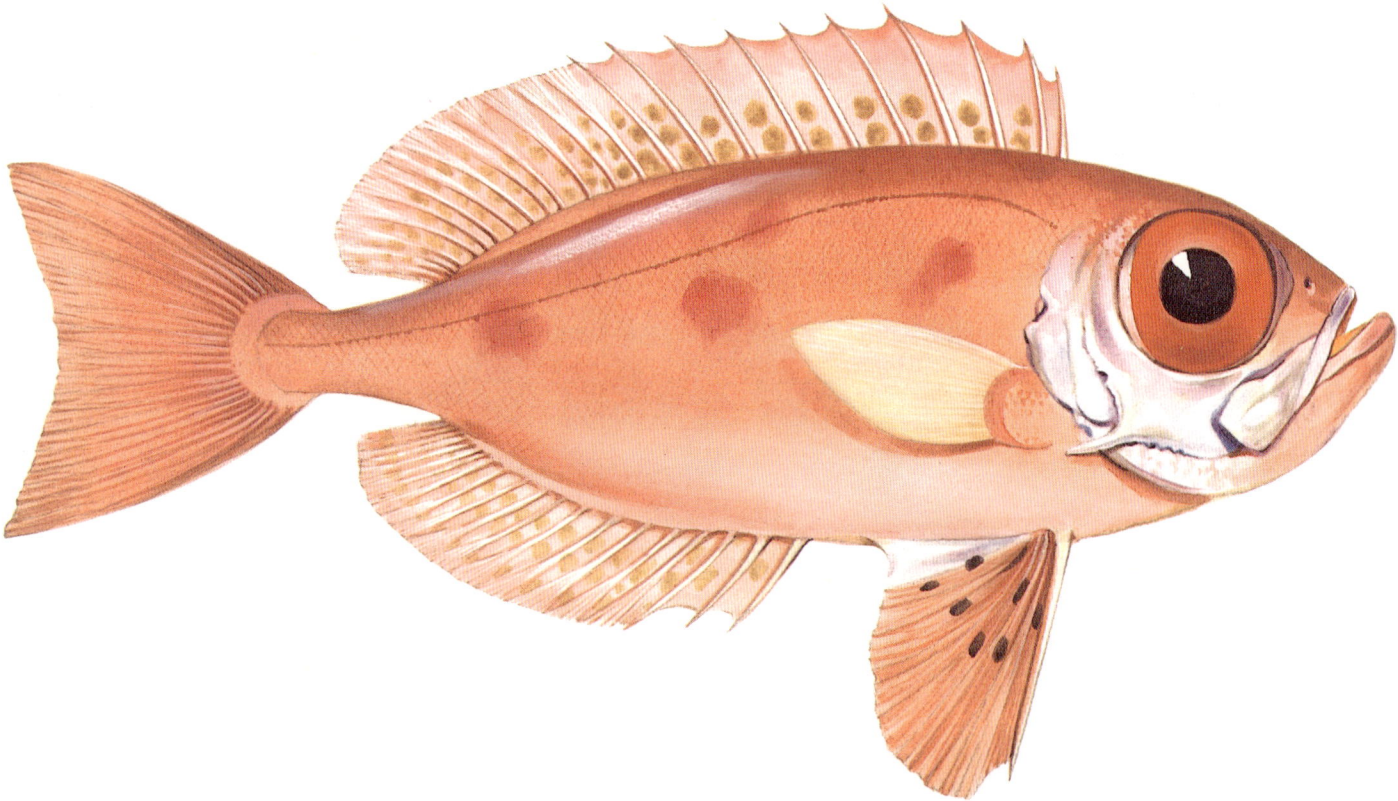

Red bullseye, *Priacanthus macracanthus*

A group of small, deep-bodied fish immediately identifiable by the orange lining of their mouths and the enormous big eyes in which large black pupils are circled in scarlet. The lining of their mouths is all the more striking because their thick, protruding jaws make their mouths open almost vertically. They are not good eating unless poached or steamed and are a bigger attraction as photographic subjects than as table fare. Bullseyes vary in size from the 140 mm attained by the slender bullseye, *Parapriacanthus elongatus*, to the 280 mm reached by mature common bullseyes, *Pempheris multiradiata*, or the 350 mm attained by red bullseyes, *Priacanthus macracanthus*.

FEATURES: Bullseyes have compressed, strongly tapering, scaly bodies, a dorsal fin with few spines and rays, and a many-rayed anal fin. They are tan or reddish brown on the back to salmon pink below, and sometimes streaked in yellow. They are nocturnal or deep water fishes that mostly spend the day sheltering beneath rocky ledges and crevices, emerging at night to forage for food. They often turn up in nets trawled by professionals who regarded them as trash fish.

FISHING TECHNIQUE: Bullseyes are caught by anglers off the entire Queensland coast, usually while fishing from wharves. They fight hard for their size, swimming in circles when hooked, grunting as they are lifted from the water. Bullseye perch and big eyes are among their many aliases. Children often catch numbers of them from boat moorings, using light lines and small hooks and squid, fish strips or molluscs for bait.

DISTRIBUTION: Over reefs and inshore waters and in shallow bays in winter when they shoal in great numbers. They are more plentiful in the warmer waters of north Queensland, though they appear right down the eastern coast. Skindivers say they are so plentiful even novice divers can get good photographs of these big-eyed foragers.

BUTTERFISH *Scatophagidae*

Spotted butterfish,
Scatophagus argus

A family of deep-bodied tropical fishes with strong dorsal fins that can inflict painful, but not fatal wounds. They grow to just over 400 mm in length and are of good table quality but suffer from a prejudice among amateur fishermen aware of their foul feeding habits and apparently unaware that they should be bled immediately after capture. Anglers stung by the sharp dorsal spines when unhooking butterfish should soak the wounded region in hot water for at least two hours. The name butterfish is wrongly applied to several different species, including the John dory.

FEATURES: Butterfish have steeply-formed heads, with snouts that protrude more with age. In all varieties, the bodies carry black vertical bars that fade near the belly. Tiny scales over the body give them a feeling akin to sandpaper. The lips are outlined in black.

VARIETIES: The two main varieties of butterfish found in Australia are the spotted butterfish, *Scatophagus argus*, known to aquarians as scat, and striped or southern butterfish, *Selenotoca multifasciata*. Juvenile spotted butterfish are quite striking fish in colour, displaying intricate patterns of dark bars and spots, reddening bodies and fins, which is why they are popular in aquariums. Adult spotted butterfish are brownish-grey, strongly washed with lilac, and densely covered in black spots. They can adapt to fresh water. Striped butterfish have what Whitley called curious helmet-like heads and are distinguished by vertical bars over the upper flanks that reduce to elongated spots under the belly.

DISTRIBUTION: Butterfish are common in the estuaries and bays of Torres Strait, the Gulf of Carpentaria, north Western Australia, and right down the Queensland coastline into New South Wales.

Striped butterfish,
Selenotoca multifasciata

BLEEDING THE CATCH: Fish such as Australian salmon, dart, tailor, yellowtail kingfish and mackerel, are more flavoursome if they are bled immediately on capture. One method is to insert a knife behind the gillcover so that it penetrates through the body at the lateral line and severs the backbone and throat vessels. Another is to cut the soft, fleshy region between the gill covers, and a third is to simply cut a notch on the underside of the fish between the vent and the tail. After bleeding, wash the fish in saltwater and store in ice.

CARDINAL FISH   *Apogonidae*

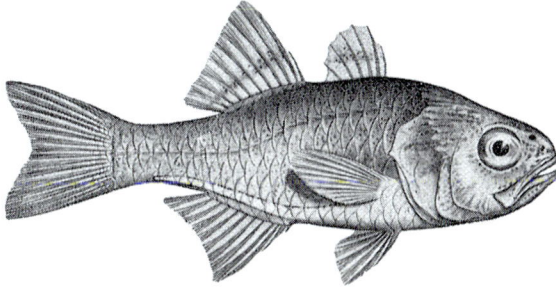

A group of saltwater fish, also known as gobbleguts and soldier fish, renowned for the astonishing manner in which the male refuses food for five weeks while the eggs of his young incubate in his mouth. Unlike their freshwater relatives, the mouth almighty, the marine members of the family sometimes venture into Australia's colder waters. The group includes the striking blue-bodied cardinal fish, *Apogon cyanosoma* in which four or five blue bands run right down the golden body; the eared cardinal fish, *Fowleria marmorata*, in which the pale brown body carries a black ear mark behind the eye rather like the thumbprint on John dory; the southern cardinal fish, *Vincentia conspersa*, the coldwater variety known in southern New South Wales, Victoria, and Tasmania, which has a deep brown body flecked with gold; and the three-saddled cardinal fish, *Apogon bandanensis*, a pale brown fish with a silvery belly that congregates in small groups in Barrier Reef pools. One group of cardinal fish have such large mouths they are known as gobbleguts, with newly born fish crowding to take shelter inside the male's mouth when threatened.

FEATURES: They have a wide gape in their mouths, and all have remarkable agility. They come in a striking variety of colours and have fairly big eyes. They live in groups and solitary fish are rare.

FISHING TECHNIQUE: Cardinal fish have no angling value, but are prized by aquarians. Even as bait fish they lack the appeal of prawns, molluscs, squid and other traditional baits.

DISTRIBUTION: Most cardinal fish prefer Australia's warmer waters, and rarely venture south into New South Wales. One or two varieties show up as trash fish in Western Australian trawlers' nets.

Gobbleguts, *Apogon rueppellii*

PLANKTON: These are the tiny creatures of the sea, plant and animal, which are too weak and helpless to do anything but drift with the current. They are the most important of sea creatures because none of the others could exist without them. Fishing both as a livelihood or hobby depends on the presence of large amounts of plankton. Vast shoals of pelagic fish such as anchovies, herrings, and pilchards follow the plankton around Australia.

CARP *Cyprinidae*

Goldfish, *Carassius auratus*

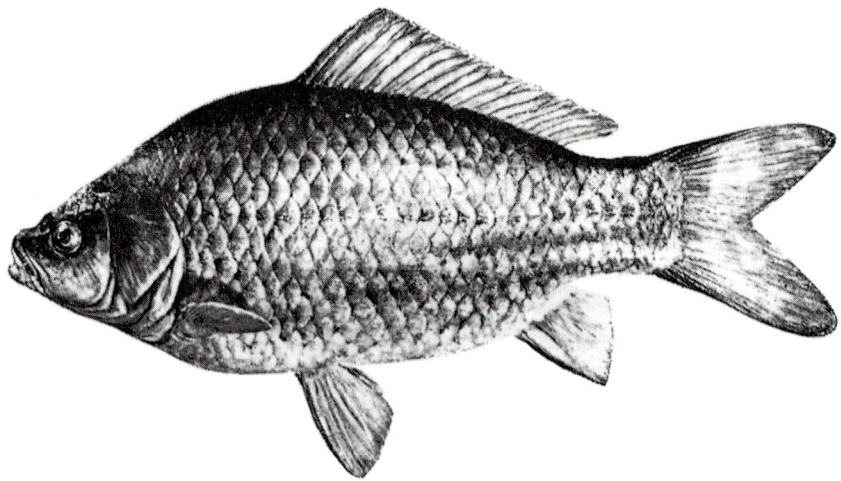

Golden carp, *Carassius carassius*

Of the 11 species of fish imported from overseas and introduced into Australian waters, the carp is the biggest pest. They are poor eating, miserable sporting fish and destroy the habitat in which many of our best native species flourish. Some migrants eat them in the belief that carp boost their virility, but the carp's only admirable quality is their ability to survive both drought and high temperatures. Overall, Australia is probably lucky to have only five of the world's 2000 carp species. Best known are goldfish, *Carassius auratus*, and European or common carp, *Cyprinus carpio*. *Carassius carassius*, also known as golden carp, are easily distinguished from the common carp by their larger scales and the absence of barbels and vary in colour from greenish-grey above with silvery sides to pinkish red. Around the States a variety of names are used, including Prussian carp, leather carp, calico carp, king carp and mirror carp, most of them hybrids. Common carp were first introduced into the Murray River in 1890 and moved into the Murray-Darling system. By 1969 they were being caught in South Australia near Renmark. They have now been declared noxious fish in South Australia and Victoria. In both States they destroy water plants by stirring up the bottom while feeding and threatening the habitat of native fish. European carp are larger and have attained a weight of 14.5 kg in Australia, way below European and American standards but proof of their ability to survive low oxygen and polluted conditions.

FEATURES: European carp have two pairs of fleshy barbels or whiskers at the corner of their mouths, which are lacking in goldfish. Both species have overcome tremendous natural barriers to enlarge their range. Goldfish vary from a brassy-grey to pink body colour and have yellow fins. European carp are golden-brown to olive over the back, merging to a shimmering yellow over the sides and a drab yellow along the belly. Cultivated carp in aquariums become dull and lustre-less.

FISHING TECHNIQUE: Despite official efforts to make carp popular table fish by publishing recipes for them, carp are virtually ignored as food fish and for sport.

DISTRIBUTION: Southern Queensland, New South Wales, Tasmania, Victoria, and Lake Burley Griffin in the ACT.

European or common carp, *Cyprinus carpio*

CABBAGE: A colloquial term used by fishermen to describe the broad-leafed weed found in rock pools. Cabbage, *Ulva lactuca*, makes ideal bait for vegetarian species such as luderick, and usually only grows where there is a constant wash flowing over it. Collection of cabbage from rocky pools should only be done at low tide, with the younger, light green leaves picked from plants rather than taking whole clumps.

CATFISH (EEL-TAILED) *Plotosidae*

Of the 1000-odd catfishes in the world, the Australian varieties fall roughly into the categories of blunt-tailed or fork-tailed. The blunt or eel-tailed variety are well distributed in both freshwater and saltwater and belie their repulsive appearance because they are among the best eating fish from our creeks, backwaters and billabongs. Some country town sportsfishermen specialise in their capture, prizing the flesh that can be baked, fried or steamed once the skin has been peeled away. They fillet the fish by working from the tail, taking out the rib and bones. In Western Australia, estuary catfish are called cobbler.

FEATURES: Some Australian catfish make a nest of sand or stones for their young, carefully guarding the eggs against predators. Young catfish can form into a ball of waving fins and tails. The dorsal fins and pectoral spines can inflict wounds, painful for hours during which the victim can only bathe the wound in hot water.

Short-tailed eel catfish, *Tandanus tandanus*

Estuary catfish or cobbler, *Cnidoglanis macrocephalus*

The throbbing pain and the numbness brought on is out of all proportion to the size of the catfish, which range from 90 cm in length to 4 kg in weight. Both freshwater and saltwater catfish have eight barbels or whiskers around the mouth, with nostrils set in the border of the upper lip. In the illustrated variety, *Tandanus tandanus*, the short-tailed eel catfish, the dark blotches that fleck the slippery brown or olive body increases anglers' repulsion. But as in the white-lipped catfish, *Paraplotosus albilabris*, and long-tailed catfish, *Euristmus lepturus*, striped catfish, *Plotosus lineatus*, and the estuary catfish or cobbler, *Cnidoglanis macrocephalus*, and in Berney's catfish, *Hexanematchthys berneyi*, the flesh is delicious.

FISHING TECHNIQUE: Catfish can be taken on most natural baits such as grass-hoppers, worms, shrimps, mussels and grubs. They need careful handling when bringing them in to avoid dorsal fins that stiffen on capture. A wire trace or leader is recommended and they should be cleaned as soon as they are landed. The offensive-looking skin will come off easily if all the fish, except the head, is dipped in boiling water.

DISTRIBUTION: All States, usually in harbours or rivers, but most of the large specimens are found in the north, where carp and redfin have not reduced their numbers as they have in the Murray, Lachlan, and Murrumbidgee rivers. In Western Australia, the white-lipped catfish or cobbler has reached 1.4 metres and the current Australian record stands at 1.24 kg for a fish caught at Bridgetown by Kazik Przybylski in 1975.

Berney's catfish, *Hexanematchthys berneyi*

Straight-backed catfish, *Neosilurus hyrtlii*

CATFISH (FORK-TAILED OR SALMON) *Ariidae*

Blue catfish, *Arius graeffei*

Australia boasts several varieties of fork-tailed catfish, all of them in tropical waters. They frequent both freshwater and saltwater and offer splendid sport on light gear biting on virtually every type of bait. Our best known species is the giant salmon catfish, *Arius thalassina*, which has been classified as a sea-going variety since 1962. They exceed a metre in length and reach 26 kg. The illustrated blue catfish, *Arius graeffei*, locks its sharp spines in an extended position when captured and the spines often have to be cut off to release them from nets. This tropical species extends as far south as the Hunter River, NSW. Threadfin catfish, *Arius armiger*, are often taken by anglers seeking barramundi in the Northern Territory. Salmon catfish, *Arius leptaspis*, occur in northern Queensland and in Papua New Guinea.

FEATURES: Fork-tailed catfish can change colour to suit their environment, their body colour ranging from silver-grey to brown or even red. They use their cat-like whiskers to locate food on muddy bottoms. They have unusual breeding habits, with the bright yellow fertilised eggs of about 122 mm in diameter carried in the mouth of the male until they hatch. Their bodies are scaleless and slimy to touch. Biologists separate each variety by the formation of their clumps of teeth and other features.

FISHING TECHNIQUE: Fork-tailed catfish take grasshoppers, fish flesh, tadpoles, bivalves, and are extremely partial to kangaroo liver. Most are taken on handlines but when the fish are big and plentiful, as they often are in Moreton Bay and Darwin, it is wise to switch to a rod and reel, with a line that will cope with whatever weight is running. Hook size 2/0, with sinker weight according to conditions.

DISTRIBUTION: Most in tidal creeks, mudflats, bays and offshore reefs in Australian tropical waters. When they are spawning in colonies, few waterholes would be considered free of them.

CLEANER FISH   *Labridae*

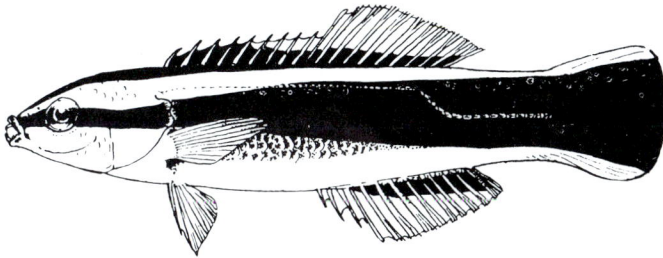

A strikingly-banded little fish that picks parasites and growths from the fins, scales, mouths and gill chambers of a variety of tropical fish, some of whom appear happy to wait for its attention. Coral trout, cod, tuskfish, emperors, and wrasse and other large fish assemble off coral outcrops as if in a hairdresser's, waiting for the cleaner fish to pick off pieces of skin from teeth inside open mouths. The cleaner fish are no longer than 10 cm in length and appear to have no fear of swimming deep into the vast mouths of some of their customers, fulfilling the same role as the crocodile bird which cleans the teeth of crocodiles of the Nile. Cleaner fish can change colour quickly but their basic colour appears to be golden yellow on top and silvery white below with a broad black band running right along the body from the snout to the tail. Above and below the black band are patches of light blue. Both the anal and dorsal fins have black bars at their bases. The astonishing thing is that the cleaner fish's customers appear to establish permanent cleaning areas to which they regularly return for servicing. Cleaner fish are also known as gadfly fish, bridled beauty, or blue streak. Whitley said blennies bite pieces out of the bodies of large fish which they approach in the guise of cleaner fish.

FEATURES: The outstanding trait in cleaner fish is their swimming style. They are darters, able to accelerate in an instant with a curious looping motion. Anglers trying to net one on a coral reef often give up in disgust, beaten by the fish's manoeuvrability.

DISTRIBUTION: Abundant in the Barrier Reef, north to the Gulf of Carpentaria, across northern Australia and right down the west coast to Rottnest Island.

Cleaner fish, *Labroides dimidiatus*

REEF FISHING: Off-shore reefs provide some of the best catches available to Australians. In the north, coral trout, emperor and sweetlip are abundant over reefs, while in the south, snapper, morwong and teraglin are plentiful for anglers who go out from major centres. Veterans know where the most productive reefs are from cross-bearings they take on shore headlands and cliffs. The best equipped boats use depth-finders to locate reefs and the sudden appearance of undersea valleys. Technique varies from drifting slowly over the reef to anchoring over deep holes but it is obvious that large numbers of fish feed on the animal life and vegetation reefs attract.

COBIA *Rachycentridae*

Cobia, *Rachycentron canadus*

A renowned gamefish which has been mastered by only a small band of Australian fishermen. They are also known as black kingfish, sergeant fish and black ling, and are recognised as one of the toughest fighting fish in Australian waters. Their blunt head and dark chocolate-brown bodies and powerful, crescentic tails give them the appearance in the water of sharks. There is a splendid symmetry in their body shape and they use their tails to leap clear of the water. The spinous dorsal fin is short and spiky, but the soft dorsal fin starts with a sharp peak and although it trails off to the tail, that peak shows up menacingly in the water. They reach a weight of 68 kg or 150 lb in Australian waters, but the Australian record stands at 61.5 kg for a fish taken off Southport in 1977 by George Walsh. The speed with which cobia make their first run repeatedly leaves fishermen with burnt fingers and even when they are fought to a standstill and brought to gaff they will sometimes smash the gaff as they come clear of the water.

FEATURES: Cobia have very small scales, sharply-pointed pectoral fins, large powerful tails with a keel on each side, and inconspicuous small teeth. Their eyes are brown with a silvery iris and black pupil. In young fish the body has three brown stripes with lighter areas between them, which is reason for the name sergeant fish.

FISHING TECHNIQUE: They will take a wide variety of lures and baits but are particularly partial to whole crabs. They are regularly taken by trolling close to manta rays or other rays beneath which they travel. Feathered jigs appear the most effective lures, though they have been taken on drone spoons and konaheads. Reef anglers fishing rocky bottoms for snapper and other reef species sometimes locate cobia searching for crabs.

DISTRIBUTION: All Australian tropical and sub-tropical waters, with stragglers reaching as far south as Jervis Bay, NSW.

BEST TIME TO FISH: The tide, changing twice every day, is the sportfisherman's friend. As it rises, the fish follow the surging waters inshore to feast on food churned up by the surf. Usually the best catches are made in the hour before high tide and the hour after it. As the tide ebbs, the fish return to deeper water.

COD *Moridae*

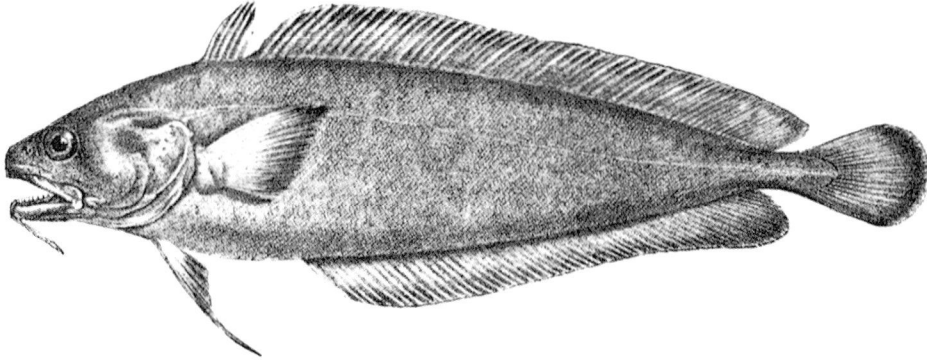

Ling, *Lotella calarias*, often mistakenly included among our cod, belong to the family *Uphidiidae*

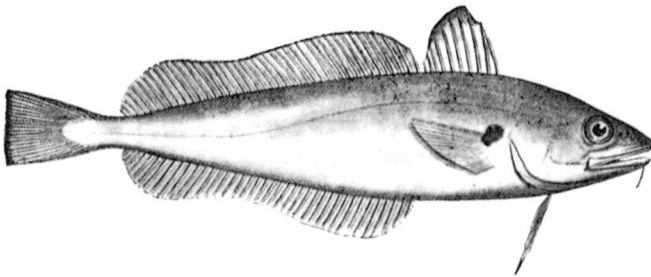

Red cod, *Pseudophycis bachus*

The name cod has been given without discrimination to a large number of Australian fish but there is only one true cod of the family *Gadidae* in our waters. The family has tremendous commercial importance in Europe, where cod are valued for their vitamin-rich liver oil and family members such as the English whiting and haddock are prized for their food value. Australia's cod belong to the family *Moridae* and all have a fleshy barbel on the lower jaw, which helps in their search for food. The best known varieties are the beardie, *Lotella rhacinus*, a shallow-water species found near caves and ledges in exposed coastal reefs, where it feeds on crustaceans and small fish; and the red cod, *Pseudophycis bachus*, which have been sold commercially since early colonial years.

The word cod is widely used in naming members of the *Serranidae* family in Australia, e.g. tomato cod, peacock cod, black cod, Chinamen cod and estuary cod, *Epinephelus tauvina*, which grows to 250 kg and is also known as the greasy cod because of its slime-covered body. Two of these black cod and estuary cod, are now fully protected in New South Wales.

FEATURES: Apart from their characteristic barbels, cods all have their ventral fins well forward, near the throat. All the fins are soft. The tails all fan out from the backbone, and the prominent dorsal, anal and tail fins are clearly separated. They all have large eyes.

Estuary cod, *Epinephelus tauvina*

FISHING TECHNIQUE: Line fishermen catch beardies up to 50 cm and 2.5 kg on small fish and crustacean baits. They are not highly rated food fish but are suitable for smoking. Ling and red cod follow suit.

DISTRIBUTION: Central and southern New South Wales, Victoria, Tasmania, South Australia, into southern Western Australia.

CLIFF-TOP FISHING: Much of the Australian coastline has lofty cliffs within easy access of major cities. Often these cliffs are sandstone, weakened by pollution and salt-water, which makes it imperative for anglers to carefully select their fishing positions. They should never stand on jutting, overhanging ledges and on squally days should beware of fierce gusts that will blow them off the edge. Sensible footwear with cleats or non-slip soles are just as essential as a stout rod that allows anglers to haul in catches while clear of the edge. Line of at least 9 kg breaking strain is recommended.

FISHING FROM JETTIES, PIERS AND SEAWALLS: Australia boasts an extra-ordinary number of man-made vantage points for fishermen. The long jetty at Carnarvon in Western Australia is 1.6 km or a mile long and a noted spot for kingfish, mulloway and Westralian jewfish. The breakwaters at the back of Sydney's Kingsford-Smith airport attract hundreds of anglers keen to try for bream, snapper and whiting. Big seawalls at Harrington, Port Macquarie, and in the north at Mackay and Townsville have all proved outstanding spots for whiting, trevally, mackerel, and tailor. Often in these places, the simplest methods work best. At Brunswick Heads on the New South Wales north coast, for example, chunks of stale bread have proved highly successful bait for bream, for anglers fishing the incoming tide from the seawall.

CORAL COD   *Serranidae*

A smaller fish than coral trout, and deep-bodied and just as colourful. They are one of the exciting family of cod taken from Barrier Reef charter boats, red-bodied fish covered in peacock-blue spots. They are excellent table fish, with skinned fillets white, firm and delicately-flavoured. The illustrated *Cephalopholis miniatus*, or coral trout cod, are taken in surprising numbers on snapper grounds, and are not to be confused with the orange cod, *Cephalopholis aurantius*, tomato cod, *Cephalopholis sonnerati*, flag-tailed cod, *Cephalopholis urodelus*, or the blue-spotted rock cod, *Cephalopholis cyanostigma*, which has conspicuous blue spots on the body, head and fins.

FEATURES: The rounded tail of the coral cod darkens with maturity, but the vivid spots remain. They seldom grow beyond 450 mm in length but will put up a fight when hooked that belies their weight.

FISHING TECHNIQUE: Again it is a question of turning a fish that will take most baits before it reaches the safety of coral reefs or crevices. They bite on almost any bait but particularly well on live small fish, and it is essential to get the bait down to where they feed on crustaceans and small crabs.

DISTRIBUTION: Coral cod are abundant along the entire Barrier Reef, with small fish taken on floating lines, larger ones on hand-lines. They are warm water fish that prefer the reefs of Torres Strait, northern Western Australian waters and the northern Barrier Reef.

Coral trout cod,
Cephalopholis miniatus

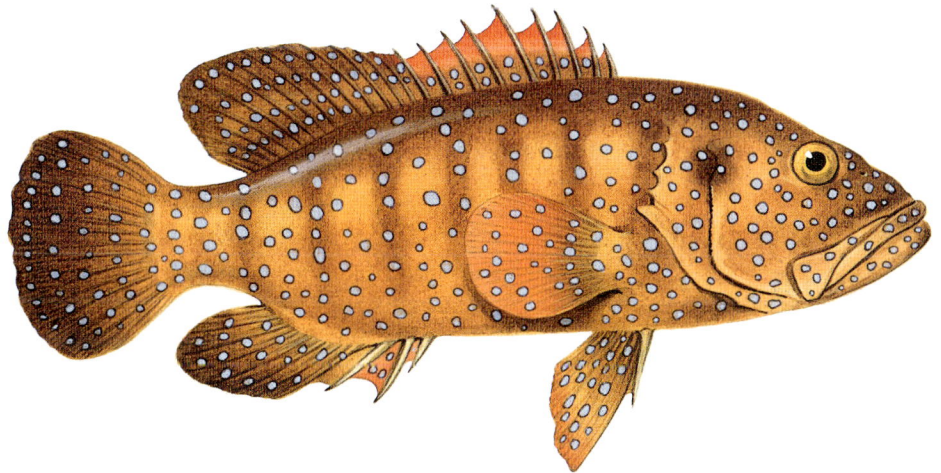

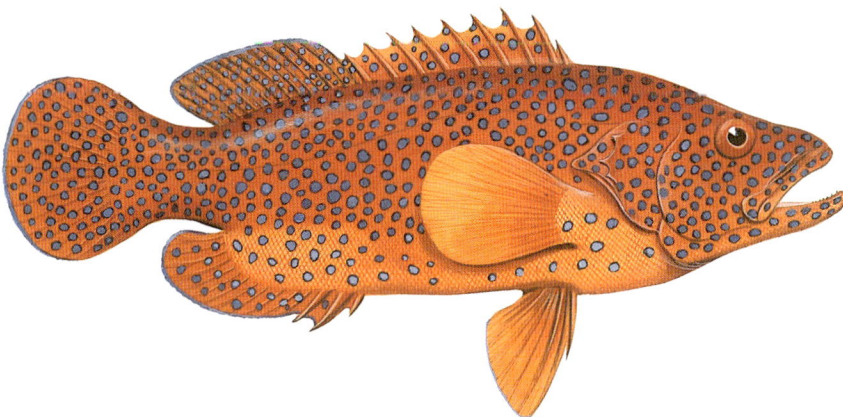

Blue-spotted rock cod,
*Cephalopholis
cyanostigma*

CORAL TROUT *Serranidae*

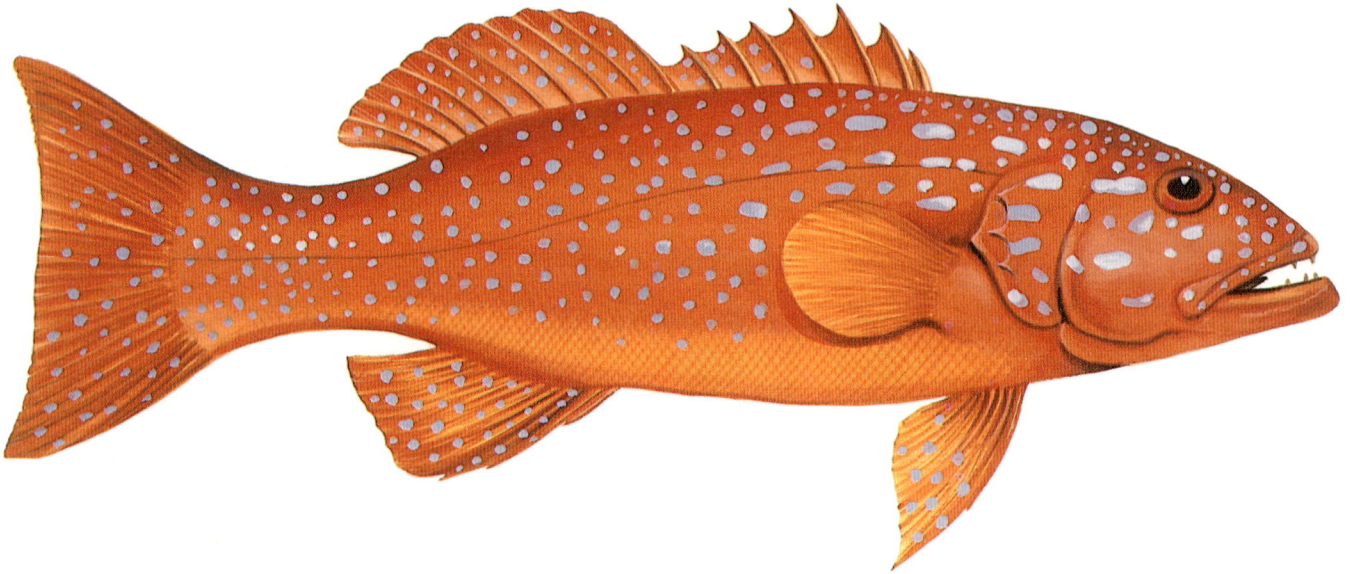

Coral trout,
Plectropomus maculatus

A colourful, contentious variety which anglers usually group with coral cod, a member of the same family. Both are vividly coloured fish that can produce spectacular gradations of colour. Coral trout, *Plectropomus maculatus*, are mostly bright pink to red in colour, with the body and fins abundantly speckled with small round blue spots, which become larger and more scattered towards the head. They have slightly forked or square-cut tails whereas the tails of coral cod are rounded. Recent work at the Australian Museum proved that five different species of coral trout occur in Australian waters. These are distinguished primarily by the size, spacing and the locality of the blue spots, with fin shape also helping to separate the species.

FEATURES: Photographs taken three minutes apart show that the "typical" coral trout has three colour-phases and that the saddles of all fish also waxed and waned from a stage of brightly decisive patterns to one where they completely vanished. All varieties of coral trout have a cluster of small blue spots over the head, and body and these are the cause of their aliases, leopard cod and passionfruit trout. Coral trout have no more than seven or eight spines in the dorsal fin, the coral cod nine. A 19.1 kg coral trout was taken off Heron Island.

FISHING TECHNIQUE: Coral trout are challenging fish which bite strongly and put up a tough fight. They use the reefs along rocky shores where they live to advantage by darting into holes and crevices and whatever snags the reefs offer. The trick is to turn them before they get the line caught in coral. They take most flesh, prawns, crabs, crustaceans and will accept metal spinners and artificial lures. Barrier Reef fishermen know to fish for them at anchor and not on the drift, working the edges of coral outcrops. They demand strong tackle and hooks from 6/0 to 10/0. Jigging the bait entices them to grab it and crush and kill it. Every moment counts once they take the bait and run.

DISTRIBUTION: Abundant among the rocky reefs of Western Australia and the coral reefs of Queensland and northern Australia. Essentially a warm water fish that thrives above the Tropic of Capricorn.

CRABS *Brachyura*

Edible crustaceans found mainly on or near the sea coast. A few specialised forms are found in inland freshwaters in Australia. Most are crawlers or burrowers in the littoral region, some have taken to the sea by adapting the last pair of legs as paddles. They provide fascinating contrasts in their walking and running styles, with some species moving sideways or backwards and others running forwards at surprising speed. They invariably contain delicious white flesh but meals of crab meat require patience as the best bits have to be removed from the tough, flint-like shells in which crabs are encased.

Crabs are equipped with gills, like fishes, on each side of the thorax. Water is moved through the gill chambers by flaps attached to the outer edge of the mouth region. They vary enormously in size, the smallest measuring only 6 mm across the carapace, while those caught commercially normally are at least 15 cm wide. The largest of all crabs is the Japanese spider crab, which has a claw span of more than 3 metres, although the body size may be only 40 cm. The second biggest crab in the world is the Tasmanian giant crab, *Pseudocarcinus gigas*, which measures 35 cm across the back and has pincers more than 45 cm long, with the biggest weighing 14 kg. They are formidable specimens when alive, with pincers that could snap a man's arm, but they are virtually harmless when they are hauled onboard trawlers, because the sudden reduction in water pressure paralyzes them. Recent studies have shown their habitat is round 90 to 150 metres off Bass Strait and eastern Tasmania. Costs involved in taking them has so far prevented their commercial exploitation.

Their diversity in size and shape allows crabs to colonise a striking range of habitats. Some are even known to climb trees in search of food. Mostly they are marine creatures, living among rocks, or burrowing in sand or mud, leading scavengers' lives on the sea bed, killing small fish with their pincers, and breaking open the shells of molluscs.

Most of the 4,000 crabs found around the world have complex life histories, but almost all of them periodically discard the bony sheathing in which they live. This moulting process continues throughout their lives and explains why some crabs are surprisingly light when captured—they are only partway through another moult. Some Australian States have long traditions of crabbing. Every summer in Perth's Swan River, for example, hundreds of families wade into the water to catch blue manna crabs in scoop nets. Right round Australia, crabs are an important bait. Commercially, crabs are caught and trapped in a valuable year-round industry. Authorities in all States now keep a close watch on the crab traps used by amateur fishermen and it is always wise to check on the legality of your crabbing methods.

Mangrove or **mud crabs**, *Scylla serrata*, grow to a weight of 5 kg and can measure 22 cm across their shells. They vary in colour from green, shortly after moulting, to brownish-green. Some have a tinge of purple or blue in their shells. They live in mangrove swamps, mudflats and estuaries, where they burrow deep holes as sanctuary against predators. Their holes are easily spotted in the dry season or when tides are out. Muddies, as they are nicknamed, have long, powerful claws, which they can use with surprising speed to bite the unwary. These claws contain meat that is rated more succulent than their body meat. They sometimes cast a claw with a contraction of muscle without injuring themselves. The break is quickly sealed with a pale blue jelly of coagulated blood and with each succeeding moult a new claw grows. Mud crabs with only one claw bring lower market prices than those with both claws. Professionals catch them alive and offer them for sale that way in the markets. Mud crabs are plentiful along the entire Queensland coast and in northern New South Wales.

Soldier crabs, *Mictyris longicarpus*, are small, militant bright blue or mauve sand-dwellers that assemble in large numbers on sandbars and beaches, disappearing at high tide but reappearing to feed as the tide recedes. They grow to only 2.5 cm across and are outstanding bait, provided they are placed on the hook so that the point protrudes from their eyes. This exploits the partiality bream have towards soldier crabs' eyes. The smallest soldier crabs can take a heavy toll of whiting if they are set three at a time on the hook.

Mud crab, *Scylla serrata*

Soldier crab, *Mictyris longicarpus*

Soldier crabs are abundant in south Queensland and along the temperate Western Australian coast.

Spanner crabs, *Ranina ranina*, also known as frog crabs, are vivid pink to scarlet sand-burrowers that often allow themselves to be stranded by the falling tide. They rest under the sand with only their eyes and the front of their shells protruding, waiting to close their claws on small whiting. They are delicious eating if their frog-like sheaths are split lengthwise so that the best of their meat can be reached. They will sometimes close their claws so tightly on baits they can be swung clear of the water. Mature spanner crabs reach a shell width of 15 cm and around 1 kg in weight. Their large claws should be cracked for the tasty meat they contain. Spanner crabs are prevalent along the south coast of Western Australia and in southern Queensland.

Ghost crabs, *Ocypode ceratophthalmus*, are greyish-white to greenish-cream amphibious shore crabs whose colouring helps their nighttime camouflage as they move across the sand scavenging for food. They are notorious for stealing anglers' baits left unguarded in the sand and will even try to attack freshly caught fish, eating out their eyes and gills. Fully grown ghost crabs span 18 cm, leg tip to leg tip, and run with a distinctive high body action that gives them the speed and manoeuvrability to evade angry anglers. They are splendid bait for flathead and most reef fishes. Parrot fishes obviously rate them highly as food for they spend a lot of time digging for them. They are widely distributed in Australia but are particularly plentiful in Queensland where they use their powerful claws to behead newly-hatched turtles as they make for the water.

Ghost crab, *Ocypode ceratophthalmus*

Sand crab, *Portunus pelagicus*

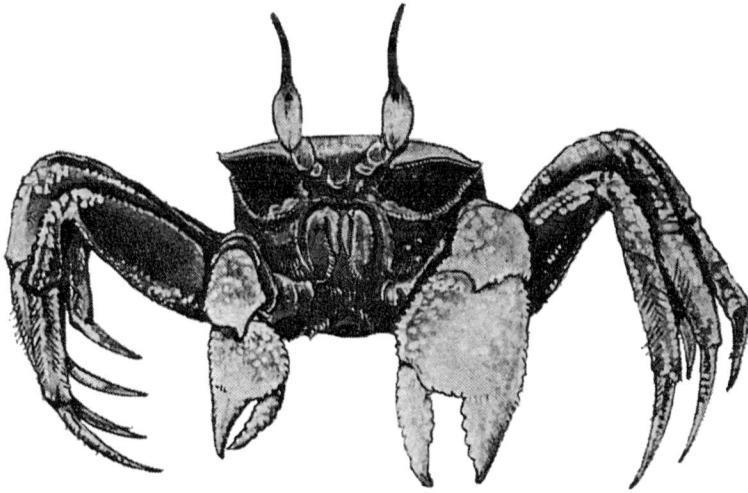

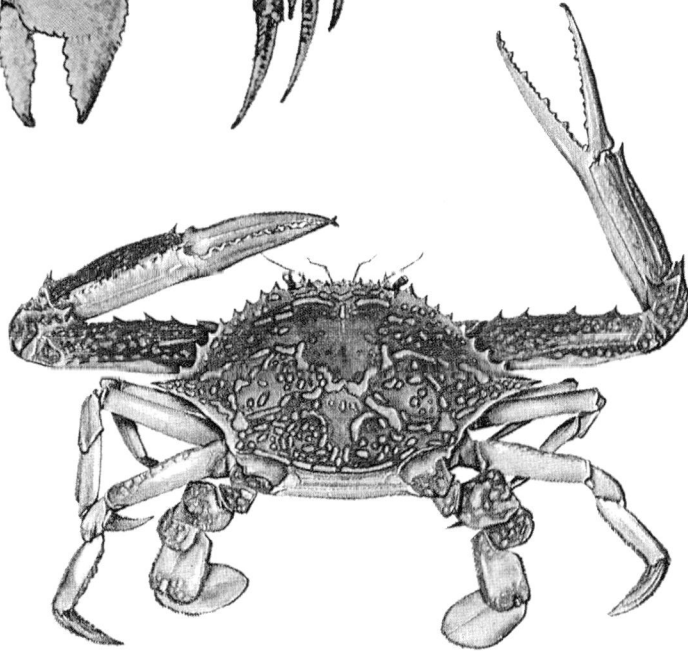

Hermit crabs, of the family *Paguridae*, have the ability to live in the dead shell of other species, moving house many times as they grow. They select their new homes before they move and once inside take such a tenacious grip on the inside they cannot be dragged out alive. The largest Australian hermit crabs reach 25 cm, including body and limbs. They are frequently caught by trawlers in deep waters. The spotted hermit crab, *Dardanus megistos*, are a brilliantly coloured tropical variety with scarlet bodies, sprinkled with white spots. Another fascinating hermit crab is the miner, *Cancellus typus*, which disdains living in shells but prefers a burrow which they cut in soft stones with the hard, bony plates on their tails.

Robber crabs, *Birgus latro*, are prominent members of the hermit crab family, also known as coconut crabs, because of their habit of feeding on fallen coconuts all over the Indo-Pacific region. They will climb to great heights to tear away the husks around the nuts. They grow to 45 cm in length and are highly rated table fare.

Sand crabs or **blue swimmers,** *Portunus pelagicus*, also known as blue manna crabs, are a fast-moving variety living in bays, estuaries and open seas that attain a shell width of 200 mm, and are generally considered to be our most delicious crab. In life their legs are mottled in white, blue and purple. Females have brownish sheaths, males thicker claws. They are always cooked before they are sent to market, usually by gently simmering in boiling water for ten minutes. Both amateurs and professionals make big catches of blue swimmers every summer in temperate Australian coastal waters and they range throughout the Indo-Pacific region. They are closely related to the red-spot crabs, *Portunus sanguinolentus*, which are bluish-grey in colour and have red-tipped claws, but are more readily identified by the three bluish-red spots on their backs. Red-spot crabs are common in Moreton Bay and sometimes offshore.

Freshwater crabs, of the family *Potamonidae*, are widely distributed in Australian inland waters and are noted for their ability to withstand severe drought. There are six known species in Australia, five of which appear to be restricted to the Cape York area. The sixth, *Holthuisana transversa*, is found throughout northern Australia. Aborigines catch them with crab hooks. They are olive-green in colour, with convex backs and rarely grow to more than 5 cm across their backs.

CRABBING TECHNIQUES: Great care should be given to the selection of the crabbing site, with boats offering a wider selection of likely spots than piers or sand flats. The best spots are those with little movement in the water, for crabs do not bite readily if the boat moves too fast on currents or winds. When there is excessive movement in the water it is wiser to kellick. Experienced crab fishermen heavily berley their mooring areas with fish pieces, meat bones and other edible scraps two or three days before they go crabbing, reasoning that by the time the bones have been cleaned the crabs will be ready to bite.

Select tough, gristly baits which the crabs cannot easily tear to pieces, setting the bait firmly on a 5/0 or a 6/0 hook, and keeping the bait on the bottom with a heavy sinker. Bring the crabs up slowly when they take the bait and try to tug it clear of the hook. A landing net with a monofilament mesh that will not entangle the crabs as badly as cotton mesh or prawn netting is preferred. Use a fish box to store the newly-taken crabs as they are hard to get out of bags.

Crab nets: Over the years a wide variety of devices have been tried for catching crabs, most of them involving nets. Single drop nets, double drop nets, spring-loaded wire nets, wire envelope traps, and the traditional baited crab pots and dillies have all earned periods of popularity. The hand-held scoop net and a bright torch often works as well as anything else but the most favoured crab traps these days are the witch's hat crab net, also known as the suicide net, the dilly net, and the envelope trap. But before purchasing any of these, crab enthusiasts should check with their State Fisheries Department about local regulations. Queensland bans catching female crabs, for example, while New South Wales allows it. New South Wales restricts the number of nets to five nets per person per boat. In Western Australia, anyone using nets to catch crustaceans must have an amateur fishing licence, and it is the fisherman's responsibility to carry accurate gauges to ensure none of the crustaceans taken are below the legal length. South Australia forbids the taking of female crabs at all times and has some restrictions on the months during which male crustaceans may be taken.

CASH FROM CRAYFISH: There are no lobsters in Australia or in the Southern Hemisphere. Lobsters are a group of decapods found only in the north Atlantic. The succulent crustaceans Australian restaurants and fish markets insist on labelling lobsters are crayfish. Despite the misnomer crayfish are a $100 million-a-year industry and provide a large proportion of Australia's edible seafood catch.

CRAYFISH   *Panuliridae—Scyllaridae*

Under their lobster pseudonym, crayfish provide a large part of Australia's edible marine catch and are the most lucrative fish in our seas. The most abundant are the western crayfish, *Panulirus cygnus*, of the family *Palinuridae*, which are the big sellers in our $100 million-a-year crayfish industry under the name of rock lobster. Their eggs float as plankton in an area of around 20,000 square kilometres in the sea between Bunbury and Shark Bay, Western Australia, returning to the shore once a year. Government biologists can accurately forecast the size of the annual catch up to three years in advance by studying the eggs. Western crayfish tails were originally sold in cans but are now marketed whole and even alive in Japan and the US. southern crayfish, *Jasus novaehollandiae*, are twice as big at 1.5 kg when fully grown, and are the main crayfish catch in South Australia, Victoria and Tasmania. In the eastern States, eastern or common crayfish, *Jasus verreauxi*, which weigh up to 8 kg, are the commonly caught variety. Bag limits apply for amateurs on all crays in Tasmania, Victoria and New South Wales. The painted or coral crayfish, *Panulirus ornatus*, are the most common of the five highly-decorated crayfish in our tropical waters. Most popular member of our other crayfish family, *Scyllaridae*, a flattened, compressed group of burrowers, are the Balmain bug, *Ibacus peronii*, which were driven out of Sydney Harbour by pollution but still appear in trawlers' nets. Balmain bugs are close relatives of the Shovel-nosed lobster, *Thenus orientalis*, found in Moreton Bay.

FISHING TECHNIQUE: Crayfish are caught in baited traps, either beehive or square in shape, made of cane or tea-tree, woven on to a heavy wire frame or of metal and heavy gauge mesh. The pots can be up to 120 cm in diameter, have an incurved entrance easy for crays to negotiate but difficult to leave. The bait is any type of offal. Western crayfish are caught in shallow water by boats averaging only 8 metres in length.

DISTRIBUTION: All Australian States have large populations of both marine and freshwater crayfish. Marine crayfish have suffered from overfishing and are subject to strict legislation, but there is hardly a river, lake, creek, pond, dam, or swamp without a freshwater species.

Western crayfish,
Panulirus cygnus

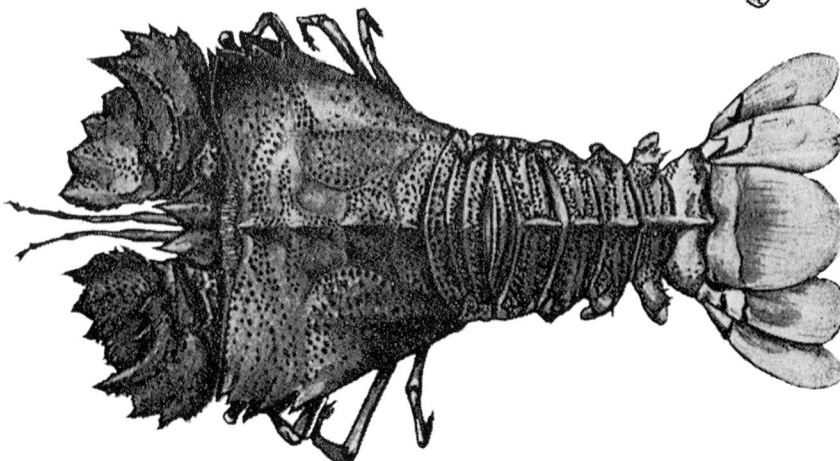

Moreton Bay bug, or
shovel-nosed lobster,
Thenus orientalis

CUCUMBER FISH *Chlorophthalmidae*

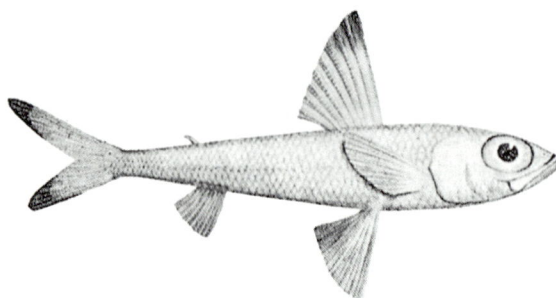

Cucumber fish,
*Chlorophthalmus
nigripinnis*

Slender little fishes not to be confused with southern grayling and cucumber herring, that grow to around 30 cm and have a distinctive cucumber-like smell that gives them their name. They are commonly trawled out near the continental shelf and are taken at depths as shallow as 40 fathoms. They have larger eyes and smaller teeth than lizard fishes and their body scales are well forward of the head. Flathead and other commercial fish feed ravenously on them.

FEATURES: Cucumber fish are easily recognised by the high fan-like first dorsal fins on their elongated bodies. They have small adipose fins, with the upper lobe of the caudal fin slightly longer than the lower lobe. The scales are cycloid, teeth villiform.

COLOUR: Their general colour is pale green above, with golden spots, silvery below. The sides and the head are silver. Young fish have bluish blotches on the sides. The tips of the first dorsal and tail fins are black.

DISTRIBUTION: Queensland, Western Australia, New South Wales, Victoria, Tasmania, South Australia and New Zealand down to 150 fathoms.

NOMENCLATURE CONFUSION: Much of the confusion about the names of Australian fish traces back to our early settlers, who called fish by the names they were accustomed to at home in England. Our biologists have made brave attempts to sort out the mess and produced names like morwong and mulloway that anglers usually ignore. Western Australian fishing writer Ross Cusack explained the name for Westralian dhufish in 1982 by explaining that "dhu" was Gaelic for "black" or "dark" and attributed the tag to a Scottish outlaw, Roderick Dhu, also named Roderick the Black or Black Roderick. Cusack was eventually forced to concede that his dhufish was in fact *Glaucosoma herbracium* or the "common jewie" and that the official name was Westralian jewfish.

DAMSELFISH   *Pomacentridae*

A family of small, brilliantly-coloured, coral-dwelling fishes, including pullers, humbugs, and sergeant majors, with around 320 species spread around the world, many of them in Australian tropical waters and three in cooler temperate Australian waters. They are generally perch-like fishes with a single nostril on each side of the head, graceful swimmers that dart in and out of crevices and the branches and fronds of coral. The group includes the yellow-tailed damselfish, *Neopomacentrus cyanomos*, which has a large black spot behind the head, delicate trailing rays from the soft dorsal and anal fins, and a vivid yellow tail; the azure damselfish *Chrysiptera hemicyaneus*, which is a striking peacock blue in body colour with the rearward part of the torso and the tail a glittering golden yellow; the white damselfish, *Dischistodus perspicillatus*, whose silvery white body has three black saddles on top and a translucent tail; and the yellow damselfish, *Pomacentrus popei*, which has a bright yellow body, a jet black spot on the pectoral fin and striking black eyes.

FEATURES: Damselfish are important food fish on Australia's northern reefs for larger fish like the emperors and coral trout. They average around 100 millimetres in length, feeding on crustaceans, plankton and algae. Many of them are lagoon-dwellers accustomed to being stranded by the tides and they are all famous for the manner in which they use weed and coral for cover.

DISTRIBUTION: The majority of Australia's large population of damselfish inhabit the warmer waters of the north. The white ear, *Parma microlepsis*, the Victorian scalyfin, *Parma victoriae*, and the one-spot puller, *Chromis hypsilepis*, are the regular inhabitants of colder southern waters.

White ear, *Parma microlepsis*

DART OR SWALLOWTAIL *Carangidae*

Northern dart,
Trachinotus bailloni

A deep-bodied trevally-like fish that rides the waves with remarkable dexterity and speed, sometimes becoming almost stranded in its eagerness to swim along the beach zone. The two main species found in Australia offer first-rate family sport because they strike the bait so fiercely even inexperienced anglers can catch them. They fight hard on light gear, turning and running with a speed that has the line spraying foam behind them. Their preference for warm, sun-drenched surf means they have to be protected from the sun after capture. Regular swallowtail fishermen preserve the flesh by burying them in trenches. They are first-rate panfish.

FEATURES: Swallowtail have deeply-curved, swallow-like tails, deep but slender bodies. They average just over 3 kg in weight, but have been taken up to 8 kg. Whitley recorded an oyster-crushing or snub-nosed dart, *Trachinotus blochi*, that reached over one metre and up to 22 kg but the common dart, *Trachinotus botla* is much smaller. The main Australian varieties are the southern swallowtail, *Trachinotus coppingeri*, which has five to seven dark blotches along the sides, usually above the lateral line, and the northern or black-spotted dart, *Trachinotus bailloni*, which has darker, circular black spots along the lateral line. They are greenish-grey on top and have touches of yellow on their fins. They have powerful pads of teeth in their throats for crushing shells, pipis or oysters.

FISHING TECHNIQUE: Use a handline or a single-handed rod and reel, with a 2 to 3 kg breaking strain line, 6 to 2 hooks, and a light sinker. Best baits are small pieces of fish such as garfish, mackerel or bonito, and worms where available. Worms rolled in dry sand to remove the slime make ideal dart bait. A two-hook rig with the hooks one metre apart and a sinker in the middle often succeeds on dart, but they will also grab at surf spinners. Be ready for their tearaway tactics once the hook is set.

DISTRIBUTION: Warmer Australian waters from the New South Wales central coast up to Gladstone on the Queensland coast and from Exmouth to Bunbury in Western Australia. They are common through the Pacific and Indian Oceans and in warm weather will sometimes bob up as far south as Perth and Sydney.

Snub-nosed dart, *Trachinotus blochi*

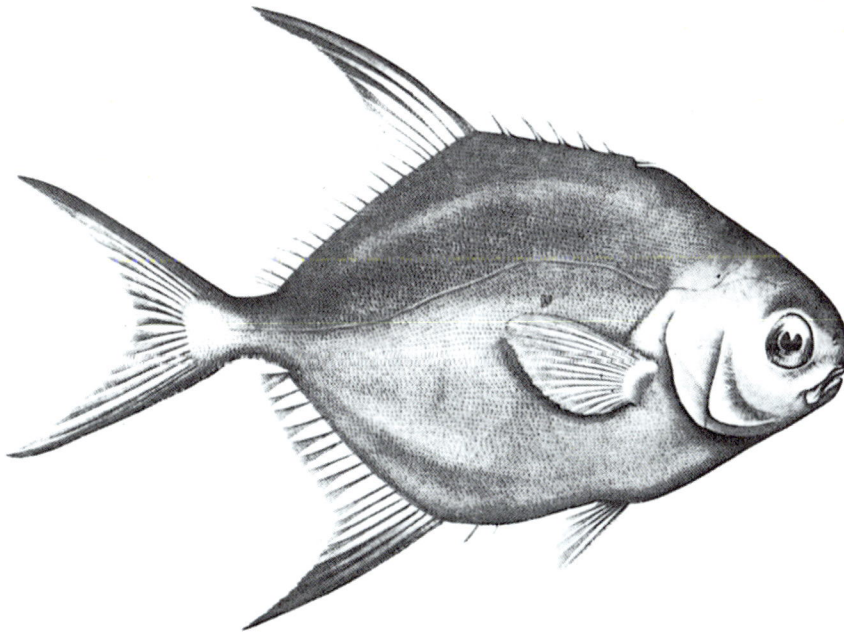

FISH WITH LEMON JUICE AND PARSLEY

INGREDIENTS

4 fillets fish
4 tablespoons wholemeal flour
60 g margarine
½ cup lemon juice
4 tablespoons chopped parsley
Freshly ground pepper

METHOD

You'll find that cooking the fish in lemon juice instead of just squeezing it on at the end makes quite a difference to the final flavour.

Dip fish in flour until lightly coated on both sides. Melt margarine in a non-stick frying pan and when it begins to bubble add fish. Sear fish on both sides. Pour in lemon juice, add parsley and pepper then lower heat. Cook for about 5 minutes or until fish is cooked through and most of the liquid is absorbed.

Serves 4

Reprinted with permission, Carolyn Dunne, *The Semi-Vegetarian Cookbook*, Bantam, 1989

DOGFISHES *Squalidae*

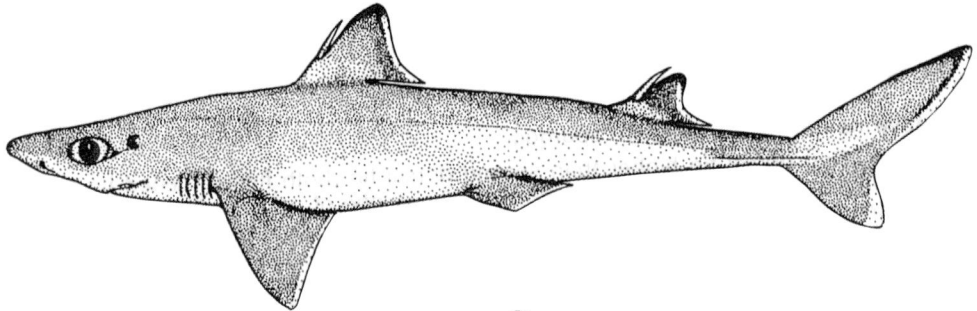

Spiked dogfish, *Squalus megalops*

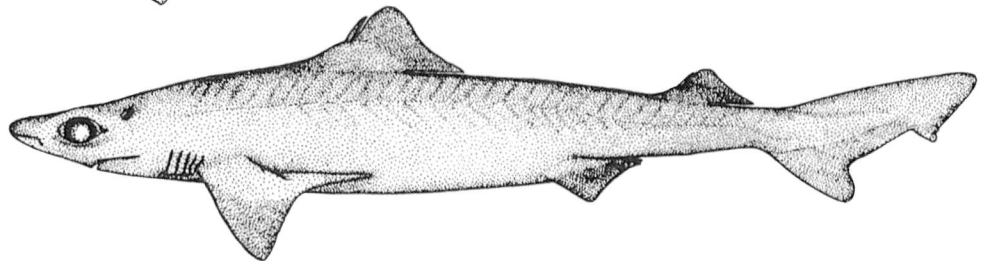

Endeavour dogfish, *Centrophorus moluccensis*

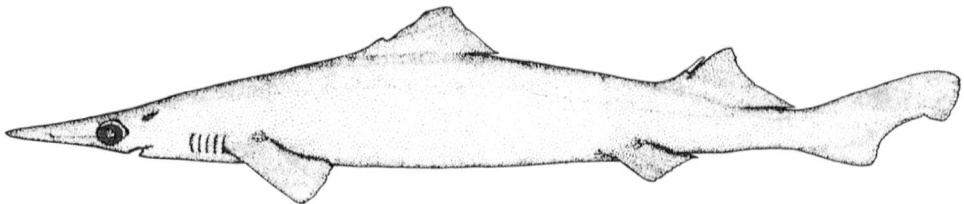

Long-snouted dogfish, *Denia quadrispinos*

A family of small, harmless sharks, generally found in deep coastal waters, identified by the long spines in front of their dorsal fins and by their lack of an anal fin. They are edible but suffer from a public prejudice. The old practice of selling them from fish and chip shops as "flake" or "sea fillets" is now illegal but they can be sold under names that do not mislead. Whitley suggested dogfishes were flattened like stingrays and then in mid-evolution changed their minds and reverted to being sharks. The most common Australian varieties are the spiked dogfish or skittle dog, *Squalus megalops*, a short, slender specimen with spines before each dorsal fin and a down-turned shallow snout; the white-spotted dogfish, *Squalus acanthias*, which has a brightly-spotted grey body and is particularly abundant in Tasmania; the golden dogfish, *Centroscymnus crepidater*, also known as the deepwater dogfish, as it has been recorded at depths down to 600 fathoms; the prickly dogfish, *Oxynotus bruniensis*, a blunt-snouted, heavily-scaled, extremely spiny character with each dorsal

preceded by a spine; the endeavour dogfish, *Centrophorus moluccensis*, which has strong spines covered by skin preceding both dorsal fins; the long-snouted dogfish, *Denia quadrispinos*, a sharp-nosed variety from the Great Australian Bight; and the strange luminous shark, *Isistius brasiliensis*, a small oceanic species said to attract prey by night with their "luminescent power".

FEATURES: Most of Australia's dogfish average one metre in length. Only a few stray into shallow coastal waters. They are mostly taken in trawlers' nets at depths below 200 fathoms. They all have five gill openings on each side of their greyish to brown bodies. Their name stems from the ancient habit of giving sharks canine names and calling their young pups. They have little angling value.

DISTRIBUTION: Every Australian State has some species of dogfish, but they are most plentiful in southern waters; Tasmania has at least 12 varieties.

Dolphin Fish   *Coryphaenidae*

Blunt-headed speedsters with dorsal fins that run right along the top of the head to the butt of the tail. They are prized light-gear fish notorious for their acrobatic displays and outstanding fighting qualities. Dolphin fish are unforgettable to bring to a boat as they undergo a series of colour changes as they die, with colours brightening and fading until they end up a dull grey. They have exceptional grace and swimming speed and will broach the surface of the sea, dodging among the waves, as they follow a trolled bait. They are warm water fish distributed right across the Pacific to the Australian east and west coasts and on to Hawaii, where they are known as morado or mahi-mahi. Hawaiian fishermen often hold a captured dolphin fish in the water to attract others close to the boat where they can be taken with baits and lures. There are two very similar dolphin fish in Australian waters.

FEATURES: Apart from their characteristic blue dorsal fins, dolphin fish have exceptionally wide, forked tails and bodies speckled by green and blue spots. The fins are a combination of orange and yellow. They reach up to two metres in length and 36.5 kg in weight. Fish attacking a lure will light up in a glowing show of colours. Large dolphin fish develop a pronounced blunt head and tend to travel alone or in twos or threes.

FISHING TECHNIQUE: Dolphin fish are caught trolling behind game boats at speeds up to seven knots. They bite readily on gang-hooked garfish and mullet and on almost any of the popular feathered lures. The ideal tackle should give this brave fish a chance—nothing heavier than light game rig is suggested. Wire traces are advisable because of their powerful mouths. A swivel will help eliminate tangles when they fight. They have a habit of congregating under pieces of flotsam, logs, rope or driftwood and to exploit this habit, Hawaiians build fish rafts just to attract them. They often take flying fish on the wing.

DISTRIBUTION: Through all warm Australian waters as far south as Bermagui in New South Wales and the Recherche Archipelago in Western Australia, but mainly in Barrier Reef waters and from Geraldton in the west to Cairns in the north. Dampier used the illustration of a dolphin fish in his *Voyage To New Holland*, published in 1701.

Dolphin fish, *Coryphaena hippurus*

DORIES *Zeidae*

John dory, *Zeus faber*

A slow-moving family of thin, flat fish represented in Australia by nine varieties, all of them outstanding food fish. They are ugly-looking fish with capacious mouths which they can extend with remarkable speed once they sight food. They provide poor sport. The largest of the family is the king dory, *Cyttus traversi*, found in the deep waters of the cooler states, a large-eyed fish that grows to 6 kg but lacks the large dark spot of the family's most celebrated member, the John dory, *Zeus faber*. The legend is that St. Peter placed the spot on the John dory when he took the fish for tribute money. John dory are unimpressive looking fish, short, deep-bodied, dullish olive-grey in colour with sickle-shaped ventral fins. Their flesh is firm and white and a delicious flavour. The mirror dory, *Zenopsis nebulosus*, is also a deep-bodied fish

but a brighter silvery-grey in colour with a distinct greyish fingerprint. They are identified by the dense, dark, first dorsal and ventral fins and by the three spines on the anal fin. Silver dory, *Cyttus australis*, are short, deep-bodied fish taken over the southern continental shelf. They lack the dark finger marks on the sides and do not have any bony plates or scutes along the midline of their backs or bellies. Silver dory take their name from their vivid silver colouring.

FEATURES: Surface and bottom fish of offshore reefs with members in all States. Few fish retain their flavour after freezing as well as the dories and fewer still give up with such little fight. They are trawled in large numbers and are caught on handlines or by spearing.

Mirror dory, *Zenopsis nebulosus*

Silver dory, *Cyttus australis*

FISHING TECHNIQUE: Dories have a marked preference for small, live fish and have a habit of drifting up to the baits and swallowing them. Their soft mouths are best handled on a single hook. Sinkers should be avoided whenever possible and hooks should be no bigger than 2/0 to 4/0. They are sometimes taken inside Sydney Harbour and the Hawkesbury River where they shelter in winter. They are such a valuable commercial fish it is surprising that not one State has imposed legal limits on the size that can be taken.

DISTRIBUTION: From Western Australia's southern coast around the bottom of Australia to South Australia, Tasmania and Victoria, and up the New South Wales coast to around Bundaberg in Queensland.

DRUMMER *Kyphosidae*

Silver drummer,
Kyphosus sydneyanus

A vegetarian family of deep-bodied, fast-swimming fish highly rated by sports-fishermen for their fighting qualities. They are not good table fare and seldom reach fish shops, but the drummer known as rock blackfish, *Girella elevata*, from the related family *Girellidae* which is only found in New South Wales, can be of good table quality if they are skinned and cleaned immediately on capture, especially if the fillets are marinated. The illustrated silver drummer, *Kyphosus sydneyanus*, offer good sport from ocean rocks when the water is rough. One weighing 12.98 kg was caught by Robert Crawford in Jurien Bay, Western Australia in 1965. Low-finned drummer, *Kyphosus vaigiensis*, are a Queensland variety often taken by spearfishermen. Southern drummer, *Kyphosus gibsoni* are found in both Queensland, Western Australia, and New South Wales. Topsail drummer, *Kyphosus cinerascens*, are greyish fish identified by their high dorsal fins and narrow, golden longitudinal bands.

FEATURES: All the drummers are tough, tenacious fighters, running fast and determinedly when hooked. They bite warily, with smooth mouths and live close to rocks or hiding places, feeding on algae, crabs and

FAR RIGHT:
Fishing from jetties, harbour walls and piers can be extremely successful with a paternoster rig. This method, where one or more wire booms are mounted above the lead, gives the fisherman a chance to experiment with different kinds of bait. Hook sizes should vary with the size of the bait used.

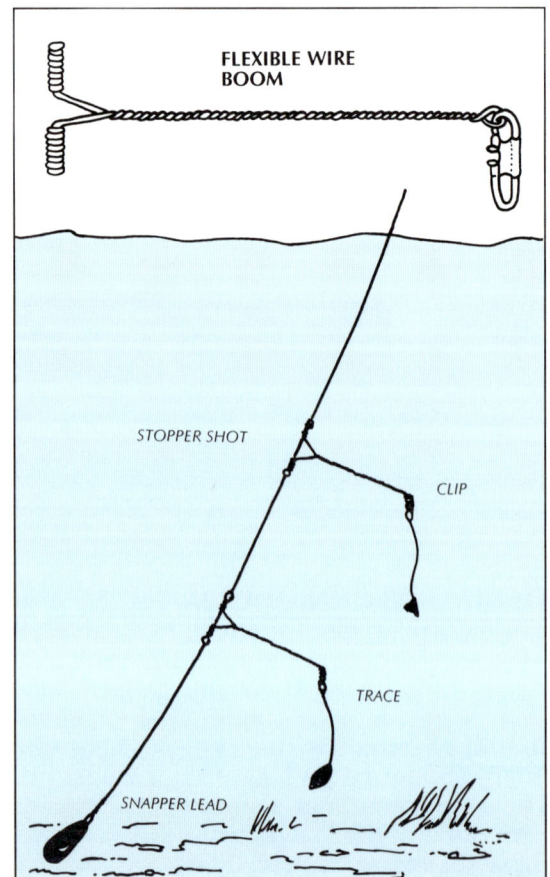

FLEXIBLE WIRE BOOM

STOPPER SHOT

CLIP

TRACE

SNAPPER LEAD

shellfish. The Western Australian variety is sometimes known as buffalo bream.

FISHING TECHNIQUE: Rockhoppers using baits of cunjevoi, weed, prawns and shellfish have learned that drummer can be berleyed with mixes of breadcrumbs and bran. They require small but strong hooks, 4 to 1/0, and lines with a high breaking strain because of their weight. Rockhoppers, using sinkers to get to the bottom, often do best with cabbage weed packed tightly on the hook. Boats that can manoeuvre close in to the shore help avoid snags and prevent the drummers reaching rocky hideaways when they make their run.

DISTRIBUTION: Black drummer are found only around the rocky cliffs and estuaries of New South Wales. Other drummer range through Queensland, South Australia and Western Australia. Topsail drummer occur in north Queensland and Northern Territory waters.

FISH WITH TOMATO ONION SAUCE

INGREDIENTS

4 fish fillets
1 tablespoon vegetable oil
1 large onion, chopped
2 medium tomatoes, sliced
2 tablespoons chopped parsley
1 tablespoon lemon juice
Freshly ground pepper

METHOD

Cooking fish this way really seals in the flavour and juices. Try this method using other combinations such as mushrooms and onions or a selection of fresh herbs.

Line a shallow baking dish with enough foil to make a closed parcel. Place the fish in and sprinkle with lemon juice and pepper. Lightly saute the onion in oil 5 minutes until softened. Add the tomato and cook, covered, for 5 minutes. Add the parsley and pour the mixture over the fish fillets. Seal the parcel and bake in a 180°C oven for 15-20 minutes or until fish is cooked.

Serves 4

Reprinted with permission, Carolyn Dunne, *The Semi-Vegetarian Cookbook,* Bantam, 1989

EELS   *Anguillidae*

Slippery, elongate fishes with bodies like snakes, in which the gill openings are reduced to a pair of slits or holes, one on either side of the head. The ventral fins and sometimes the pectoral fins are absent. There are more than 650 species spread around the world, about 145 of them occurring in Australia, mostly in tropical waters. Some are excellent eating, but the few Australians ready to try them usually stick to the freshwater varieties. Years ago freshwater eels were strung up in fish shops but this practice has faded out. Eels have always been surrounded by superstition and mystery and the awe with which they were held increased when their amazing breeding habits were documented.

Freshwater eels: All eels, including those that live in freshwater as adults, spawn in the sea. They are chiefly nocturnal, and spend the daylight hours under rocks or crevices and among weeds, occasionally basking in the sun. Sometimes the freshwater varieties leave the water and travel overland, especially when the grass is wet. The main species of freshwater eels in Australia are the short-finned eels, *Anguilla australis*, an olive-green to brown variety with short dorsal fins stretching half their body length that is common in dams, swamps, rivers and estuaries, and the long-finned eel, *Anguila reinhardtii* an olive-green to brown variety, sometimes silvery with the lateral and dorsal areas mottled and covered in darker blotches. Short-finned

eels grow to 5 kg, long-finned eels to 20 kg and both are delicious when smoked. They often travel huge distances to reach the sea to spawn, travelling overland through inland farms and dams to reach their spawning grounds, which are thought to centre in the deep water north of Australia around New Caledonia.

Saltwater eels: Australia's warmer marine waters carry a wide range of eels, varying in length from half a metre to almost four metres. Most are equipped with fang-like teeth that can inflict nasty wounds on fishermen and which they use to tear their prey apart when feeding, but their bite is not poisonous to humans. Some are shy when approached by divers, others will take food from the hand or even wrap themselves playfully around divers. Best known varieites in Australian waters are: *Moray eels* of the family *Muraenidae*, a group with heads like birds and strongly muscled jaws. Morays can be plain, mottled, spotted or banded. They have no pectoral fins and very small gill slits, but the vertical fins are usually well developed. The ancient Romans reared them in ponds and fed them on unwanted slaves. The tessellated moray, *Gymnothorax favagineus*, is a common coral reef variety often seen by holiday-makers when wading through lagoons and grows to one metre in length; the green eel, *Gymnothorax prasinus*, which lives around the southern half of Australia; the mottled reef eel or leopard moray, *Gymnothorax*

Short-finned eel, *Anguilla australis*

Tessellated moray,
Gymnothorax favagineus

Green eel, *Gymnothorax prasinus*

undulatus, is a savage, fearless variety that can be berleyed out of their caves and crevices with fish pieces; the white-spot moray, *Gymnothorax prionodon*, are readily identified by the circular white spots over their bodies and tails and the serrated teeth that provide their alternative name, saw-toothed eel; the long tailed catfish eel, *Euristmus lepturus*, are the world's largest reef eels, morays that grow to 3.8 metres: the mosaic moray, *Enchelycore ramosus*, a striking variety with a characteristic mosaic pattern and curved, open jaws lined with needle-sharp teeth. Arrow eels of the family *Cyemidae* are short, deep-bodied eels with dorsal and anal fins ending abruptly to form a fork. Their jaws are beak-like and do not close properly. The family contains one common species, *Cyema atrum*, which is distributed worldwide in tropical and warm temperate regions, usually well out to sea. They are inky black in colour, sometimes with lateral black spots, and minute nipples or papillae stud their heads and bodies.

Conger eels of the family *Congridae* are a scaleless, elongate variety, similar in appearance to the freshwater eels with upper jaws that overhang the lower. They are usually found in shallow water or along the continental slopes. The southern conger eels, *Conger verreauxi*, are the largest eels found in Australia's southern waters, reaching 25 kg in weight and two metres in length. They are extremely active at night when they feed on small fish. They were once regarded as an important commercial variety but are seldom offered today in the markets. They are no threat to humans but care should be taken removing them from

Long-tailed catfish eel,
Euristmus lepturus

Mosaic moray,
Enchelycore ramosus

Short-finned conger eel,
Conger wilsoni

craypots as they can inflict painful bites. The little conger eels, *Gnathophis habenata*, are an offshore species that reach only 400 mm in length and appear frequently in trawlers' nets. They are uniformly pale brown to yellowish above, lighter below and have prominent silver eyes. They are found in Tasmania, Victoria, New South Wales, South Australia and southern Western Australia. There are some curious congers like the ladder conger, *Scalanago lateralis*, which have a branched lateral line; the fringe-nosed conger, *Gnathophis umbrellabius*; and short-finned conger eel, *Conger wilsoni*, which grows to two metres in length and has been taken with a gaff or large hook and then skull-dragged to the shore.

Snake eels or **worm eels** of the family *Ophichthidae* are small, elongate eels with tongues that adhere to the lower jaws and have a posterior nostril within or piercing the upper lips. Snake eels lack a true tail, or caudal fin, whereas worm eels lack pectoral fins but possess tails. Both forms are often brightly coloured, spotted or banded like sea snakes, though the snakes, of course, have scales and breathe through the lungs. The short-headed worm eels, *Muraenichthys breviceps*, are the most frequently encountered members of the group, common in sheltered bays and estuaries in Tasmania, Victoria, South Australia and Western Australia. They are pale-greenish in colour, speckled above with minute brown dots, and are often sighted by flounder spearmen at night. They have been sighted swimming near the surface but are trawled at depths down to 70 metres. There are at least 35 species of snake or worm eels in Australian waters.

Pike eels of the family *Muraenesocidae* are widely known among anglers for the damage they do to their tackle and their catches. They have vicious long teeth, grow to a metre and a half in length and create absolute mayhem for those unlucky enough to haul them into a dinghy, tangling lines, biting at everything that moves. They are grey on top, silvery along the sides and their fins have a broad black margin. They have large mouths, with three rows of teeth in each jaw, and are usually found in brackish backwaters. Queensland boat-owners sometimes provide customers with a piece of heavy hardwood to deal with pike eels as they are hauled on board.

FEATURES: The young freshwater eels or elvers emerge from their eggs and float about the sea for a time in a larval stage that shows them as slender, transparent creatures often mistaken for fish. When they are about 7 cm long they head for land, drifting down the coast, seeking an estuary or harbour that is fed by freshwater. They move upstream to the source of the river and spend their lives in remote billabongs and waterholes. In England they are taken in vast numbers at the elvers stage, pounded into paste and fried in butter, for sale as fish cakes. In Australia the entire eel population spend their lives in their chosen waterholes until the spawning urge overtakes them and they head for the sea. Our knowledge of the astonishing breeding habits of eels stems from the work of Johannes Schmidt, appointed early in the 1900's by the Danish government to find the reasons for an alarming decline in eels. In 20 years of research Schmidt traced the baby fish-like eels from their birthplace in the Sargasso Sea to their fresh-water homes in Europe. Armed with proof of the eel's extraordinary powers, Schmidt came to Australia in 1929 and found evidence that Australia's eastern eels bred in deepwaters to the north and those from north-western Australia bred in waters near Sumatra.

FISHING TECHNIQUE: Although they are prized table fare elsewhere in the world, eels are seldom fished for in Australia. They are most vulnerable after rain when they venture out in search of food. Amateurs catch them by fishing with two or more rods from the shore, with the rods propped up on rod rests. The lines are cast with baited hooks and allowed to lie on the bottom. Worms, prawns, pieces of meat or fish are all effective baits. Commercially they have been caught until recently in Lake Colac, Glenaire, Sale, Lake Purrumbete and Maffra Lagoon in Victoria, but Tasmania is now increasing its annual eel catch. All the Australian eel catch is exported. The professionals use conically-shaped fyke nets which are like airfield windsocks, with the nets divided into compartments by cane hoops which act as a frame. The entrance to each compartment is controlled by a conical valve of netting that prevents the eels escaping.

EMPERORS AND SWEETLIPS *Lethrindae*

Sweetlips emperor,
Lethrinus chrysostomus

Both the emperors and sweetlips are plentiful in Australian waters, where they are known collectively as *Lethrinads*. They are a colourful group of sea perch of excellent table quality (very similar to bream in shape but far more ornate), caught commercially inside the coral reefs north from Gladstone in Queensland. Southern visitors often are surprised by the frequency with which they attack the bait. Emperors have rows of scales over their cheeks, sweetlips cheeks are bare. Emperors grow to 18 kg or over 40 lb, but are mostly taken around 5 kg to 8 kg. Sweetlips grow to 9 kg or 20 lb, but usually are caught at around 2.3 kg or 5 lb. Both emperors and sweetlips are notable in that mature fish retain the same splendid flavour of younger fish. The sweetlips emperor, *Lethrinus chrysostomus* are the most abundant of the family and bite readily and fight fiercely. Sweetlips emperors are olive-green above, silvery beneath. Their vivid dark vertical body stripes fade quickly after death. They are also known as red throats, tricky snappers and lippers. Other common emperors are the long-nosed emperor, *Lethrinella miniatus*, the yellow-tailed emperor *Lethrinus mashena*, and the handsome spangled emperor, *Lethrinus nebulosus*, all of north Queensland. They are also known as government bream and king snapper.

FEATURES: Sweetlips do not have a notch on the rear lower edge of gill cover or preopercular flange, which is invariably present in emperors. They have bronze cheeks and are pale pink along the head, with olive-brown bodies tending to silvery over the belly. The dorsal fin is a vivid scarlet and the tail varies from greyish-brown tinged in pink to brilliant pink. There is an unmistakable scarlet blotch at the base of the pectoral fin. Fish taken in freshwater have dark vertical bars over the body that fade on death. One of their most distinctive features is that the inside of their mouth is bright red. Fish captured at night are silvery, with the dark bars showing only after they are thrown on the deck.

FISHING TECHNIQUE: Best hauls of emperors and sweetlips are taken by berleying the fish up from the coral bottoms to within a few metres of the surface. They come up in remarkable numbers and from then are easily caught on handlines, biting strongly on all types of fish baits, molluscs and crustaceans. Grant says they enjoy newly-born turtles. Emperors and sweetlips fight strongly when hooked and the angler's main problem is to prevent them darting back to the coral. Best rigs are those that allow the baits to swing free as the sinker takes them down, with swivels to take the twist from the line.

DISTRIBUTION: Mainly in the tropical waters of Queensland and the Northern Territory, though they occasionally stray south as far as Caloundra and Cape Moreton.

Note: The striking sea perch *Lutjanus sebae* is universally known throughout the Barrier Reef as the red emperor although it is not an emperor at all and is a genuine member of the *Lutjanidae* group. It is one of the prized fish of the Barrier Reef region, growing to 22 kg, fighting tenaciously when hooked, and providing an outstanding meal even in the larger sizes. They are caught on everything from octopus to cut fish. Red emperors are fish of tropical seas and are caught right across northern Australia into the Indian Ocean.

Painted sweetlips,
Plectorhynchus pictus

97

ENGLISH PERCH OR REDFIN   *Percidae*

The most controversial fish in Australian waters, persistently blamed for the reduction of native species. Arguments about the wisdom of introducing them has continued for more than a century, with thousands of anglers claiming they clear good waters of food and through their high fertility rate and remarkable resilience take over entire waterways. Others rate them excellent sport, tough enough to survive droughts and dramatic changes in water temperature. There are an estimated one million English perch in Eildon Weir alone, which demonstrates how well they have done since first shipped to Tasmania in 1862, when 11 specimens arrived. They were first introduced into Victoria in 1862, New South Wales in 1888, and can now be caught in most waterways in those States, as well as in South Australia and Western Australia. Only in Queensland where water temperatures are presumably too hot for them have English perch, *Perca fluviatilus*, failed to build up in dense shoals.

FEATURES: They take their name from the red tinge on the pectoral, ventral and anal fins. Their backs are a darkish olive-green, the sides striped with five or six vertical bars. They pale quickly when frightened and this allows them to merge into their surroundings. They have the ability to take on the colour of their environment, which is why some are indistinct and drab in colouring, others brightly tinted. They have reached a weight of 10 kg or 23 lb in Australia but are far smaller in Europe.

FISHING TECHNIQUE: Redfin bite well on crayfish and shrimps. A growing band of redfin anglers regularly take good numbers using small lures, which they jig and bob close to the bottom. Novices appear to catch just as many redfin as veterans, fishing the same locations. Redfin flesh is white and sweet but they are impossible to scale quickly. Better to cut the head and shoulders away and skin the fish.

DISTRIBUTION: All States except the Northern Territory, northern Queensland and only in the south of Western Australia.

English perch, *Perca fluviatilus*

FIREFISH   *Scorpaenidae*

Spectacular, warm water members of the scorpion fish family with fan-like fins, also known as butterfly cod, lionfish, zebrafish, and featherfins. The Arabic name for them means hell. They grow to only 45 cm and short of 1 kg in weight but they are among the most picturesque fish in the sea, great favourites in aquariums and with underwater photographers. They have a habit of swimming very slowly with all fins extended, dazzling their prey in a show that makes fin colours glow and wane as in a coal fire. They have venomous dorsal spines, contact from which can inflict painful stings that endure for days. Victims frequently suffer periods of heavy sweating and shortness of breath but there is no record of any fatal stings from this highly attractive fish.

FEATURES: Firefish are known for their colour changes and the graceful undulations of their long and narrow fins. The membranes of the front dorsal and sometimes the pectoral fins are deeply incised. Older fish have spiny heads or cheeks with a band of prickles. The illustrated red firefish, *Pterois volitans*, has 13 spines to the dorsal fin and 14 rays in the pectoral fin, all of them unbranched and free of membranes. The yellow body is vertically striped with golden brown, some of them black-edged, often with yellow or scarlet on the tassel-like flaps of the head. There is a dark tentacle over each eye. They feed on crustaceans or small fish which they pick out of small shoals, driving their prey into corners and sucking them into their mouths with swift, violent attacks. The dwarf firefish, *Dendrochirus zebra*, is more aggressive than other scorpion fish and has at times approached scuba divers. They grow to only 180 mm and have reddish-brown bodies carrying seven or eight vertical brown bars, with slender, needle-shaped dorsal spines.

DISTRIBUTION: Several Indo-Pacific species have reached tropical Australia, through Western Australia, the Northern Territory, and down the Queensland coast to northern New South Wales. Red firefish have reached Sydney but are commoner in northern coral reefs.

Red firefish, *Pterois volitans*

FLAGTAILS   *Kuhliidae*

A group of freshwater and saltwater fishes that take their name from the prominent markings on their tails. They are also known as mountain trout but the varieties known as jungle perch are the ones that have excited amateur fishermen. Southerners on trips to northern waters have been delighted by the eagerness with which jungle perch take sophisticated lures. Queenslanders argue that they catch just as many using baits like green frogs. The best known jungle perch is the illustrated species, *Kuhlia rupestris*, sometimes known as rock flagtail, which is brown across the back, fading to green and silver beneath. The scales are spotted in black and there is a dark smudge on the tail. They grow to two-thirds of a metre and 2.5 kg or 5 lb and have to be carefully stalked in idyllic mountain settings, where they compete for food with sooty grunter and mangrove jack. They are both outstanding sport and table fare.

Jungle perch, Kuhlia rupestris

FEATURES: Jungle perch have distinctive tails and are renowned for their shyness.

They have an ability, similar to ocean-run salmon, to penetrate rapids and waterfalls. The coastal variety, the five-bar flagtail, *Kuhlia mugil* is a brilliant silvery colour with several black bars in the tail. Another relative of this fascinating family, the tripletail, *Lobotes surinamensis*, is described elsewhere in this book.

FISHING TECHNIQUE: Southerners are adamant that the best sport comes from using fly tackle with black streamers or longtails, though not many anglers take such gear into jungle rivers. Queenslanders use grasshoppers, crayfish, shrimps and frogs. The adventurous might try a surface popper.

DISTRIBUTION: Queensland, New Guinea, New Caledonia and the western Pacific. The coastal forms get down from southern Queensland into northern New South Wales, but have also appeared in the southern section of the Barrier Reef.

FLATFISH

There are around 110 species of flatfish in Australia including flounder, sole and Queensland halibut, and most are delicious eating. They are far smaller than the flatfish of Europe and nowhere near as abundant, and there are never enough of the more edible varieties caught to satisfy the demands of Australian hotels and restaurants. New Zealand has taken advantage of this by sending big quantities of frozen flounder to Australia.

They are not fishes that provide outstanding sport, and are so easy to spear that most fishermen tire of taking them once they have enough to satisfy immediate demand. They are more fun when taken by casting small baits over beaches and mudflats, but the test of angling skill ends when they take the hook, for they show no fight and make no attempt to free themselves.

Their life styles are intriguing. They are born with eyes on either side of their heads and remain pelagics, swimming close to the surface, until they reach around 12 mm. Then they become bottom-dwellers as one eye moves to the same side as the other eye and they become either left-eyed or right-eyed fish. Once the eyes are in place they head for the bottom and spend the rest of their lives grubbing for crustaceans, and small marine creatures. Some of them are masters of camouflage, and experiments have shown they have amazing ability to change colour to merge into their surroundings. They often cover their bodies with sand, leaving only the eyes clear, and they can be very difficult to detect.

Europe's notable flatfish, plaice, turbot and halibut are not found in Australian waters, though we do have a flatfish known as Queensland halibut, at 10 kg the biggest of this delectable group of fishes.

See Flounder page 108, Queensland halibut page 201, and Sole page 248.

FISH MARINADES: The flavour of most fish can be improved by soaking pieces ready for cooking in a liquid marinade, usually a mix of salad oil, vinegar, lemon juice and parsley. An hour in the marinade should be enough, though some cooks prefer to leave the fish in the marinade for four hours. The fish should be drained before cooking but the marinade can be used as a baste during the cooking process. Marinades vary enormously. Some include yoghurt, ginger, garlic, curry, paprika and chilli powder for a Tandoori-style flavour, others include vermouth or white wine, basil, pine nuts, olive oil and garlic. For devilled fish cutlets, the recommended marinade combines chutney, tomato sauce, worcestershire sauce, vinegar, mustard and pepper.

FLATHEAD *Platycephalidae*

Flathead are poor sporting fishes, but are much sought by anglers because of their outstanding edible quality. There are at least 41 varieties in Australian waters but only about a quarter of these are regularly fished for by sportsmen. Millions of kilograms are taken annually by trawling, inshore netting, and by line, and although some species are a little dry, flathead consistently feature on restaurant menus in all States and are a basic part of the fish and chips trade.

Flathead are elongate, bottom-dwelling fish with flattened, depressed heads and both eyes set on top of their head after centuries of burying in the sand. There are usually two longitudinal ridges on the head, one of which ends in two sharp spines, on the preopercular margin. These spines have caused many painful wounds among anglers who tried to handle flathead without wearing a glove or using an old piece of towelling.

Anglers seeking a good meal have a wide range of flathead habitats from which to choose. They are caught from seawalls, jetties, sandbars, offshore reefs, and are just as common in estuaries as large harbours. The majority of those caught in Australia belong to the family *Platycephalidae*, the cooler water variety. This group includes the largest of Australia's flatheads, a fish that grows to 1.2 metres and 14 kg, the mud or dusky flathead. No flathead are found in America and Europe, but they range from China to the tropics, through Indonesia and down Western Australia and Queensland to the southern States. Australia also boasts a family of spiny flatheads of the family *Hoplichthyidae*, a deepwater variety that resembles other flatheads in shape but lacks scales and has a row of spiny scutes along each side of the body. This family has large eyes, flattened heads, and is found at depths between 360 and 800 metres. In the tropics the genus *Suggrundus* is more common than *Platycephalidae*. This group can be identified by their sculptured heads. All the flathead families are exceptionally good eating despite their frequently grotesque appearance.

Tiger flathead, *Platycephalus richardsoni*: For more than half a century this was the main species of flathead caught off New South Wales, but over-fishing has heavily reduced their numbers. They are mottled brown above, creamy below, with red-brick and white spots and dark streaks near the tail. The teeth are large and prominent. In Tasmania, their body colour turns light-brown or pinkish-grey. They average around 65 cm and 1.3 kg in New South Wales but in southern waters get up to

Tiger flathead,
Platycephalus richardsoni

Dusky flathead,
Platycephalus fuscus

Bar-tailed flathead,
Platycephalus indicus

2.5 kg. They are a major commercial species in Tasmania with the annual catch exceeding 100 tonnes. In spring, large adult tiger flathead migrate into Tasmania's coastal bays and provide a big attraction for anglers. Their flesh is white, tender and flavoursome and remains edible for long periods in storage.

Dusky flathead, *Platycephalus fuscus*: A depressed, elongated variety common in east coast estuaries, also known as mud flathead. Their teeth are small but needle-sharp and removing hooks from their large mouths requires care. They are greyish to olive brown on top with bony ridges along the upper surface of the head. The sides are mottled black but they take their names from the dusky colour of their heads, which are brown-spotted. Both the ventral and dorsal fins are brown-spotted, and there are further dark blotches on their tails. They are much paler in colouring in Queensland where the name dusky appears a misnomer. Grant prefers to use the names northern and southern dusky flathead, but they appear to be the same species with only pigmentation differences, with the Queensland specimens living in sand rather than mud. They reach 1.2 kg and at that size require wire traces to prevent their teeth slashing lines. Most flathead specialists stab duskies through the head with a knife or crunch a boot over their heads to avoid a painful sting from their preopercular spines as they remove the hook.

Bar-tailed flathead, *Platycephalus indicus*: A warm water variety common in the estuaries of north-western Western Australia, the Northern Territory, and north Queensland seldom sighted south of the Tropic of Capricorn. The smaller specimens are the tastiest and at their maximum size of one metre and 5.8 kg in weight, they lack flavour. Their upper bodies are sandy-brown in colour and liberally spotted in a darker brown. They are white below and there are ill-defined dark blotches across the back. The tail is brown and splashed with orange-yellow and gives them their name. Bar-tailed flathead usually are caught on fish baits but are unusual in that they will rise to a trolled lure or plug.

Fringe-eyed flathead, *Cymbacephalus nematophthalmus*: A small, heavy-bodied variety that inhabits weed beds, and congregates around jetty piles in the Gulf of Carpentaria, across the Northern Territory into north-western Western Australia and New South Wales. They take their name from the fleshy eyebrows above their eyes. They have cinnamon-brown bodies covered in irregular dark brown or black bands, one of which extends into the spinous dorsal fin. There are numerous dark spots on top. They seldom reach more than 40 cm, are excellent eating, and notable for the squeaky grunts they produce on capture.

Tassel-snouted flathead, *Thysanophrys cirronasus*: A small, brown flathead with a body heavily studded with greenish-grey to purple crossbars which take their name from the fleshy tissue on the snout. They are among the finest eating of all fishes, and are found in the coastal waters of southern Western Australia, South Australia, Victoria, New South Wales and southern Queensland. They grow to only 380 mm.

Marbled flathead, *Platycephalus marmoratus*: A heavily-bodied, deepwater variety found in Western Australia south of Rottnest Island, New South Wales and southern Queensland. They are immediately recognisable by their marbled and cream flecks on pale brown bodies and by the six to eight broad dark-brown crossbars. Their tails are cinnamon-brown with light brown

Fringe-eyed flathead,
*Cymbacephalus
nematophthalmus*

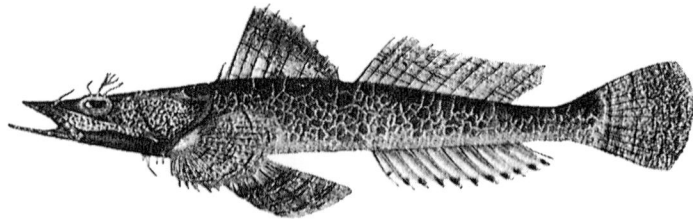

Tassel-snouted flathead,
Thysanophrys cirronasus

Marbled flathead,
Platycephalus marmoratus

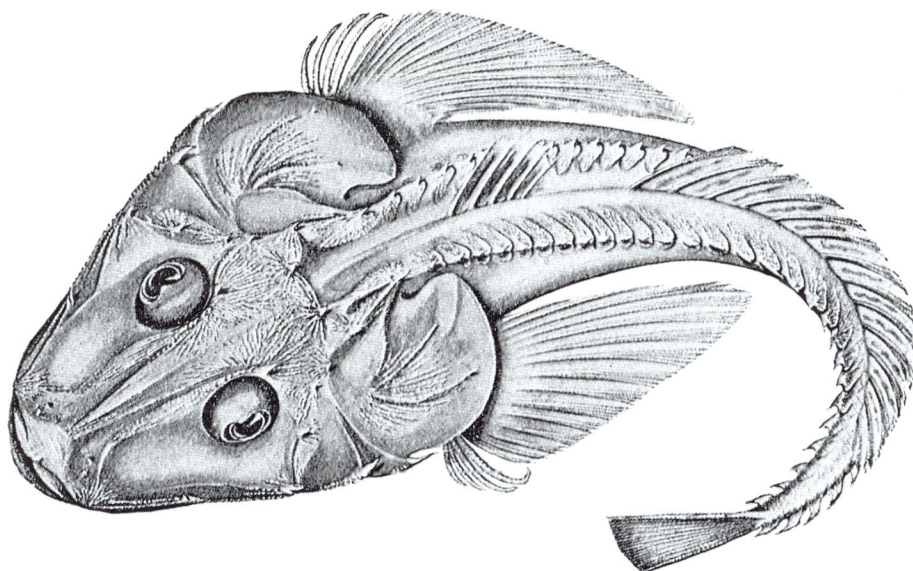

Deep-sea flathead,
Heplichthys haswelli

spots and are white-tipped. The large head is deeply mottled. They grow to half a metre and are usually taken at a depth of 25 fathoms and are only occasionally taken by deepwater line anglers drifting over coastal reefs.

Grassy flathead, *Platycephalus laevigatus*: A cool-water species known in Victoria as black or rock flathead. Their bodies are more rounded than other flatheads. They inhabit grassy zostera flats and are frequently exposed to the nets of trawlers in areas where there are sharp falls in the tide. They are generally not sighted in the open by day but lie buried in sand beneath

algae stands, becoming active just before dusk, moving out from the sand to the edges of reefs to feed on small marine creatures. Mature specimens average around 50 cm and they are found off New South Wales, Victoria, South Australia, Tasmania, and Western Australia.

Flag-tail flathead, *Platycephalus arenarius*: A beautifully marked flathead that frequents warm water estuaries, bays and inlets in Queensland and the Northern Territory. They are mottled along the top with greenish-brown dots that almost completely cover their elongate silvery bodies, and have characteristic tails patterned in light blue, green and white. They grow to 35 cm, live on fish and crustaceans, and are a very tasty member of the flathead family, frequently caught on prawn bait.

Blue-spotted flathead, *Platycephalus caeruleopunctatus*: Another species, seldom caught by anglers, which find their way frequently on to the table. They are largely restricted to southern Queensland waters and are readily identified by the clusters of thick blue spots all over their bodies. They provide outstanding white meat and are known in the fish trade for their sustained good flavour after long periods of storage. They must be quickly chilled on capture.

Deep-sea flathead, *Heplichthys haswelli*: A deepwater flathead rarely encountered by anglers but of excellent table value. They are compressed, elongate, and have ridged, broad heads with flattened snouts and tough, bony bucklers or shields on the lateral line along the sides. Most are taken at 35 to 40 cm in length, at depths between 300 and 400 metres, but they get down as far as 1500 metres. They can be identified by the black blotches above the preoperculum, which is armed with two vicious-looking spines.

Sand flathead, *Platycephalus bassensis*: A light brown flathead with a prominent preopercular spine and a tail spotted on the upper part with a dark blotch on the lower half. They are taken both on lines and in nets when sheltering on the bottom of bays, inlets and estuaries in South

Sand flathead,
Platycephalus bassensis

Grassy flathead,
Platycephalus laevigatus

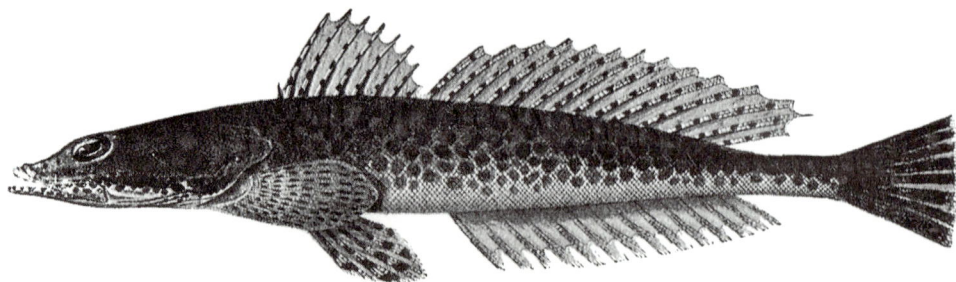

Australia, Tasmania, Victoria and New South Wales. Skindivers find they can approach them to within a few metres. They are identified by the "flag" set in their tails. Sand flathead are not a large variety, rarely exceeding 45 cm and averaging close to 30 cm. But they bite on small cut fish baits, peeled prawns and yabbies, and will take artificial lures as eagerly as any bait. They are also known as slimy flathead.

FISHING TECHNIQUES:

1. Drift-Fishing
A highly successful method used in all States in which one or more lines are presented to the fish from short rods or spool casters. The motion of the boat drifting with the tide wobbles the bait just enough to attract the fish. To prevent the lines snagging, the best approach is to go out with companions who can take turns paddling to stop the boat fouling the lines. The chained hook rig is often used as the top hook holds the bait clear of the bottom while the rig itself is dragged across the bottom. Fish taken by this method usually are big enough to require 6/0 hooks.

2. Spinning
This technique has the angler retrieving lures across the top of weed beds at just the right speed to entice the flathead into biting. A strong two-metre spinning rod and a vigorous, deliberately erratic retrieval will catch plenty of flathead. The ABU range of lures, particularly the shiner, the killer, spoons and swaybacks have all proved effective. The rod has to be worked energetically from side to side during the retrieval to get plenty of movement on the lures.

3. Handlining
From piers, wharves, and seawalls, thousands of flathead are caught every year by anglers who follow the fundamentals. Baits of prawn, squid, beach worm, octopus, mussel, and mullet gut must always be fresh. Berley should be used even when flathead are known to be nearby, and all baits must be firmly attached to hooks; flathead are adept at picking loose baits or baits that are too soft from hooks. Live baits such as yellowtail, mullet, anchovy and pilchard should be hooked through the back, behind the dorsal fin. The weight of the bait generally is enough to take the hook down. Keep the bait moving. Sinkers that are too big will merely anchor it in one spot and lessen the prospects of catching a big flathead. Keep a glove or old towel handy to safeguard against the flatheads' nasty spines.

FLATHEAD DRIFTING RIG

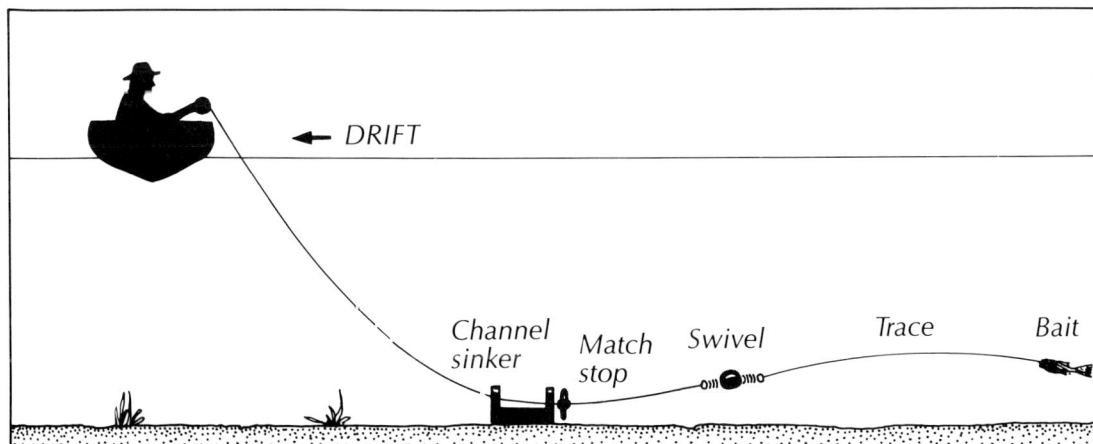

FLATHEAD DRIFTING RIG: As flathead are bottom feeders the rig should ensure that the bait is kept close to the bottom. Either a rod or handcaster may be used.

FLOUNDER *Bothidae*

Yellowbelly flounder,
Rhombosolea leporina

Australia boasts a large number of appetising flounder, but anglers seldom take big catches of them. They are taken mainly in nets, by underwater divers, and occasionally by sportsmen in flat bottom boats equipped with lights and spears. They cling to the bottom sand, often almost disappearing, feeding on small sea worms, crustaceans or small shellfish. Flounder are often prettily patterned on top where both eyes watch proceedings, but are uniformly white or yellow on the blind side. They are fish of high table quality but most people who eat them do not know the difference between flounder and sole.

FEATURES: Flounder begin life in the same form as other fish, with an eye on each side of the head, swimming close to the surface until they are about 12 mm long. Then one eye either moves round the head or through the head to the same side as the other eye. From then on they swim with both eyes upwards in a wavy motion of

their bodies which Whitley compared to the motion of a flying carpet. They invariably have a more prominent lower jaw than soles, and the preoperculum edge of the cheek-bone is free. Flounder produce millions of eggs that float and then grow to mostly small fish, averaging around 30 cm in length.

FISHING TECHNIQUE: Some small catches of flounder are made with light rods and small hooks baited with earth worms slung below a sinker and fished on the bottom on rising tides. A No. 1 hook is big enough and in some spots a No. 4 or 6 hook is better. Flounder prefer sandworms, which are more easily baited on a No. 4 or 6 hook than the larger sizes. The moment the hook is set, the angler should haul in the line. Flounder seldom offer any resistance. In the absence of sandworms, craytail, marine worms or prawns are good alternative baits, but the most successful method of catching flounder is to use a single-pronged spear with a light attached. Batteries are usually fitted into the hollowed out handle of the spear. Flat-bottom boats can be used, but generally the spearfishermen simply wades barefoot through the shallows, and the light finds the flounder. Australia's best known flounder are:

Large-toothed flounder, *Pseudorhombus arsius*: Found on the east and west coast, they are brown in colour with or without dark blotches and pale spots. They take their name from the exceptionally large teeth on both jaws, and grow to a little over 30 cm, though some have reached 40 cm. They take prawns or flesh baits when fished over estuary banks. Off-shore they get down to depths around 50 metres. Large-toothed flounder are a delectable variety found in Western Australia, South Australia, New South Wales, Queensland and the Northern Territory.

Small-toothed flounder, *Pseudorhombus jenynsii*: Another fine table fish, brown or grey in colour, with five or six large white spots with a dark centre—eye spots—spread around the body. The fins are spotted and the large, canine teeth so evident in the large-mouthed flounder are notably absent. Small-toothed flounder reach 36 cm and are found in all mainland States, but are mostly taken in Queensland and around beaches of Bass Strait islands.

Long-snouted flounder, *Ammotretis rostratus*: A delicious-eating species, light brown in colour, with or without small dark spots. The snout is extended and modified to produce a soft fleshy hook. They grow to around 30 cm, and range from southern New South Wales, Victoria, South Australia, southern Western Australia, and Tasmania, where they are incorrectly labelled as sole in the markets.

Bass Strait flounder, *Arnoglossus bassensis*: A greyish brown variety, with several conspicuous blotches and spots on the upper side. There are several dark blue spots over the body, two of them on the middle line towards the tail, both ringed in black. Bass Strait flounder are taken off South Australia

Large-toothed flounder, *Pseudorhombus arsius*

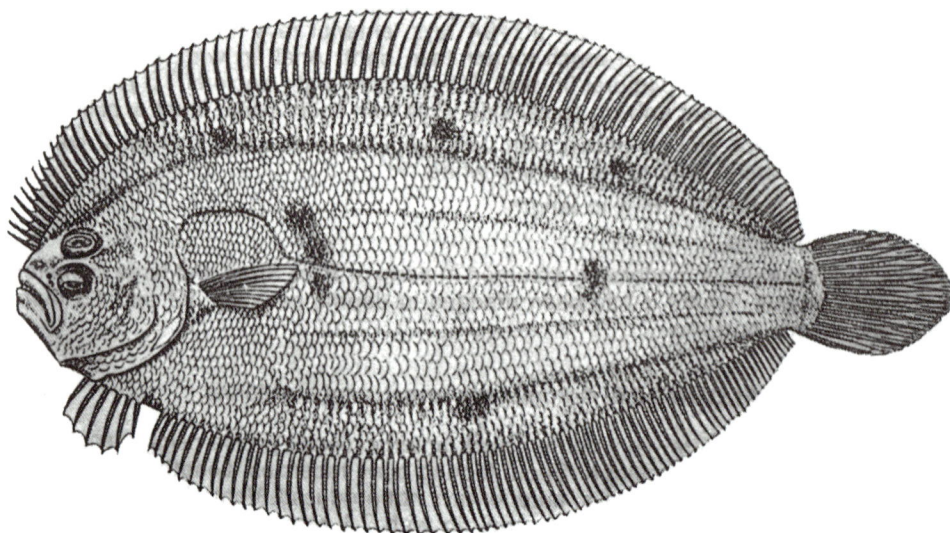

Bass Strait flounder,
Arnoglossus bassensis

Greenback flounder,
Rhombosolea tapirina

as well as from the coast of Tasmania, at a depth of around 30 fathoms. They grow to 24 cm in length.

Greenback flounder, *Rhombosolea tapirina*: A valued food fish but not enough of them are caught to satisfy demand. The anal and dorsal fins, running from head to tail, are extended, giving the fish the appearance of a giant pancake. They are also known as the Melbourne flounder. Mature specimens range in colour from greyish-green to cinnamon-brown, with the body

studded by dark blotches. The fins are white-edged. After death the body turns a dull green, which gives this variety its name. The long bony slivers of bone comprising the side fins can be easily removed during cooking. Like all flounder, they should be cooked whole. They are caught in southern New South Wales, Victoria, Tasmania, South Australia and southern Western Australia.

Crested flounder, *Lophonectes gallus*: The most abundant flounder in Tasmanian waters, where they are often caught in scallop dredges. The scales are larger than in most flounders and are present only on the top side. They are light tan to dark brown in colour, with darker marking on the dorsal surface. They reach 20 cm and are found in all States. Easily recognised by the prominent crest-like rays on the dorsal fin.

Leopard flounder, *Bothus pantherinus*: A prettily-marked left-eyed flounder. They are a tropical member of the family which undergoes amazing colour changes, varying from light green to a pinkish brown over which there is an irregular pattern of dark spots and blotches. Towards the tail on the midline of the body, there is a black spot. The fins are all mottled in white. Large leopard flounders are regularly caught in the Gulf of Carpentaria by prawn trawlers but they are also taken in smaller sizes along the Barrier Reef. They reach 300 mm in length and are delectable eating.

Large-scaled flounder, *Ammotretis macrolepis*: A right-eyed variety found only in Bass Strait and Storm Bay, where they occur on muddy bottoms at depths between 40 and 80 metres. The top surface is yellowish brown or pink with numerous grey and golden spots on the head and body, and the lower surface is white. The fins are yellowish, with dark grey dots. They reach 100 mm in length.

Crested flounder,
Lophonectes gallus

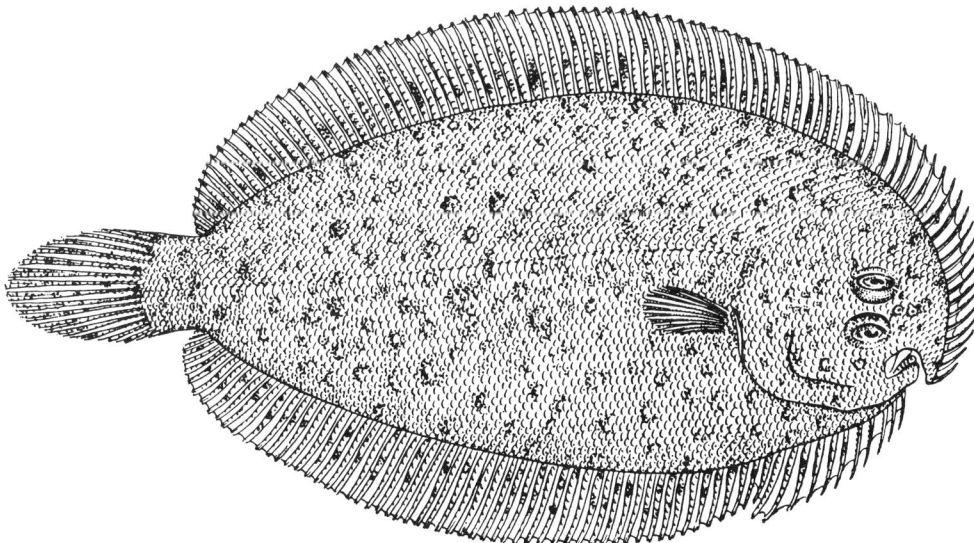

Large-scaled flounder,
Ammotretis macrolepis

FLUTEMOUTH *Fistulariidae*

A small group of very long fishes with tube-like snouts and tails in which the middle rays form a whip-like trailing filament. They are related to trumpet fishes and are sometimes known as cornet fishes. Whitley said First Fleeters called it the "Tobacco Pipe Fish". The most common varieties in Australian waters are the deepsea flutemouth, *Fistularia petimba*, which has a bright pink to brownish body and darkish fins, and the smooth flutemouth, *Fistularia commersonii*, which are brownish-green in colour and have pale blue streaks over the upper body that run from eye to tail. They both measure just over one metre in length, and up to 3.4 kg in weight.

FEATURES: Flutemouths are common along rocky coastlines and are sometimes cast ashore in storms. They are usually seen floating harmlessly about the surface like tree pieces, preying on surface shoals of smaller fish. They gather themselves into position for attack with their pectoral fins and make the strike with surprising speed, reversing back from their targets. They are a splendid table fish.

FISHING TECHNIQUE: Flutemouths can be successfully line-fished on baits of peeled prawns or squid pieces. The deep sea variety gets down to depths of 100 fathoms but the smooth flutemouth is most active in eel grass in estuaries. They usually are caught by mistake when they rush in to take baits anglers have cast out for other fish.

DISTRIBUTION: The deep sea flutemouth ranges along most Australian coastlines. The smooth flutemouth inhabits the bays and estuaries of New South Wales, Queensland, the Northern Territory and round to Western Australia. In deeper waters it is preyed upon by sawfishes and other large fishes.

Deepsea flutemouth,
Fistularia petimba

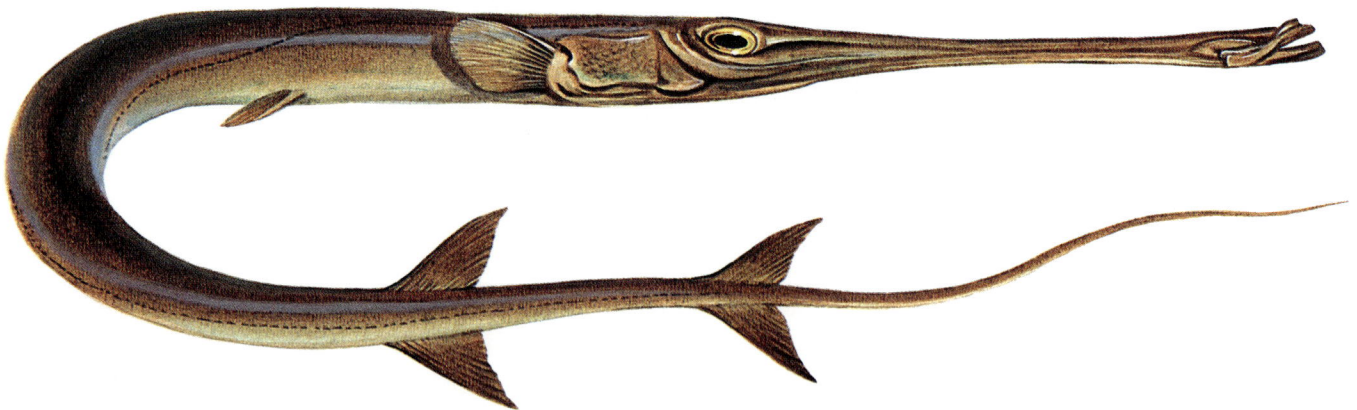

THE LAW ON LEGAL LENGTHS: All States now impose fines for amateur fishermen who catch certain species that have not reached what is regarded as their legal length. These legal lengths are based on the species having had the chance to spawn twice before they can be caught and are more scrupulously adhered to by amateurs than professionals. Illegal undersized fish regularly show up in commercial catches in every State. See page 20.

FLYING FISH   *Exocoetidae*

Speedy, pelagic fishes that can fly for half a minute at speeds up to 25 km/h. The distance covered in one flight depends on factors such as whether the flight path is upwind or downwind and whether take-off began on the crest of a wave. Flying fish have been known to fly for around 180 metres at a height of several metres. On windless days flights of around 65 metres are common. The wing-shaped pectoral fins are raised as the fish launches itself into the air, simultaneously sculling and pushing off with a powerful tail and extending the ventral fins to form supporting wings. They mostly fly well away from land to escape from dolphin fish and other large fish that feed voraciously on shoals of flying fish. For many years scientists argued over whether flying fish flapped their wings in flight, but modern high-speed cameras have shown that the wings remain rigid. Juvenile flying fish often move their pectoral wings while swimming and in making practice hops while learning to fly, but once airborne the flying fish becomes a glider.

FEATURES: The most common Australian flying fish is the illustrated great flying fish, *Cheilopagon pinnatibarbatus*, which has a wing span of up to 45 cm, grows to a length of 42.5 cm, and has 11 anal rays on view in gliding. The base of the dusky pectoral fins are silvery, and the V-shaped tail is dark. The body is a bluish-purple. They are extremely active at night and, when attracted by lights, often land on small craft. Underwater they fold their fins against the

Great flying fish,
*Cheilopagon
pinnatibarbatus*

body. African and South American flying fish have freshwater habitats but the 19 species known in Australia are all oceanic, enjoying waves thrown up by ships.

FISHING TECHNIQUE: Although flying fish are much prized as food, they are seldom caught on rod or line. They are mostly taken in dip nets. West Indian and Californian commercial fishermen lure them into their nets with torches. Noted American fishing expert A. J. McLane recorded that flying fish have been taken in the Gulf Stream by anglers with fly rods and light flies. He also added that flying fishes have been hunted by expert clay target shot-gunners using light loads. The fish floated after being shot and were collected for food.

DISTRIBUTION: Most Australian flying fish prefer the tropics, but Rondelet's flying fish, *Hirndichthys rondeletii*, ranges as far south as Tasmania and into the southern Indian Ocean. The leaping flying fish, *Cheilopagon nigricans*, known for the crossband on their deep-blue pectorals, are abundant off the Western Australian coast.

BIGGER FISH TO COME? Alf Dean, the market gardener who has caught six fish weighing more than a tonne, including the world record 2664 lb (1209 kg) white death shark, believes there are far bigger fish in the sea. "In 1954 I played one I estimated at 4000 lb for four hours and lost it," Dean says. "I had cramp in both legs after three and a half hours, but went on with the battle. He was only hooked in the mouth, but he was such a tough customer he pulled our 36 ft cutter 12 miles in the struggle."

TAGGING THE CATCH: Tagging of fish and returning them to the water helps evaluate fish populations and can influence government policies on bag limits, closed seasons, and quotas. The technique ranges from clipping the fins of hatchery-reared fish to the insertion of darts and internal tags made of plastic or metal. In freshwater, biologists can stun fish long enough to tag them by passing an electric shock through the water but in saltwater the electric current spreads too quickly, so nets or traps are used. For large oceanic fish, such as marlin, dart tags with plastic heads are used, the head carrying a plastic streamer and message. The dart tag is fitted to the end of a tagging pole and jabbed into the fish when it nears the boat.

FORTESCUE *Scorpaenidae*

Venomous, prickly little scorpionfish closely related to bullrout, stingfish and soldierfish, inflicting painful stings with their head or spine fins. Pain from their sting can last for days. They are heavily armoured, with sharp spines over their head, spines around the underlip, and 16 dorsal spines that originate behind the eyes and trace back towards the soft dorsal fin. One wit suggested they would be more aptly called "Forty Skewers", but their name has aboriginal origins. They are adept at lying inert in trawlers' nets and experts recommend that they should only be picked up by the pectoral fins, which put the dorsal and head spines out of reach. Moreton Bay trawlermen have frequently had to seek medical help after being stung clearing a net of fortescue.

FEATURES: Of the two main varieties in Australian waters, the eastern fortescue,

Centropogon australis, has lighter, more defined markings. They are greyish underneath, light brown across the body, with four to five dark cross bands, including one band that crosses their eyes and another halfway along the dorsal fin. The bands also extend to the soft dorsal and tail. The western fortescue, *Centropogon latifrons* has a darker body colour and blunter head. They are heavily blotched over their dark brown bodies with two dark bars crossing the tail and rear body.

DISTRIBUTION: Fortescue have no interest for anglers. The eastern variety is common from southern Queensland estuaries to Eden, NSW. The western version is usually taken at night by trawlermen off the central and southern New South Wales coasts, and is known from South Australia to Western Australia.

Eastern fortescue,
Centropogon australis

FRESHWATER SUNFISHES *Melanotaeniidae*

Crimson spotted
rainbowfish,
Nematocentris fluviatilis

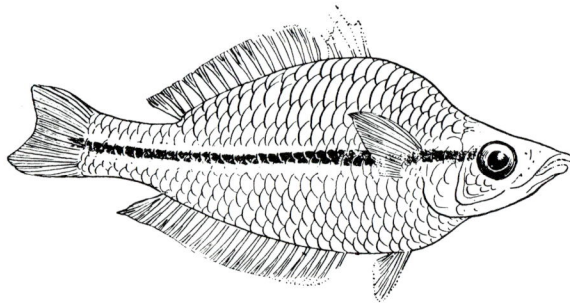

Striped sunfish,
Melanotaenia trifasciata

Highly attractive aquarium fish, also known as rainbowfish, jewelfish or pink ears, found mostly in Australia's northern coastal freshwaters. They are variable in form, finnage and colouring and naturalists have difficulty classifying them. Males usually are deeper-bodied than females and have brighter colouring. Both sexes have much longer anal fins than hardyheads, blackmasts or blue eyes, the fin usually originating before the level of the hind border of the first dorsal fin. Soft-spined sunfish, *Rhadinocentrus ornatus*, have flexible dorsal spines, with tails shorter than the anal base and blue-spotted bodies. Red-banded sunfish, *Melanotaenia splendida*, are olive to yellow with white breasts and mouths that reach the front of the eyes and a row of enlarged teeth along the outside of the upper jaws. Striped sunfish,

Melanotaenia trifasciata, are deep-bodied fish with bands of very small teeth on the outside of the jaws and a broad blackish bar along each side of their light brown bodies.

FEATURES: Sunfish have a single hard spine in front of each dorsal as well as the anal fin. Their small mouths do not reach below the eye, the jaws are equal. They are of no table or angling value except as baitfish but are of great value in aquariums.

DISTRIBUTION: Strictly limited to freshwater creeks, lakes and streams. The soft-spined sunfish ranges as far south as Coffs Harbour in New South Wales, but the family mainly inhabit north Australian freshwater as well as Papua New Guinea. They favour swimming in small groups.

FUSILIERS *Caesionidae*

A brilliantly-coloured group of small reef-dwellers. The scissor-tailed members of the group belong to the family *Caesonidae*, which inhabit the northern area of the Barrier Reef and the Coral Sea. These include the gold-banded fusilier, *Caesio caerulaura*, whose glowing blue-green body has a broad golden ribbon stretching from head to tail; the red-bellied fusilier, *Caesio cuning*, which has a deeply forked canary yellow tail and a shimmering silver-blue body that turns rosy red on death; and the black-tipped fusilier, *Pterocaesio chrysozona*, whose slender blue body has two brown stripes running from eye to tail, all of them found in northern Australia. The most striking fish in the group, however, is the southern fusilier, *Paracaesio xanthurus*, which belongs to the family *Xanthurus*, and is identified by the brilliant royal blue across the top of its head and on the margins of its forked tail. The southern fusilier, which is illustrated, is bright yellow on top, silvery blue beneath. All the fusiliers are above average panfish and offer good sport.

FEATURES: The fusiliers are a gregarious schooling species identified by their tails and the stripes along the lateral line, bottom-feeding reef fish with elongate profiles that average between 250 mm and 450 mm in length. They are notable for the glow in their vivid colouring, and even in the darkest areas of reefs they show out like neon lights.

FISHING TECHNIQUE: Fusiliers bite on baits of prawn and cut fish presented on light tackle. Although they usually feed on the sea bottom, on the surface they feed on plankton when they are shoaling. Commercial fishermen favour them as bait for larger fish that dwell on the sea bottom.

DISTRIBUTION: The *Caesionidae* side of the family is restricted to Torres Strait, the Northern Territory, northern Western Australia, and the coral reefs of north Queensland. The southern fusilier ranges from southern Queensland to southern New South Wales and is a very popular fish among holiday-makers on Lord Howe Island, where it is called Painted Lady.

Southern fusilier,
Paracaesio xanthurus

GALAXIAS *Galaxiidae*

Jollytail, *Galaxias maculatus*

Flat-headed galaxias, *Galaxias rostratus*

Mountain trout, *Galaxias truttaceus*

There are at least 21 species of this family in Australian waters. The name means the Milky Way and apparently was bestowed on them because of their milky coloration and the dotted bodies that looked like stars. Country folk often confuse them with small trout, but the trout has scales and an adipose fin whereas galaxias have neither and have a much smaller mouth than trout. They have similar feeding urges to trout and one species, the mountain trout,

Galaxias truttaceus, is just as effective a destroyer of mosquitoes and flies. Galaxias have been trained in aquariums to take chopped worms from attendants' fingers. The most famous galaxia is the jollytail, *Galaxias maculatus*, which New Zealanders call whitebait. Sadly, they are not as abundant in Australia as they sometimes have been in New Zealand. A species of dwarf minnows, also known as striped galaxias, is represented in Australia by a

Victorian species, *Galaxiella pusilla*, and a Western Australian variety, *Galaxiella nigrostriata*, which breed in peaty water. They are conspicuously striped on an orange, yellow or white body.

FEATURES: Galaxias have scaleless bodies, with well-rounded bellies. They usually are between 6.8 to 17.5 cm in length, but specimens up to 24 cm have been identified. They have no adipose fins, about 10 branched anal rays and less than 60 vertebrae. They are so variable only experts can provide precise identification. They do this by studying the form of the tail fin, the relative positions of fins, the protrusion of the lower jaw, as well as their colouring. They are fish of extraordinary hardihood and have been dug out alive from mud-clogged drains and from under logs and stones. One shrivelled specimen, dunked in formalin, revived and began swimming again. But they are essentially freshwater fishes that cannot stand long periods in saltwater.

DISTRIBUTION: Galaxias range from southern Queensland to New South Wales, Victoria, Tasmania, and south-western Australia, with relatives in New Zealand and adjacent islands. Species are found from the Alps to the coast and some like to burrow in soft clay. They are believed to have been left behind when lands and rivers down to the Antarctic broke up or dissolved.

SUCKER BAIT: North Queensland aborigines enthralled Douglas Ogilby with their ingenious technique for catching turtles. Ogilby, curator of fishes at Queensland Museum, discovered that the aborigines caught a sucker fish, *Remora remora*, to which they fitted a strong cord. They then took the sucker fish out in a canoe and when they sighted a giant turtle flung the fish at the turtle. The sucker fish immediately attached itself to the turtle, leaving the aborigines hauling on the cord to bring in both fish and turtle. The aborigines knew the pads on the sucker fish were so powerful the fish would not separate from the turtle.

THE BIGGEST TROUT: Sir Robert Hamilton, then Governor of Tasmania, caught the biggest trout ever landed in Australian waters in 1887 in the River Huon. The fish, a brown trout, weighed 12.7 kg or 28 lb, and is still on display in the Hobart Museum. The world record was a brown trout of 18 kg or 39.4 lb, taken at Loch Awe, Scotland, in 1886.

GARFISH   *Hemiramphidae*

Slender, bony fishes up to 35 cm in length which provide flesh of exquisite flavour. They are keenly sought by anglers aware of their outstanding table qualities despite the small amount of flesh in each fish and the large number of bones in their narrow bodies. There are around 18 varieties in Australian waters but only about a dozen of them attract sportsfishermen. Most have sharp, protruding beaks on their lower jaws, but there are two snub-nosed varieties. They can be distinguished from the related long tom by the absence of a protruding upper jaw; in the long tom, both jaws protrude. The rarest Australian garfish is the long-finned garfish, *Euleptorhamphus viridis*, which has only been identified six times. According to Grant, five of those leapt aboard launches. The most plentiful are the sea garfish, *Hyporhamphus australis*, or "beakie" of southern fish markets, and the river garfish, *Hyporhamphus regularis*. Both are often used by anglers with ganged-hook rigs seeking bigger fish. Most of the big garfish catches are made at night. The black-barred garfish, *Hemiramphus far*, is a heavy-bodied species used by commercial fishermen as a trolled bait for large mackerel and marlin, a silvery fish with four to nine vertical black blotches across the body on the vertical line. The snub-nosed garfish, *Arrhamphus sclerolepis*, has a short, red-tipped beak on the lower jaw, a chunky shape light green on top and silvery below, and is one of our finest table fish. The three-by-two garfish, *Hemiramphus robustus*, has a large black spot on the sides beneath the dorsal fin, a brilliantly silver fish with a deep blue tip on the lower tail.

FEATURES: Garfish swim slowly at the surface, feeding on minute organisms, sometimes leaping with a chopping noise. They prefer quiet water out of the wind. They assemble over shallow flats containing weed bed. Those over 4.7 kg in weight and 45 cm in length are rated exceptional fish. Sea garfish frequently enter estuaries in large numbers but seldom travel more than a couple of kilometres from the open sea.

FISHING TECHNIQUE: This has developed into a popular sport but it can only be undertaken in calm weather as garfish cannot easily be located in choppy

Sea garfish,
Hyporhamphus australis

River garfish,
Hyporhamphus regularis

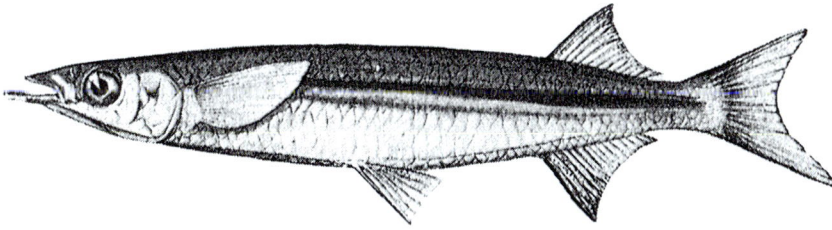

Snub-nosed garfish,
Arrhamphus sclerolepis

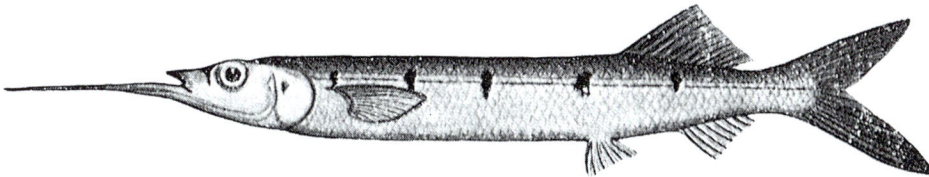

Black-barred garfish,
Hcmiramphus tar

water. The secret of big catches is in effective berleying. Choose a location where stale bread, bran, pollard or whatever berley used will not be swept away, throwing in finely chopped prawns, stale yabbies, crabs or shellfish. A small amount of berley should be mixed with wet sand and the rest kept dry. The sanded berley is sprinkled around the boat to lure the garfish. Then dry berley, usually stale bread well crumbed, is tossed on to the water surface to bring the fish to the top. Use a light, whippy rod. In a boat a threadline reel is preferable. Plastic bubble and cigar floats allow the bait to be brought up near the surface. A lot of garfish are caught from jetties and some anglers claim their best catches come at night from lighted jetties.

The strike should be made as soon as the float disappears. Best baits for garfish are beach worms, blood worms, squirt worms, kelp, maggots, mussels, pipis, freshwater shrimps, peeled prawns, tripe, bacon rind, and ham fat. But whatever the bait used it should be broken up into pieces small enough for the garfish to take into their mouths. Garfish will provide superior fillets to whiting and before they are dropped into the pan the fine bones can be made edible by using a bottle filled with iced water as a rolling pin on fish to crush the bones.

DISTRIBUTION: Found in every State. Generally larger and more plentiful in tropical waters than in southern States.

GANGED OR CHAINED HOOKS: The terms used when two or more hooks are linked by forcing the point of one through the eye of another so that cannot slip out. They are often used with whole garfish or other small bait when fishing the surf for tailor, mackerel, flathead and tuna. They need to be smeared with fish oil and wrapped in foil to prevent snagging.

GEMFISH *Gempylidae*

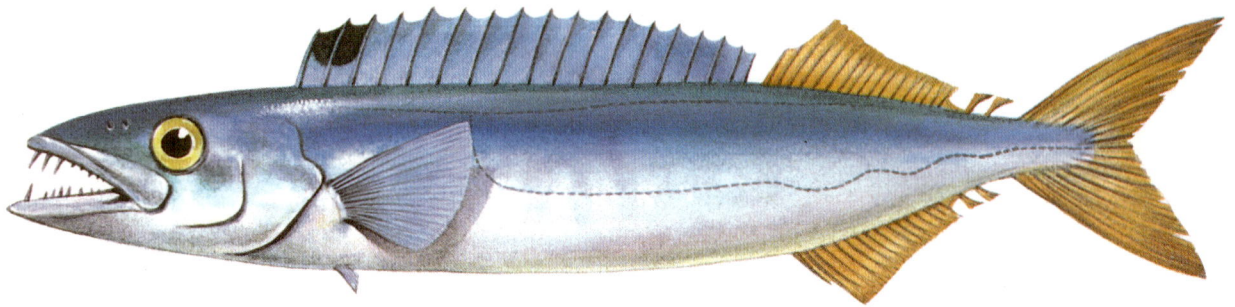

Common gemfish, *Rexea solandri*

A family of large, elongate, small-scaled mackerel-like fishes which form an important part of commercial catches in some Australian States. They seldom appear in coastal waters or near the surface and are usually caught well offshore at depths down to 800 metres. The flesh is edible and is improved by smoking. Gemfish were originally known by names such as king barracouta, hake, and kingfish but had their name changed to what was considered a more marketable label when they became so prominent in the markets. Their long, scaleless bodies resemble their close relatives the barracouta, and their mouths are armed with a frightening array of fang-like teeth. Two species of the family, the illustrated common gemfish, *Rexea solandri*, and the barracouta, *Thyrsites atun*, occur in large numbers in Australia, but the gemfish has completely overshadowed its relative in the markets, where dealers remain suspicious of the sometimes milky texture of barracouta flesh. Gemfish enjoy a contrasting reputation for their high edible quality.

FEATURES: Gemfish are bluish above, silvery below, with a black blotch on the anterior point of the first dorsal fin. The second dorsal, anal and tail fins are greyish or orange. The narrow body is covered in minute deciduous scales. The lateral line divides the fish into two portions; the upper portion extending back to below the middle of the soft dorsal; the lower portion branching off the upper portion below the sixth or seventh spine of the dorsal fin and extending right along the middle of the body to the tail. Gemfish reach 8 kg in weight and 1.1 metres in length.

FISHING TECHNIQUE: Because of the depths at which it is caught, the gemfish has very little interest for anglers, who prefer to direct their attention to the more accessible barracouta.

DISTRIBUTION: Tasmania, Victoria, New South Wales, South Australia, Western Australia.

ORANGE GINGER GEMFISH CUTLETS

INGREDIENTS

4-6 cutlets
3/4 cup orange juice
1 tablespoon grated orange rind
1/2 cup golden syrup
1/3 cup gingerwine
1 tablespoon chopped ginger

METHOD

Combine orange juice, rind, golden syrup, gingerwine and ginger. Mix until well combined.

Add cutlets. Marinate 2-4 hours, or overnight. Drain. Place onto a well greased BBQ plate or grill. Cook approximately 3-4 minutes each side, basting frequently with marinade.

GOATFISH *Mullidae*

Black-spot goatfish,
Parupeneus signatus

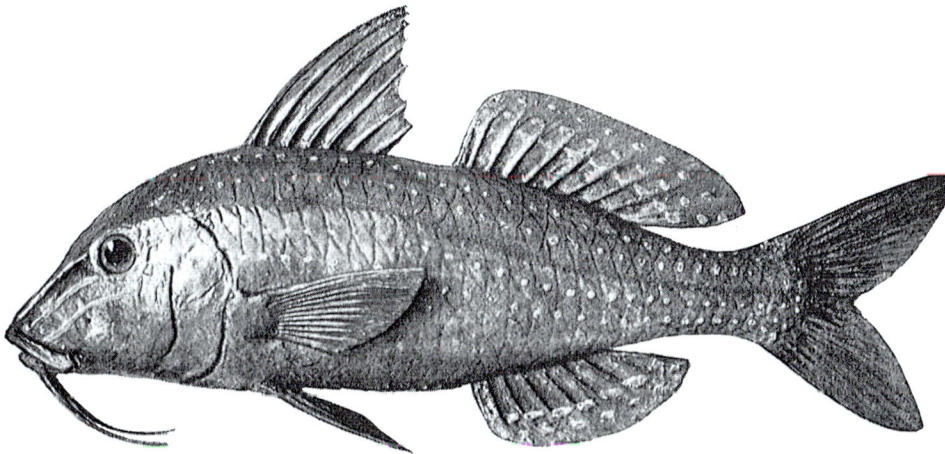

A family of brightly-coloured marine fish, also known as red mullet, with barbels on the lower jaws that resemble the beards of goats. They are sometimes caught by anglers in inshore waters, reefs and bays and are exceptionally good eating. They use their whiskers to detect food on the sea floor, usually crustaceans, rock crabs and weed. In New Zealand and in the Mediterranean, where they are also prized as food fish, they are known as red mullet. In some parts of the Pacific they are known as dreamfish because eating them causes hallucinatory fish poisoning bringing on

Red mullet, *Upeneichthys vlamingii*

123

bizarre dreams and nightmares but this is unknown in Australia. Among the best known Australian specimens are the double-barred goatfish, *Parupeneus bifasciatus*, which has five black saddles set over the pink back and sides; the illustrated black-spot goatfish, *Parupeneus signatus*, one of the larger varieties (average weight 1.3 kg), which has a conspicuous black spot towards the upper base of the tail; the gold-saddled goatfish, *Parupeneus cyclostomus*, a small tropical form (50 mm), a bright pink fish with purple reflections and a vivid golden saddle at the rear of the soft dorsal fin; the mottled goatfish, *Upeneus tragula*, which has a brown or yellow body with brown mottling, dark bands on the tail, and a dark bar extending right along the body, and red mullet, *Upeneichthys vlamingii*, distinct from the other species because of their vivid reddish colour and steep head profile.

FEATURES: Goatfishes are carnivores capable of vibrating their barbels rapidly over sandy bottoms. Their small, separate dorsal fins, large scales, and forked tails are also characteristic. They were often brought to the table live during Roman orgies so that the changing colours and tones could be admired before the fish was cooked. Australia's 18 species are separated by their teeth structures, colour, fins and scaly sheaths.

FISHING TECHNIQUE: Regularly caught on handlines in the Barrier Reef by anglers using whiting, squid, worms, and crustaceans for bait.

DISTRIBUTION: All Australian States but most plentiful in the tropics. Only a couple of species occur in the south.

TAHITIAN RAW FISH SALAD

INGREDIENTS

750 g very fresh fish (use chunky fibred fish such as snapper, gemfish or ling)
200 ml freshly squeezed lime juice (or lemon if lime is unavailable)
2 medium onions, very finely sliced in rounds (optional)
Vegetable salt to taste
2 teaspoons green peppercorns
1 cup thick coconut milk
1 tablespoon chopped chives

METHOD

The fresh juice marinade has the effect of making the fish white and opaque, like cooked fish. The flavour is indescribably delicate and incredibly delicious.

Remove any skin and bones from the fish and, using a stainless steel knife, cut into thin strips or bite-sized pieces. Place the fish pieces in a glass or earthenware bowl and pour over enough lime juice to cover. Add onions, salt and peppercorns and mix with a wooden spoon (don't use any metal utensils at all). Cover with plastic wrap and refrigerate at least 8 hours, stirring once or twice while marinating.

Drain off the juice and add the coconut milk. Line shells or small bowls with lettuce leaves and serve fish salad garnished with chopped chives.

Serves 6

Reprinted with permission, Carolyn Dunne, *The Semi-Vegetarian Cookbook*, Bantam, 1989

GOBIES *Gobiidae*

Bridled goby,
Arenigobius bifrenatus

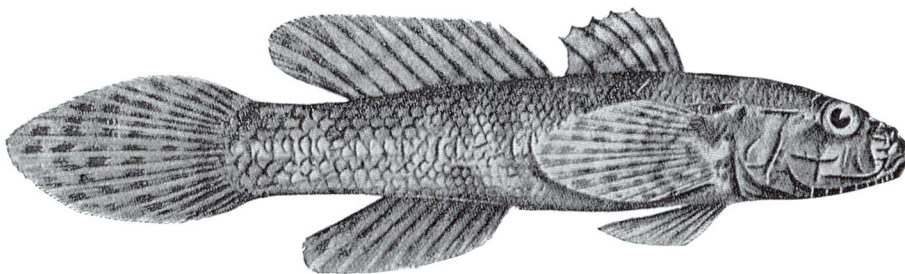

Sculptured goby,
Callogobius mucosus

Small coastal fishes, common in shallow water, where they adhere to stones. They average between 15 and 30 mm when fully mature. A few venture into freshwater but most of Australia's 300 odd species are marine. Tasmania alone has 14 species and there are at least 1800 species of goby around the world. They defend their territory and some guard and fan their eggs which are sarcophagus-shaped and stuck on rocks and shells. The Tamar goby, *Favonigobius tamarensis*, the most common goby in Tasmanian estuaries, enters freshwater but also shelters in marine habitats. The redhead goby, *Paragobiodon echino-cephalus*, is found in coral, and its body is oval and scaly and the head has an abundance of warts. The four-bar Maori goby, *Gobiodon citrinus*, has no scales and may be covered in granulated slime. The bridled goby, *Arenigobius bifrenatus*, has broad black bars on the head and cheeks, from the eye to the pectoral fin. The sculptured goby, *Callogobius mucosus*, has mucous organs in raised ridges on the head. The ornate goby, *Istiobius ornatus*, are common on the Barrier Reef. The girdled or orange-spotted goby, *Nesogobius hinsbyi*, have a mouth reaching behind the anterior of the eye. Blue-spotted goby, *Pseudogobius*

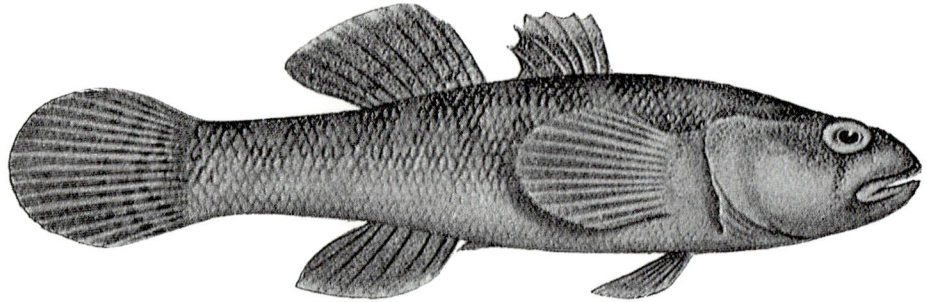

Desert goby,
Chlamydogobius grenius

olorum, penetrates upstream into fresh-water from marine lagoons and estuaries.

FEATURES: Gobies are mostly dull brown with mottling to harmonise with sand and mud, but some have ornate markings. One is transparent and almost invisible. Generally they are only 2.5 to 5 cm long. Several species are taken in nets with prawns and they form a valuable food fish for larger species but have no interest for anglers even as bait.

DISTRIBUTION: There is a bewildering number of goby species spread round Australia and new varieties appear to be discovered each year in most States. They are also widely distributed through the Indian and Pacific Oceans, ranging north to the coral regions of southern Japan. The desert goby, *Chlamydogobius grenius*, is a freshwater variety with rare powers of endurance during droughts.

THE BIGGEST AUSTRALIAN FISH: White pointer sharks are by far the biggest fish in Australian waters. Naturalist David Stead dredged white pointers' teeth from the Pacific Ocean floor measuring five inches or 12.7 cm across. Sharks with teeth so wide would be from 34.5 to 27.5 metres long (80 to 90 feet), said Stead, but no proof of the existence of such monsters has emerged since his 1906 calculation.

OUR SMALLEST FISH: The smallest Australian fish is the goby, which measures only 13 mm in length when fully grown. The goby has a relative in the Philippines that grows to 3 mm. The lightest Australian fish is the Floater, which lives in our coastal waters and can only be caught in fine gauze. The problem then becomes one of finding a scale delicate enough to weigh one, as they weigh less than one-thousandth of a gram.

GOBLINFISH *Scorpaenidae*

Ugly marine fish with rough, ill-shaped heads and strong, extended dorsal spines that frequently carry venom. Several species are found in Australian waters. They are also known as saddlefish or saddle heads because of the pommel-like shape of their heads. The northern Australian stonefish is one of the family. They have little interest for anglers and usually are taken in trawls and dredges at depths down to 30 fathoms. Goblinfish grow to 22 cm and have small mouths, tiny teeth and large eyes which dominate their heads.

FEATURES: Goblinfish must be treated with caution because of the venomous spines in most varieties. The most dangerous of them is believed to be the saddle-head. *Glyptauchen panduratus*, which Grant describes as highly venomous. They have a deep chasm at the nape of the neck and two curved spines at the upper lip, beneath their large eyes. The spines are very well defined on the dorsal surface.

DISTRIBUTION: Goblinfish usually are found in shallow inshore waters close to reefs, where they apparently lie around for extended periods waiting for food to turn up. They inhabit coastal waters of New South Wales, Victoria, Tasmania, South Australia and the bottom of Western Australia as well as northern marine waters.

Goblinfish, *Glyptauchen panduratus*

GOLDEN PERCH   *Percichthyidae*

A native fish of sluggish, often turbid inland rivers, highly popular with anglers because of their delicious table quality. They are also known as callop or yellowbelly. They have been introduced to dozens of Australian streams as part of government restocking schemes and appear to do best in water where the flow has not been interrupted by dams. They lie in shady spots, darting out periodically to feed on passing creatures. Golden perch can live in crowded conditions with silver perch, Macquarie perch and Murray cod, but they are not outstanding sport fish in dams because of their habit of biting only spasmodically. They have been taken up to 10 kg in weight and a 19 kg golden perch was recorded from the lower Murrumbidgee River at Wagga. The maximum record length is 76 cm.

FEATURES: The colour varies from olive green, or dark grey to silvery on the back and golden-cream or yellowish-white below. Purple or reddish tints on the head are common, with occasional reddening of fins before and after capture. The fins are yellow, often with white margins on the median fins. Smaller specimens have a mottled brown or intense golden colour. Older specimens have a pronounced lower jaw. The tail is rounded and the body is strong, deep and muscular in profile. A strong pointed anal spine and razor-sharp gill covers can inflict painful but not dangerous wounds.

FISHING TECHNIQUE: Golden perch have gained wide respect from anglers in recent years, showing that they will take a variety of lures and flies. They take the deep-diving lures at feeding depths, and a wide range of spoons. Flies can only be used in clear water. Hamill's Killer, Mrs. Simpson, Craig's Night-time and flies with a display of orange materials have proved successful. Best results come in late afternoon and immediately after dark. They bite and fight strongly.

DISTRIBUTION: Murray River system, Bulloo, Bacannia and Lake Eyre drainage systems. Their northern limit is the Georgina River, between Lake Eyre and the Gulf of Carpentaria. Natural populations in rivers such as the Fitzroy near Rockhampton and Clarence and Richmond Rivers in northern New South Wales. Widely known throughout New South Wales, Victoria and the ACT. Also introduced for a time into Western Australia.

Golden perch,
Plectroplites ambiguus

GRAYLING *Prototroctidae*

A small, elongate freshwater fish that resembles the herring whose numbers need to be closely monitored because of their sensitivity to environmental changes. Over the last few years there were fears that this important Australian fish would follow its close New Zealand relative, *Prototoctres oxyrhynchus*, into extinction but research has disclosed small populations in western Tasmania, King Island and in limited areas of southern New South Wales and Victoria. Their numbers have been heavily depleted, however, since the days when early settlers found them in most of Australia's cooler streams and much of their territory has been taken over by the introduced trout. They bear little resemblance to their distant relatives in Europe, which are far bigger fish and more exciting for anglers.

FEATURES: Australian grayling, *Prototoctres maraena*, are well rounded fish with the single dorsal and small adipose fins common in trout, olive-green on top, and silvery along the sides with a thin yellow line stretching from the head to the base of the tail. They grow to 300 mm in length, have small heads, short snouts, and a dorsal fin that has its origin behind the ventral fins. They are sometimes referred to as cucumber fish because they give off a smell like cucumbers when caught.

FISHING TECHNIQUE: Australian grayling are fully protected in Tasmania and should be treated as an endangered species wherever they are found.

DISTRIBUTION: Tasmania, southern New South Wales and Victoria.

Australian grayling,
Prototoctres maraena

SPEAR FISHING ETHICS: Underwater fishermen have dramatically changed their attitude to big fish in the past 20 years. Gone are the days of spearing fish on every outing. Today the emphasis is on photography, and only fish of record size are speared. Instead of articles on how to make spearguns, today's scuba diving books show how to photograph the fish encountered.

GRINNERS *Synodontidae*

A family of little fish with huge eyes towards the top of their spherical heads, also known as smilers, pugs, harlequins, and monkeyfish, which bite out burrows near rocky or coral shores, entering tail-first. They appear to signal to each other by lowering or raising their dorsal fins. They are closely related to lizardfish. Best known Australian species are the painted grinner, *Trachinocephalus myops*, an expert at ambushing other small fishes; the variegated grinner, *Synodus variegatus*, whose speckled brown body is tinged in red and has needle-sharp teeth with which they destroy passing morsels; the threadfin grinner, *Saurida filamentosa*, a deepwater variety similar to Sergeant Baker; the large-scaled grinner, *Saurida undosquamis*, which are a first rate trolling bait; and the slender grinner, *Saurida gracilis*, which has brown crossbands on all fins and the tail.

FEATURES: No two grinners are alike, but all of them are ornate in their markings and colouring. They can be marbled cream, blue, gold, brown and silver with various spots and streaks. They are generally elongate in shape with a silhouette like a big cigar. Some experience a dramatic colour-change after death.

FISHING TECHNIQUE: In our northern waters grinners are often collected as live bait by fishermen who realise their bright colours will show out. They are firm-fleshed and can be trolled at high speeds without breaking up.

DISTRIBUTION: Queensland and New South Wales provide figured varieties, but others are found in the Northern Territory and Western Australia, in the Albrolhos Islands region.

Large-scaled grinner,
Saurida undosquamis

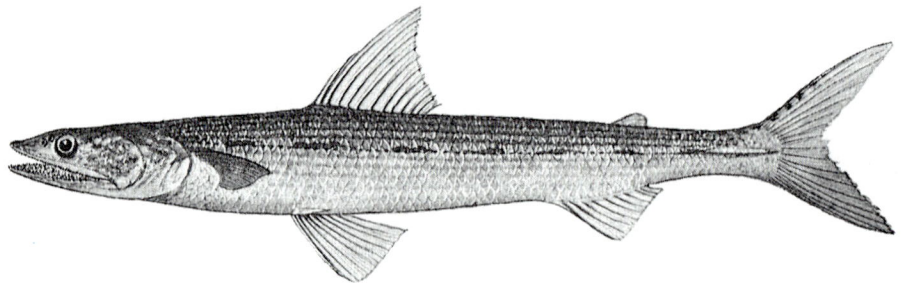

TROLLING TECHNIQUE: The critical factor in trolling is in controlling boat speed. Some lures only work at a slow trolling speed. Large outboard motors usually will not operate at a speed slow enough for plug-type lures such as the Helin Flatfish or Shakespeare Flap Jack. This can be overcome either by fitting a low-pitch propellor or by towing a bucket, but either way the motor must be well-tuned.

GROPER   *Labridae and Serranidae*

Giant Queensland groper, *Promicrops lanceolatus*

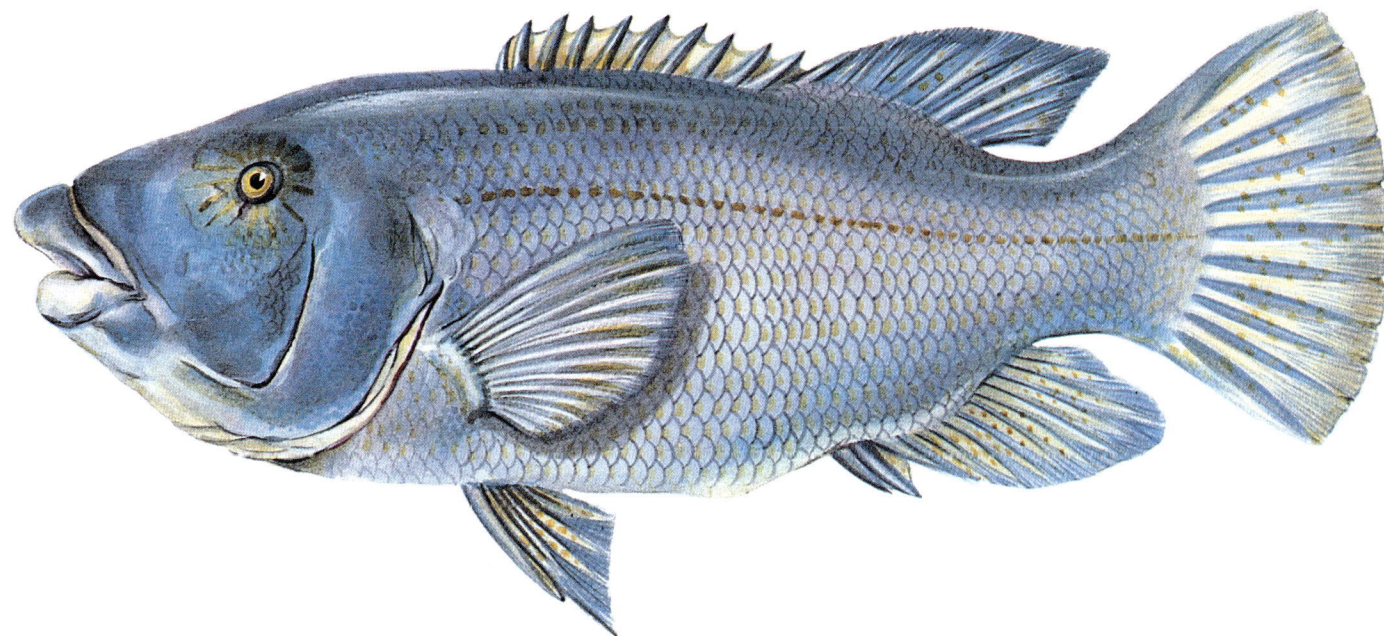

Blue groper, *Achoerodus gouldii*

The name given to a group of large salt-water fish, highly prized by anglers, most of whom hope one day to land a big one. Unfortunately wrasses and rock cods are included in this common name which has resulted in confusing classifications. They are all fish of immense strength, tenacious enough to dash for a hole or crevice when hooked. The giant Queensland groper, *Promicrops lanceolatus*, is a cumbersome fish of great curiosity, forever eager to peer into wrecks and caverns, where it takes up

Hapuku, *Polyprion oxygeneios*

residence and frightens many divers. Their mouths can enfold a diver's leg but there is no confirmed case of a Queensland groper deliberately attacking a swimmer. They are essentially warm water fish of the rock cod family *Serranidae*. The southern blue, brown and red gropers of the wrasse *Labridae* family are distinguished from their northern relatives by their thick, rubbery lips and are so easily taken by spearmen, New South Wales authorities imposed bans on taking them when they appeared likely to be killed off. Fisheries experts still advise anglers to return them quickly to the sea. Stories of their boldness and curiosity are common among underwater explorers. The New Zealand hapuku is often called a groper but it belongs in the family *Percichthyidae*. A lot of the groper's weight is in the head and the mouth of a fully grown specimen is frighteningly large. Queensland groper up to 287 kg have been reported, but the Australian Anglers' Society record is 150.45 kg for a fish caught wide of Byron Bay in 1976 by L. West. The biggest blue groper so far taken by a sportsman was a specimen of 38.70 kg by Gordon Hume at Reef Head, South Australia, in 1966.

FEATURES: Whitley's explanation of the colouring contrasts in groper was that the red comes from carotenoid pigments, black dots are due to melanine which produces

a grey shade, whilst the blue is an 'optic' colour from transparent cells. Reds are usually females and blues males, but hermaphrodite or intersexed gropers have been identified. In Western Australia, grey gropers are females. Young groper usually are green, the older, larger ones grey to olive with white checkers.

DISTRIBUTION: Queensland groper inhabit the warmer waters of New South Wales, Queensland, and Western Australia but sometimes stray into other regions in warm conditions. The southern red, brown and blue groper (illustrated) is not a tropical fish but is found in Queensland, New South Wales, southern Western Australia, and occasionally in Tasmania.

FISHING TECHNIQUE: Groper mostly eat crabs and small fish, but will rise to most baits, particularly when they are trolled. They demand strong tackle, generally 90 kg lines and are frequently caught from banks on lines tied to trees. Lighter gear can be used from boats, but they always require strong wire traces. They are not afraid to swim in close to the shore so it is unnecessary to attempt long casts. Live catfish, rays, whole fish, salmon heads and flaps from rays have all landed big groper, but the best bait is undoubtedly squid or octopus. Gropers appear to eat anything; these predatory creatures have even been caught with birds in their stomachs. They seem to swallow most of their food whole. Even in deep water berley is strongly recommended.

When they are taken in very deep water, groper appear unable to adjust to changing water pressures; the air-bladder is broken and a reversed stomach appears in their mouths. But groper will come to the surface under their own buoyancy and surface as fast as anglers can retrieve their lines. There is a Maori superstition that says allowing gropers to touch a boat as it is landed brings bad luck.

COOKING TECHNIQUE: Groper carry so much fat, they are ideal for grilling, baking, frying or steaming. They have a splendid flavour and are ideal for dishes featuring raw fish. The meat is less coarse near the head and steaks are preferable to cutlets. A gourmet's delight comes from cutting the flesh between the gills and the under-part of the head and from the thorax. Professional fishermen call these the tongues and throats and often take them home when they send the rest of the fish to the market. Boiled groper heads provide excellent soup.

Groper have a heavy bone structure, but give diners no problems. They are so big they represent a carving problem for chefs. Most find that the best cutlets come near the tail where there is the least fat, whereas the most appetising steaks come from near the head. Any reasonably developed groper provides an excellent meal.

BAKED FISH WITH GRAPEFRUIT

INGREDIENTS

4 fillets fish
1 tablespoon margarine
6 shallots, finely chopped
2 heaped tablespoons wholemeal
    breadcrumbs
2 grapefruit
Freshly ground pepper
2 tablespoons chopped parsley

METHOD

Eating grapefruit in any form always makes you feel slimmer and healthier, regardless of the facts. Baked with fish gives this dish an added zing.

Saute shallots in margarine until soft. Stir in breadcrumbs, pepper and parsley. Squeeze the juice from one grapefruit. Cut the other grapefruit in half and then divide into small segments making sure there is no pith attached. Place fish in a shallow greased casserole. Pour grapefruit juice over the top. Add grapefruit segments topped with breadcrumb mixture. Cook for 15-20 minutes at 180°C.

Serves 4

Reprinted with permission, Carolyn Dunne, *The Semi-Vegetarian Cookbook*, Bantam, 1989

SMOKING THE CATCH: Most Australian anglers are now aware of the benefits of smoking their catch, either by hot or cold smoking. Hot smoking involves the use of smoker cookers, which are sold in most tackle shops and produce appetising results from well scaled and cleaned fillets. Cold smoking involves storing brined fish in a room through which smoke is channelled for three or four days or longer, with the temperature in the room containing the storage racks strictly controlled. Ardent anglers build their own smoke houses for cold smoking, knowing that surplus fish from big catches can be preserved for months by this method.

GRUNTER   *Terapontidae*

Freshwater terapon perches that form an important group, provide first-class food, and splendid fishing. Grunters are exceptionally hardy fish that can endure long periods in dried-out waterholes. They have provided big problems for ichthyologists trying to classify them, for many have been identified by only single specimens or from fish sent to our museums. One of the best known grunters is the sooty grunter of which we have at least four varieties, durable fish that fight hard when hooked. Grant reports that in northern Queensland coastal streams sooty grunter are also known as purple grunter, black bream and even Barcoo grunter so the confusion is obvious. Among the best known Australian varieties are spangled or jewel grunter, *Leioptherapon unicolor*, black-banded grunter, *Amniataba percoides*, silver

perch or bidyan, *Bidyanus bidyanus*, coal-black grunter, *Hephaestus carbo*, leathery grunter, *Scortum hillii*, English Wyandotte or yellowtail grunter, *Amniataba caudavittata*, and banded grunter, *Hephaestus trimaculatus*; Barcoo grunter, *Scortum barcoo*, a silver-black variety with 13 dorsal spines; Welsh's grunter, *Bidyanus welchi*, an olive-green fish from Central Australia named after a member of the ill-fated Burke and Wills expedition; sooty grunter, *Hephaestus fuliginosus*, a sooty, blackish purple fish that have been taken in bore water of 32 degrees Celsius; and Ord river grunter, *Hephaestus jenkinsi*.

FEATURES: All grunters take their name from the noise they make with their swimming bladders when taken from the water. Some say it's an expression of scorn

Banded grunter,
Hephaestus trimaculatus

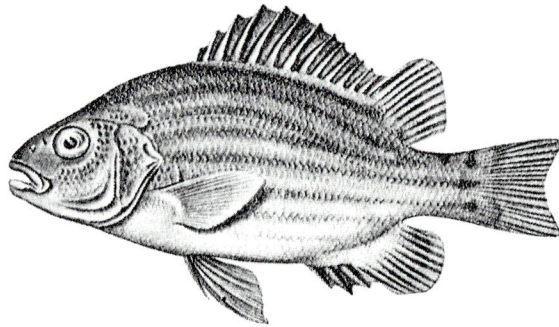

Spangled grunter,
Leioptherapon unicolor

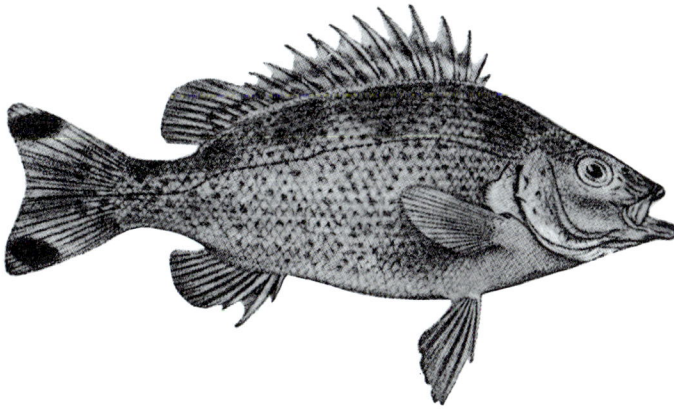

English wyandotte or
yellowtail grunter,
Amniataba caudavittata

at naturalists' attempts to classify them. They come in a bewildering array of colours but all of them have the unmistakable shape of perch. They usually have large yellow eyes. They prefer sunny Australia, but can prosper in rapids, lagoons or still-water. They get further up stream than barramundi or jungle perch, often sharing their habitat with eel-tail catfish.

FISHING TECHNIQUE: Grunter eat most freshwater insects and bite well on worms, prawns, and shrimps. They are not popular angling fish despite their excellent flavour because of their numerous bones. They are strong fighters when hooked and most are ideal for smoking. They have big potential for fish farming as they will spawn in ponds and small dams. Queenslanders catch a lot of grunters on streamer flies and bellbrook lures, frequently hooking them while seeking barramundi.

DISTRIBUTION: Grunters have a wide temperature tolerance that has enabled them to spread to all mainland States, populating bore drains, small pools, isolated billabongs, dams of all sizes and even the remotest rivers.

See sooty grunter page 251.

THE FISH'S HEARING: The hearing ability of fish varies according to variations in their hearing mechanism. The fish that hear best are those with ears coupled to their swim bladders. Australia's many species of grunter vibrate their swim bladders to create the noises that give them their name. Some fish grumble when disturbed by using their gill-covers, mouth or spines. In some species these noises are associated with courtship or the breeding season. They use the noises both to attract friends and frighten enemies. Scientific tests have shown that river catfish communicate in this way.

GUDGEON   *Eleotridinae*

Australia has around 50 of the 300 varieties of gudgeon found around the world. Most inhabit fresh or brackish water, but some occur in saltwater. They are usually small fish between 30 and 100 mm in length, but in the waters of northern Queensland the sleeper gudgeon, *Oxyeleotris lineolata* reaches several kilograms in weight and 500 mm in length. They are often difficult to identify because of their small size. They are closely related to gobies, but little is known of their breeding habits although all species attach their eggs to the bottom where they hatch in a few days. They are sometimes carried across land by winds that lift them from shallow pools. They are all ideal aquarium fishes and are often introduced to give colour to garden pools.

FEATURES: Gudgeon are sluggish, dormant fish that laze about in pools, withstanding drought in dried-out dams and outback waterholes. Many of them feed on the larvae of mosquitos. They are a brightly-coloured family. Snakehead gudgeon, *Ophieleotris aporos*, have crimson spots along

Carp gudgeon,
Hypseleotris compressa

Striped gudgeon,
Gobiomorphus australis

brown sides, an orange belly, and two or three oblique purple bars from the eye to the operculum. The dorsal fins are yellow, blue and crimson. Firetail gudgeon, *Hypseleotris galii*, matures from a light yellow colour to adulthood's vivid markings. Trout gudgeon, *Morgurnda adspersa* is a lovely chunky fish with bright flecking and mottling of reddish-brown and purple over a yellowish-brown body and rows of red spots over the base of both dorsal fins, the tail, and the anal fin. The illustrated striped gudgeon, *Gobiomorphus australis*, is deep chocolate along the body, with a large purple spot at the base of the pectoral fin, and scales speckled in purple and yellow. Carp gudgeon, *Hypseleotris compressa*, grow to only 100 mm in length, are a dull yellowish-green in autumn and winter and become bright green in the summer breeding season; western carp gudgeon, *Hypseleotris klunzingeri*, are greyish with a black spot edged in white on the upper pectoral fin; flat-headed gudgeon, *Philypnodon grandiceps*, have a huge gape in the mouth that reaches past the middle of the eye, and dark bands along the side towards the tail.

FISHING TECHNIQUE: Gudgeon bite on freshwater prawns and yabbies, but only the sleepy gudgeon is worth catching for the table.

DISTRIBUTION: All Australian States, though some varieties are not found in Tasmania and Western Australia.

FRESHWATER FISH: Overseas visitors frequently are shocked to discover that Australia has so far identified only 183 freshwater fishes, a strikingly low number for a country covering a vast 7,682,000 square kilometres. By contrast there are 600 species in North America, which is roughly comparable in size to Australia. Africa boasts 1,400 inland species, China 600, South America 2,000. Dr. Gerry Allen in his book on Australian freshwater fish blames the scarcity of species on Australia's isolation and on the harsh, arid conditions that exist in central Australia. With the exception of the Murray-Darling system, Australia's inland waterways are near the coast and vast areas of the inland are dry and featureless. Gudgeon of the family *Eleotridinae* are one of our major freshwater fish species, with 25 varieties commonly encountered.

GURNARD *Triglidae*

Red gurnard,
Chelidonichthys kumu

Bottom-dwelling fishes with well-armoured heads and slender, tapered bodies whose wing-shaped pectoral fins sometimes cause them to be mistaken for flying fish. They walk along the bottom feeling out food, occasionally emitting a crooning noise from their swim bladders. Some look capable of flight when they extend their pectoral fins wide, but even the flying gurnard, *Dactyloptena orientalis*, cannot fly. They use the wide spread of their pectoral fins to cling close to the bottom, rather than make them airborne. Australian gurnards include the illustrated red gurnard, *Chelidonichthys kumu*, which has large fan-like pectorals and grows to a weight of 3 kg; the butterfly gurnard, *Lepidotrigla vanessa*, which occurs well out to sea at depths unlikely to be touched by sportsmen; the spiny gurnard, *Lepidotrigla papilio*, the handsomest of all gurnards, with a striking red body and bright blue infra-marginal band at the edge of the pectoral fins. Most gurnards are plentiful in the catches of trawler fishermen who send big quantities to market annually, with the sharp-beaked gurnard, *Pterygotrigla polyommata*, a superb foodfish.

FEATURES: All gurnards are expert burrowers and all are fine panfish. Their distinctive feature is the box-like bony head which is often rough or spiny. They are distinguished from Sergeant Baker by their pectoral rays and their two dorsal fins. Sergeant Baker have only one dorsal fin. They use their bony snouts to dig for worms and shell fish.

FISHING TECHNIQUE: Most gurnards are accessible only to anglers with boats capable of getting to offshore reefs. They inhabit gravelly bottoms in deep water but are regularly taken by line-fishermen with the gear to get down to depths between 30 and 50 fathoms. A heavy sinker and a two- or three-hooked rig attached to rings and swivels will take baits of cut fish or crustaceans down to where they live.

DISTRIBUTION: All States and New Zealand. They are most plentiful in New South Wales and Victoria, and in South Australia and Western Australia, where they are known as red rock cod and are subject to minimum legal length, 210 mm in SA and 229 mm in WA.

HAIRTAIL *Trichiuridae*

Australian hairtail,
Trichiurus coxii

A brilliantly-silver, eel-shaped fish with razor-sharp teeth that provide exciting sport for anglers in small areas of Australia. Even experienced anglers cannot forecast when hairtail will bite but when they appear in large shoals they will attack whatever baits are offered with those long, intermeshed teeth for half an hour and then suddenly become reluctant biters that toy with the line. In this period they have to be teased to bite with the angler gently lifting and lowering the bait. Then just as unpredictably as they appeared they will disappear, sometimes leaving the angler with 18 fish for his 30 minutes' work. Three species have been identified in Australia, the Australian hairtail, *Trichiurus coxii*, the northern hairtail, *Trichiurus haemula*, and the spiny hairtail, *Trichiurus savala*. They are also known as cutlass fish. They are far from unique to Australia, ranging from the sea of India through the East Indies to Japan, where they are sought in Tokyo Bay. For their length, hairtail are surprisingly light, and despite those teeth the skin is thin and delicate. They are first-rate food fish.

FEATURES: Hairtail grow to a length of 2.2 metres and weigh approximately 5 kg, but usually average around a metre and 1.5 kg. They have scaleless bodies, tapering to a long, slender thread of tail. The continuous dorsal fin runs from the back of the head to the start of the tail thread and has 140 soft rays. There is a dark blotch between the first and fourth rays. The pectoral fin is dark in colour and there are no ventral fins. The pointed head and snout hold a single row of vicious-looking teeth in each jaw. The lower jaw is slightly longer than the upper, which has two pairs of enlarged barbed teeth in front. A lot of fish are lost because these formidable teeth take the bait without the hook penetrating the lower jaw or throat.

FISHING TECHNIQUE: Handlines are normally used, though rod and reel anglers also get good results. Lines of 7 to 9 kg breaking strain are normal. Gloves or well-padded finger stalls are essential. Sinkers are obligatory but two or three split shot crimped on the line will take it down to where the hairtail feed. The vital part of the exercise is deciding on the depth at which they are feeding. In boats carrying several fishermen it's advisable for each angler to try a different depth until the first fish is caught and the others can adjust to the same depth. Live yellowtail, plentiful where the hairtail roam, are the best bait. Best time is the hour after dusk, particularly on a high tide. Successful hairtail anglers go out to the known grounds with strips of wire trace already prepared. They have

the bait at one end and a curtain ring or swivel at the other end. When the fun starts they simply unhook the trace and hand it and the fish to a companion, clicking a fresh trace into place as the helper dispatches the captured fish. Every moment counts if the angler is to fully exploit the limited period in which the hairtail will remain biting.

DISTRIBUTION: The Australian hairtail is found in New South Wales and Western Australia, the northern hairtail in Queensland, and the spiny hairtail in Queensland, the Northern Territory and Western Australia. The most specialised hairtail spot in Australia is in the Cowan Creek arm of the Hawkesbury River, where they are caught every month of the year and are most plentiful in early winter. They have also appeared in numbers recently inside Sydney Harbour and in Botany Bay.

TRACES: The term used for a length of heavier material linking the main line to the hook, which may be either wire or heavier line. Its purpose is to prevent break-offs, loss of sinkers or bait when casting or to eliminate the risk of sharp-toothed fish biting through the line as they are brought in. Ready-made traces, rigged with swivels and clips, are available at tackle shops. Modern braided trace wire is springy, and resistant to kinking. Traces are essential for fish like barracouta and hairtail but bream, whiting, jewfish and snapper are repelled by wire.

BARBECUING THE CATCH: Make sure the hot plate or grill is well greased to prevent the fish catching. Do not place the fish directly over the flame. Let the flame die down to a bed of glowing embers. If you are using gas or electrically-powered barbecues, use only medium heat. Baste the fish frequently with a marinade, turning once only. The fish is ready when it flakes easily on a fork.

HARDYHEADS   *Atherinidae*

Small, energetic fishes which school in vast numbers near jetties and shorelines where they like to play leapfrog over floating objects. Hundreds of kilograms have been taken in a single haul of the net so densely do they assemble. They form a food supply for sea birds, sharks and many fishes and are among our most commonly used bait-fish with their silvery to straw coloured sides flashing in the sea. The most abundant form are the common hardyhead, *Atherinomorus ogilbyi*, one of the largest of the species at a maximum length of 8.8 cm.

They form in dense shoals that darken the sea in inshore coastal bays. These hardy-heads are identified by their two widely separated dorsal fins and their scaly heads and thorax. The silverfish (known in WA as the Swan River hardyhead), *Atherinosoma presbyteroides*, takes over from the hardy-head in colder waters. They are known as prettyfish and Tamar hardyhead in Tasmania, and reach 5.5 cm in length. Marjorie's hardyhead, *Craterocephalus marjoriae*, a dull, yellow fish with widely separated dorsal fins and a vivid silver mid-

Marjorie's hardyhead, *Craterocephalus marjoriae*

Fly-specked hardyhead, *Craterocephalus stercusmuscarum*

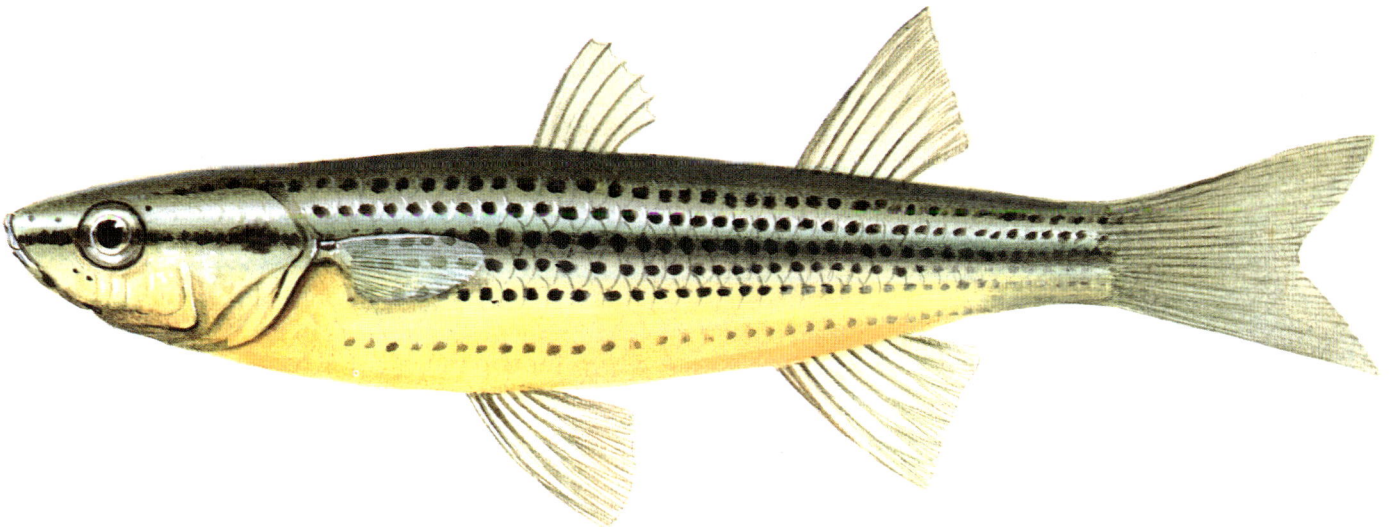

lateral stripe, and the fly-specked hardy-head, *Craterocephalus stercusmuscarum*, a prominently spotted, slender yellow fish with a black-edged silvery band running from tail to snout, is found in marine waters but generally favours freshwater rivers.

FEATURES: The abundance of large, tough scales and their bony heads make the hardyhead unsuitable for canning and unrewarding as table fish. However they have the appearance of silvery ribbons in the water, which makes them an unsurpassed allround bait for bream, tailor, coral trout, sweetlip, flathead and even tuna—when they are fresh.

FISHING TECHNIQUE: Hardyheads congregate in such large numbers around wharves and boatyard planks they can be easily taken in small mesh hoop nets. Berley in the form of stale white bread will soon bring them to the net, and they can be taken out to sea easily enough in buckets.

DISTRIBUTION: All States have some species of hardyhead. Apart from the offshore varieties there are some that will enter lakes and freshwater. Western Australia has the Swan River hardyhead, which is *Atherinosoma presbyteroides*, and the Barrier Reef a variety known as Capricorn hardyhead, *Atherinomorus capricornensis*.

ANCHORS AND ANCHORING: In buying an anchor, anglers should consider where they intend to use it and the weight of their boat. The three main types, the plough, the grapnel, and the kedge or common anchor have special uses. The plough type (CQR) is designed for sandy or muddy bottoms, the grapnel for reefs, rocky ledges, and crevices, and the kedge type for all round holding. Well equipped boats should carry at least two anchors to allow for losing one that becomes snagged and cannot be retrieved. Ideally, anchorage should be achieved with the boat facing up-current and only when the skipper is certain the anchor is holding should the motor be stopped.

BAIT NETS: These are best operated by two men, each holding a pole attached to the end of the net. They walk along in shallow water, the shorter man holding the pole nearest the beach. As they reach the end of the beach, they move in close to each other, bringing in the baitfish it contains. Bait nets are made from 3 cm mesh and are about eight metres long x five metres deep, with lead holding the lower edge on the bottom and bobby corks keeping the net afloat on the surface. Bait nets should not be confused with cast nets, which are illegal in some States.

HERRING *Clupeidae*

Freshwater herring,
Potamalosa richmondia

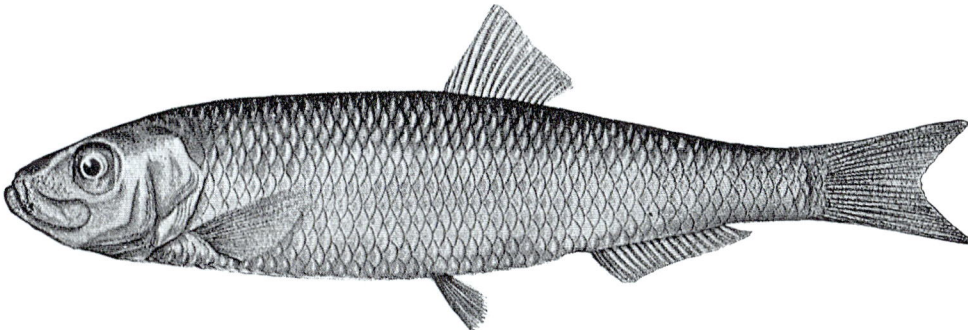

Sprat, *Sprattus novaehollandiae*

The herring family, according to Roughley, is easily the most important of the world's fishes judged on the number marketed. The family includes about 32 species in Australian waters. These small, slender fishes that spend most of their lives in oceanic waters, have not been judged as valuable commercially in Australia as they are in Europe, despite the presence of shoals of herring off the Australian coast. The family includes sprat, sardines, and pilchards. Southern herring, *Herklotsichthys castelnaui*, are deep-bodied little fish with three bronze bars running the length of their bodies and are top-class baitfish. Steamed with ginger they are a gourmet's delight. Maray or round herring, *Etrumeus teres*, are a bluish-purple variety distributed from Tasmania to Queensland and the southern waters of Western Australia. Gold-spot herring, *Harengula ovalis*, have shiny golden spots on their shoulders. Wolf herring, *Chirocentrus dorab* in the related family *Chirocentridae*, are voracious, extremely bony fish that often leap high out of the water and are rated exceptional bait. Sprat, *Sprattus novaehollandiae*, are a dark blue to silvery herring, and form one of the big schools that congregate in southern Tasmania. Freshwater herring, *Potamalosa richmondia*, are found in coastal rivers, and are coloured greenish on top with silvery sides.

FEATURES: All herrings school in remarkable numbers. Most have elongate bodies and lack a lateral line or adipose fin, have scaleless heads, and prominent yellow eyes. The freshwater variety contains keeled or spiny scales in the upper and lower edges of their bodies.

FISHING TECHNIQUE: Highly prized as baitfish, herrings are a migratory species that appeals to most large fish. In marine waters, the wolf herring offers exciting sport on light tackle and will bite readily at trolled baits, only to be cut into fillets for mackerel bait when captured. In freshwater *Potamalosa richmondia* will rise to the fly and provide good meals for campers, and at an average weight of 350 grams are good panfish.

DISTRIBUTION: All Australian States have reported incredibly large shoals of herring that darken the water for hundreds of metres.

DETERMINING A FISH'S AGE: Scales grow with the fish and show rings that indicate the years' growth. Scientists can reliably assess the age of a fish from the distance between the scale rings. Experts describe fish by counting the scales along the lateral line and down the transverse line from the start of the dorsal fin to the start of the belly. On fish like the herring, which has no lateral line, the count is made between the shoulder and the tail, where the line would otherwise occur.

THE RELIABLE MAGGOT: Herring are the most common fish in Western Australian waters, but frequently they will not bite, except on maggots. Hence many keen anglers in the west dabble at some time or other in maggot-breeding. Maggots are known as "wogs" in that part of the world and every fisherman's ambition is to breed some "super wogs". One characteristic of the Perth super-wogs is that they can be stored in old jars or tins and left for months in the fridge. They come to life and are ready for the hook fairly quickly, after being thrown into the tackle box.

HUMBUGS   *Pomacentridae*

A genus of small coral-dwellers named after the popular two-coloured confectionery. They float around among the branches of staghorn coral, clinging by their spiny fins and become so attached to their homes they allow themselves to be taken from the water when the coral is removed and, what Whitley called their "fairy grotto", is disturbed. They are closely related to pullers and are also known as moonstones. The most common are the banded humbug, *Dascyllus aruanus*, also known as the white-tailed footballer, gleaming white fishes with three vivid black crossbars, the first running back from the mouth through the eyes to the nape, the second from the black ventral fins upwards to the mid-dorsal, and the third from the anal to the soft dorsal fin. Their tails are always completely white, which separates them from the black-tail humbug, *Dascyllus melanurus*, which have black tails with the three black bars crossing the body in a more vertical position. The reticulated humbug, *Dascyllus reticulatus*, are pale brown with silvery reflections and two faint vertical bands crossing the body.

FEATURES: Humbugs are all less than 10 cm in length, separated from other damsel fishes by their conic teeth. They spend their lives congregating in shoals around stands of staghorn coral on the Great Barrier Reef, retreating reluctantly on the approach of divers.

DISTRIBUTION: Humbugs stick to Queensland's Barrier Reef, but other members of the family are found all around Australia.

Banded humbug,
Dascyllus aruanus

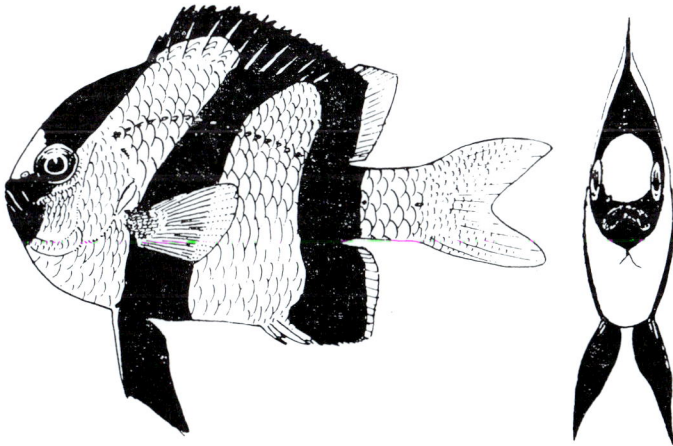

CHRISTMAS TREE RIG: This device consists of a series of colourful, flashing blades, spaced a few metres apart back from the hook, which itself holds a bright, flashy lure. Usually four blades painted in bright colours are used, with an anti-twist paravane a metre or two behind the last blade. None of the blades carry hooks and the theory is that the flashing of the blades annoys the fish into attacking the lure on the hook.

HUSSARS   *Lutjanidae*

A brilliantly-coloured family of sea perches, snapper-like in shape, with exceptionally large mouths. They are appetising panfish but are mostly used cut-up for bait for larger fish. Typical hussars, *Lutjanus adetii*, are bright pink in colour with a vivid yellow band running horizontally from the gill covers to the tail. The snout and eye are splashed with yellow. On top a series of pale yellow bands run back towards the pink tail. They are also known as yellow-banded sea perch. Striped sea perch, *Lutjanus vitta*, are called hussars in the Cairns region but differ in the dorsal spine count. Hussars have 11, striped sea perches 10. Other members of the family include the blue-banded sea perch, *Lutjanus kasmira*, which have golden to lemon-yellow bodies and four violet-edged stripes running lengthwise from head to tail, and the Moses sea perch, *Lutjanus russelli*, which have a vivid black spot above the lateral line on their pale-pink to olive-green bodies. The Chinaman fish, *Lutjanus nematophorus*, is a reef-dweller known to have caused ciguatera, a form of tropical fish poisoning, in northern Queensland.

FEATURES: Hussars usually have two isolated rows of scales along the temples. The preopercular margin is serrated and often notched to receive a knob on the interoperculum. They have broad, boomerang-shaped teeth and no molars. Colouring differs widely according to the species and their habitat, but fish from shallow waters are much paler. Their colouring intensifies for a few minutes after death.

FISHING TECHNIQUE: Hussars are rated nuisance fish by amateur fishermen because of their habit of mutilating bottom baits intended for larger fish. The Moses perch will rise to trolled lures and baits.

DISTRIBUTION: The northern half of Australia, with a few varieties venturing into New South Wales.

Chinaman fish, *Lutjanus nematophorus*

JAVELIN FISH   *Haemulidae*

Spear-shaped fish with a strong spine along the anal fin from which they take their name. They are often confused with black bream and in Queensland are known as grunter bream because of their habit of producing loud, croaking grunts on capture, a noise created by grinding the teeth. The sound is amplified by the swim bladder. Javelin fish grow to 6 kg and are regularly caught around 4.5 kg. They are distinguished from bream by their tails; bream have forked tails, in javelin fish the tail is square cut. Largest of the family is the spotted javelin, *Pomadasys kaakan*, which is illustrated. They reach 55 cm in length. The small spotted javelin, *Pomadasys argenteus*, grow to 30 cm. Blotched javelin, *Pomadasys maculatum*, are another smaller variety, reaching 40 cm. All javelin fish fight hard when hooked.

FEATURES: Young javelin fish have twelve or more faint vertical bars, made up of tiny black spots, between the rays and spines of the dorsal fin. These disappear completely in mature fish. The lower lobe of the tail is blotched in white near the tip. The bulge over the eye is more pronounced in older fish.

FISHING TECHNIQUE: Javelin fish take small spinners, wobbled and plastic frogs, but bite best on baits of cut fish, live prawns, small frogs, pilchards and herrings. Hooks should be 2/0 to 6/0. Snapper and reef rigs are suitable. Over coral, lacquered spinners showing bright colours often attract good fish.

DISTRIBUTION: Found in coastal waters and estuaries in Western Australia, the Northern Territory, Queensland and northern New South Wales. They often hang close to gravel bottoms.

Spotted javelin, *Pomadasys kaakan*

JOB-FISH *Lutjanidae*

Green job-fish, *Aprion virescens*

These members of the hussar family are fork-tailed, edible warm-water fishes known for their saddened look. When their mouths are closed they look as if the world is against them, bearing all the troubles of the biblical Job. The family includes the small-toothed job-fish, *Aphareus rutilans*, which have graceful filaments trailing from the tails of their bodies. They are bronze on top with coppery-red tinges, have pale brown fins and frequently turn up in the catches of trawlers seeking mackerel. Also in the family are the green job-fish, *Aprion virescens*, which grow to 15 kg and have a lovely bluish-purple tinge along their olive-green bodies; the rosy job-fish, *Pristipomoides filamentosus*, the snapper-like variety with dull blue scales and pink sides and back; and the large-eyed job-fish, *Etelis coruscans*, a deepwater species with scarlet bodies and silvery bellies, and tails that trail out into frail filaments.

FEATURES: A heavy-shouldered species easily recognised by their deeply-forked tails and trailing filaments. They are sometimes known as king snapper because of the belief that they take control and lead every shoal of snapper. They strike hard at all baits and are splendid table fare.

FISHING TECHNIQUE: Job-fish are bottom-fished at night over coastal reefs at depths around 25 metres on baits of squid, prawns, and cut fish. They rise savagely to trolled plugs or spoons and fight doggedly from their first high speed run, turning suddenly from side to side in their efforts to break free.

DISTRIBUTION: All Australia's northern regions through the warm waters of the Indian and Pacific Oceans, down to the New South Wales border.

PEPPERED JOB-FISH CUTLETS

INGREDIENTS

4-6 cutlets
½ cup oil
¼ cup wine vinegar
2 tablespoons pickled green peppercorns
2 tablespoons crushed pepper
2 tablespoons chopped parsley

METHOD

Combine oil, vinegar, peppercorns, pepper, and parsley. Mix until well combined.

Add cutlets. Marinate 2-4 hours, or overnight. Drain. Place onto a well greased BBQ plate or grill. Cook approximately 3-4 minutes each side, basting frequently with marinade.

KNIGHTFISH   *Monocentrididae*

Heavily-armoured golden-yellow fish covered in thick scales and stout spines, they are a curiosity of Queensland waters and along the New South Wales continental shelf. They are also known by the more appropriate name, pineapple fish, coat-of-mail, and as port and starboard light fish. This refers to a luminous organ on each side of their lower jaws. Whitley stated that the light was caused by symbiotic bacteria and was probably used to attract prey. A great many interesting features are packed into the 28 cm body of the knightfish, a species of high photographic appeal but of little value for anglers. They sometimes stray from their natural habitat in water down to 80 fathoms into harbours and bays where they are taken in lobster pots.

FEATURES: Not the least interesting feature of knightfish is that the leading spines of both the dorsal and ventral fins can be locked erect or folded down into grooves in the lower back and sides. They have bright patches of red or bright yellow on either side of the lips. Grant says that when given the freedom of a bucket of water to swim in, pulses of green light are visible at each corner of the knightfish's mouth. These pulses are in rhythm with the fish giving out a series of loud croaks which become more rapid if the fish is alarmed.

FISHING TECHNIQUE: Of no angling value but recommended for underwater cameramen.

DISTRIBUTION: Central Queensland coastal waters, south down the New South Wales continental shelf. They appear only occasionally on the Barrier Reef. Latest research has indicated that a sub-species reported in Western Australia is synonymous with the knightfish.

Knightfish, *Cleidopus gloriamaris*

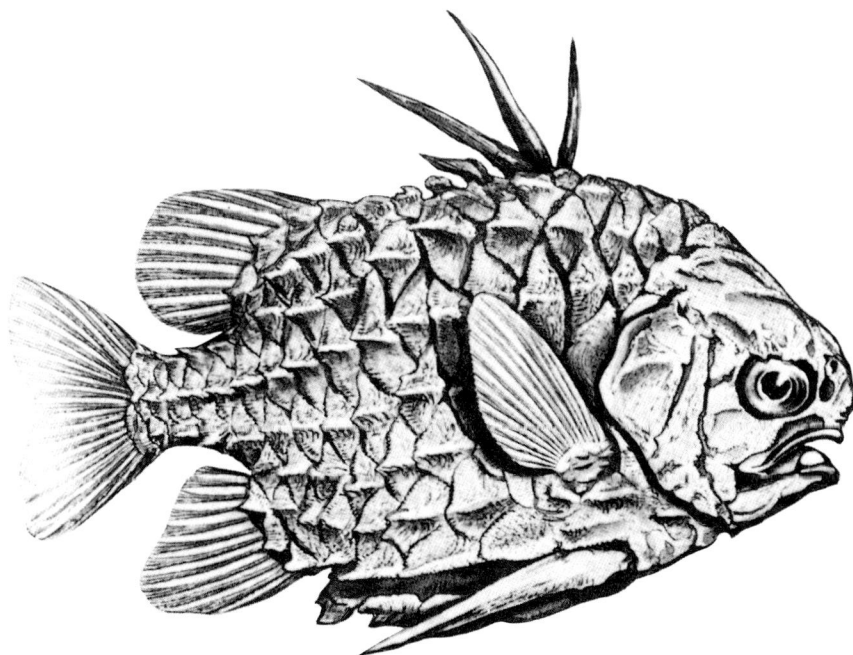

LAMPREYS *Petromyzontidae*

Short-headed lamprey,
Mordacia mordax

One of the lowest forms of fish-life, eel-shaped creatures with seven gill openings on each side and with only one nostril on top of the head. The 31 species in the world are spread around three families in nine genera. They breed in freshwater streams, ascending rivers from the sea to spawn. At sea they attack other fish, rasping away with a toothed tongue as they lack true jaws but have a sucking oral disc on the head. Two of the three sub-families in the group, *Geotriinae* and *Mordaciinae*, are found in Australia, both of which lay eggs that produce eyeless, toothless young that live in burrows in wet sand or mud. *Geotriinae* are a wide-mouthed variety, *Mordaciinae* are short-headed with a pouch-type throat.

FEATURES: The illustrated short-headed lamprey, *Mordacia mordax*, has teeth in concentric circles and not surrounded by fringes, with two patches of three larger teeth on each side of the mouth-opening. They are parasitic on other fishes and grow to 55 cm, grey or bluish in body colour with fins that are sometimes yellowish or reddish. They grip rocks with their suckers when ascending waterfalls and make nests of stones which they carry in the sucking disc. Some males have a bag of skin at the throat.

DISTRIBUTION: New South Wales, Victoria, Tasmania and South Australia. Throughout the world, the distribution is anti-tropical, occurring in the northern hemisphere above 30 degrees north and in the southern hemisphere below 30 degrees south.

LEATHERJACKET *Monacanthidae*

Tough, misshapen little fishes notable for the strong spines above their heads which they can lock into position to prevent larger fish swallowing them. They have rough, scaleless skin beset with prickles, knobs or tiny denticles, a limited number of teeth sharp enough to cut through wire, and are excellent eating despite their appearance. Australia, in fact, is one of the few countries in the world where leatherjackets are eaten. One of the remarkable habits of this much maligned fish is that it can disappear and reappear at will. This is explained by its exceptional manoeuvrability; it can swim very fast, hover, or swim backwards at will. There are more than 50 species spread round Australia. Elsewhere in the Pacific they are regarded as poisonous. Leather-jackets are closely related to triggerfish of the family *Balistidae*. Leatherjackets have two dorsal spines, the second only rudimentary, whereas triggerfish have three dorsal spines and prominent scales.

All leatherjackets can move one eye independently of the other. Many of them are carriers of crustacean parasites that burrow into their flesh.

The name leatherjacket was first used by Captain Cook's men who knew similar species in the West Indies. Mostly they inhabit shallow waters around Australia's coastline, but a few are pelagic in oceanic waters. Small leatherjackets were once used as bait for craypots but a decline in their numbers has stopped this. Despite its toughness, the skin of the leatherjacket peels off easily and resembles the shagreen of a shark. Their flesh is white and firm and of a pleasing flavour and their bones are far less trouble than those of many small fish. They average between 35 and 45 cm in length but the Chinaman leatherjacket reaches 68.7 cm in length and 3.5 kg in weight. They can be great pests to snapper fishermen anchored over an underwater reef by stealing well-prepared baits, but

Yellow-finned leatherjacket, *Meuschenia trachylepsis*

they often brighten the lives of small boys fishing from jetties. They are the worst of small pickers and there are times when they are hard to get away from.

Yellow leatherjacket, *Nelusetta ayraud*: The largest of Australia's leatherjackets, also known as Chinaman leatherjacket. They grow to 70 cm but average between 45 and 50 cm. Their skin is so rough it is wise to wear gloves in handling them. They are easily recognised by their yellow sides and belly and by their yellowish-brown backs. They are voracious fish and will sometimes dispute among themselves for an appetising bait. They have even been caught by hand when they have lost perspective in seeking surface baits. Traps

Yellow leatherjacket, *Nelusetta ayraud*

Spiny-tailed leatherjacket, *Bigener brownii*

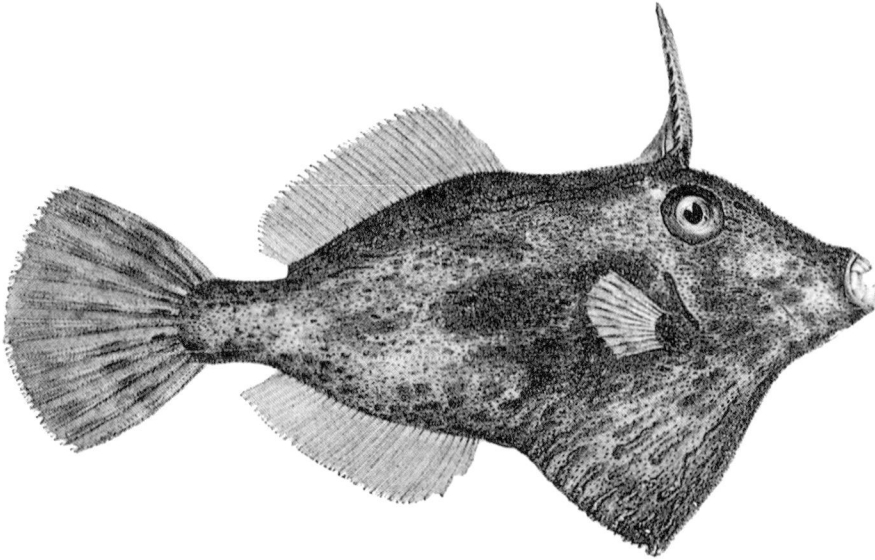

Rough leatherjacket,
Scobinichthys granulatus

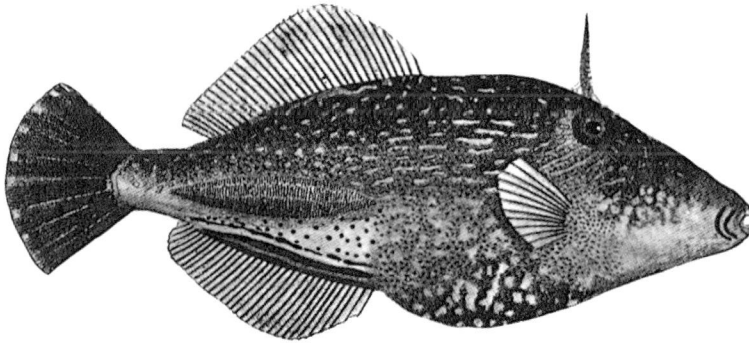

Toothbrush
leatherjacket, *Penicipelta
vittiger*

containing baits sometimes only have to be lowered a metre over the side before they are returned to the boat with several yellow leatherjackets.

Rough leatherjacket, *Scobinichthys granulatus*: One of three leatherjackets found in New Zealand where schoolboys often get their first satisfaction from angling by catching them. They bite very hard and will take virtually any bait. New Zealanders adept at catching them use very light tackle with wire traces, sinkers on the bottom with the first hook and trace 60 cm above it. They live in weedy conditions, feeding on crabs, shellfish and marine eggs down to 55 metres.

Horseshoe leatherjacket, *Meuschenia hippocrepis*: An attractive variety found in all States except Queensland. There are broken blue lines across its olive-green body, and a crescent shaped cross band on its bluish tail. The mid region is yellow with backward facing black horse-shoe markings, the centre of which is usually green. Most abundant in Bass Strait, where it is often found in groups of 10 or a dozen around shallow reefs.

Toothbrush leatherjacket, *Penicipelta vittiger*: A small-mouthed variety with incisor-like teeth, and a prettily-marked brownish-yellow body speckled with blue lines and spots. The males of this leatherjacket are usually studded about the head and belly with purple or pink spots. The soft dorsal, anal and pectoral fins are olive, yellow or orange, the tail pink or olive. In contrast to all this colour the female toothbrush leatherjacket is uniformly grey, white, brown or orange with creamy blotches. There are no spots on the snout or body.

Bridled leatherjacket, *Acanthaluteres spilomelanurus*: Another leatherjacket in which there is a marked difference between males and females. In males the upper surface of the body usually is light green or brown, with a thin blue line extending from the chin through the eye to the mid region of the body. There is a thin black line or bridle extending from the anterior margin of orbit to the dorsal surface. The lower surface below the midline is light green or greyish with many bright blue spots. The tail fin is bright yellow or light brown with a black vertical line. In females, the upper surface is greenish, pale blue or brownish and the lower surface light yellow. The dark bridle is usually present before the eyes, and the vivid colouring of the male is missing.

Beaked leatherjacket, *Oxymonacanthus longirostris*: A beautiful little fish easily identified by the long straight tubular snout, which changes colour from yellow in juveniles to red in adults, but always with a bright blue ring towards the tip. The orange or red pelvic flap is edged in black and has a bold black blotch on the body. The beaked leatherjacket is common throughout the Barrier Reef. The bright blue body has seven rows of brighter orange circular spots that become red in older fish. This colourful little fish reaches 90 mm in length.

Bridled leatherjacket,
*Acanthaluteres
spilomelanurus*

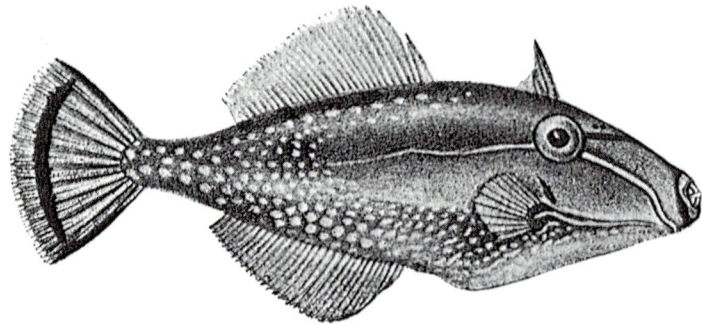

Beaked leatherjacket,
*Oxymonacanthus
longirostris*

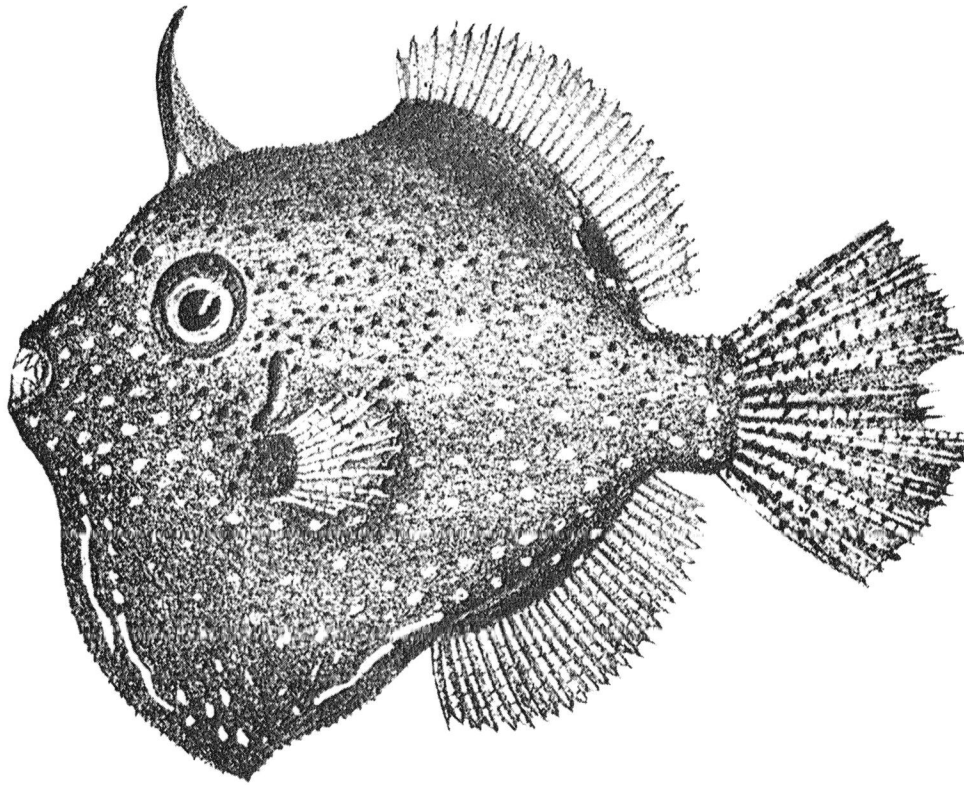

Pygmy leatherjacket, *Brachaluteres jacksonianus*: The smallest member of the leatherjacket family, found across the southern half of Australia, attaining a maximum length of 90 mm. They are found near the bottom among sea grasses and algae, where they are often difficult to spot until they move. They have short, deep bodies, rounded and moderately compressed, with unusual distensible bellies. The body and head vary in colour from brownish, greenish, purplish to whitish, often with faint longitudinal stripes or rows of white-edged spots. The fins are brownish or translucent. The ventral surface below the head and the region near the soft dorsal and anal fins carries thin bluish lines or small dots.

Mosaic leatherjacket, *Eubalichthys mosaicus*: An oval-shaped variety in which both males and females are golden yellow, with rows of narrow blue stripes running from head to tail, curving over the face and cheeks into a show of short blotches and scattered blue spots. All the fins are pale blue-green. This is one of the most edible of all leatherjackets, reaching a weight of 3.3 kg. Juveniles of this form have a habit of sheltering beneath the tentacles of the large blue jellyfish. Distributed off southern Queensland, New South Wales, Victoria, Tasmania, South Australia and southern Western Australia.

Velvet leatherjacket, *Meusehenia australis*: A greenish member of the group with dark spots and blotches across the body and a tail without spines. The body is covered with small, closely-set spines, giving the fish a velvety feel to the touch. The dorsal spine is rounded in front, flattened behind, with a small ventral flap. It has been known to bite divers. Found in deepwater in

Pygmy leatherjacket, *Brachaluteres jacksonianus*

Tasmania, Victoria, South Australia, southern Western Australia and New South Wales.

FISHING TECHNIQUE: They prefer rocky bottoms along the beaches, in bays, and in estuaries. Big quantities are caught over reefs and rocky grounds while anglers are fishing for snapper and these deepwater specimens are much larger than those caught inshore. Standard boat, surf and rock tackle is used to catch leatherjackets, but it is essential to include hooks with extra long shanks and a short wire snood to prevent their sharp teeth cutting through the line. They will take most saltwater baits, particularly pieces of craytail, prawns, mussels and crushed pipis. In the estuaries a No. 4 to No. 1 hook is big enough but outside a No. 1 hook is more suitable.

Velvet leatherjacket,
Meuschenia australis

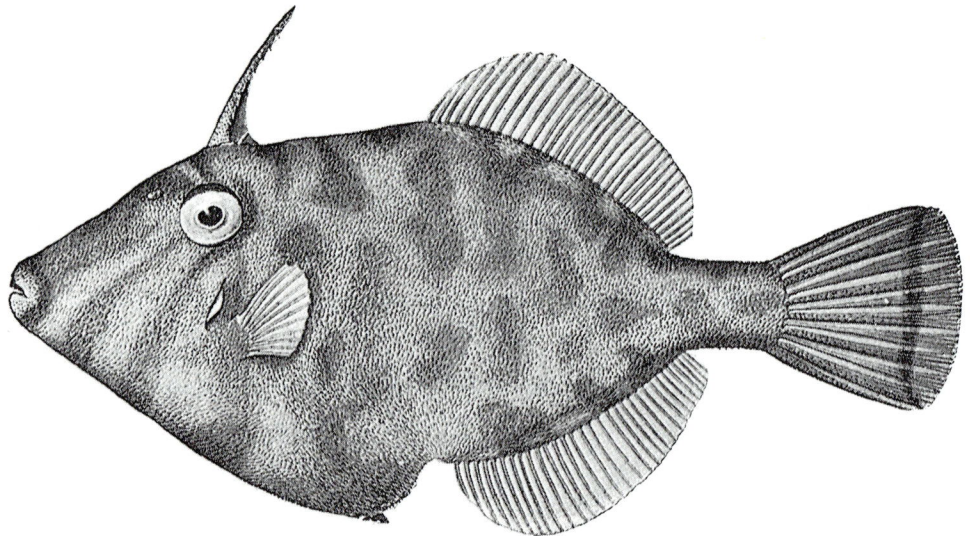

ARTIFICIAL REEFS: All Australian States now have schemes in hand to improve sporting fishing by building artificial reefs, which have been shown to dramatically increase fish population. The problem of costs has been overcome by dumping worn-out trams, derelict motor cars, old ferries, and used tyres. These structures promote plankton and algae growth and provide shelter for fish. Surveys have shown that within two or three years large schools of luderick, bream and leatherjackets inhabit the reefs, but the locations need to be carefully chosen. Fisheries officials discourage construction by amateurs.

LEATHERSKIN *Carangidae*

Big-mouthed scrappers that offer outstanding sport for anglers in Australia's tropical waters, frequently leaping clear of the surface, and exploiting their exceptional speed to run out plenty of line. They are outstanding acrobats and will continue to fight within sight of the boat. At least four varieties are seen regularly in Australia where they are also known as queenfish, whitefish, charlia and skinnyfish. They are splendid foodfish if they are chilled immediately on capture, otherwise they quickly become too dry to eat. Like all members of the trevally family they have prominently forked tails. Their scales are spear-shaped and embedded deep in their leathery skins, whereas the scales in another family member, the darts, are small and rounded. They grow to around 15 kg in weight, and 1.5 m in length. Australia's leatherskin include the deep-barred leatherskin, *Scomberoides tala*, the slender leatherskin, *Scomberoides tal*, the giant leatherskin, *Scomberoides commersonnianus*, and the illustrated large leatherskin, *Scomberoides lysan* which has a characteristic double line of spots along the flanks and an upturned lower jaw.

FEATURES: No keels or scutes. Silver to satiny white in colour. They are distinguished from queenfish by the rows of dark blotches along the lateral line. Queenfish have two rows of these blotches, one above and one below the lateral line, leatherskin have just the one row above the lateral line.

FISHING TECHNIQUE: Leatherskin bite at even the biggest baits and will take chrome spoons and feathered lures, but prefer moving baitfish. They are taken trolling at speeds that discourage other reef fish. Traces up to two metres long are advisable, otherwise that big mouth will slice through the line. Linked hooks work well, especially those carrying garfish. Small leatherskin bite well at night in shallow water, the larger ones out among the reefs. The vital point to remember is that they will exhaust themselves if you remain calm as they repeatedly broach the surface.

DISTRIBUTION: Australia's tropical north around the Northern Territory to north-western Western Australia. They have been sighted as far south as Noosa, but are more abundant north of Bundaberg.

Large leatherskin,
Scomberoides lysan

LINGS *Ophidiidae*

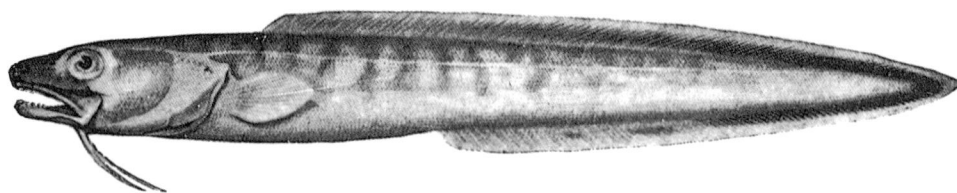

Pink ling, *Genypterus blacodes*

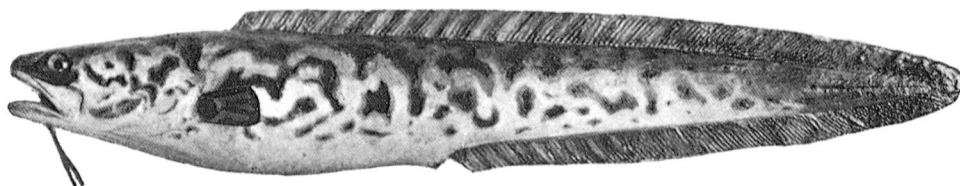

Rock ling, *Genypterus tigerinus*

Long, tapering eel-like fishes distinguished from eels by the presence of cod-like gill openings. Along with their relation, the beardie, they are easily recognised by the whiskers or barbels on their chins. Their scales are small and frequently number several hundred in the lateral line. Principal members of the family are the pink ling, *Genypterus blacodes*, known by their distinctive red to pink body colouring and extended length (1.5 metres); and the rock ling, *Genypterus tigerinus*, which are grey or white in body colour with the upper two-thirds of their bodies and their heads mottled in black. Both are important commercial fishes with densely textured flesh that makes delicious eating.

FEATURES: All the fin rays are soft, and the dorsal, anal and tail fins are connected, whereas in the related beardies and bearded rock cods these fins are separated. There are paired nostrils on each side of the head.

FISHING TECHNIQUE: Pink ling are common on the continental shelf where they are taken by trawlers and dropliners as they burrow in soft sand or mud. Rock ling are less abundant and are generally caught in shallow coastal areas at depths down to 600 metres. In summer juveniles are found among sea grasses in bays and estuaries. Small quantities are caught in gill-nets and cray pots.

DISTRIBUTION: Colder waters of Australia's southern States. In Tasmania, they are extremely important commercial fish that bring high prices in the markets.

LONG-TOM   *Belonidae*

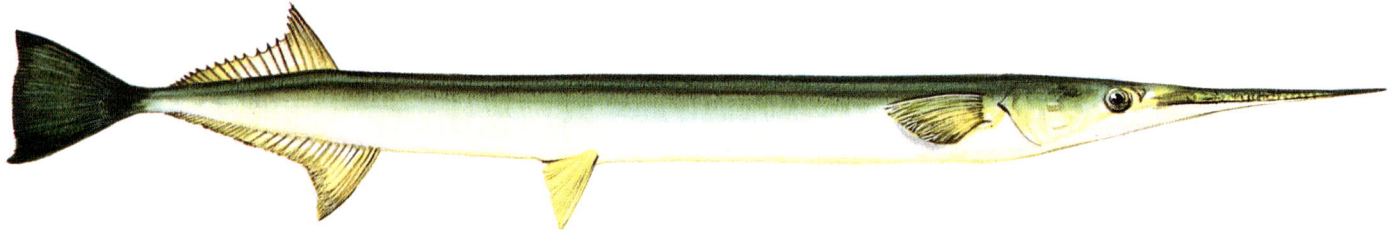

Slender long-tom,
Strongylura leiura

Black-finned long-tom,
Tylosurus acus

A group of slender fish with lengthy beaks armed with needle-sharp teeth. There are at least 11 species of long-toms in Australian waters, all close relatives of garfish and flying fish. They are also known as needle fish or skippers because of their habit of getting up on their tails and skittering along the top of the water at speed. Long-toms have two long beaks or jaws, garfish only a long lower jaw and most long-toms reach a far greater length than garfish. Australia's long-toms include the illustrated slender long-tom, *Strongylura leiura*, the variety most common in southern waters; Krefft's long-tom, *Strongylura kreffti*, a shorter specimen well stocked in northern rivers; the stout long-tom, *Tylosurus gavialoides*, found off the New South Wales and Queensland coasts: and the illustrated black-finned long-tom, *Tylosurus acus*, a warm-water variety found in Queensland and the Northern Territory; black-spot long-tom, *Strongylura strongylura*, a small variety (450 mm) that ranges through the warmer waters of the Northern Territory, north Western Australia and Queensland, easily recognised by the black blotch near the tail base; crocodile long-tom, *Tylosurus crocodilus*, identified by the three faint lines that run along the back and by the prominent keel at the tail base. Despite green bones, all long-toms are good eating.

FEATURES: Long-toms form into schools around rocky outcrops and coral reefs and are particularly plentiful over the sandy bottoms of Barrier Reef waters. They invariably put on a spectacular display when hooked, leaping high out of the water, twisting in mid-air to free themselves of the hook, tail-walking and lunging at the angler. Professionals often take them in seine nets. They are regarded in New Guinea as a bigger menace than the shark because of having pierced the chest and abdomen of fishermen, causing internal bleeding and death. They are known to attack anglers carrying lights in the dark.

FISHING TECHNIQUE: They bite eagerly on baits of fish strip, prawns or weed that are flicked across the surface. They are difficult to hook on lures because of their narrow throats and sharp teeth. They have been known to leapfrog turtles and there is a record of a long-tom, attracted by lights,

leaping aboard a small boat and killing a Japanese seaman in New Guinea waters.

DISTRIBUTION: Long-toms are most plentiful in tropical waters, but some varieties come south in summer. Rare in Tasmania and South Australia, they are only lured into southern waters by the shoals of anchovy, herring, and hardyhead on which they feed.

Krefft's long-tom,
Strongylura kreffti

Stout long-tom,
Tylosurus gavialoides

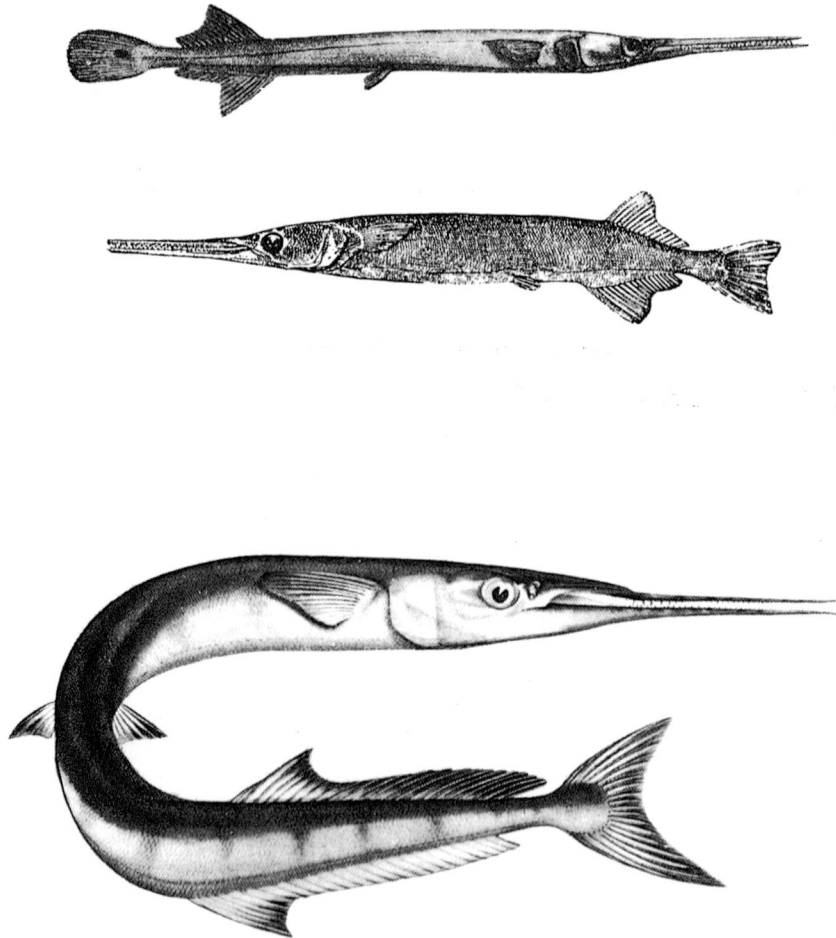

Barred long-tom,
Ablennes hians

LUDERICK   *Girellidae*

Luderick, *Girella tricuspidata*

A fish of many aliases, including nigger, blackfish, darkie, and the Maori name parore. Luderick are outstanding sporting fish eagerly sought by hundreds of specialist anglers. Luderick devotees are said to rival the numbers of trout fanciers. These fish are often hard to get at, as they are vegetarians which feed chiefly on weed along rocky coastlines, but this does not lessen the enthusiasm of dedicated luderick fishermen. Although the largest fish are taken from rock walls and cliffs, and off ocean beaches, they sometimes venture into rivers. The dark, vertical bars that cross their flanks from the eye to the tail are more pronounced in ocean-caught fish. Newly-caught esturine fish have a purplish glow that fades on death. They are black or brown on the sides, silvery below, with yellow pectoral fins. Luderick flesh is soft but has an appealing taste if the fish are bled and the fillets washed in seawater on capture. They are closely related to zebrafish, *Melambaphes zebra*, which have an olive-brown body colour with black tapering bars running vertically across the belly. Rock blackfish, *Girella elevata*, which have the same shape as luderick but are a drab blackish-brown in colour, are another important member of the family, and have their own entry in this book.

FEATURES: Their dorsal fins have up to 16 spines. Their mouths are small with the teeth arranged in rows. This allows them to cut the ulva or cabbage that grows on surf-washed rocks and their favourite eel-grass, *Zostera*, into neat pieces of an edible size. *Girella tricuspidata*, which is illustrated, move over muddy shallows and sea-washed rocky pools, feeding on red, brown or green algae. It is a shy fish, difficult for skindivers to approach.

FISHING TECHNIQUE: Luderick fishing is a science all its own, but an expert who gets among a spawning school can catch 100 in an outing. They are very responsive to berley but the right mixture of chopped weed, bran, pollard, stale bread and even minced meat needs to be prepared beforehand. Rock fishermen cannot carry large amounts of berley down cliffs so they scrape weed from the rocks with their cleated-shoes and let the tide carry it out. Luderick will bite on pipis, worms, cunje and prawns but weed is by far the best bait for them. Small hooks, No. 8, 10 or 12, usually snecks, are advisable because of their small mouths. Luderick rods are around three metres long, fitted with centrepin or threadline reels. The closely related rock blackfish, *Girella elevata*, is taken on baits of cunjevoi or rock crabs. Both luderick and rock blackfish smash a lot of gear, putting up a fight out of all proportion to their size.

DISTRIBUTION: From the southern waters of South Australia around to Victoria and Tasmania, and up the New South Wales coast to Maryborough in Queensland.

FLOATS FOR LUDERICK

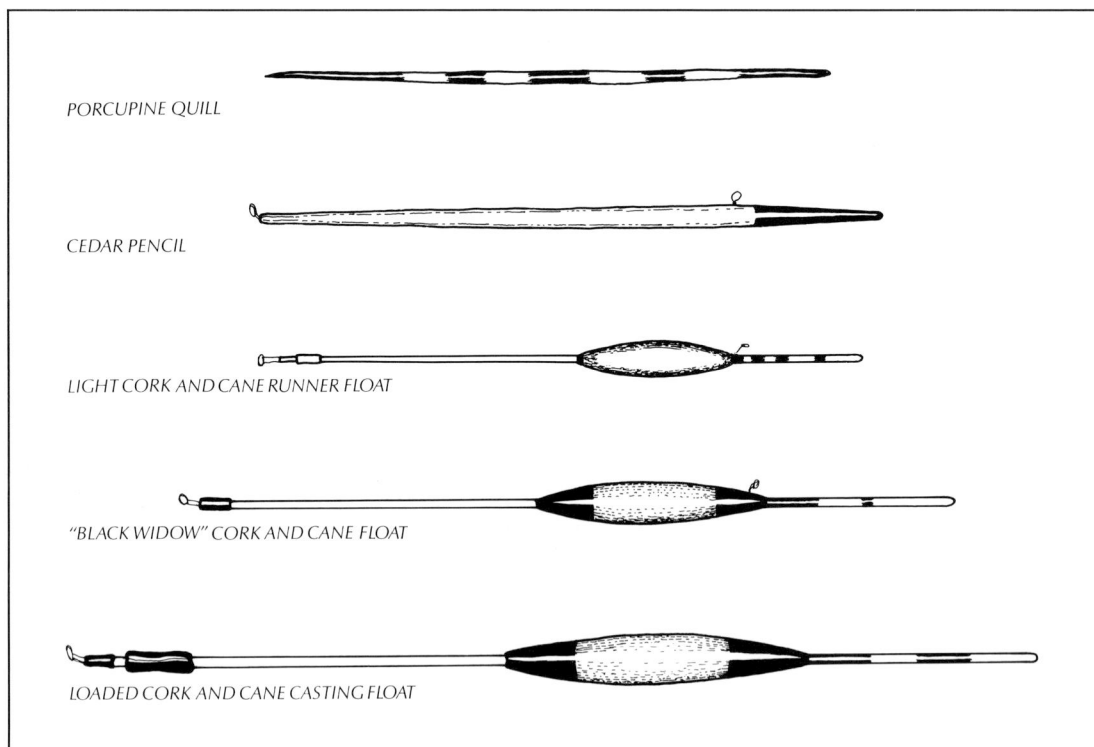

PORCUPINE QUILL

CEDAR PENCIL

LIGHT CORK AND CANE RUNNER FLOAT

"BLACK WIDOW" CORK AND CANE FLOAT

LOADED CORK AND CANE CASTING FLOAT

LUNGFISH   *Ceratodontidae*

One of the world's most remarkable fish, believed to be more than 200 million years old. They are closely related to South American and African lungfish and are breeding well in coastal waters and lakes of Queensland, where they are fully protected and must be released immediately on capture. The lungfish, *Neoceratodus forsteri*, is a living fossil, sluggish of movement but curious by nature. They have powerful eel-shaped tails which they use as a paddle, very small eyes, teeth like crushing plates, and are usually covered in slime. The body is covered in over-lapping scales similar to those in a bony fish. Their skeletons are of cartilage, not bone. They grow to 1.8 metres and a weight of 45 kg. Carefully packed in foam-lined, water-saturated boxes Ern Grant had no difficulty transporting the species as far as Tokyo.

FEATURES: Lungfish are olive-green to dull brown along the back, sides, tail and fins, yellow to orange on the chin, with reddish bases on the chest and belly. The eyes are brown. Their teeth are probably the most remarkable feature in a remarkable fish with dental plates similar to those found in deposits of the Cretaceous period. They usually breath through gills but can rise to the surface to swallow air into the lungs if the water is foul. They die quickly if taken out of water and cannot move about on land. They feed on snails, waterplants, freshwater shrimps and worms in their native habitat, but have taken chopped liver in aquariums. They spawn between August and October.

FISHING TECHNIQUE: Although early settlers ate lungfish, referring to them as "Burnett salmon", lungfish have been fully protected since it was discovered that they had survived millions of years of geological change.

DISTRIBUTION: Originally known only from the Mary and Burnett Rivers of southern Queensland, lungfish stocks were moved by bullock waggons to the Brisbane valley in 1895-96 and became firmly established in Enoggera Reservoir, the Stanley River, and the Pine and Bremer Rivers. They have further shown their toughness in several aquariums.

Lungfish, *Neoceratodus forsteri*

MACKEREL *Scombridae*

Slimy mackerel, *Scomber australasicus*

The perfectly proportioned fish of the *Scombridae* family are fast, powerful swimmers, pelagics of the temperate to tropical regions of all oceans, and include renowned fighters albacore, bonito and tuna. They are very tasty if smoked or canned and will keep for a week or more if salted on capture, but they are not rated good table fish because of their soft flesh. They rate highly as bait and are readily taken by most flesh-eating fish. Freshly caught, they make the best of all strip baits for the surf because of their toughness.

There are literally millions of mackerel in Australian waters, for they are migratory fish of the open sea whose seasonal movements have been made in such dense schools they have excited scientists for more than a century. Peron observed vast schools in south-western Australia in the 19th century, and many highly-regarded biologists since then, such as Roughley and Whitley, have reported aerial sightings in which the mackerel were so thick they could not be counted.

Slimy mackerel, *Scomber australasicus*: A slender, elongated variety that grows to 1.5 kg but is more generally sighted around 0.5 kg. They have iridescent green bodies with irregular dark green or bluish oblique or blotchy markings, and are silvery below. The fins are yellowish-green or bluish, some edged in black. There is a wide gap between the dorsal fins and no keel on either side of the tail as in tuna. They get their name from their soft and slippery touch. The eyes are large and partly covered by an adipose eyelid. Both jaws contain a single row of sharp, pointed teeth, with those in the lower jaw larger than those in the upper jaw. They range from southern Queensland, along the New South Wales coast, Victoria, Tasmania, South Australia, and southern Western Australia. They are known in Tasmania as blue mackerel.

Spotted mackerel, *Scomberomorus munroi*: One of the smaller Australian mackerels. Although they have reached 10 kg in weight they are more often caught around 2.5 kg. They are bright silvery fish, bluish-green across the top with four irregular rows of dark spots that become more conspicuous on death. The first dorsal is a vivid blue, and the inside of the pectoral fin is dark blue to black. They are a popular quarry for Queensland anglers who drift-fish for them on ganged hooks, using pilchards or garfish for bait. They will also take spoons. Grant rates them a highly edible fish if they are chilled in crushed ice on capture with the fillets cut obliquely into steaks and grilled with lemon juice.

Narrow-barred mackerel or **Tanguigue,** *Scomberomorus commersoni*: Also known as Queensland kingfish and in Western Australia colloquially as Spaniards. Hooked in big numbers in Queensland for food and highly regarded as sport fish. They migrate northwards inside the Barrier Reef to spawn from October to December, laying millions of eggs. Juveniles are common in Torres Strait. They are the largest of Australia's mackerels, having been recorded at 60.4 kg in weight and 2.2 metres in length. Under their international name, tanguigue, the record stands at 44.9 kg or 99 lb and fish of that size have been trolled off Lizard Island in the northern section of the Barrier Reef. The Game Fishing Association of Australia record is 38.75 kg for a tanguigue caught off Rottnest Island, Western Australia, in 1982 by Barry Wrightson. Narrow-barred mackerel have a deep purple tint across the back that fades to silvery blue over the sides, which carry 40 narrow, wavy, bluish-grey bars. The first dorsal fin is vivid blue and the tail deeply forked. Anglers take them from boats or rocky headlands from which they float out baits under balloons. They will bite during the day but by far the best time is at dusk, when they feed on anchovies, sardines, garfish, hardyheads, sprats and flying fish. Yet again, they rate poorly as table fish if thrown under a wet sack but will provide outstanding meals if chilled immediately on capture and cut in obliquely-sliced fillets. They are distributed throughout the northern half of Australia down to Victoria. They are wellknown in the Sea of Japan, and right across the warmer sections of the Indian and Pacific Oceans.

Shark mackerel, *Grammatorcynus bicarinatus*: Also known as the large-scaled tuna because of the ease with which their body scales fall off when they are handled. They are common all round northern Australia and are one of the major targets of visitors to the Barrier Reef, schooling when they are immature but preferring a solitary life in adulthood. They are regularly caught from holiday boats on outriggers, plastic handlines and by trolling with rods. Best baits are small fish and spoons. Shark mackerel are easy to identify because of their double lateral line and take their name from their shark-like smell when gutted. They provide an appetising meal if bled and cleaned immediately after capture.

Frigate mackerel, *Auxis thazard*: A sub-tropical variety infrequently found in cooler waters, although small quantities are caught by purse seine nets in south-eastern

Narrow-barred mackerel, *Scomberomorus commersoni*

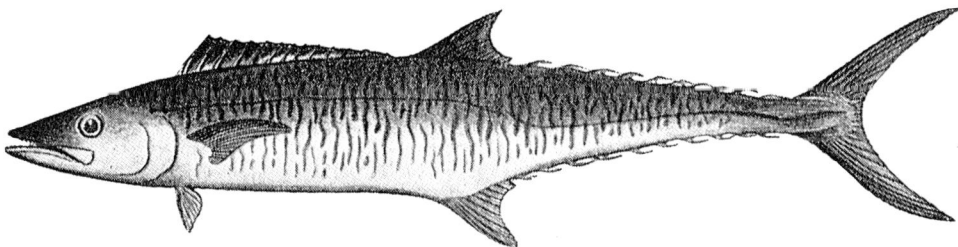

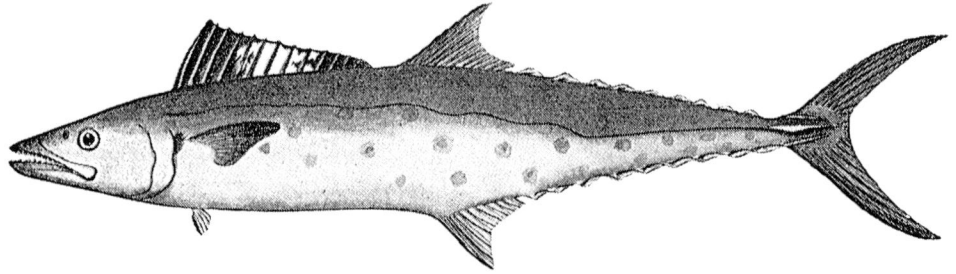

School mackerel,
*Scomberomorus
queenslandicus*

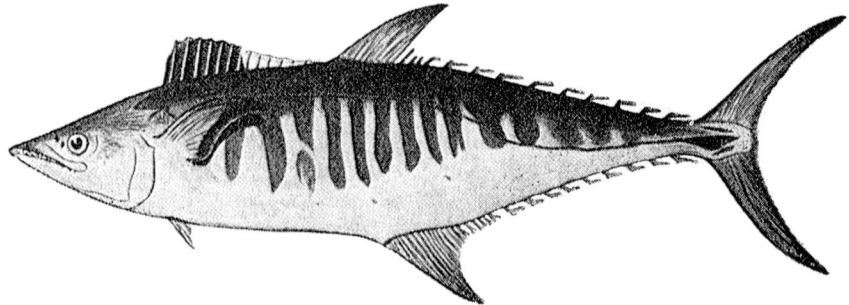

Broad-barred mackerel,
*Scomberomorus
semifasciatus*

Australian waters by trawlers fishing for skipjack tuna. They are dark bluish-grey on top, silver below with wavy oblique bars and blotches on the upper surface behind the pectoral fins. They reach 7 kg in weight but are usually taken around 1.4 kg. Their teeth are extremely small. Frigate mackerel are normally used as baitfish for larger game fish.

School mackerel, *Scomberomorus queens-landicus*: Found in northern Western Australia, the Northern Territory, Queensland and northern New South Wales waters in winter. Big shoals attract professionals with mesh nets. They are bright silvery little fish generally taken at around 2.5 kg. Their blue-green backs have a particular glitter. The flanks are silvery-white with two or three rows of dark blotches. When the first dorsal fin is extended, the leading half is jet black, the bottom half white. They take their name from the dense formations when they enter places like Tin Can Bay, Queens-

land and provide outstanding sport if they are fished on the drift with gang-hooked pilchards or live whiting.

Scad mackerel, *Grammatorcynus bilineatus*: Small versions of the shark mackerel which reach only 560 mm in length. They are an unusual pale green along the back and both the belly and upper sides are silvery. The tail is deeply forked like all members of the family and they are easily identified by their large eyes. They are not a true scad, which belong to the genus *Caranx* but the name has met with such universal acceptance authorities have gone along with it. A prime bait every season for marlin fishermen off Cairns.

Broad-barred mackerel, *Scomberomorus semifasciatus*: An exceptionally deep-bodied variety, identified by the black first dorsal fin and the prominent broad vertical bars across the torso. After capture the broad bars fade and the silvery sheen on the fish

Horse mackerel,
Trachurus declivis

becomes a dull grey, which is why they are sometimes called grey mackerel. Broad-barred mackerel grow to 7.7 kg but average around 2.5 kg and on the Barrier Reef and in the major harbours down the Queensland coast are important fish for the holiday trade.

FISHING TECHNIQUE: All mackerel bite well on fish pieces and small live fish. The common mackerel usually are taken on handlines without sinkers. The larger varieties roam the big inlets and may be trolled for there, but they are more likely to bite when they go out to sea. The larger mackerel also will take spoons and feathered lures if they are trolled at the right speed. Minnow-type lures invariably attract their attention.

DISTRIBUTION: Mackerel are caught off all Australian States but the larger specimens are caught on the Great Barrier Reef. Every year southern State anglers make the pilgrimage north in search of this great sporting fish, eager to sample a brand of fishing Queenslanders have developed into an art form.

MALAYSIAN FISH CURRY

INGREDIENTS

2 tablespoons vegetable oil
2 medium onions, chopped
2 cloves garlic, crushed
4 cm fresh ginger, grated
2 red chillies, finely chopped
2 strips thinly peeled lemon rind
1 tablespoon good curry paste
200 g thick coconut milk
500 g fish fillets
50 ml water
50 ml pineapple juice
250 g pineapple pieces

METHOD

A mild tasting curry with an interesting blend of sweet and savoury flavours.

Fry onions for about 5 minutes until soft but not brown. Add garlic ginger and chillies and stir for another minute. Add curry paste and stir for about 2 minutes. Add coconut milk, water and pineapple juice. Bring mixture to the boil, lower heat and simmer for 5 minutes. Add fish, cut into bite-sized pieces. Add pineapple pieces, and cook for 5 minutes or until fish is cooked. Serve with brown rice and side dishes.

Serves 4

Reprinted with permission, Carolyn Dunne, *The Semi-Vegetarian Cookbook*, Bantam, 1989

MACQUARIE PERCH *Percichthyidae*

An outstanding native freshwater angling and table fish, restricted to the cooler rivers, creeks and dams of eastern Australia, where it is also known as white-eye perch, mountain perch and silver eye. Abundant in some areas, the Macquarie perch is threatened by competition from introduced species such as carp, redfin and trout in many of the regions where it formerly prospered. It is unsuitable for breeding in farm ponds. The fish was named *Macquaria australasica*, in honour of New South Wales Governor Lachlan Macquarie, and according to Whitley, was discovered in either 1802 by Barrallier or 1817 by Alan Cunningham. Siltation and the erection of weirs and dams has restricted its spawning grounds. Fertility of Macquarie perch was shown in tests by the late John Lake, an authority on Australian freshwater fishes, who discovered that a 1 kg fish would probably produce 200,000 eggs. They have been taken up to 3.5 kg in weight, but average closer to 1 kg.

FEATURES: A broad-shouldered fish, grey on top and dull yellow below, with a blunt head, snub nose, several mucous cavities on the head, a small mouth, and deep purple dorsal, anal and tail fins. The purple fins quickly distinguish it from golden perch.

FISHING TECHNIQUE: Taken on flies and spinners, and baits such as worms, freshwater shrimps, and the very effective blowfly larva or maggot. These 'gentles' are probably freely taken because they show up clearly over sand. The angler has to keep out of sight as Macquarie perch become very wary of man in the heavily fished regions. They have the annoying habit of toying with the bait before taking it. They should always be allowed to run a few metres before the hook is set. A 2.7 metre floppy fly rod fitted with a threadline reel is most frequently used. Fishing in a current, a small sinker should be set on the line above the leader. They bite at all times but are at their hungriest at night.

DISTRIBUTION: Higher reaches of the Murray-Darling system. Common in the large dams of the Murrumbidgee River such as the Burrinjuck and Cotter, the Wyangala dam on the Lachlan, and Eildon Weir on Victoria's Goulburn River. Also found in Sydney's water supply dams and the Shoalhaven and Kangaroo Rivers, where it was probably introduced. Lake recorded them as far north as Fraser Island and the Mary River and as far south as the mouth of the Murray River.

Macquarie perch,
Macquaria australasica

MANGROVE JACK *Lutjanidae*

One of the Lutjanus group of hussars, sea snappers and perches, which includes about 20 members, the mangrove jack, *Lutjanus argentimaculatus*, is an important fish, equally at home in freshwater and saltwater, and a great challenge for anglers. They are an outstanding species for lure fishing because they appear to have feelings about their rights to the waters in which they live, and are prepared to defend them on principle even when not hungry. Almost every member of their family has an alias and mangrove jack are no exception. They are known as creek red bream, red snapper, rock barramundi, dog bream, purple sea perch, and most damagingly and wrongly as red bass. The Northern Territory name, mangrove snapper, is probably most appropriate. Recent research has shown that mangrove jack live in estuaries, rivers and tidal creeks until they reach maturity at a weight of around 3 kg, when they move to offshore reefs and grow to at least 10 kg. Hence they can be caught well up freshwater streams or off the coast.

FEATURES: There is no pit before the eye of the mangrove jack as there is in red bass.

The scales of mangrove jack are easily dislodged whereas in red bass they are tightly lodged and difficult to move. Mangrove jack are splendid eating but red bass are known to have caused the ciguatera form of fish poisoning.

FISHING TECHNIQUE: Strong tackle is essential fishing for mangrove jack. A stout spinning rod, a saltwater reel able to cast the 3.63 kg breaking strain line, heavy duty hooks and lures are mandatory. Best baits are prawns, mullet, fiddler crabs in mangrove country. Garfish on ganged hooks are also recommended. A system of instant retrievals, which begin when the cast strikes the water forces the jacks to burst free of cover. Leave no slack line so that the jacks can be struck hard the instant the hook is set.

DISTRIBUTION: Coastal waters of northwestern Australia, through Torres Strait, into Queensland down the coastal rivers and foreshores into central New South Wales.

Purple sea perch,
Lutjanus superbus

MORWONG *Cheilodactylidae*

A fish of many aliases also known as sea bream, king snapper, black perch, silver perch, sea carp, red moki, five fingers, queen snapper, strongfish, and jackass fish, to which they are related. They are very important fish to the Australian trawling industry which markets large numbers of them and although they grow to considerable sizes and fight hard they are not highly rated as sports fish. The confusion over their name is increased in north Queensland where sweetlips and emperors often are erroneously called morwong. There are 12 kinds of morwong in Australian waters, perch-like fishes but with 15 instead of 17 tail rays and the lower rays of the pectoral fins forming fingers with which they feel around rocks. They differ from trumpeters of the family *Latrididae* by having moderate-sized scales and an anal fin base much shorter than the second dorsal fin, which has less than 36 rays. They grow to 15 kg, but average 6.5 kg.

There is wide confusion about morwong and jackass fish owing to their general similarity, but they can be readily distinguished by the broad black vertical band extending from in front of the dorsal fin to behind the gill-cover. Jackass fish, *Nemadactylus macropterus*, are deep-bodied, silvery-grey over the flanks and belly, with the lower rays of the pectoral fin lengthened into a trailing filament that extends back past the start of the anal fin. Jackass fish flesh is white, firm and delicious to eat.

Grey morwong, *Nemadactylus douglasii*: The true porae of New Zealand, easily identified by the elongated fifth ray from the bottom of the pectoral fin, the almost oblong anal fin, and the branching soft rays in the upper half of the pectoral fins. They are greenish-grey to orange on top, have purple tints, are greenish-yellow on the sides, and silvery below. The membrane of the spinous dorsal fin is canary yellow and the

Jackass fish, *Nemadactylus macropterus*

Grey morwong,
Nemadactylus douglasii

Banded morwong,
Cheilodactylus spectabilis

membranes of the soft dorsal and anal fins are flecked in the same yellow. New South Wales anglers have found summer the best time for these morwong on the south coast and autumn and early winter on the north coast.

FISHING TECHNIQUE: Morwong feed on the same foods as snapper, marine worms, crustaceans, molluscs and small fish. They have ravenous appetites and when they are feeding will take prawns, whitebait, squid, octopus and fish baits such as mackerel, bonito, garfish, yellowtail and pilchards. Regular snapper tackle is used for morwong. However, they have smaller mouths than snapper and require smaller hooks, say 2/0. For boat fishing an ordinary snapper rod and reel and a 4.8 kg breaking strain line are ideal, with sinkers heavy enough to hold the bait on the bottom.

DISTRIBUTION: New South Wales and southern States.

Banded morwong, *Cheilodactylus spectabilis*: The largest of all morwongs, growing to 15 kg in weight. They have reddish-silvery bodies crossed by up to eight vertical brown bars. All the fins are reddish-brown, and black or light blue at the tips. They are also known as red moki.

FISHING TECHNIQUE: Occasional fish are caught by line anglers exploiting this morwong's taste for shellfish and crustaceans, but most are taken by spear or are gill-netted. They are ideal for baking.

DISTRIBUTION: Tasmania, Victoria, New South Wales and New Zealand. Throughout their range, they rarely exceed 1 metre in length and 15 kg in weight.

Dusky morwong, *Dactylophora nigricans*: A light-green variety heavily flecked in brown, with heavy orange-brown spots over the cheeks and eyes. They are also known as strongfish. Dusky morwong

Red morwong,
Cheilodactylus fuscus

attract the attention of groups of specialist anglers who regularly fish the same holes for them. Younger fish around 2 kg in weight are first-rate table fare but the flesh from mature fish, double that size, is dry and flaky.

FISHING TECHNIQUE: Freshly peeled prawns and wriggler worms are the best of a range of baits taken by this fish. Tackle as for snapper.

DISTRIBUTION: New South Wales, into Victoria, Tasmania, South Australia and southern Western Australia, with stragglers as far north as Queensland's Gold Coast.

Magpie morwong, *Cheilodactylus vestitus*: A graceful variety with silvery and whitish fins dominated by oblique black bars across the face and body. Their yellow-to-orange lips are ringed with chocolate-brown. This is a shallow water variety taken by spearmen. Their flesh is firm and tasty and they attain a weight of 2 kg.

FISHING TECHNIQUE: Like most morwong the magpie is very wary of taking a hook, although they eat worms and shellfish. They are difficult to hook because of their rubbery lips and small mouths but they will respond to berleying. Pipis on small hooks are recommended.

DISTRIBUTION: Common only along the east coast of New South Wales and southern Queensland.

Blue morwong, *Nemadactylus valenciennesi*: This is the queen snapper of southern Australia, a striking blue-bodied fish, with a pattern of bright yellow lines on the snout radiating out from the eyes. The membrane of the soft dorsal fin is spotted. An irregular black blotch across the body disappears as the fish matures. They grow to more than 10 kg in weight, which makes them an important quarry for trawler skippers.

FISHING TECHNIQUE: Blue morwong are line-fished on baits of peeled prawns but will also take shellfish, crab and cunje. They are such outstanding food fish they are much sought by commercial net fishermen and spearmen.

DISTRIBUTION: New South Wales, through Victoria, South Australia and southern Western Australia.

Magpie morwong, *Cheilodactylus vestitus*

173

MOSQUITO FISH   *Poeciliidae*

An incredibly fertile fish originally introduced into Australian freshwaters to control a mosquito plague. There is no evidence that this succeeded. Indeed most Australian ichyologists believe several of our native fish are more effective mosquito eaters and this has been shown by the examination of fishes' stomachs. John Lake said the mosquito fish may in fact have been responsible for the reduction in native fishes because of its habit of nibbling the fins of immature natives. Our indigenous fishes are certainly scarce in waters where the mosquito fish, *Gambusia affinis*, abound. The mosquito fish have an amazing history. Originally found only in the rivers of North America that flow into the Gulf of Mexico, they have been introduced into Austria, Germany, Spain, Italy, Israel, South Africa, Thailand, Japan, the Philippines, China and Russia as well as Australia. Grant cites one study which revealed that a female mosquito fish ate 225 large mosquito larvae in an hour, but this has not occurred in Australia. What has been shown beyond all doubt is that the mosquito fish is one of the most durable of fish, able to withstand drought, bush fires and extreme hot and cold temperatures.

Mosquito fish, *Gambusia affinis*

FEATURES: First brought to Australia in 1925, mosquito fish were introduced to all States except Tasmania within five years. Dark green to olive in colour, they have touches of light blue on the body and near the eye and transparent fins and tails. There is a horizontal ridge along the entire body. They breed three or four times a year, with 80 or more young produced each time. The anterior rays of the male's anal fin form an organ known as the gonopodium, with fertilisation occurring when this is inserted in the female. Live fish are released after developing inside the female which reach maturity within two months.

DISTRIBUTION: Apart from *Gambusia affinis*, which is widely distributed in Western Australia and Australia's eastern states, the closely related domingo mosquito fish, *Gambusia dominicensus*, is found in the warmer regions of the Northern Territory and South Australia. *G. dominicensus* is a smaller variety which grows to 35 mm compared with 60 mm by *Gambusia affinis*. They are also separable by their dorsal fin count, which is 7 or 8 in *gambusia* and 9 in the domingo mosquito fish. Females of both varieties grow to double the size of the male.

MOUTH ALMIGHTY *Apogonidae*

Mouth almighty,
Glossamia aprion

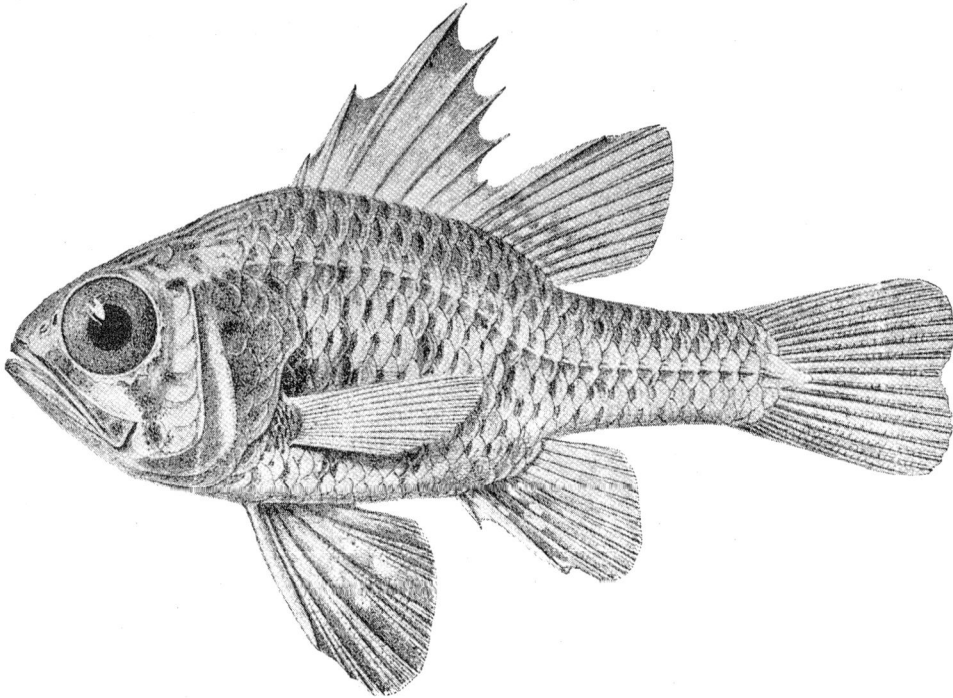

Australia has a wide range of fish known collectively as cardinal fish, siphon fish or soldier fish, all found in warmer temperatures, and most in saltwater. The males in this family of small, bright little fish always carry the eggs of the young in their mouths until they hatch and even after they incubate the youngsters crowd to take shelter in the parent's mouth when threatened. The mouth almighty, *Glossamia aprion*, is one of the very few Australian freshwater varieties. The unflattering names of flabby and stinker are often given them but they remain fascinating creatures because of the manner in which the young are born. The female lays a little bag of eggs which the male rips open with the point of his jaw and picks up one egg after another, refusing food while he is carrying them for five weeks. Grant reports that although they could never rank as a sportsfish they are highly rated among northern anglers as a panfish.

FEATURES: Mouth almighty grow to 700 grams or 1.5 lb whereas the smaller relative known as the Queensland mouthbreeder, *Glossamia aprion gilli*, is far smaller, reaching only 180 mm or seven inches. Like the oceanic members of the family our freshwater Glossamia are heavily-bodied, with a huge gape to the mouth and teeth on the tongue. They are golden-brown to whitish-brown in colour with irregular dark bar markings over the body.

FISHING TECHNIQUE: Of little interest to sportsfishermen although they are used occasionally as baitfish for larger species. They are of keener interest to aquariums because of the exceptional energy they show in the water and their breeding habits.

DISTRIBUTION: The mouth almighty in Queensland, the Northern Territory, Western Australia, and New Guinea, the Queensland mouthbreeder in southern Queensland and northern New South Wales.

MUDSKIPPER *Gobiidae*

A fascinating goby with eyes like periscopes and an ability to survive out of water for long periods. They take their name from their skill at skipping over mudflats at surprising speed and they can even climb over rocks and the roots and trunks of mangroves. They enjoy basking in the sun and lolling about mudflats at low tide, when they busy themselves searching for insects and small crustaceans. There are eleven species in Australia's tropical waters. They are carnivorous and quarrelsome, moving about in dramatic bursts. They are also known as kangaroo fish, johnny jumpers, climbing fish, and goggle-eyed mangrove fish. Former Superintendent of New South Wales Fisheries, Theo Roughley, called them a piscatorial paradox, fish that drown if they spend too much time underwater. Australian mudskippers include the blue-mudhopper, *Scartelaos histophorus*, an exceptionally slim-bodied goby with long bases to the second dorsal and anal fins; the common mudskipper, *Periophthalmus argentilineatus*, a small variety of around 100 mm which moves about by using the pectoral fins the way a cripple uses crutches; and the great mudskipper, *Periophthalmodon fraycineti*, which is illustrated. They grow to about a fifth of a metre, brownish fish known for their large eyes, and the dorsal fin is edged in black and red.

FEATURES: Mudskippers will often remain motionless in the mud for several minutes. They are sustained out of water by a primitive form of lung. The enlarged cavity that forms the gills encloses air as well as water and the surrounding tissue absorbs oxygen from the air. When disturbed, they can skip across water just as easily as they move over the mud.

FISHING TECHNIQUE: There is no point in catching these endearing little fishes. Better fun comes from watching them skip about, a spectacle Cook's men enjoyed in 1770. They are as nimble as frogs in Queensland's mangroves.

DISTRIBUTION: Tropical Australia, Queensland, the Northern Territory, and north-west Western Australia.

Great mudskipper,
*Periophthalmadon
fraycineti*

MULLET *Mugilidae*

Nimble pelagic fish which skitter around Australian bays, lagoons and estuaries performing impressive feats of acrobatics. They are important fish commercially but have only limited interest to anglers who do not rate them highly as food fish or as sportfish. Australia has around 30 species of mullet but only about half a dozen of these capture the attention of sportsmen. They have very small teeth or no teeth at all and eat only microscopic amounts of weed, worms and maggots, but they have an exceptionally high iodine content. Experiments in America showed they contain 900 times more iodine than top quality beef.

Australia's mullet have a wide variety of common names, most of them confusing. Names like tallegalane (sand mullet), lano (sand mullet), poddy mullet (sea mullet), bully mullet, hardgut mullet (both sea mullet), flicker (fantail mullet), wide bay and gold gill (tiger mullet) only add to the confused array of official names.

All species of mullet are essentially river fish, although some of them move from freshwater to saltwater. The sea mullet migrates to the sea to spawn, and other species only move freely into rivers during flood tides. The mullet's reputation as a poor food fish is especially unfortunate for sea mullet, which are among the best Australian edible fishes when they are skinned, and deep-fried or grilled. Yellow-eyed mullet and tiger mullet are others that are good eating, providing firm white fillets ideal for cooking.

Huge catches of mullet are often sent to pet food manufacturers during periods of market glut, but millions of dollars worth are still sold commercially around the States. Whitley said Queensland aborigines used dolphins to help them round up big mullet schools, whose arrival they forecast by observing the presence of certain birds. Mullet shoals several miles long have been sighted from the air. Mullet gut is excellent bait for many other fishes.

Mullet will not usually strike at baits or lures, lacking the teeth to do so, but some Australian anglers float-fish for them with dough and flour mixed with cotton wool. In freshwater, where they use a vacuum-cleaning method of feeding, they will take stale bread, earth worms, spaghetti, pollard and prawns. Overseas they are taken regularly on fly rods and cane poles and are rated ideal baitfish for tarpon, sailfish and kingfish. New Zealand anglers share Australians' poor opinion of them as food fish and inferior sport fish.

Sea mullet, *Mugil cephalus*: A major component of the fish-and-chip trade in

Sea mullet, *Mugil cephalus*

some States. They are olive-green above and silvery below in ocean waters but become darker on entering estuaries or rivers. There is a small dark spot at the base of their pectoral fins. The eye is covered by a transparent and gelatinous eyelid that has a small slit in it over the pupil. The head is bluntly-rounded and there are eight rays on the anal fin. They grow to 8 kg in marine waters, but average around 1 kg. Experiments by CSIRO scientists have shown them to be a remarkably nomadic fish, massing in estuaries and then leaving in a succession of schools for their annual spawning migrations. Despite persistent attacks by sharks, tailor, luderick and net fishermen, they move north along the coast, spawning on the surface of the sea. The eggs are carried southwards until the fry are big enough to enter harbours and bays. Juvenile fish stage a trial migratory run by moving out to sea for a short period around the age of two, before returning to their home waters. Several months later they move out for their first spawning runs with mature fish.

FISHING TECHNIQUE: Victorian anglers have been fishing for sea mullet for half a century with fly rods up to three metres long, tapered line, and a nylon leader. The fun comes from experimenting with fly patterns, but one of the most successful is a black-spider dry fly pattern tied on a No. 10 or 12 hook. Anglers with fly rods

position themselves on river banks where they can cast out to the main current where the mullet can be seen jumping. The fly is cast in front of the sea mullet and allowed to drift. The mullet takes the fly without fuss, apparently believing it is a shrimp or insect or maybe just because they look helpless.

DISTRIBUTION: Sea mullet occur world-wide in both temperate and tropical regions and in all Australian States. They appear in Tasmania only in summer.

Yellow-eyed mullet, *Aldrichetta fosteri*: A slender-bodied variety found in Australia's cooler waters. They are olive-brown in colour along the top and on the dorsal fins and silvery to yellow below. The eyes, which are a bright golden colour, give it its name. There are no dark spots above the pectoral fins. Two distinct stocks are believed to flourish in our waters; a western stock that spawns in mid-winter and an eastern stock that breeds in summer and early autumn. They grow to 950 grams or 2 lb in weight.

FISHING TECHNIQUE: Yellow-eyed mullet feed in estuaries on algae, nutrients from detritus, and worms. Dense pods of them are often sighted nibbling at moss on rocks and the weed on wharf piles. They can be tempted to swim to hooks baited with prawns and worms by berleying.

Yellow-eyed mullet,
Aldrichetta fosteri

DISTRIBUTION: Yellow-eyed mullet are found in southern New South Wales, Victoria, South Australia and southern Western Australia, and are probably the most widespread and abundant fish found over sandy bottoms near the Tasmanian coast. There, sheltered bays and estuaries act as a nursery for large schools of juveniles.

Blue-tailed mullet, *Valamugil seheli*: The largest of Queensland's mullets, growing to 10 kg, also known as black-spot mullet, blue-spot mullet, long-armed mullet, long-finned mullet, and sand mullet. They are easily identified by their light blue tails and blue soft dorsal fins. Their yellow pectorals have a prominent blue or black spot at the base. Their bodies are deeper than in most mullet and have a vivid silvery sheen from the gill covers to the tail.

DISTRIBUTION: Blue-tailed mullet are common in estuaries north of Cairns, but stragglers are seen as far south as Rockhampton. They are abundant in Princess Charlotte Bay and throughout the Gulf of Carpentaria. Bundaberg appears to be the limit of their southern range.

Fantail mullet, *Mugil georgii*: Smallest of all Australian mullet, also known as flickers, silver mullet, tychuree, and small fantail mullet. They reach 30 cm in length but average nearer to 25 cm. Plentiful in shallow flats in southern Queensland where large numbers reach fish shops. They are a brilliant silver colour, with a thick upper lip, and an almost straight tail. In large shoals, they have a habit of flicking at the surface.

Flat-tail mullet, *Liza dussumiera*: One of the smaller mullets, destined to be sought mostly for bait. They grow to 45 cm in length and 1 kg in weight but most are only half that and the ideal size for baitfish. They are steely-blue to silvery on top and along the sides and white below. There is a small black spot at the base of the pectoral fin preceded by a golden blotch. They are not good sport and only a few are taken on bream baits or dough, on standard mullet tackle. Mostly they are taken in seine nets. Flat-tail mullet are taken in most states except Tasmania, seldom in Victoria, with catches improving along the New South Wales coast into Queensland. They are plentiful throughout tropical Australia,

Flat-tail mullet, *Liza dussumiera*

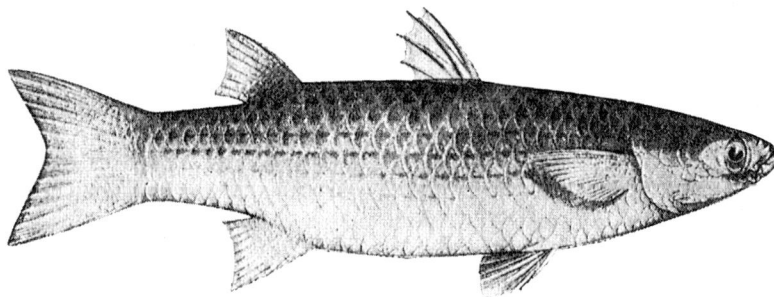

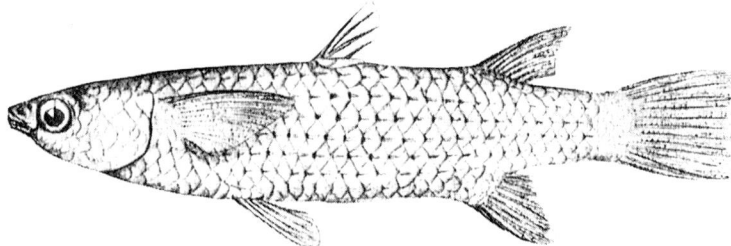

Diamond-scale mullet, *Liza vaigiensis*

Sand mullet, *Myxus elongatus*

where they are sometimes used as bait for barramundi.

Diamond-scale mullet, *Liza vaigiensis*: One of the heaviest Australian mullets, which prospers in our warmer marine waters. They reach 10 lb or 4.5 kg. Fish biologists rate them good table fare but in a region where appetising fish abound they lack popularity. Diamond-scale mullet have broader heads and larger scales than other mullet, and are easily identified by their black pectoral fin, the square-cut yellow tail, and the six broken brown streaks running along a body that is olive-green above, silvery along the flanks, and a dull yellow beneath. They are a favoured trolled bait for marlin and even the smaller specimens yield several good fillets.

DISTRIBUTION: Tropical Australia. Abundant along the northern Queensland coast and on the northern tip of the Barrier Reef.

Sand mullet, *Myxus elongatus*: An unusual mullet because of its row of well developed teeth. It is also known as lano and tallegalane. They are also one of the few mullets acceptable as panfish, yielding an

outstanding meal if the fillets are skinned before cooking. They are dark olive-green on top, and have no fleshy eyelid like sea mullet. There is a prominent black spot in the axil of the pectoral fin. They grow to 40 cm but average around 25 cm.

FISHING TECHNIQUE: Sand mullet offer good sport for anglers using a light rod, a small float, and a No. 6 hook with a No. 8 hook 45 cm below it. They will take the same baits as yellow-eye mullet, marine worms, prawns and dough.

DISTRIBUTION: The open bays of southern Queensland, New South Wales, Victoria, Tasmania, South Australia, southern Western Australia, and around Lord Howe Island.

Tiger mullet, *Liza argentea*: Takes its name from the dark longitudinal stripes that run from head to tail, each formed by the black and silver on the body scales. They are also known as gold-gill because of the prominent golden smudge that overlies the gill covers. The anal fin has ten rays and the tail is unusually deep and flattened. Apart from their stripes, tiger mullet are silvery-brown on top and bright silver

Tiger mullet, *Liza argentea*

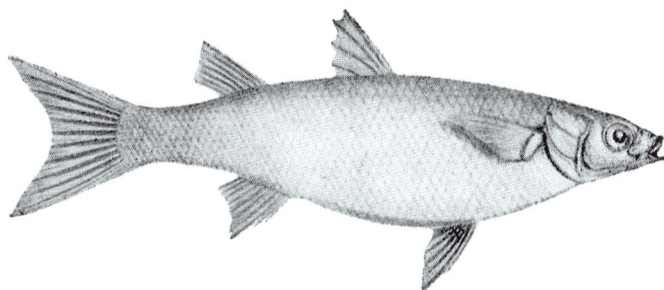

Freshwater mullet, *Trachystoma petardi*

along the flanks. They grow to 45 cm but are more commonly taken at 30 cm. They are also known in South Australia as jumping mullet, a name that would be appropriate to almost any member of the family.

FISHING TECHNIQUE: Mostly captured by seine netting, the tiger mullet can be persuaded to rise from the deeper waters around jetties by berleying and on occasions they will bite wildly on dough, worms, or squid in a feeding frenzy. They are one of the best table mullet.

DISTRIBUTION: Every Australian State except Tasmania.

Freshwater mullet, *Trachystoma petardi*: A small to moderate sized fish generally found where deep pools slow the flow of rivers. They feed on plants and animals.

They vary considerably in edible quality according to the conditions in which they are caught. They are remarkable in that they have fine teeth in both lips and larger teeth in the upper jaw. They are dark, almost black along the back, with brilliant orange-yellow eyes, heads tapering to a point. They are also known as pink eyes because their eyes become bloodshot when they are iced down. They cover substantial distances in times of flood. They have no interest for anglers but are taken in seine nets when they move downstream into brackish water.

DISTRIBUTION: The inland sections of coastal streams in southern Queensland, the eastern rivers of New South Wales, as far as the George's River just south of Sydney. When floods recede they will feed in company with the sea mullet.

MULLOWAY *Sciaenidae*

Mulloway, Argyrosomus hololepidotus

The official name for the fish universally known as jewfish. Of all the names agreed on at the drawn-out series of conferences between the states to decide on uniform Australian fish names, this is the one least likely to be accepted by anglers. They are also known as kingfish in Western Australia and elsewhere as butterfish, dhufish and dewfish, but the only name likely to gain general acceptance was jewfish. For the large jewfish have achieved a special affection among sportsmen, many of whom will fish for nothing else. They are an important game and table fish right across the southern half of Australia and fight with a pugnacity matching their large (length 1.8 metres and weight 55 kg) maximum size, always making two or three determined runs before they are brought to gaff. Opinions vary about their eating quality but there should be no complaints if they are bled and chilled on capture.

FEATURES: Mulloway, *Argyrosomus hololepidotus*, should not be confused with the fish known as river perch or lesser jew, *Johniops vogleri*, a small silvery fish found in New South Wales and Queensland rivers. In southern Australia mulloway is the largest fish anglers can catch in harbours, estuaries and tidal rivers. They are silvery grey along the back, silver on the sides, with lighter, spaced, burnished spots along the lateral line. There is a dark blotch on the pectoral base, and they are

orange or dullish red inside the mouth. Small mulloway up to 7 kg tend to remain in saltwater estuaries where they are known as 'school jew', but specimens smaller than that are usually referred to as 'soapies', because of their soft flesh.

FISHING TECHNIQUE: All the best mulloway are caught at night, usually during washouts when heavy rain brings coastal rivers down in flood conditions. They gather in gutters at the river mouths, chopping into food fish carried downstream. They will take small fish like mullet, whiting, tailor, herring and yellowtail, plus squid, prawns and beach worms. Mulloway take the bait in their front teeth and lips and carry it several metres before deciding to swallow it, so it is essential to give them free line and offer no resistance until they take the bait well into their mouths. Let the mulloway make its first run to make sure the hook is set, gradually increasing the pressure until it is turned. They tire quickly after their initial fight and the angler must be prepared to give them a lot of line. With 150 metres on the reel or spool, you can cope with the biggest mulloway. Avoid a test of strength but never allow the fish any slack line.

DISTRIBUTION: Southern Queensland coastal waters and estuaries, New South Wales, Victoria, South Australia and southern Western Australia.

MURRAY COD *Percichthyidae*

The largest and most famous of Australia's native freshwater food fishes, the Murray cod has great bulk and a delicious flavour. It has also been heavily depleted in recent years by over-fishing. They are keenly sought by sportsfishermen and are caught commercially in some states. There is an old bushmen's tale that tree-markings on the swim-bladder of Murray cod are a map of the fish's birthplace. They were first recorded in 1813 by G. W. Evans near Tarana, New South Wales, and have been an important part of our inland fishing ever since. They were split into six species more than a century ago but only one species was recognised until the 1970s when they were split into two species—the Murray cod, *Maccullochella peeli* and the trout cod, *Maccullochella macquariensis*. Murray cod have been recorded to a weight of 79.13 kg and 1.8 metres in length. It has been scientifically accepted that they can be separated from trout cod by the way in which the upper jaw overhangs in trout cod, which has a straight snout and head slope, compared with the concave head slope of Murray cod.

FEATURES: Slightly convex tail, head profile concave. The lower jaw protrudes in larger specimens. Margins of the fins sometimes red, body olive-green with small brown spots, pale yellow below. Short dorsal spines. Pectoral fins rounded, behind the level of the ventral base.

FISHING TECHNIQUE: Best baits are crayfish, yabbies and mussels and small fish such as the common carp. But specialist Murray cod anglers prefer to troll for them with large propellor lures. They stage a surprisingly stubborn and sustained fight when hooked. Anglers should look for dead trees and other snags in rivers and places where stagnant water gives the Murray cod a chance to feed. Deep pools with a good log cover where frogs, crayfish and mussels

Murray cod,
Maccullochella peeli

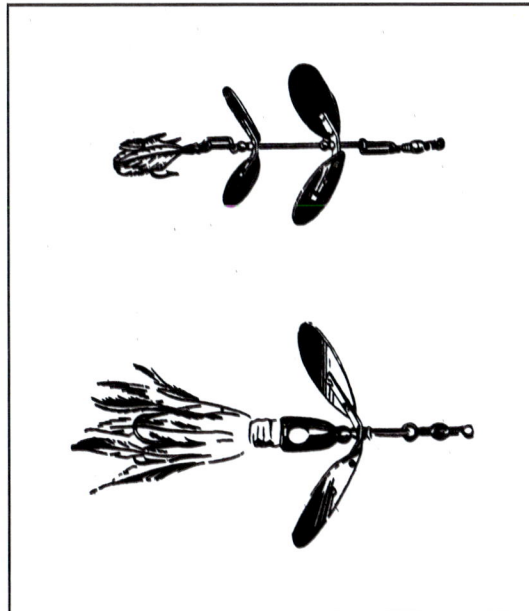

TOP: The aeroplane spinner features free-spinning nickel and red blades.

BELOW: Feathered cog jig with propeller head and white feathered body.

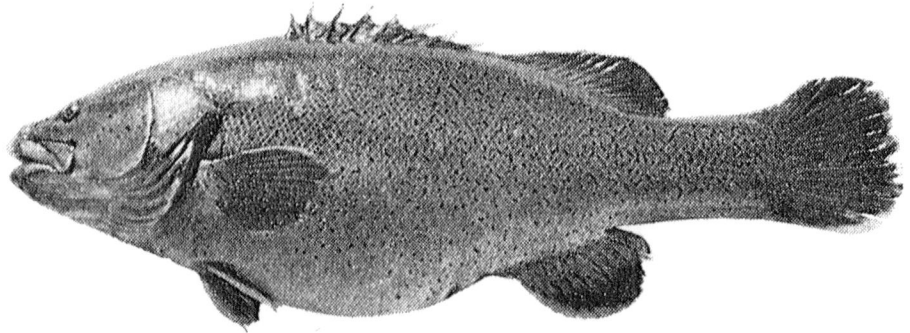

Trout cod,
*Maccullochella
macquariensis*

are easily located are typical Murray cod habitat. They need heavier tackle than other freshwater species because of their sheer size. A lot of Murray cod anglers tether their catches with cord tied through the lower jaw to keep them alive and fresh while they fish for others.

DISTRIBUTION: Murray cod are consistently caught in the Murray River and its tributaries, the Edwards, Wakool, Murrumbidgee, and in Victoria in the lower reaches of the Ovens and Goulburn Rivers.

Good fishing is also found in the slow-flowing Darling River and its tributaries the Macintyre, Gwydir, Namoi, Macquarie, Bogan, Castlereagh, and the Warrego and Culgoa, which drain into Queensland. In Queensland the Condamine, Balonne, Weir and Moonie Rivers are reliable Murray cod waters, as are the Warrego and Culgoa. In South Australia, the Murray River still provides good cod catches. Efforts to introduce Murray cod into Western Australia early this century failed.

A selection of freshwater lures that have proved highly effective in catching Murray cod.

NANNYGAI   *Berycidae*

A fish of ancient lineage found in all Australian States and important in the markets of South Australia and Victoria, where they are first-class table fare. Nanny-gai are handsome deep-pink fish, studded with iridescent metallic tints, that reach half a metre in length. They were first identified in Australian waters in 1829. Australian specimens include the swallowtail nanny-gai, *Centroberyx lineatus*, a small form often referred to as red snapper, which is iden-tified by its deeply-forked tail, large eyes and cavernous mouth; the common nanny-gai, *Centroberyx affinis*, another deep-bodied variety which is identified by the silvery-green line that runs from head to tail; and the bright redfish, *Centroberyx gerrardi*, which make up a third of the nannygai catches in southern oceans, where trawlermen insist on marketing them as red snapper or Bight snapper. The name nannygai is a corruption of aboriginal words Moora nennigai. They average around 60 cm in length and the biggest of them reach 2 kg in weight.

FEATURES: The mouth gape of nannygai is large, the body short and deep and they are conspicuous by their colouring, red with violet and silvery reflections. The fins are red, the eyes large and gold, tinged with red. Their scales are extremely rough. They prefer rocky or broken ground in deep water but occasionally enter harbours and bays to feed.

FISHING TECHNIQUE: Nannygai are heavily trawled with nets in South Australia and Victoria but amateurs mostly catch them with handlines. They try to twist the line when hooked by swimming in circles so they should be firmly drawn to the boat once the hook is set. Best baits are worms, squid, starfish, prawns and cut fish. Sinkers capable of taking the bait down to them are advised.

DISTRIBUTION: Southern oceanic water from south Western Australia across the Australian Bight to Victoria and up the east coast to southern Queensland. Most plentiful in the cooler waters of South Australia and Victoria.

Common nannygai,
Centroberyx affinis

NURSERY FISH *Kurtidae*

Nursery fish, *Kurtis gulliveri*

One of the most remarkable fish in Australian waters, also known as the incubator fish, the hunchback or the humphead. Nursery fish *Kurtis gulliveri* inhabit the muddy rivers of the tropics, where many experienced line fishermen rate them superior eating to the legendary barramundi. Their reputation rests, however, on the freakish role the male plays in the birth of their young. The mature male develops a hooked projection on the top of the head that grows forwards and downwards until it forms an almost closed ring. With the approach of the breeding season, a thickened skin appears, covering the ring. The female deposits a nest of large eggs within the ring, with filaments on the male holding them in place. The male then carries the eggs about like a bunch of grapes until the young hatch. The nursery fish's smooth-skinned body is golden brown on top, creamy along the belly and the flanks, head and tail are a bright, diaphanous silver. The dorsal fin and lobes of the tail are black-tipped. They grow to 60 cm in length.

FEATURES: Males have a dark spot towards the side of the hump or hook, females eight tubercles along the back. The tail is deeply forked in both males and females, and both have heavy lower lips.

FISHING TECHNIQUE: Their main diet is small fish and as they move about stretches of brackish water, they are captured by anglers with baits of freshwater shrimps. They have been known to take spoons but not feathered lures.

DISTRIBUTION: The coastal lagoons and rivers of the Northern Territory, and the rivers of New Guinea. They are often caught in Queensland's Norman River and in Cambridge Gulf, Western Australia.

OXEYE HERRING (TARPON) *Elopidae*

One of the fastest fish in Australian waters which will resist until exhausted, leaping clear of the surface, turning and running out a lot of line. The combination of fighting qualities and a vivid silver body that shimmers in the sun as they speed through and out of the water make oxeye herrings outstanding fish for sportsmen. They have too many fine bones, however, to be ranked highly as table fare. Oxeye herrings are also known as bony mullet or tarpon after their close relation, the American sportfish *Tarpon atlanticus*. The American variety grow to a weight of 43 kg or 100 lb but the biggest caught in Australia have been around 1.5 metres in length and 2.60 kg in weight. For their size they are amazing fighters and it is not uncommon for them to die quickly after a fight even if returned to the water. Grant records that juvenile oxeye herrings are so adept at leaping, they hurdle across the floatline to escape when netted. They demand split-second reactions from anglers eager to land them.

FEATURES: Large black eyes, bright silvery bodies with large scales, and a trailing filament on the single dorsal fin.

They often shake hooks free of their bony-plated jaws and mouths. Their heavily-forked tails and all fins are yellowish to pink.

FISHING TECHNIQUE: Sharp hooks are essential. Spinning at dawn or dusk with spoons, light-headed jigs and fast retrieved flies work better than baits. Once the hook is set, the best technique is to let them exhaust themselves by allowing them lots of line. They congregate in large shoals under moored buoys in crowded waterways like Moreton Bay, where a wire trace above the fast-moving lure is advisable. The younger fish prefer lagoons above tidal influence, older fish deeper reaches where they can feed on mullet, garfish, gobies and small bony bream. They often fall to anglers fishing for barramundi with barra frogs and bellbrook lures.

DISTRIBUTION: All of tropical Australia, from Moreton Bay in the south to Papua-New Guinea in the north, the Northern Territory and the warm waters of Western Australia. Only occasionally in New South Wales.

Oxeye herring, *Megalops cyprinoides*

PARROTFISH   *Scaridae*

Surf parrotfish, *Scarus fasciatus*

An attractive, brightly-coloured family of coral-chewers seldom caught by anglers and frequently confused with Australia's 450 species of wrasses. The teeth of parrotfish are fused together to provide a beak-like appearance that gives the family their name, whereas the teeth of wrasses are separate, peg-like crushing stems. The difference between the two remains hidden to most fishermen and because of this a lot of wrasses have been called parrotfish. Wrasses are large, groper-like fish capable of breaking lines and often are susceptible to trolled baits. Parrotfish have small mouths and rarely change their coral diet and because of this it is doubtful if any have been caught regularly by anglers. Australia's best known parrotfish are the illustrated surf parrotfish, *Scarus fasciatus*, a brilliantly green fish with salmon pink blotches over the cheeks and a table fish of the highest rank; the illustrated six-banded parrotfish, *Scarus sexvittatus*, which have bright silvery triangles on the edges of their body scales that form a striking latticed pattern; the blue-barred parrotfish,

Scarus ghobban, which grow to one metre in length and are found at Rottnest Island in Western Australia as well as on the Barrier Reef; the violet-lined parrotfish, *Scarus globiceps*, which have the unusual habit of forming mixed shoals with the surf parrotfish and take their name from the tracery of violet bars that radiate around the eyes of the females; and the rosy parrotfish, *Pseudolabrus psittaculus*, which are common in rocky reef waters in southern States.

FEATURES: The surf parrotfish is a very pretty fish with numerous markings. The male is pale bright-green on the upper body with the base of some scales showing through as coral-red. On the underside the colours fade into a dull red or pinkish red. The head is a salmon-orange colour overlaid by a network of pale green lines. The female differs, with bright greenish-blue bodies, each scale edged in yellow. The face and gill covers are yellow and blue lines radiate from the eyes. There is also a blue line along the upperlip and two or three

Six-banded parrotfish,
Scarus sexvittatus

on the chin and throat. The tail fin is yellow, etched in blue.

FISHING TECHNIQUE: On very rare occasions parrotfish will take baits of cut fish or prawns. They have such a marked preference for shallow water, some reef-walkers have approached feeding shoals and then chased spooked fish into shallower water until the exhausted parrotfish is gathered in by hand. The secret is that the hunter has to be in better physical shape than the fish to bring in a splendid panfish.

DISTRIBUTION: The western Pacific right down the southern section of the Barrier Reef often in shoals of several hundred fish.

KANGAROO MEAT AND FENCING WIRE: The biggest fish ever caught in Australian inland waters was a Murray cod of 114 kg or just over two hundredweights in the old imperial scale. The fish was more than 182 cm long, and was caught during the 1902 drought when bridge builders were camped at the four-mile crossing of the Barwon River near Walgett, New South Wales. Aroused by activity in the river, the bridge builders rushed into Walgett and got the local blacksmith to make a big hook on to which they put a big lump of kangaroo meat, with a piece of fencing wire as a trace. Despite the primitive technique of the bridge builders, the Murray cod took the bait.

PEARL PERCH *Glaucosomidae*

Pearl perch, *Glaucosoma scapulare*

A deep-bodied fish widely regarded as Australia's best table fish. They are restricted to the coastal reefs of southern Queensland and to New South Wales and are nowhere abundant. They take their name from the pearly lustre of prominent bone above the pectoral fin, which is covered by a dark and delicate skin that easily rubs off. They have unusually large eyes which apparently helps night vision. Some have a black spot set on the back towards the rear of the soft dorsal fin. The body colouration of the pearl perch, *Glaucosoma scapulare* is a silvery green, with dashes of brown over the back and golden brown spots on each scale. They grow to a weight of 5.4 kg or almost 12 lb.

FEATURES: Pearl perch stay in the same area for months at a time. Skin-divers report that although an occasional solitary fish is sighted, they are mostly seen in small schools, usually near rock faces, gutters,

and crevices. They are frequently caught in late afternoon on handlines by fishermen seeking snapper. They bite best after dark and feed hungrily until just after 10 p.m. when they disperse, reappearing just before dawn to feed again. They disappear shortly after sunrise.

FISHING TECHNIQUE: Like their relatives, the Westralian jewfish, pearl perch are mainly midwater feeders, readily taking baits of cut fish, squid and prawns that are held well clear of the bottom. They need strong, sharp hooks because of their exceptionally large mouths which they use to crush crustaceans and molluscs. A wire trace is advisable when seeking big specimens.

DISTRIBUTION: Southern Queensland and New South Wales, right down the New South Wales coast, but rarely in Victoria.

PERCHES *Serranidae*

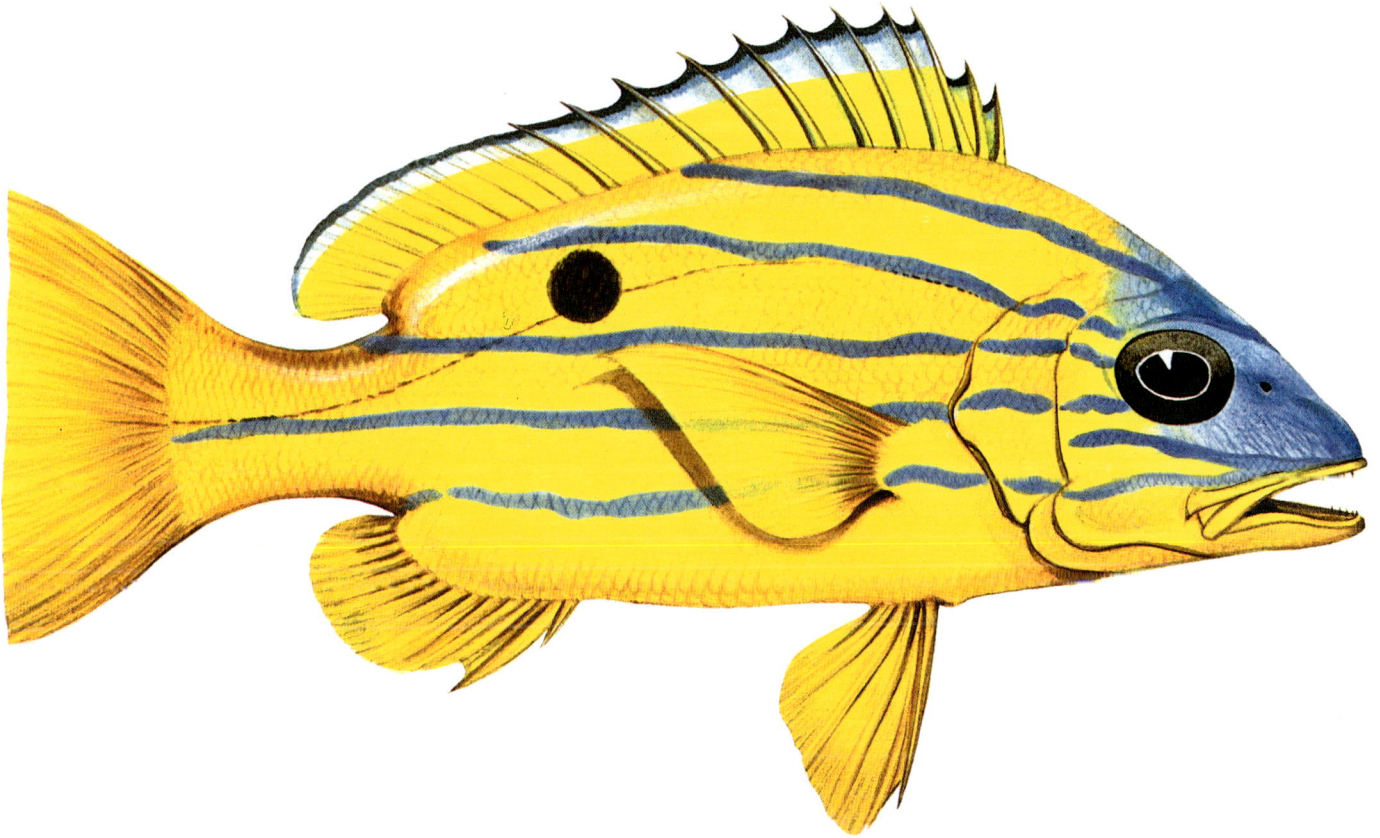

The family *Serranidae* includes a large number of perch-like fishes that are referred to as cod although they are not true *Gadidae* or cod. Australia's cods inhabit rocky reefs, coral or rough bottoms, usually in warmer seas. They include the brown-spotted cod, *Epinephelus suillus*, which grows to 225 kg in weight and two metres in length; black cod, *Epinephelus damelii*, a reef-dweller that reaches more than a metre in length and 103 kg in weight and has been heavily depleted by spear-gunners; butterfly perch, *Caesioperca lepidoptera*, also known as red perch, which at one time was marketed in large numbers by New South Wales trawlers but today appears in sizes too small for the markets; splendid perch,

Callanthias allporti, a deepwater variety from the southern States which is just as colourful as any Barrier Reef fish; the black-banded sea perch, *Hypoplectrodes nigrorubrum*, an excellent panfish found in the shallow waters of New South Wales, Victoria, Tasmania and South Australia; potato cod, *Epinephelus tukula*, whose white body and head is studded with potato-sized black blotches; and the blue-banded sea perch, *Lutjanus kasmira*, which has five narrow blue bars extending from the head to the tail, and sometimes a black spot beneath the second dorsal fin. The estuary perch, *Macquaria colonorum*, is a close relative of the bass.

Blue-banded sea perch,
Lutjanus kasmira

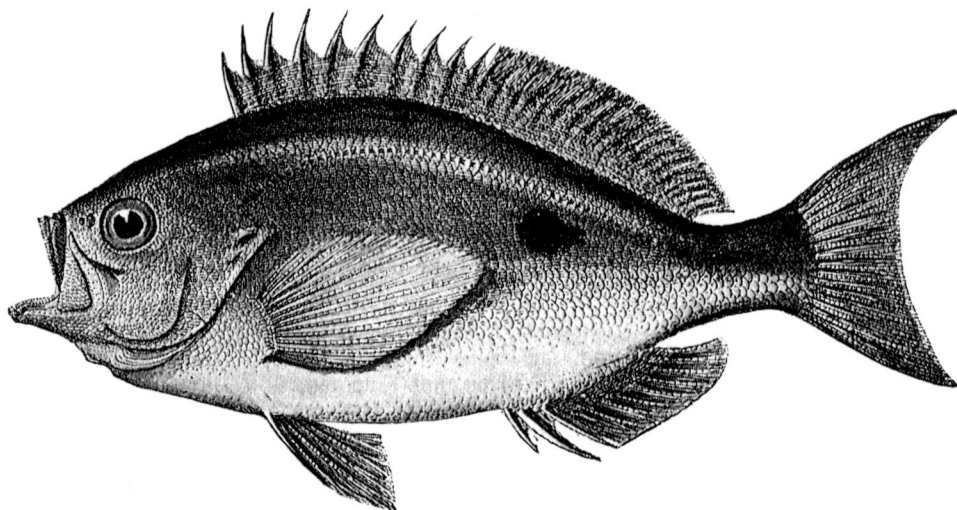

Butterfly perch,
Caesioperca lepidoptera

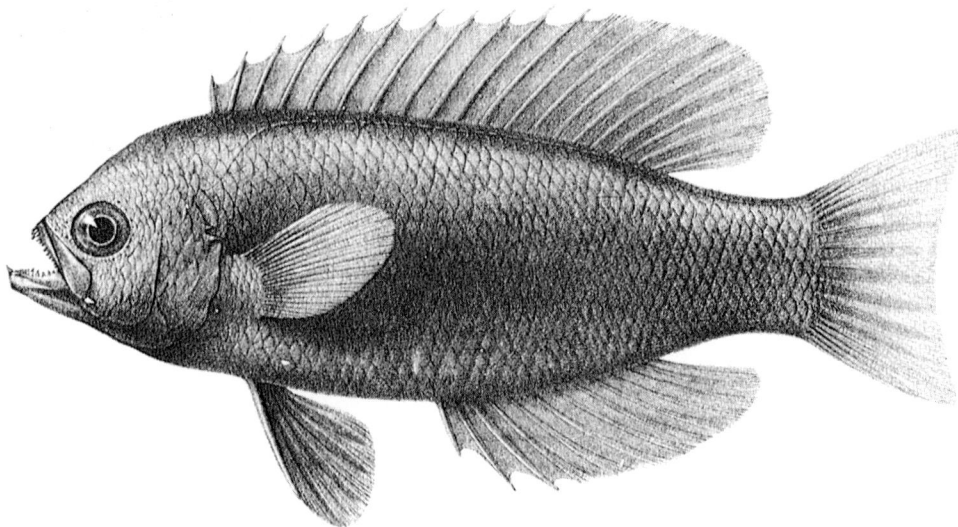

Splendid perch,
Callanthias allporti

FEATURES: Moderately short to elongated bodies, strong lower jaws. At least two spines on the opercle. Several species are hermaphrodites from birth while others change sex later in life. Australia's two splendid perches provide an interesting contrast in shape and habitat. The shallow water variety, *Callanthias australis*, from the warm waters of the Barrier Reef is a deep-bodied fish whereas *Callanthias allporti*, which is found in much deeper and colder water off eastern Tasmania, Victoria and southern New South Wales is a slimmer fish. They are both colourful fish, with breeding males developing a golden hue over their pink sides.

FISHING TECHNIQUE: Mostly taken on handlines at depths below 50 metres on prawn, cut fish and crustacean baits.

DISTRIBUTION: All Australian States boast some varieties of *Serranidae* but they are most abundant on the Barrier Reef, where their ability to change colour quickly has hamstrung biologists seeking to document bona fide species. The splendid perch, *Callanthias allporti*, is found in deep water off Tasmania, Victoria and southern New South Wales.

PILCHARD *Clupeidae*

Small, appetising members of the herring family which feed more people in the world than any other fish group. The family includes herring, sprat, milkfish and bony bream. Important as they are to canneries, the main value of pilchards to anglers is as a baitfish. They are one of the most consistently successful of all baits, especially in summer when they contain plenty of oil. All of our game fish bite avidly at pilchard baits, especially when they are presented whole on ganged hooks. Pilchards have more slender bodies than herring and are far more lively than the docile sprat, a factor which becomes important when they are used as live bait. Australia's pilchards include the northern pilchard, *Amblygaster sirm*, which has two enlarged anal rays and 10 or 11 dark spots along the upper flanks; the illustrated common pilchard, *Sardinops neopilchardus*, a chubby-bodied pilchard found in dense shoals in the open coastal waters of Western Australia, South Australia, Tasmania, New South Wales and southern Queensland. Great numbers of this species, which is very similar to the sardine of Europe, darken the sea every winter. Most commercial catches are made at night when the big shoals light up the surface and crowding is so intense there is a plopping noise as if rain is falling. They attain a length of 240 mm.

FEATURES: Steely-blue above, silvery below, with a row of dark spots along the lateral line, above which there are more dark specks. The tip of the tail is dark and the operculum bears radiating grooves. The belly is serrated. One dorsal fin consists entirely of soft rays.

FISHING TECHNIQUE: Mostly caught in nets by professionals, who freeze them and sell vast quantities for bait. They are ideal bait for salmon, mackerel, tuna, sweetlip and snapper and are being used increasingly for game fish. The average angler buys them frozen at bait shops or tries to pick up a few in scoop nets.

DISTRIBUTION: All Australian States. It is a fish of migratory habits. The Western Australian variety, which occurs as far north as Carnarvon, is the most favoured among anglers.

Common pilchard, *Sardinops neopilchardus*

PIPEFISHES *Syngnathidae*

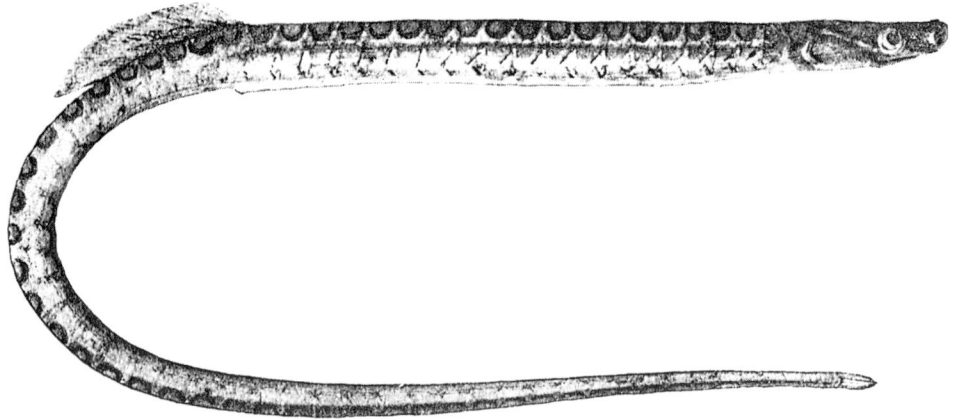

Ring-back pipefish,
Stipecampus cristatus

Slender, whip-like fishes closely related to seahorses and sea dragons, usually found among seaweeds which they resemble in shape and colour. Their bodies are encased in rings of bony armour. Some have a tiny tail fin to assist their feeble swimming power. Australia boasts more than 90 different pipefishes, but only two of these are found in freshwater, the small-headed pipefish, *Hippichthys heptagonus*, and the black-skinned pipefish, *Hippichthys penicillus*. The most common saltwater varieties are the double-ended pipefish, *Syngnathoides biaculeatus*, which is thickest in the middle and tapers towards the snout and tail; the ring-back pipefish, *Stipecampus cristatus*, which is attractively marked with creamy-white blotches on a pale brown body and has a fan-shaped tail; the ladder pipefish, *Festucalex scalaris*, whose pale brown body has 13 to 16 darker crossbands resembling a ladder and a tiny caudal fin at the end of a slender tail; the knife-snouted pipefish, *Hypselognathus rostratus*, readily recognised by its long snout, upper surface of which is raised into a knife-like ridge; Verco's pipefish, *Vanacampus vercoi*, which has a single keel and operculum and a brown body with four cross-bars on the trunk and ten or more on the tail; the mess-mate pipefish, *Corythoichthys intestinalis*, a coral-reef inhabitant with up to 17 delicate dark crossbands across its light brown body and an orange fan-shaped tail; and the deep-bodied pipefish, *Kaupus costatus*, which has a deeply compressed body bearing a sharp keel and an elevated dorsal fin.

FEATURES: Pipefishes are noted for their camouflage and even to veteran skindivers are often almost invisible. They generally are brown or green to match their surroundings amid weeds. Few exceed 30 cm in length, and the largest is the brushtail pipefish, *Leptoichthys fistularius*, 56 cm. The females lay eggs on the lower surface of the tail of the male who guards them in folds of skin or a pouch until they hatch.

DISTRIBUTION: Saltwater pipefish are found in all Australian States, the freshwater species, the black-skinned and small-headed pipefish, in the rivers of southern Queensland and northern New South Wales.

PORCUPINEFISH *Diodontidae*

Pear-shaped fishes with prominent spines, closely related to puffers, tobies and toad-fishes, with an ability to inflate themselves into a ball by absorbing water or air. Heavily protected by the tough armour of spines, they have earned the universal hatred of professional and amateur fishermen alike because of the damage they do to nets or human hands when handled incautiously. Whitley credited one porcupinefish with gnawing its way out of a shark that had been unlucky enough to swallow it. They can drift while inflated and travel long distances in this manner. There is an Aboriginal legend that porcupinefish were smooth until, treacherously betrayed, they ate spiny anteaters whose spines stuck through the skin. South Sea islanders wear helmets made of porcupinefish when in battle dress.

FEATURES: They have only two teeth, one upper and one lower, housed in bear-like jaws, and oddly shaped swimming bladders that resemble a seated female figure. All species of porcupinefish, including the brown-backed porcupinefish, *Diodon liturosus*, and the illustrated three-barred porcupinefish, *Dicotylichthys punctulatus*, are poisonous and should never be eaten. They have greenish-grey bodies studded with white dots that stretch to the tail and belly, and heavy black bars across the head and sides.

FISHING TECHNIQUE: Useless as bait or for the table, porcupinefish require a special technique to remove them from nets. A knife should always be used as they generally respond to capture by inflating their bodies and increasing the tautness of the netting.

DISTRIBUTION: All States have at least one variety of porcupinefish, most of them white in body colour, some with black spots or a black "chinstrap".

Three-barred porcupinefish, *Dicotylichthys punctulatus*

195

PRAWNS AND SHRIMPS *Peneidae*

The names given to swimming crustaceans with five pairs of walking legs under their heads and five pairs of swimming legs beneath their abdomens. Hundreds of species have been discovered around Australia but only a dozen are of importance to amateur or commercial fishermen. They belong to two main groups, penaeids, which shed their eggs in the sea, or carids, which carry their eggs under their tails. Most of the world's prawn trade involves penaeid prawns. There is no zoological difference between prawns and shrimps and none of the world's leading dictionaries attempt to separate them. One of Australia's leading experts on the subject, Nick Ruello, uses prawn in describing the penaeid species and shrimp when referring to carids. Ruello was involved in a prawn-tagging scheme conducted by the New South Wales Fisheries Department which showed some remarkable movements by prawn schools. Prawns tagged off Lakes Entrance in Victoria showed up in trawler catches in Hervey Bay and Moreton Bay, Queensland.

Prawns are of enormous indirect value to amateur fishermen and are an important part of the fish trade in all States. They are a valuable source of food for all gamefish and are readily obtainable as bait. The Japanese breed them in hatcheries but the bulk of all prawn catches are taken by commercial trawlers, usually at the mouths of estuaries during an outgoing tide in the dark phases of the moon. Heavy rain improves prawn catches throughout the year, but the theory that they are attracted by bright lights is a fallacy. The lights' main value is in helping to spot prawns on the surface.

Penaeid prawns usually are of two sexes, with females growing to much larger sizes than the males. After mating the females shed the fertilised eggs into the sea and these shed larvae which moult repeatedly for just on a month, when they begin to resemble the shape of tiny prawns. Most species then enter coastal rivers and bays and spend their lives in estuaries, but some deepwater varieties live out their lives in the ocean. Recent research into prawn movements has shown that the school prawn moves out to sea and migrates north along the New South Wales coast, while the eastern king prawn may cover as much

as 1000 km along the coast to spawn off Queensland. The seaward run from the estuaries remains a rewarding period for all prawn fanciers but an increasing number are taken each year at sea. Stocks in Shark Bay and Exmouth Gulf in Western Australia have produced important harvests and since the early 1970s a prawn known as the royal red prawn has been taken in commercial numbers at depths down to 300 fathoms off the New South Wales coast.

Banana prawns, *Penaeus merguiensis,* are a valuable export item for Queenslanders and taken in vast numbers in the Gulf of Carpentaria by trawlers based at Weipa, Karumba and Thursday Island between March and July each year. Spotter aircraft watch for the annual "mud boil" produced at sea by vast schools of banana prawns and guide the fleet to the prawns. Grant says it is not uncommon for one trawler to catch as much as 30 tonnes (60,000 lb) in a day, as the contents of the nets are spilled onto the decks and the prawns are literally shovelled into brine tanks below. Amateur anglers often catch them in coastal rivers with cast nets and find them ideal bait as well as splendid eating. Banana prawns grow to 23 cm.

Eastern king prawns, *Penaeus plebejus,* reach 30 cm in length, and are among Australia's biggest and best known varieties. Ruello rates them the champion swimmer among our prawns, capable of 6 km per day and migration movements of around 1200 km. They are very popular with amateur fishermen because they swim near the surface and can be easily caught with a scoop net and lamp. The spectacular annual scene of thousands of sportsmen's lights dotted around Tuggerah Lakes focuses on

FAR RIGHT:
Eastern king prawn,
Penaeus plebejus

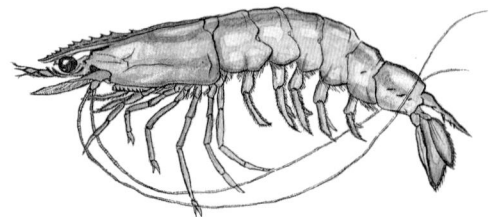

196

the movement of eastern king prawns to the sea. In Queensland, immature king prawns are fished in the shallow waters of Moreton Bay during spring and early summer after which the mature kings move out of the bay into deeper water. The off-shore distribution extends from the Queensland border to Rockhampton in late summer and early winter, and catches over 200 kg in a day are commonplace. The king prawns' colour usually is light-brown to reddish-brown with two parallel grooves running the full length of their bodies.

Western king prawns, *Penaeus latisulcatus,* also known as blue-legged prawns because of the colour of their walking legs, are the most abundant species in South Australia and Western Australia. Commercial boats take large numbers of them in Spencer Gulf and Gulf St. Vincent. They are also occasionally taken in New South Wales and the Gulf of Carpentaria.

School prawns, *Metapenaeus macleayi,* are the most plentiful species in the rivers of northern New South Wales and southern Queensland and are so tolerant of low salinity they may be found as far as 60 km up-river from the sea. They are fairly small at 15 cm when mature but their cheapness and abundance has made them the most popular bait prawn among New South Wales and Victorian anglers. They resemble the greentail or greasyback prawn, but differ in having a smooth shell. They are also much paler in colour and are more densely spotted. Heavy rain or flooding sends them downstream in huge dark schools that hug the banks and make them easy picking for amateurs with bait nets and scoops. Around Noosa they were once offered as live bait by trawlermen who caught them in traps that floated on the surface.

Tiger prawns, *Penaeus esculentus,* are brown, vividly-marked prawns that take their name from the crossbands over their heads and tails. They grow to 28 cm in length and in the last few years have become one of Australia's most important commercial species. They are distributed in our northern oceanic waters from Shark Bay in Western Australia to central New South Wales and appear to be most plentiful in Torres Strait and in the Gulf of Carpentaria, south to Princess Charlotte Bay in northern Queensland. They can be taken in these waters all the year round but some boats prefer to leave tiger prawn grounds to get behind the spotter planes leading to the vast schools of banana prawns. A close relative the giant tiger or leader prawn, *Penaeus monodon,* grows to 30 cm which makes it the world's largest prawn, dark-blue or grey in life with a series of white crossbars.

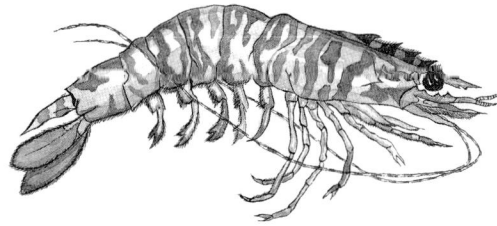

Tiger prawn, *Penaeus esculentus*

Greentail prawns, *Metapenaeus bennettae,* also known as greasybacks, are named after the fan-like tails of dark green and the mat-like hairs that cover the shell. They are almost transparent in life and in Queensland are probably more highly rated as food than as bait. They are abundant in New South Wales, particularly in Tuggerah Lakes, and in eastern Queensland. They mature at only 7.6 cm which makes them Australia's smallest

FAR LEFT:

School prawn, *Metapenaeus macleayi*

Greentail prawn, *Metapenaeus bennettae*

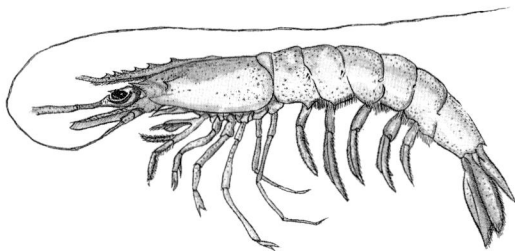

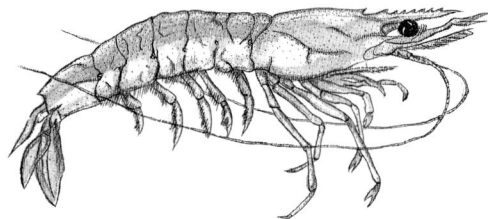

commercial species, but their lack of size does not worry the Brisbane River fishermen for whom they provide a handsome living. The greentail is one of the few prawns to breed in estuarine waters; freshly-hatched prawns move upstream to brackish waters before migrating downstream as they mature. Their close relative, the western school prawn, *Metapenaeus dalli*, is found in Western Australian coastal waters from Broome to Mandurah and is eagerly sought by amateurs each summer in the Swan River.

Rainbow prawns, *Parapenaeopsis sculptilis*, also known as coral prawns, are an extremely colourful variety with four pale crossbands evenly spread between tails and heads, and yellowish patches along the bottom of the head. They have little commercial value because their large heads restrict the amount of meat they offer, but they are an extremely potent bait on the central Queensland coast, probably because their colouring attracts fish. They grow to 150 mm, and often show up in the catches of boats seeking banana prawns in the Gulf.

Endeavour prawns, *Metapenaeus endeavouri*, also known in Queensland as bay prawns or brown prawns, are a light brown variety with a blue fantail, which carries large spines. Their shells have patches of matt-like hairs. They grow to around 20 cm and are found from Shark Bay in Western Australia to Bundaberg in Queensland.

Red-spot king prawns, *Penaeus longistylus*, were identified in Australian waters decades earlier but only became a commercial proposition in the 1980s. They are named after the prominent red spot on each side of the tail above the third pair of swimming legs. They are common in northern Australians reefs, in the China Sea, and in Malaysia.

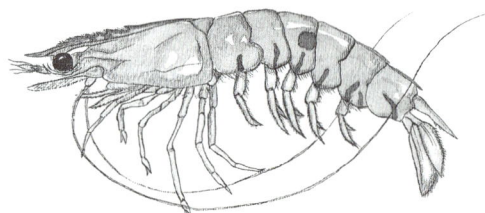

Banded coral shrimps, *Stenopus hispidus*, are colourful shrimps found in the tropical waters of the Indian Ocean and the Pacific, and belong to neither the carid or penaeid families, but have features of both. They grow to only 10 cm, with flowing white feelers and a large pair of third legs. Their white bodies and arms are banded with scarlet. They act as cleaners for coral reef fishes, waving their long feelers apparently to attract business. Magically, far larger fish remain still while the shrimp picks away the parasites, damaged tissue or fungi on their bodies. The shrimp does all this without leaving their crevices while fish queue up around their "cleaning stations".

Mantis shrimp: Australia has more than 30 species of mantis shrimp, ranging in size from 2.5 cm to 30 cm, all of them taking their name from their close resemblance to the praying mantis insect. The most common form in southern waters is the smooth mantis shrimp, *Alima laevis*, which frequently appears in the Sydney markets, a succulent variety snapped up by European migrants aware of their high edible quality. Mantis shrimps are downwardly-flattened crustaceans, usually pinkish-brown in colour, with strong spines on the outer edges of the tail that can prove painful to careless handlers. Under the

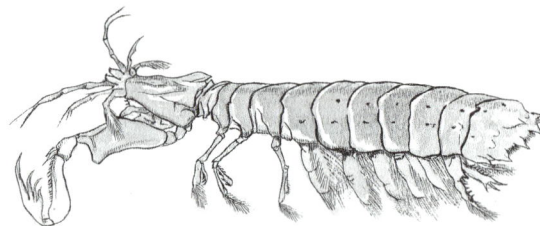

head, they have a strong pair of toothed claws which they use like the blades of a clasp knife to hold prawns, small fish, and other creatures. They regularly appear in catches of prawn trawlers, usually with a prawn clutched in their claws. Some scientists describe them as the "thugs of crustaceandom".

Yabbies: Carid shrimps of the order *Alpheus* which have been highly regarded as food and bait by Australian anglers for more than a century. The marine variety have a pair of legs modified into heavy nippers, one of which is invariably larger than the other.

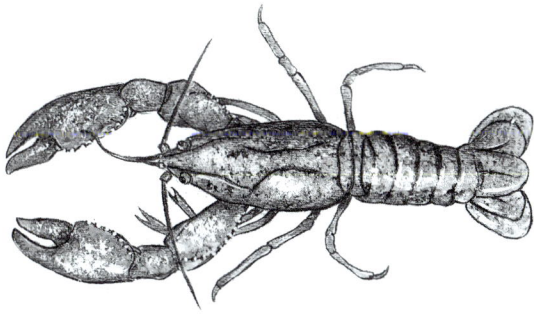

A peg-like projection on the movable part of this nipper fits into the socket on the fixed part. The sudden closing of the peg into the socket produces a sharp crack like the noise of a pistol. They are also known as ghost nippers or burrowing shrimp, names that should be reserved for *Callianassa australiensis*, a saltwater yabby with a massive claw that it uses to dig holes, two-thirds of a metre deep. Amateur fishermen catch them with special yabby pumps, professionals with a powered sand pump. On the best yabby sand banks amateurs can collect up to 100 yabbies in an hour. They make excellent bait for bream, flathead, whiting, tailor, and snapper.

FISHING TECHNIQUE: Australians catch most of their prawns in scoop nets or dip nets, usually operating in groups of two or more. In many areas they wade through the dense schools of prawns with a person on each side of the net, scooping them into kerosene tins while others light cooking fires on the bank. Freshwater yabbies are excellent eating and used to catch cod, yellowbelly, redfin, often as live bait, and are trapped in pots or simply by dangling a piece of meat in the water on a piece of string. The yabbies attach themselves to the meat as they attack it and are brought to the surface in a scoop net. Some anglers build themselves yabby rakes for use in our rivers. On the beaches, few specialist anglers would be without a yabby pump.

DISTRIBUTION: There are yabbies and prawns in all Australian States and some prawn species form valuable commercial operations, bringing in millions of export dollars.

FAR LEFT ABOVE:
Freshwater yabby, of the family *Parastacidae*

FAR LEFT BELOW:
Burrowing shrimp,
Callianassa australiensis

WATCH THE BIRDS: Saltwater hot spots often can be found by watching sea birds, particularly mutton birds and terns. The birds follow schools of fish, waiting to swoop on scraps after predators strike and often reveal the depth at which the fish are swimming by the height at which they fly. When the birds drop to the surface, it is a sure sign the schools are under attack and predators have begun leaving fish pieces. In freshwater the presence of cormorants and pelicans often reveals the existence of shrimp, small fish and other aquatic life that will attract sizeable fish.

PRETTYFINS *Plesiopidae*

Blue devil, *Paraplesiops meleagris*

A family of carnivorous, brightly-coloured coastal fishes with seven genera and 17 species in Australian waters, also known as roundheads, longfins, guinea fowl fish and blue devils. The family is characterised by numerous dorsal spines, a disjunct lateral line and four soft pelvic rays. Most have graceful, trailing soft dorsal and anal fins. Although the illustrated blue devil, *Paraplesiops meleagris*, grows to 400 mm and is a very tasty panfish, most of our pretty-fins are too small to be marketed commercially. Like Bleeker's devilfish, *Paraplesiops bleekeri*, the blue devilfish spends most of the daylight hours beneath deep ledges and caves. All bar *P. bleekeri* (which are protected), can be caught on a line, but mostly they are subjects for under-water cameramen, completely disproving the notion that southern fishes are not as colourful as those from tropical waters.

FEATURES: In *Paraplesiops meleagris*, the dark blue head and body is studded with glowing blue to purple spots. The head is darker than the peacock blue tail, which shows clear purplish tints. *P. bleekeri* is easily identified by the four black vertical bands across the body and the yellow tail. Alison's devilfish, *Paraplesiops alisonae*, is an exceptionally slender member of the family with 11 dorsal rays rather than 12 and an almost circular tail. They grow to around 100 mm and have reddish-brown bodies, with heavily studded blue spots around the snout. They have little angling appeal but provide vivid photographs for underwater cameramen.

DISTRIBUTION: The best known blue devils are found in the southern half of Australia. *P. meleagris* is confined to South Australia and Western Australia, *P. bleekeri* to New South Wales, and *P. alisonae* to Victoria and South Australia. *Trachinops caudimaculatus*, or southern hulafish, is common around the shallow coastal reefs of Victoria, Tasmania and South Australia.

QUEENSLAND HALIBUT   *Psettodidae*

A tropical flatfish that reaches a larger size than any other in Australian waters (10 kg) and should be more widely sought because of its outstanding table qualities. They are mostly taken by trawlers in the far north fishing to a depth of 45 metres, but bring poor prices and some trawlermen do not bother sending them to market. Anglers lucky enough to catch and cook one readily understand the frustration of biologists because our halibut is ignored by the fish-eating public. The Queensland halibut, *Psettodes erumei*, unlike other Australian flatfish, will travel in an upright position in deep water, lying over on its side when it enters shallow water on a rising tide. One eye lies near the top of the head as it moves along the bottom in the flatfish's customary undulating style.

FEATURES: Flounders, soles and tongue soles all differ from the Queensland halibut in having the dorsal fin extending forward over the head at least to above the eye. None of the halibut's rays are spinous and there are no spines on the ventral fin. They are brown on the eyed top side and lighter on the blind bottom side, having begun life in the normal manner as flatfish with eyes on each side of the head and undergoing the transformation in which one eye moves across the head to the same side as the other.

FISHING TECHNIQUE: Few flatfish are taken on lines, though they are sought by anglers drifting over mud and sand in estuaries. Most are taken by fishermen using handspears from flat-bottom boats.

DISTRIBUTION: The Queensland coastline to the Northern Territory and northern Western Australia.

Queensland halibut,
Psettodes erumei

MAPPING THEIR BIRTHPLACE: There is an aboriginal legend which says that all Murray cod carry a map of their birthplace on the membraneous walls of their stomachs. The fish are said to have made the maps lying in the shade of gum trees during the heat of the day. Some anglers have gone forth seeking Murray cod under gumtrees, eager to open their stomachs and study the maps. They have been sadly disappointed, for there are no maps, only big fish sheltering at the coolest depths of the largest waterholes.

QUEEN SNAPPER *Cheilodactylidae*

Queen snapper,
*Nemadactylus
valenciennesi*

A large, appetising member of the morwong family, also known as blue morwong. They are favourites with underwater cameramen, charter boat skippers, and amateur anglers and appear with unfailing regularity in fishing magazines. Their appeal stems from their photogenic quality, for few marine fish provide such good clear closeups. They have bright blue bodies, with scales edged in yellow, the juveniles with alternating blue and yellow longitudinal lines. The dorsal, anal and caudal fins are blue with yellow spots or wavy lines. Their most distinguishing feature is the blue and yellow marks radiating from the eyes in what has become known as a "highwayman's mask", which sits on a dusky patch that crosses the snout and nape.

FEATURES: Queen snapper, *Nemadactylus valenciennesi*, have moderately elongate bodies and 16 spines in the dorsal fin, and 15 rays on the pectoral fin. The anal fins

have three spines. The lower rays of the pectoral fin forms fingers for touching rocks. Early settlers called them "five fingers".

FISHING TECHNIQUE: Queen snapper are reef-dwellers which respond to crustacean baits, peeled prawns, cut crabs, and worms. They are occasionally caught in gill-nets, and will respond to berley that is well presented. Anglers should remember that this is a large fish that grows to 12 kg and adjust line strength and hook sizes accordingly.

DISTRIBUTION: Queen snapper are found in New South Wales, Victoria, South Australia and Western Australia. They have been netted off King Island in Bass Strait but whether they have ventured into Tasmanian waters is unknown and Tasmanian biologists would welcome specimens.

RAINBOWFISHES *Melanotaeniidae*

A colourful group of small, mainly fresh-water fishes which has eight genera and around 50 species spread around the world, five genera and 22 species in Australia. They are also plentiful in New Guinea and surrounding islands. They are also known as jewelfishes and sunfishes, and are keenly sought for aquariums because of their wide range of body colours, which in most varieties become even more striking with the onset of the breeding season. They provide such a wide range of colours and finnage it is difficult to give a uniform general identification, but they are easily spotted in tanks, where they feed on dried foods and breed without problems. Some ichthyologists consider they are more effective in controlling mosquito larvae than the introduced mosquito fish. The blue eye, *Pseudomugil signifer*, was included in the rainbow fish family in a review published in 1982 but is now thought to be a separate species more closely related to the hardy-heads.

FEATURES: The illustrated chequered rainbowfish, *Melanotaenia splendida inornata*, is a beautiful little fish that grows to around 90 mm and has nine or ten coppery lines running from head to tail on bright greenish-brown bodies. Rows of pale blue spots become more intense near the tail, providing a chequered effect that extends to both dorsal and anal fins. There is a dark blotch above the gill covers and the cheeks are bright orange in colour. Just as striking is the toothed or red-striped rainbowfish, *Melanotaenia splendida rubrostriata*, a pink-bodied variety from New Guinea, with orange-red lines running along the body in which the anal and dorsal fins of the male take on a vivid red tinge during the breeding season. The Australian rainbow-fish, *Melanotaenia splendida*, has a silvery-blue body with translucent fins and scales. A prominent crimson spot at the rear of the gill cover is emphasized by the orange or brown stripes along the side.

Chequered rainbowfish, *Melanotaenia splendida inornata*

Red-striped rainbowfish,
*Melanotaenia splendida
rubrostriata*

DISTRIBUTION: The chequered rainbow fish and the toothed rainbow fish are among our northern varieties, found in coastal streams in Queensland and the Northern Territory, particularly in Cape York Peninsula rivers that flow into the Gulf of Carpentaria. The pink-eared rainbow fish is found in subtropical streams in southern Queensland and New South Wales. The controversial blue eye dwells in sea water in brackish mangrove areas.

Crimson-spotted
rainbowfish,
*Melanotaenia splendida
fluviatilis*

RAINBOW RUNNER *Carangidae*

A powerful, streamlined fish of the open seas, found throughout the world in tropical and sub-tropical waters. They grow to 1.3 metres and are rated as highly as sporting fish as they are table fish. The Japanese prepare special sauces for this fish, rightly regarded as a gourmet's delight. They are built for speed, with slender, cigar-shaped bodies and a magnificent crescentic tail. In Australia, they are mostly fished for on the fringes of the Great Barrier Reef, where *Elegatus bipinnulatus* are a favoured trolled bait for the giant marlin caught off Cairns and where juvenile rainbow runners around half a metre in length are common in small schools.

FEATURES: They are deep purple to green along the top and a bright silvery colour along the belly. In between there are bright blue narrow stripes edged in yellow. Both the anal and soft dorsal fins lead to a short, pointed finlet just ahead of the tail. All this adds up to a sleek fish that swims in tropical waters, fins sticking in the air, with two conspicuous blue lines stretching from eye to tail on each side and giving the fish its name. They reach weights up to 4.7 kg in Australian waters, but one weighing 8.6 kg was caught years ago by American president Franklin Roosevelt in the Galapagos Islands.

FISHING TECHNIQUE: Runners are mostly taken on trolled lures and feathered jigs. They offer superb sport on light tackle, staying near the surface on the first run where anglers can see their striking colours. They generally follow it with two lesser runs as its reserves of stamina ebb away. They often swim alongside large sharks, trevally, suckerfish, groper, and pilotfish. Whitley said they bred at about 60 cm.

DISTRIBUTION: Northern half of Australia down to New South Wales in December to March. New Guinea, Lord Howe Islands, and warm Indo-Pacific seas.

Rainbow runner, *Elegatus bipinnulatus*

RAYS *Rajidae*

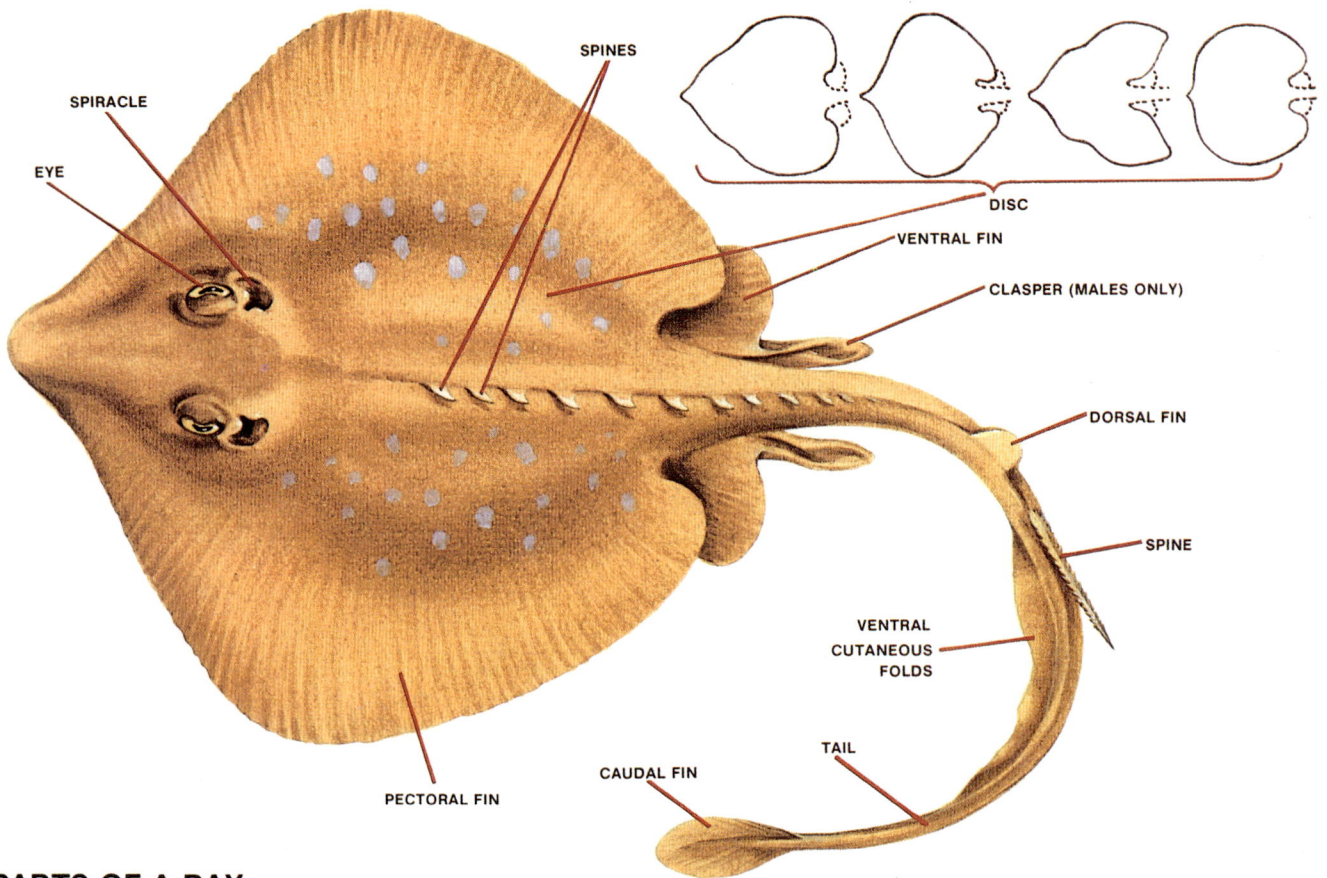

PARTS OF A RAY

(This is a composite illustration—no ray has all the features we have mentioned).

Rays are closely allied to sharks but differ in their flattened appearance and in having the pectoral fins fused to the head. The gill-slits on rays are on the ventral surface and their spiracles are large, whereas in sharks spiracles are sometimes absent. Rays were at one time considered true fishes but they are now regarded as a separate class, grouped with sharks and sawfish, all of whom have cartilaginous skeletons.

In keeping with their flattened shape, rays are bottom-dwellers that seek cover by burrowing in sand and mud so that only the eyes and spiracles are visible. This life-style probably is the reason Australians regard them suspiciously as table fare, for despite their often appealing taste, rays are not popular as food. This unpopularity is increased by the difficulty in removing the

rays' tough skins. It involves cutting the most edible part, the flaps from the carcass, and immersing them in boiling water. The skin then falls away to disclose white meat which should then be soaked in cold water and vinegar for 20 minutes. The fillets are now ready for cooking.

Australian waters are rich in rays and sharks, with no less than 50 rays and skates and 90 sharks caught by anglers. Some grow to enormous sizes but they are seldom dangerous despite the excitement they cause among the unknowing when sighted for the first time. The devil or manta ray, for example, reaches a width of 6 metres and weighs up to 750 kg. Their young are born alive and weigh around 9 kg.

Rays do not need strong tails for swimming, so few have any tailfins, only a slender whip-like appendage. There are no gill covers and five slits from the gill chamber. Most of them produce their young alive but some members of the group such as skates, of the family *Rajidae*, deposit eggs that are protected in tough, horny envelopes. There are often marked differences in male and female rays of the same family. Males can have large spines, but not the females, and there can be marked differences in the teeth of male and female rays.

The principal Australian ray families are the electric rays, *Torpedinidae*, in which electric organs are present; the stingarees, *Urolophidae*, which usually have a serrated barb in the tail; the skates, *Rajidae*, which have blunt-tipped tails and swim by undulating their disc flaps; *Myliobatidae*, eagle rays, which have wide and angular flaps; *Dasyatididae*, stingrays, which have one or more sharp, serrated barbs capable of inflicting painful wounds; *Rhinobatidae*, shovelnose rays also known as guitarfish,

banjo-shaped rays with prominently marked bodies; *Mobulidae*, devil rays, with vast mouths and exceptional width, which includes manta rays and diamond fish; *Gymnuridae*, rat-tailed rays, sometimes marketed as flake.

Numbfish, *Hypnos monopterygium*: Also known as crampfish, electric rays and torpedoes, which are armed with organs that produce electric discharges or shocks. Some can inflict a severe shock when touched, but at times the storage cells appear to run flat and the shock is imperceptible. They are used by the numbfish to frighten off would-be attackers and to stun and disable prey. They have extremely short tails and terminal tail fins set closely behind two posterior dorsal fins. The tails are shorter than their discs, which are broader than they are long. Numbfish are rusty brown or reddish above, white or creamish beneath. They are fairly plentiful in shallow waters on coasts south

Numbfish, *Hypnos monopterygium*

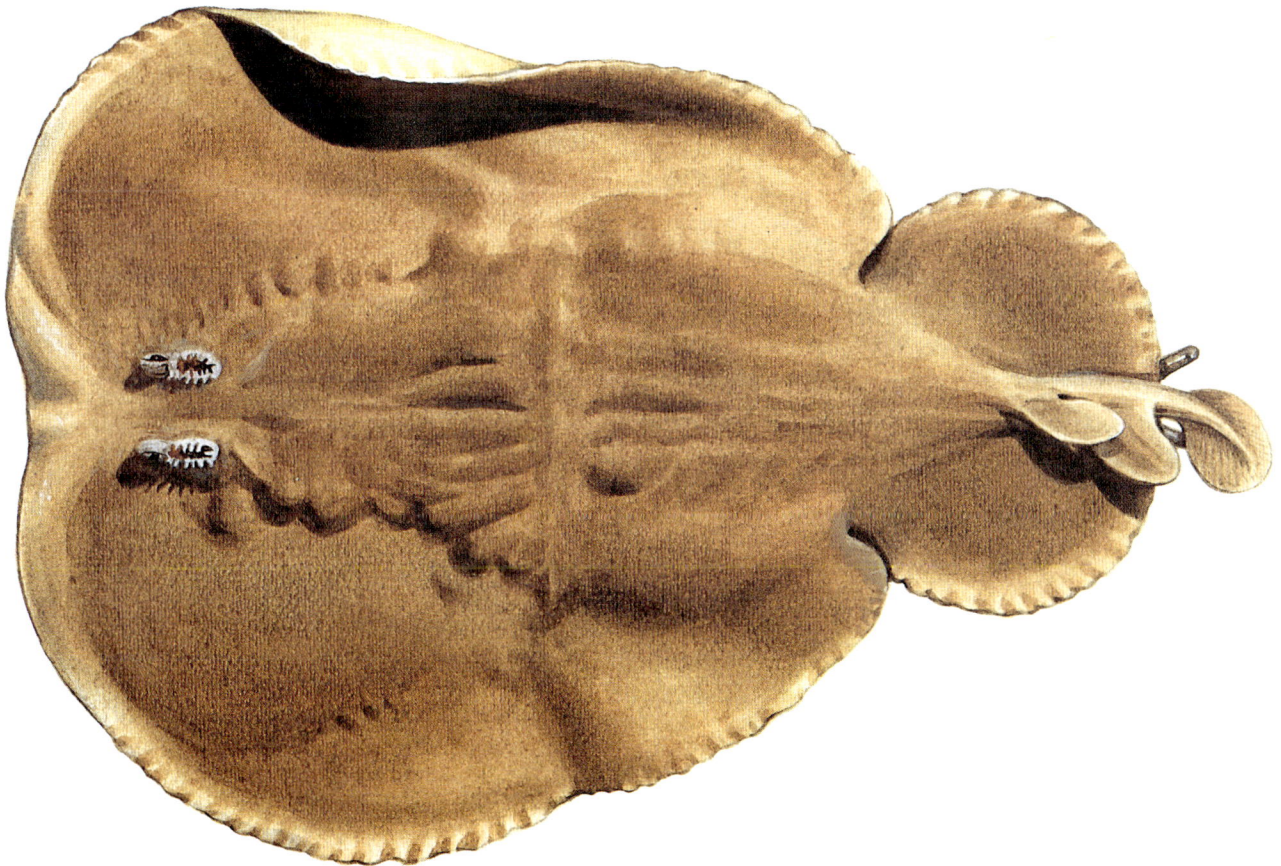

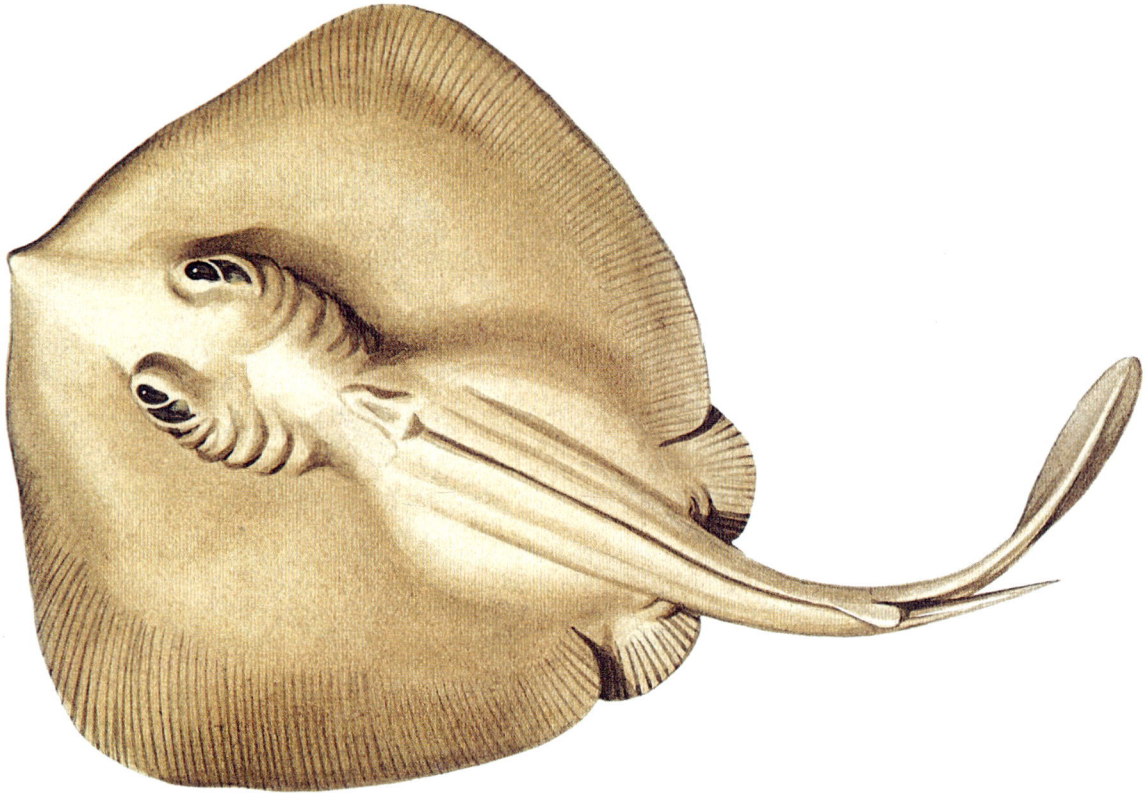

Common stingaree,
Urolophus testaceus

of the tropics. The Tasmanian numbfishes, *Narcine tasmaniensis*, are commonly taken in scallop dredges and by trawlers on soft, muddy bottoms. Numbfish have a remarkable ability to expand their mouths to take in large prey.

Common stingaree, *Urolophus testaceus*: A small, common ray also known as sand ray, plentiful in offshore, shallow sand flats and in bays and estuaries, but also found in deep water offshore. They can grow to 75 cm in length, but average around 40 cm in length. Their short tails end in flat, paddle-like terminal fins, close behind venomous spines that have a small residual posterior dorsal fin set just in front. They range in colour from a deep chocolate brown to light brown on top with pale brown margins to the wings. Larger specimens have blackish tails. The sting from the spines on their short tails can inflict wounds requiring medical help. They range from southern Queensland to New South Wales, Victoria and through Bass Strait to South Australia.

Estuary or **brown stingray,** *Dasyatis fluviorum*: An olive-brown ray, around one metre across the flaps, with clusters of tubercles on the back and numerous small spines along the dorsal line. Their tails are particularly long and have small flanges of skin running along the top and bottom behind the venomous spine or spines. Rated the best eating of the big stingaray. Common in Queensland bays and estuaries, where they cause a lot of damage to oyster leases, and in New South Wales.

Smooth stingray, *Dasyatis brevicaudata*: A dangerous ray to waders if stepped on, 2.1 metres wide and 4.2 metres long, with a very long tail. One specimen caught off Adelaide, South Australia, weighed 326 kg or 750 lb and measured 2 metres (or 6.6 ft) x 4.25 metres (or 14.2 ft). Captain Cook was so impressed by a big one that he recorded in his diary of 5 and 6 May, 1770, that he had named the place where it was caught Stingray Bay. Later Banks and Solander gathered so many plants from the same locality, they altered the name to Botany

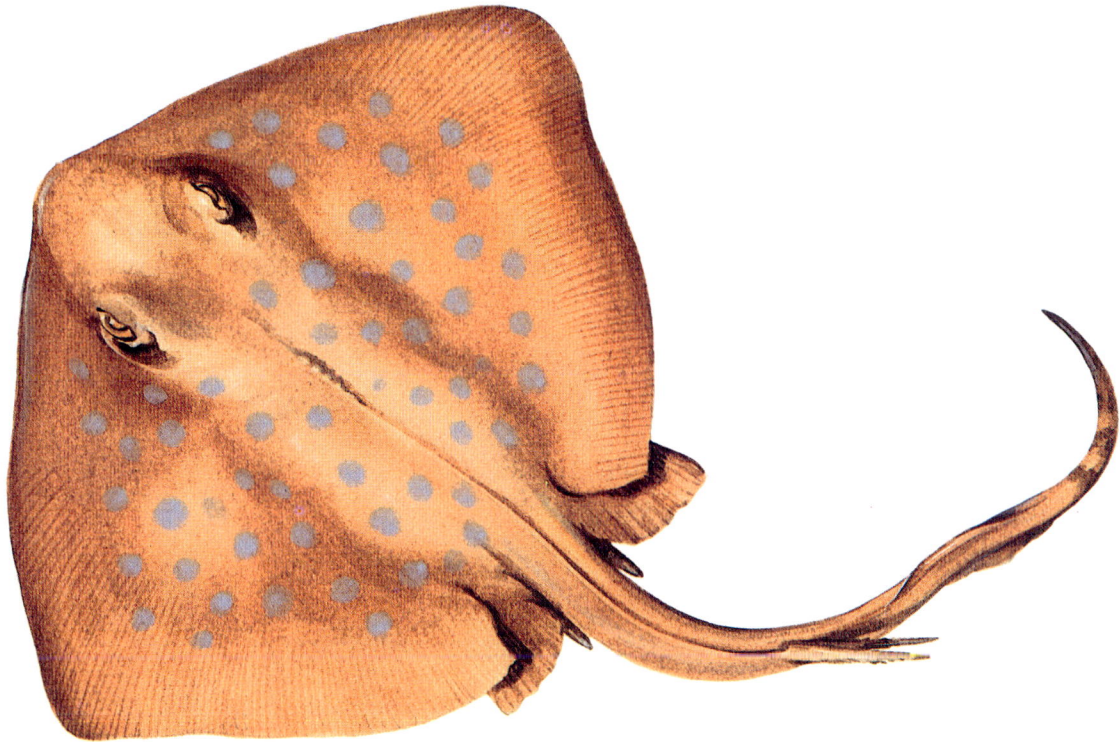

Blue-spotted stingray,
Amphotistius kuhlii

Devil ray, *Manta alfredi*

Bay. The disc of the smooth stingray is broader than it is long and the tails of captured specimens often have been mutilated. They have only one small tubercle in the middle of the back, are greyish to brown above, white below, and carry a large, nasty spine halfway down the tail. They take their name from the smooth texture of the skin. There is a cold-water variety that ranges from Western Australia across the Great Australian Bight to South Australia and Victoria and around Bass Strait into New South Wales and occasionally into southern Queensland.

Devil ray, *Manta alfredi*: The world's largest known rays, members of the *Mobulidae*, some of which reach a width of six metres. The diamond-shaped disc is wider than it is long and the flaps are pointed and wing-like. They are slow, graceful swimmers and sometimes allow divers to approach and touch them. They move by beating their wings, feeding as they swim by frightening small fish into a huddle they can sweep up with their head fins. The 1500 to 2000 teeth in strap-like bands in their lower jaws are functionless and hidden by skin. Despite their size, they are harmless to man as their short, whip-like tails carry no spikes

or spines, but there are well documented accounts of devil rays leaping clear of the surface and descending on small boats carrying men trying to harpoon them.

Manta ray, *Mobula diabolus*: Another enormous ray frequently confused with the devil ray. They are very similar in size and habit, and both prefer the coastal waters of tropical Australia from Queensland across to Western Australia. Both have their eyes set at the end of paired cephalic fins or horns, but in the manta ray these horns are curved whereas they are straight in the devil ray. Grant reports that Barrier Reef fishermen have recently discovered that manta rays will respond to berley put down for far smaller creatures, surfacing close to the berley can. Though the experience of one of these giants appearing near your boat may be frightening, Grant advises calm. The manta rays often have cobia and other much sought-after game fish sheltering beneath them, the manta rays acting as a fish attracting device (FAD).

Fiddler ray, *Trygonorhina fasciata*: Also known as guitar fishes and members of the same family (Rhinobatidae) as shovelnose rays. They can be separated from shovel-

Fiddler ray, *Trygonorhina fasciata*

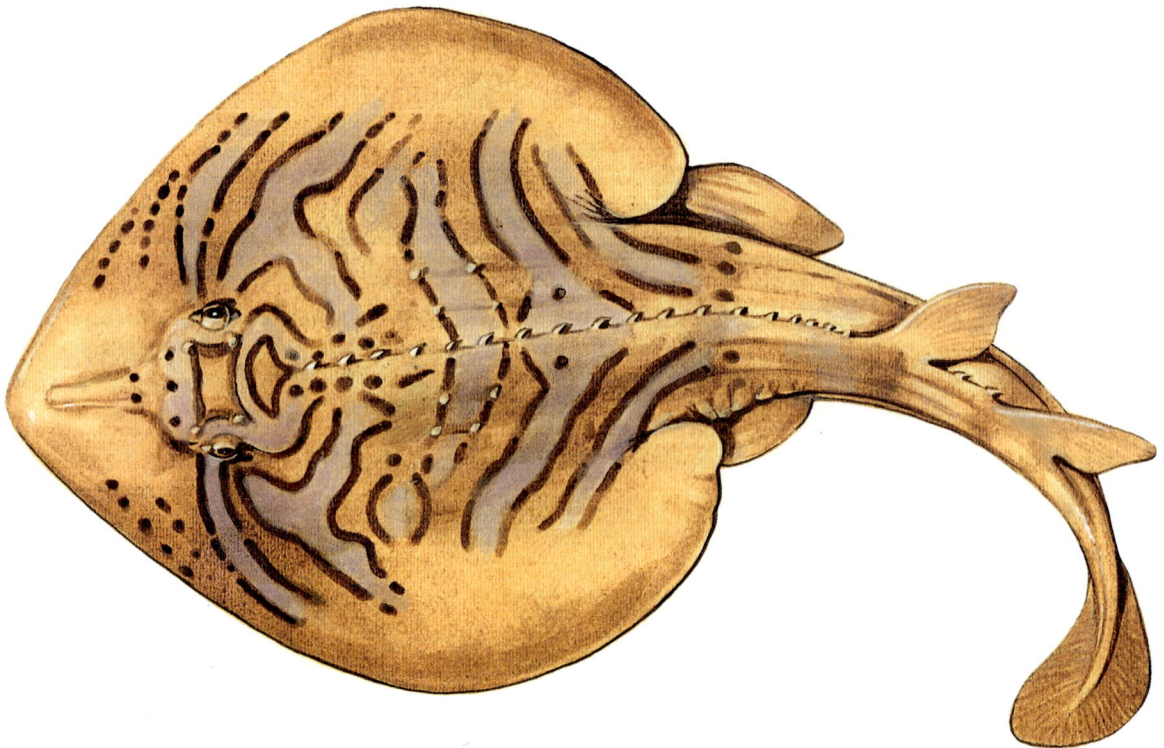

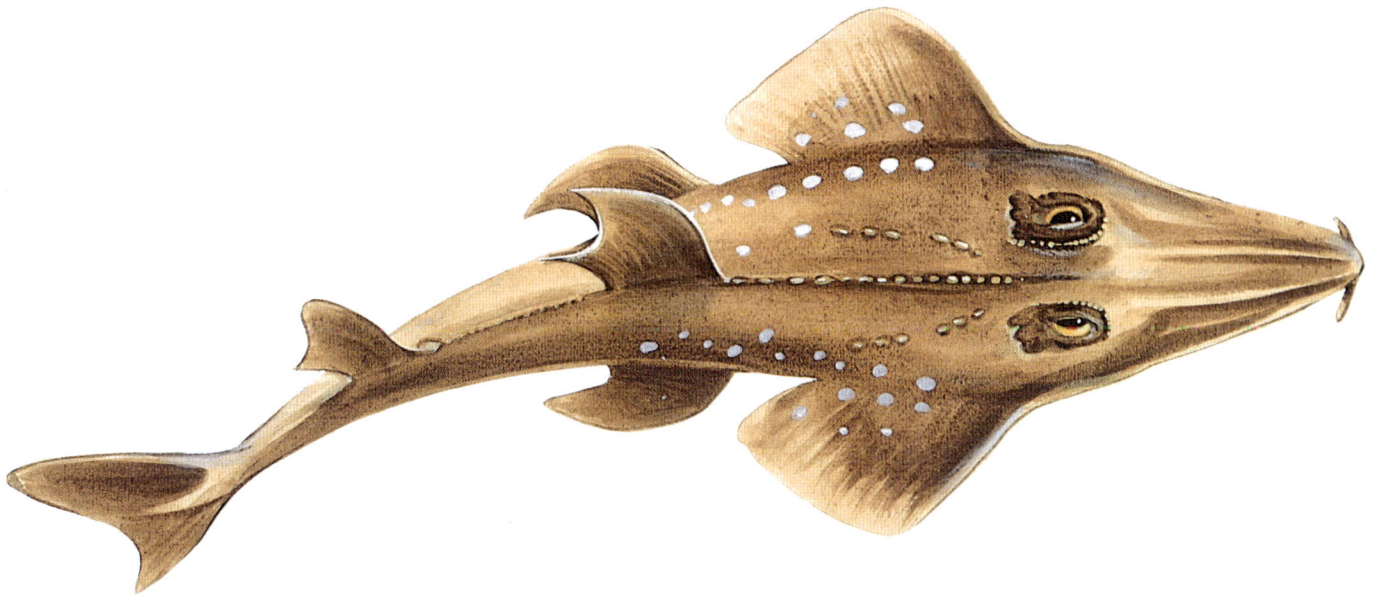

Whitespot shovelnose ray, *Rhynchobatus djiddensis*

nose rays by their snouts, which are rounded and obtusely pointed, not sharply or acutely pointed. Their bodies, usually light brown above, are elaborately patterned with darker cross-bands over the back and dark spots anteriorly. The edges of the pectorals and ventrals are lilac, the lower surfaces white. The body markings resemble a violin. The southern fiddler ray, *Trygonorhina melaleuca*, have more rounded snouts and prominent bands on the body, and lack the dark triangular markings behind the eye present in *T. fasciata*, which are restricted to southern Queensland, New South Wales, Victoria and Tasmania. The southern fiddler ranges from South Australia to southern Western Australia.

Shovelnose ray, *Aptychotrema rostrata*: A slender form with a pointed snout and triangular shape something like a guitar and prominent spines on the back, extending on to the tail. There are also spines in front of their eyes. They come closer to the shape of sharks than other rays because of their long bodies. They are mostly caught at 1.5 metres in length but mature examples reach 2.7 metres and despite their powerful tails and spines are harmless to man. They feed on crabs and other shellfish. *A. rostrata* are distributed in the inshore coastal waters of Queensland and New South Wales. The whitespot shovelnose ray, *Rhynchobatus djiddensis*, a lighter sandy colour with conspicuous white spots scattered across the top, range

across the top of Australia from Western Australia to central New South Wales. The southern shovelnose ray, *Aptychotrema vincentiana*, is a sandy coloured variety from South Australia and southern Western Australia, identified by sharply pointed snouts and upper bodies that are armed with a row of long spines behind the eyes.

Bull ray, *Myliobatus australis*: A close relative of the eagle ray, with a large angular body and a flap spread of 1.2 metres. They enjoy cruising at water level but seldom leap, mostly being content to sprawl out on sandy bottoms covered in silt. They are sandy green to deep olive in colour, with a pattern of blue bars and spots set in crescents. Their tail carries a long spine which does not connect with the body spine. Bull rays have flattened, plate-like teeth that are ideal for crushing the shellfish on which they exist. They prefer seas off southern Australia right across the Great Australian Bight into Western Australia, never losing the bull-like stare in their eyes.

Cowtail ray, *Hypolophus sephen*: An abundant ray in Australia's warmer waters, also known as fantail or banana ray and readily recognised by their very long tails, which are longer even than those of the whiptail rays. They demand careful handling as this strong tail leads back to a barb at the base, powerful enough to pierce an arm or a leg. They are closely related to the superbly marked long tail ray.

Bull ray, *Myliobatus australis*

Their tails are much heavier at the base than those of other rays, tapering down to a whip, with a deep fold of skin running along beneath half the length of the tail. They are an Indian Ocean species that enters warmer waters in northern Australia and New South Wales.

Long tail ray, *Himantura uarnak*

RAY'S BREAM   *Bramidae*

A large, compressed, mostly deep-bodied fish that is pelagic or bathypelagic in the open sea. Ray's bream have an erratic life style, occasionally appearing in large numbers when they are eagerly sought by gourmets before disappearing and becoming rare fish. They taste like chicken and have splendid flesh, but grow to only 2 kg in weight. They should not be associated in any way with the bream family, for they appear to be fish of the open ocean whose rarity ends only after violent storms. They are purplish, becoming grey after death.

FEATURES: Ray's bream, *Brama brama*, have between 80 and 90 scale rows along their uniformly silver bodies that often are bluish-black above. The fins are bluish grey, the head blunt, and the dorsal profile rises steeply above the mouth. Both dorsal fins are slightly stiff and scaled. The pectoral fins carry 19 rays. They grow to two thirds of a metre in length, but are a rather drab fish until you eat one.

FISHING TECHNIQUE: Ray's bream are periodically linefished in our deeper coastal waters, but more often are sighted stranded on our beaches than at the end of a fisherman's line. Among the little facts that are known about them is the certainty that they take squid and small fish pieces.

DISTRIBUTION: The deeper waters of New South Wales, Victoria, South Australia, and Tasmania, where museums would welcome specimens. Widespread in the Atlantic, Indian and Pacific oceans. Whitley cited an even rarer second species, *Taractichthys steindachneri*, which is known from Indo-Pacific waters, with around 45 transverse series of scales on their bodies, blue eyes, body grey, fins mostly blackish with yellowish tips to the rays. They are not related to bream of the *Sparidae* family.

Ray's bream, *Brama brama*

RED INDIANFISH *Pataecidae*

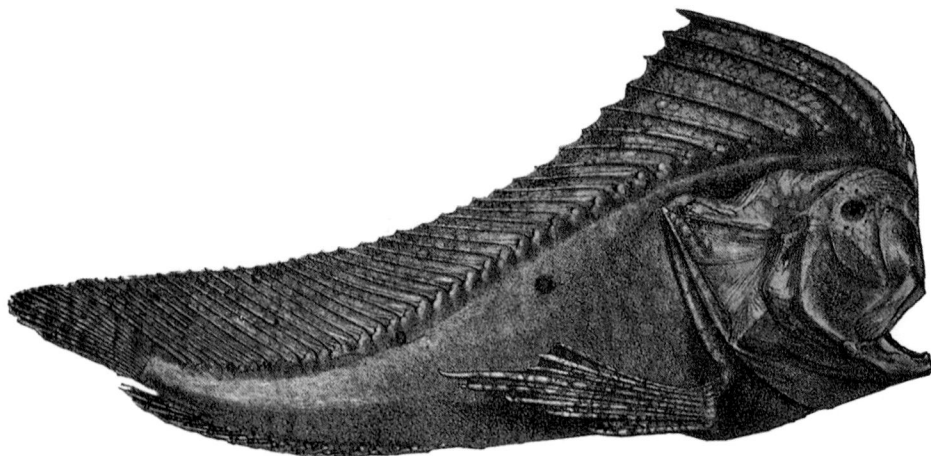

Red Indianfish, *Pataecus fronto*

The best known of Australian prowfishes, a bright red variety whose outline strongly resembles a Red Indian chief in full eagle-feather regalia. Viewed from the front they are as thin as a lath. They are also known as foreheadfish. Whitley said that in 1844 Governor George Grey sent a specimen back to England from South Australia. Fish expert Richardson named it *Pataecus fronto*, a name which suggests the likeness of this fish to the prows of ancient ships. Apart from *Pataecus fronto*, Australia's prowfishes include the whiskered prowfish, *Neopataecus waterhousii* and the warty prowfish, *Aetapcus maculatus*, whose warty skin feels like sandpaper.

FEATURES: Prowfishes are known for their absence of scales and their lack of ventral fins. They cling to rocks with finger-like fin rays, leading inactive lives, existing on crustacea, and are frequently found washed up on beaches after storms.

FISHING TECHNIQUE: Prowfishes are coldwater forms frequently seen by skin-divers lurking around the entrance to caves. They are occasionally taken on small hooks by linefishermen. Examination of their stomachs has shown many small crab nippers, which suggests these are best for bait.

DISTRIBUTION: Although they sometimes venture into southern Queensland waters Red Indianfish are more often seen in south-eastern Australia, South Australia, Tasmania and southern Western Australia. The warty prowfish is frequently taken in South Australia's gulfs, and the South Australian Museum receives regular specimens.

ROCK BLACKFISH *Girellidae*

A deep-bodied member of the same family as the luderick and the zebrafish which attracts a large number of specialist rock fishermen on the cliffs of New South Wales and Queensland. They provide outstanding sport in their efforts to free themselves when hooked, and offer first-rate table fare if they are bled and chilled on capture and not held alive in a keeper net. Dozens of dedicated rock hoppers would prefer to match their skills against a rock blackfish than against a trout or a marlin. They are wily, pugnacious fighters adept at using their large square-cut tails to lock themselves in crevices and rocky outcrops. This, coupled with the fact that they bite best in rough weather during huge ocean swells, makes them a match for the most seasoned fishermen.

FEATURES: Rock blackfish, *Girella elevata*, are uniformly blackish-brown, sometimes with a tinge of grey, and have exceptionally small heads. They grow to around 15 kg, far bigger than luderick. In matching sizes they can be distinguished from luderick by the 13 spines in the soft dorsal fin, compared with 14 or 16 spines in the luderick. They can also be separated from black drummer by the spine count—which is only 11 in the drummer.

FISHING TECHNIQUE: Blackfish are the special target of cliff-top fishermen equipped with specially designed rods. These rods keep the line clear of the edge and have powerful sidecast reels that provide the required casting distance and strength to winch up a heavy fish. Operating from eroded platforms deep in the cliffs with metal cleats on their shoes to maintain a foothold, these anglers prefer the lofty cliffs beyond Sydney Harbour's South Head where blackfish are attracted by the rich supply of cunjevoi and weeds washed off the rocks by pounding seas. In stormy weather, catches are often prolific and a lot of gear is smashed. Experts aim their baits of cabbage (green seaweed), cut crabs, and fresh cunjevoi at the shallow reefy areas or ledges where the sea breaks below them.

DISTRIBUTION: Rock blackfish range along the rocky coast of New South Wales and southern Queensland. They are not to be confused with the Western rock blackfish, *Girella tephraeops*, a slate-blue coloured fish of Western Australia, where they are known as chad.

Rock blackfish, *Girella elevata*

ROCK COD *Scorpaenidae*

Red rock cod, *Scorpaena cardinalis*, also known as scorpioncod

Australia has about 80 of the world's estimated 350 species of scorpionfish, spread through 33 genera in temperate waters. Most of them are inhabitants of the Indian or Pacific Oceans. They are not rated good food fish, because of the difficulty of getting at their flesh through needle-sharp fins and spines. The red rock cod, *Scorpaena cardinalis*, is typical of the species and need to be handled carefully. A mild sting from one can cause a burning sensation, a severe sting paralysis and swelling in the affected limb. The victim's breathing may become laboured and chest pains develop. The pain and the hampered breathing usually stop after two hours but the swelling will take a day or two to clear. Other prominent Australian scorpionfish include red firefish cod, *Pterois volitans*, a favourite with Barrier Reef visitors, the Guam scorpionfish, *Scorpaenodes guamensis*, a dark brown member of the group with dark cross bars and spots, and the painted stingfish, *Parascorpaena picta*, which has a dark green body mottled in yellow and pink.

FEATURES: The red rock cod is characterised by a bony strut or suborbital stay on their cheeks and by their nasty spines. They are capable of only short, sharp dashes for cover because they are not strong swimmers. They are plentiful up to 45 cm in length but are seldom marketed as they are rarely taken in nets. They have a variety of aliases, including Billy Bougain, fire cod, prickly heat and red scorpion cod.

FISHING TECHNIQUE: Nobody deliberately fishes for rock cod because of the inconvenience their stings cause and their heavily armoured torsos. They are hard to detect because of their ability to vary their colouring according to their habitat. They are often mistaken for stonefish and like stonefish require gloved hands or sugar bags in handling. Experienced anglers regard their capture as a good sign that splendid reef fish such as snapper are about. Grant recommends frying or boiling their flesh so that it can be picked away from the bones and used in salads like crab meat.

DISTRIBUTION: Rock cod prefer coral or rocky inshore reefs or deeper offshore terrain amid the reefs of the continental shelf, where they are often found motionless on the bottom. They are abundant off the coast of Queensland, New South Wales and Tasmania, and in New Zealand where they are known by the Maori name matua-whapuku, and frequently appear along rocky outcrops off the Western Australian coast.

ROUGHY *Trachichthyidae*

A group of wide-eyed, big-mouthed southern marine fishes with saw-like scales that includes sawbellies and sandpaper fish. They take their name from the rough, irregular arrangement of their bodies, the exposed bones in some of their heads and rasp-like sides. Some anglers claim they are a fish the Almighty did not finish but the water pressures at the extreme depths they inhabit is probably a better guide to their misshapen profile. Australian roughies include Darwin's roughy, *Gephyroberyx darwinii*, which has a grotesque vertical mouth, a head covered with ridges and granular patches, and is found at around 400 fathoms. The slender roughy, *Optivus elongatus*, is one of the few in the group within range of underwater cameramen, at whom they peer from beneath ledges. They are slightly green by day but become an overall light brown colour at night. The illustrated common roughy, *Trachichthys australis*, is reddish-brown in colour with a white vertical bar set into the cheeks. Roughies are often washed ashore after storms and are completely different in appearance and habits to the Tommy ruff.

FEATURES: Apart from their misshapen bodies, roughies are usually cinnamon-brown in body colour, with dark vertical bars on the operculum. The fins are dark-brown with white margins and the dorsal and ventral fins have white basal bars. The head is armed with a long and sharp spine over the eye and another at the lower angle of the gillcover. The tail is forked and the gape of the mouth turns strongly upwards.

FISHING TECHNIQUE: Roughies are of little angling interest because they grow to only 8 inches or 20 cm, but have been taken by line fishermen in six States, with only the Northern Territory excluded. They are often seen around crayfish pots. Those who want to claim the honour of landing this unique little fish should use cut fish, squid, octopus and crustaceans for bait and fairly strong hooks.

DISTRIBUTION: Abundant in the Great Australian Bight off Western Australia and South Australia, usually at 100 fathom depths. Also found on coastal reefs and rocks in Queensland, New South Wales, Victoria and Tasmania.

Common roughy,
Trachichthys australis

RUBBERLIPS *Haemulidae*

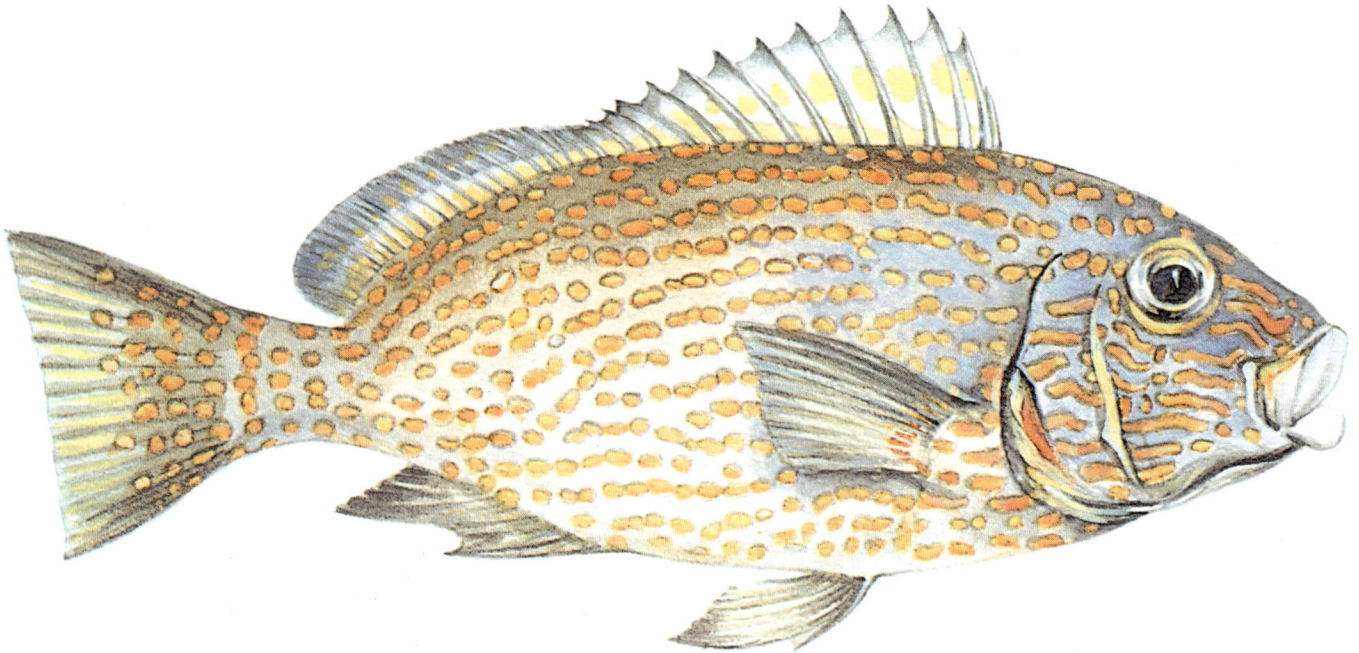

Gold spot rubberlips,
*Plectorhynchus
flavomaculatus*

A group of soft-mouthed fish related to the javelin fish also known as blubber-lips and sweetlips which have thick, fleshy lips and are often confused with morwong of the *Cheilodactylus* family and sweetlips of the *Lethrinus* family. Grant classifies them as blubberlips but they are sold commercially as rubberlips. The group, also classified as *Pomedasyide*, includes the gold-spot rubberlips, *Plectorhynchus flavomaculatus*, which are brown to olive-green in colour and have dark horizontal stripes on the upper body encircling yellowish spots; blackall, *Diagramma pictum*, which are a glittering bronze over the head and body in the water but fade to slate-grey when caught, which accounts for its other name, slate bream; and the lined rubberlips, *Plectorhynchus goldmanni*, which have a pattern of white lines running up and along their cinnamon coloured bodies.

FEATURES: Rubberlips use their fleshy mouths to vacuum the bottom of rocky reefs and headlands. Their flesh is fairly coarse but can be improved by gutting and washing in saltwater on capture. They are all graceful swimmers and usually grow to two-thirds of a metre in length. They are rarely taken by line fishermen but are easy targets for spearfishermen. Some are valued aquarium species. They use their lips to suck up vegetable matter from the bottom.

FISHING TECHNIQUE: Blackall are the best fishing in this family and will take fish baits from lines cast near to coral outcrops. They fight pugnaciously when hooked, giving a fine account of themselves for fish that seldom weigh more than 4 kg, but they are extremely disappointing table fare.

DISTRIBUTION: Mainly in warmer northern waters and the northern part of the Barrier Reef but occasionally ranging down the Queensland coastline into northern New South Wales.

SAMSON FISH *Carangidae*

Samson fish, *Seriola hippos*

A large, powerful game fish which fights ferociously when hooked. It grows to 70 kg but the current Australian Anglers' Association record is 53 kg for a specimen taken off Windy Harbour, WA, in 1974 by Charles Crombie. Samson fish *Seriola hippos* are deep-bodied fish with well-rounded heads, related to the yellowtail kingfish, but they more closely resemble turrum. They lack the long, sickle-shaped pectoral fins prominent in trevallies and off the Western Australian coast they are frequently confused with amberjack. They are also known in those waters as sea kingfish. Their upper bodies are bluish-green and silvery-gold beneath. The first dorsal fin is dark blue, the other fins greenish-gold. Juveniles have blotchy dark vertical bands on their sides. They are splendid table fish if they are bled and chilled on capture and juveniles are far better eating than adults.

FEATURES: There is a greenish-grey in their tails absent in yellowtail kingfish which are always bright yellow. Another tell-tale sign is their reddish teeth. A wavy line runs right along their flanks from gill covers to the tail, and there are only 23 to 25 rays in the second dorsal fin. Juveniles

shoal in numbers but mature samson fish seem to prefer moving about in pairs. Spearfishermen who kill one often sight another swimming around their dead mate.

FISHING TECHNIQUE: Samson fish normally are taken by snapper anglers in deep, offshore waters close to reefs and underwater cliffs. They can be taken with handlines or by deepwater trolling with rods. They search for food with great concentration and will take squid, whole fish, molluscs and octopus. They fight so savagely, high-breaking-strain lines are mandatory, along with 5/0 to 10/0 hooks, with rings to take the strain when using a fixed sinker rig. A minimum legal length of 60 cm applies in Western Australia where samson fish replace yellowtail kingfish south of Shark Bay.

DISTRIBUTION: Southern Queensland and New South Wales, occasionally in Bass Strait, and frequently off the south and south-west coasts of Western Australia. Plentiful around Rottnest Island and the Albrolhos Islands. Rare in South Australian waters.

SARATOGA   *Osteoglossidae*

Vicious, primitive native freshwater fishes whose origins can be traced back 50 million years to the Eocene age. The first Australian species was identified by explorers with Leichhardt's party in 1845. The southern saratoga, *Scleropages leichhardti*, originally was a native of the Fitzroy River system in southern Queensland, but has since been taken in rivers such as the Mary, Dawson, Burnett, and Burdekin. *Scleropages leichhardti* have also been successfully introduced into the Noosa and Brisbane river systems and dams in the Southport area. They are also known as Dawson River salmon. A second variety known as the northern saratoga, *Scleropages jardini*, occurs in rivers flowing into the Gulf of Carpentaria, across the entire Northern Territory and in New Guinea. Both are top-class sportfish.

FEATURES: The southern saratoga have compressed bodies, olive-green on top, silvery below, with exceptionally large scales that carry bright red tints which form a vertical streak. The protruding lower jaw slopes upwards and includes two short, fleshy barbels. The single dorsal fin is way back near the rounded tail and like the anal fin is black-edged and tinged with pink.

Southern saratoga,
Scleropages leichhardti

Northern saratoga are differentiated from the southern variety by the large curved red bands on the bigger scales and their darker olive green colouring.

FISHING TECHNIQUE: Both saratoga will rise readily to plugs, lures and active baits such as frogs and toads. They often take baits intended for barramundi. They usually swim in small groups with one fish striking quickly at lures cast a few metres ahead of it. They broach the water in exciting fashion as they try to shake free of the hook, a tactic with which they frequently succeed as the hooks strike bony plates in their mouth. Fishing magazines publish regular accounts of saratoga attacking large wobblers and leaving the safety of their lily-pads to slash at live frogs. Unhappily, the larger saratoga (900 mm in length and 3.5 kg in weight) are virtually inedible and only examples around half that size have any flavour. They are extremely bony.

DISTRIBUTION: Southern saratoga in the rivers listed, northern saratoga in tropical Australia and New Guinea.

SAWFISH   *Pristidae*

The largest of Australia's rays, frequently confused with the saw shark family, *Pristiophoridae*. They are mostly marine but will enter freshwater. Their snouts are flattened blades with teeth on the sides, all of them needle sharp, which they thrash around through schools of fish to disable their prey. The principal Australian varieties are the green sawfish, *Pristis zijsron*, the largest of the family which reaches 7.3 metres or 24 feet, and causes great damage to the nets of northern commercial fishermen; and Leichhardt's sawfish, *Pristis pristis*, which grows to around 2.5 metres or 8 ft 4 ins, has a distinctive lower lobe in its tailfin and five pairs of gill openings underneath the head.

FEATURES: Young sawfish are born free swimming after male and female have engaged in a hectic mating battle which often leaves their saws and bodies scarred. The saws have a gelatinous cover to protect the mother in giving birth. The body colouring in all species ranges from sandy-brown to olive-brown. They are mainly caught thrashing about in professionals' nets, but are fairly timid when encountered alone. Leichhardt's sawfish is marketed for food, and anglers seldom capture one.

DISTRIBUTION: Northern Western Australia, Northern Territory around Darwin, the Gulf of Carpentaria into Queensland and northern New South Wales. Specimens caught in New Guinea are all slightly longer than those caught off Australian coasts. They have been recorded in freshwater 240 km from the sea.

Green sawfish, *Pristis zijsron*

CEPHALOPODS: The scientific term for the group of molluscs that includes octopus, cuttlefish, and squid, all of them highly regarded as bait, and all of them are fine table fare. Australian octopuses include *Octopus australis*, the larger white, pink or brown octopus, *Octopus pallidus*, and the dreaded blue-ringed octopus, *Hapalochlaena maculosa*, which has caused at least two deaths in eastern Australian waters.

SEA DRAGONS   *Syngnathidae*

Remarkable little fishes that resemble in colour and shape the seaweed in which they live. They grow to only 30 cm and their bodies are almost three times deeper than they are wide, living in perfect safety among the weeds in which they feed on worms, minute crustaceans and other tiny creatures. They take their name from the curious leaf-like outgrowths arising from the spines on the head and body. The principal Australian species are the leafy dragon, *Phycodurus eques*, a light brown variety washed with pink with white bars across the upper body and patterns of fine white bars falling from the eyes; and the weedy sea dragon, *Phyllopteryx taeniolatus*, which have yellow bodies with brown lines and yellow spots across the body and brownish-purple lines over the chest.

FEATURES: Leafy sea dragons have a profusion of branched leafy appendages developed in clumps along the upper body and tail. The Reverend J. E. Tennison-Woods said in his Fish and Fisheries of New South Wales: "The sea dragon is the ghost of a sea horse with its winding sheet all in ribbons around it and even as a ghost it appears in the very last stages of emaciation, literally all skin and grief . . . If this is development, it stopped here only just in time; one more step and it would have been a bunch of kelp."

DISTRIBUTION: Restricted to Australia's cooler waters. The leafy sea dragon is found in South Australia and Western Australia, the weedy sea dragon in Victoria, Tasmania and South Australia.

Weedy sea dragon,
Phyllopteryx taeniolatus

SEAHORSES *Syngnathidae*

One of the strangest fish in the sea, with a head bent at an angle that gives it a horse-like appearance. Whitley says naturalists in olden times were uncertain whether to class it as a fish or an insect. There is no doubt that it is a true fish, however, despite bodies encased in armour which limits its swimming power. Seahorses have small mouths at the end of a tubular snout through which they snap up crustaceans and other food. They breath through small, tuft-like gills and swim by vibrating their pectoral and dorsal fins, moving vertically through the water with eyes working independently of each other surveying the scene, conveying a curious but comic dignity. Females lay their eggs in the pouch of the male and at hatching time, he ejects batches of tiny seahorses that head for the surface, where they swim horizontally like other fishes, until they gain strength to swim vertically in the traditional seahorse posture. Sea horses have been credited with a long list of uses. Their ashes were said to cure baldness and were also used as medicine for horses.

FEATURES: Seahorses usually are brown to blackish in colour but some are green. They have curled, prehensile tails which they use for clinging to seaweed. They can all change colour to match the weeds in which they hide. The best known Australian species are the illustrated common seahorse, *Hippocampus whitei*, which has a coronet on its head, the pot-bellied seahorse, *Hippocampus abdominalis*, a coldwater variety with a permanently rounded belly, the spotted seahorse, *Hippocampus kuda*, which has a short, central body ridge that does not reach below the dorsal fin, the short-headed seahorse, *Hippocampus breviceps*, which has a mass of small spots over the head and body and grows to only 75 cm, and the low-crowned seahorse, *Hippocampus planifrons*, a warm-water variety that averages around 100 mm in length but lacks the ornate crown of its relatives.

DISTRIBUTION: All States have at least one variety in their waters, with the Western Australian seahorse, *Hippocampus angustus*, known only in the west and tropical north.

Common seahorse,
Hippocampus whitei

SEA PIKE *Dinolestidae*

The long-finned pike, found only in Australian marine waters is no relation of the European pike, which are freshwater fish of the family *Escodidae*. Until 1971 they were included in the Australian family *Apogonidae*, but since then they have had individual status, endemic to Australia. They are not to be confused with the yellow-finned sea pike, *Sphyraena obatusata*; barracuda, *Sphyraena barracuda*; or snook, *Australuzza novaehollandiae*, which have similar pointed heads and have more commercial importance than *Dinolestidae*. Like the *Sphyraenidae*, however, they have voracious appetites, preying on schools of small fish. They are splendid sporting fish and will leap well clear of the water when hooked on light tackle.

FEATURES: Our lone *Dinolestidae* has a cylindrical body and is an extremely robust fish with an elongate profile and a large mouth with canine teeth. They differ from other cardinal fishes in having only one anal spine and 25 to 28 rays, 17 to 19 dorsal rays and an auxillary scale at the pelvic base. They are golden brown in colour above, silvery below, with a yellow tail, and reach a length of around 51 cm. Their mouths have a large gape, extending almost to the front edge of the eye, and the lower jaw is considerably longer than the upper jaw. Both the head and body are covered with moderate sized cycloid scales, which are larger and denser on the lateral line.

FISHING TECHNIQUE: Long-finned pike are mostly taken trolling, some on jiggled strip bait. They are not hard to catch when they gather over shallow inshore reefs in big schools, but wire traces are advisable. The art of catching a good haul depends on careful timing of the strike while they are making their run with the bait, and strong pressure that prevents the pike's teeth slashing through the line. Small sea pike are outstanding bait for Spanish mackerel and cobia. Barrier Reef fishermen use three or four on ganged hooks with the first hook set under the lower jaw. Sea pike are also known as sennit and yellowtail, names that are thankfully fading out.

DISTRIBUTION: Western Australia, South Australia, Victoria, Tasmania and in the colder waters of Queensland. They have been caught at the rate of one a minute when schooling off Queensland but they are not rated highly as table fare.

Long-finned pike, *Dinolestes lewini*

SERGEANT BAKER *Aulopidae*

Prettily-marked, pike-like fishes, the sole Australian representatives of a group of grinners and lizard fishes. They are said to have been named after a sergeant who first spotted them when the First Fleet sailed in. *Aulopus purpurissatus* are a striking fish when first encountered because of their vivid colouring but the excitement soon disappears when they are opened up and they give off a strong, odious smell. Their flesh is white and firm but their odour ruins their appeal as table fish. They grow to a third of a metre and in Western Australia cannot be caught until they reach a legal limit of 30 cm.

FEATURES: Their bodies are splashed in purple, red and orange, sometimes with crimson, and their caudal and dorsal fins are splashed with yellow. All the scales are edged in red and the tail is strongly forked and mottled in orange and gold. The high dorsal fin is made up entirely of soft rays rather than hard spines. Slender filaments grace the high dorsal fin in males. The eyes are orange and crimson. They have similar compressed heads to gurnards and live very similar lives on rocky bottoms.

FISHING TECHNIQUE: Mostly caught on snapper gear by fishermen using lines up to 9.07 kg breaking strain and 2/0 to 6/0 hooks. Handlines land just as many as rods. They bite on all kinds of cut fish, crustaceans, and occasionally on squid and octopus. They lurk in weeds and rocks, so the best rig is one with a sinker snapped on the end to take the line down, with two or three hooks spaced back along the line, two or three metres apart.

DISTRIBUTION: Temperate Australian seas, down the southern Queensland coast to New South Wales and Victoria, South Australia and Western Australia, and northern Tasmania. They seldom stay north of Busselton in Western Australia.

Sergeant Baker, *Aulopus purpurissatus*

SHARKS

Of the 250 varieties of shark distributed around the world, around 90 are found in Australia. Some of them are recognised as the most dangerous known to man, one of them is the biggest creature in the sea, and another the heaviest fish consistently taken by rod and reel. Sharks' teeth have been dredged from the ocean floor around Australia that were 15 cm or six inches long, which scientists said must have come from sharks 24.24 metres or 80 feet long. Australian newspapers headline shark attacks so frequently that even the species acknowledged as harmless create fear when they appear off our beaches.

Technically, sharks are not fish at all because they have bodies of gristle and cartilage instead of bone. They do not carry scales but are encased in a tough skin which in most cases is studded with rough little denticles. Unlike fish, sharks have no air bladder to give them hydrostatic stability. They cannot float easily or swim backwards which is why they swim round and round in our aquariums, but they are almost the perfect shape for speedy swimming,

pushing their huge frames through the water for vast distances.

They have several gill slits on each side of the head instead of one and they seldom breathe through their nostrils. They take in water for this purpose through spiracles, small holes behind the mouth, or through the mouth, and the water passes over the oxygen-absorbing membranes of the gills before it is discharged through the gill slits. They also differ from bony fish in their method of breeding. All have internal fertilisation and some produce their young alive and sufficiently developed to take care of themselves. Tiger sharks have been found to contain 56 well-developed embryos in their ovaries. Wobbegongs have been dissected to disclose 37 perfectly-formed young. This contrasts sharply with bony fish which eject their ova into the water where it is fertilised. Some sharks produce eggs but they are fertilised internally by copulation.

There is undoubtedly more fishing for sharks in Australia than in any other country. In America, sharks are so docile

PARTS OF A SHARK

(This is a composite illustration—no shark has all the features we have shown)

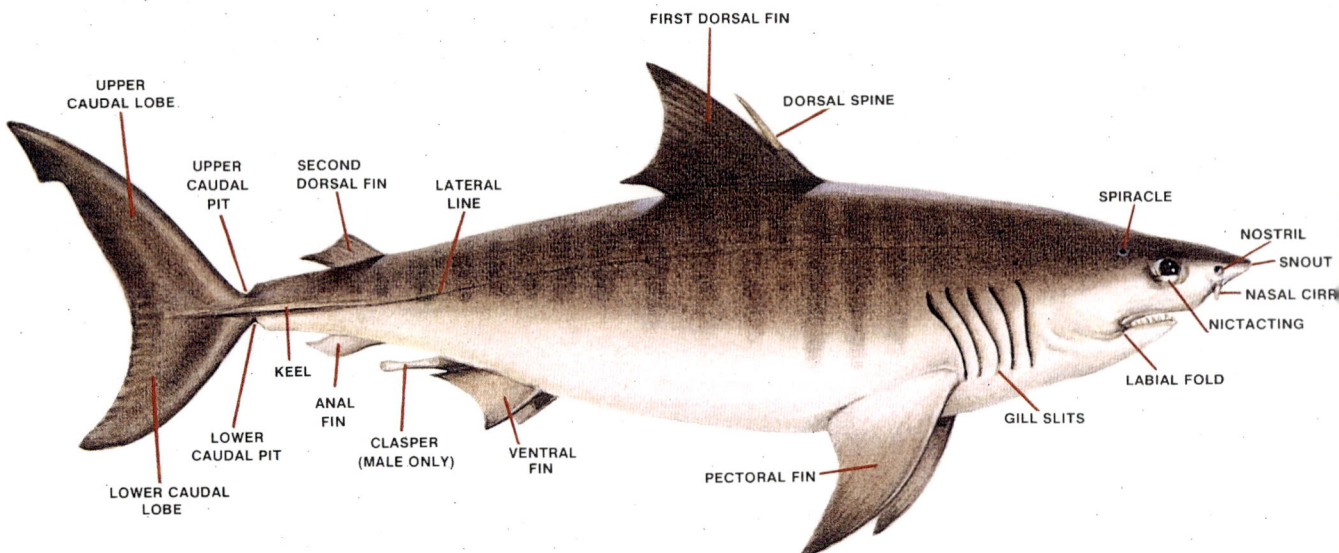

Port Jackson shark,
*Heterodontus portus
jacksoni*

they are not rated game fish, which amazes any Australian who has fought a tiger, mako, white or whaler shark. Eight sharks weighing more than an imperial ton have been caught in Australian waters, but to the Americans, these catches do not count because the weight of a shark can be too easily increased by chumming, a form of berleying with a bullock's head, a dead kangaroo or the side of a sheep. Australia tried to fall in line with this idea by banning sharks caught near the old whaling station at Albany, Western Australia, where sharks regularly fed on offal. But it seems unjust that a feat such as Alf Dean's capture of a 1208.38 kg or 2,779 lb white shark off Ceduna, South Australia in 1960 has not had world-wide recognition.

Port Jackson shark, *Heterodontus portus jacksoni*: One of the oldest of all sharks, said by some scientists to be living fossils. They are also known as bullhead, oyster crusher, and by the aboriginal name jabbigaw. They were discovered by members of the First Fleet and have attracted interest ever since as relics of a bygone age, living representatives of sharks found in carboniferous rocks. They live off molluscs, crustaceans and sea eggs, feeding mainly at night and have no value for anglers.

FEATURES: The mouth is small, the teeth pointed, often cusped in front for grasping food, with enlarged crushers at the back. They are grey to light brownish in colour with a dark blotch on the snout and eyes. There are a series of blackish stripes, rather like a harness, on the body. The head is blunt, the shark's disposition subdued.

DISTRIBUTION: South Queensland, New South Wales, Victoria, South Australia to southern Western Australia.

Wobbegong shark, *Orectolobus maculatus*: Harmless unless disturbed by waders, this variety has fang-like teeth that have ripped a leg off fishermen. They lurk among rocks, under wharves, in deep and shallow water, where they merge with the surroundings. They feed on crabs, small lobsters, octopuses and sometimes cause problems by straying into lobster pots. The flesh is edible and clean and because of its pretty markings the skin has been used for handbags and shoes but they have no attraction for anglers.

FEATURES: Brown, heavily ornamented brown bodies and faint cross bands. All fins and the tail are brightly spotted.

DISTRIBUTION: Southern Queensland, New South Wales, Victoria, South Australia, Tasmania and Western Australia. Other species of wobbegong have a more restricted range.

227

Wobbegong shark,
Orectolobus maculatus

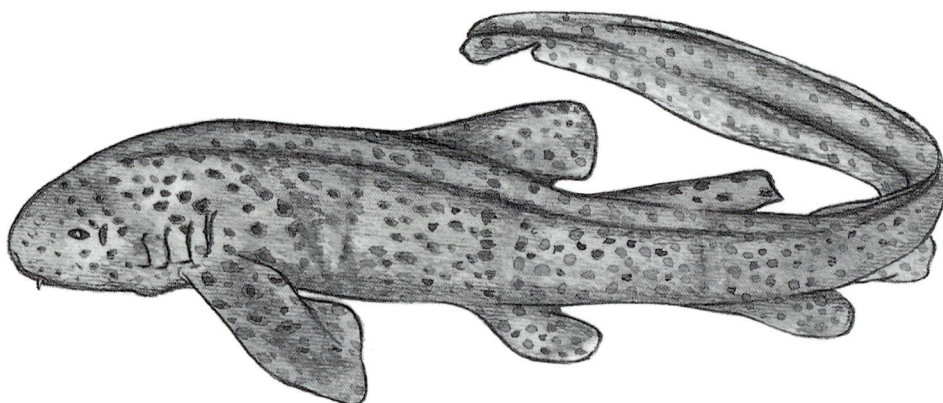

Zebra shark, *Stegostoma fasciatum*

Zebra shark, *Stegostoma fasciatum*: A harmless, attractively marked shark easily recognised by the exceptional length of the black-ridged tail fin and the large pectoral fins. They hug the sea bottom, feeding on molluscs through their very small mouths and seldom move about with any speed, but they provide good colour photography for underwater cameramen and make appealing aquarium exhibits.

FEATURES: Young zebra sharks are covered in pale stripes across their dark brown bodies, but as they mature the stripes fade and are replaced by numerous dark blotches and the body colour turns to a dusky yellow. They are narrow-bodied sharks that sometimes reach 3 metres in length but have little interest for anglers.

DISTRIBUTION: Western Australia, northern Australia, Queensland, down to Sydney.

Whale shark, *Rhincodon typus*: The largest shark in the world, reaching 15 metres in

length but harmless to man. Their mouths are on their heads and not underneath as in most sharks and they feed on small floating creatures like jellyfish, crabs and young fish. They were first identified in New South Wales waters in 1938, having previously been regarded as a tropical variety. Skindivers are regularly photographed climbing about their vast frames underwater.

FEATURES: The back and side are greenish-grey, with numerous white spots and there are several white lines on the sides of the head and body. There are several interesting keels or ridges along the sides. The eyes are small and set just behind the mouth. The teeth are small and pointed and there are about 6,000 in each jaw.

DISTRIBUTION: Of no interest as sports fish, the whale shark's range has been confined to Australia's east and south coasts, though they have been sighted as far away as Table Bay, South Africa. Often seen in New Guinea.

Basking shark, *Cetorhinus maximus*: The second biggest shark in the sea but somewhat smaller than the whale shark and equally harmless. Sometimes seen in Australian waters floating idly on its back, drifting with the currents, feeding on small crustaceans and krill. Recognised by the gill openings, which stretch completely around the neck and separate it from other sharks.

FEATURES: The basking shark's gill arches resemble very long teeth and appear to act in the same way that whalebone does in the mouth of a whale, straining the seawater for tiny living things upon which

the basking shark subsists. The head is pointed, the mouth huge, and in the young, the snout is very long and bizarre in shape. They are blackish-brown on top, lighter below. They grow to more than 6 metres and as long as 11 metres. Australian records are hazy but European basking sharks have weighed almost 3,478 kg or 8,000 lb.

DISTRIBUTION: Victoria, Tasmania, New South Wales, South Australia, Western Australia.

Bronze whaler, *Carcharhinus brachyurus*: A dangerous shark that grows to three metres

Basking shark,
Cetorhinus maximus

Black whaler shark,
Carcharinus macrurus

Grey nurse shark,
Carcharias taurus

in length and 353 kg in weight. They take their name from their bright bronze colouring on the whole of the top of the body. Fishermen often refer to how they shine "like a new penny". Their bodies are more rounded than in common whalers and they have no hesitation in entering harbours and inlets. Even experts have trouble distinguishing between Australia's numerous whalers.

FEATURES: The teeth are broad at the base in both upper and lower jaws, serrated in both jaws, with the cusps very narrow in the lower jaw and much broader in the upper jaw. They have 32 teeth in a row in each jaw compared with 30 in the common whaler. A grey or creamy strip appears along the sides from the eyes, and the lower colouring of the body is also creamy white.

DISTRIBUTION: Southern Queensland, New South Wales, Tasmania, South Australia, Western Australia.

Grey nurse shark, *Carcharias taurus*: A slow-moving creature of sleepy habits often wrongly described as a man-eater. There is no evidence of a grey nurse attacking humans. The misconception may be the result of the grey nurse's fearsome teeth, which can be protruded to grasp their prey.

FEATURES: The grey nurse shark is easily identified by the large dorsal fins, the first slightly in advance of the ventral fins, and by the long pointed, awl-like teeth, with two small spine-like cusps on either side. The third eyelid is not present in this shark,

and it has five gill slits in front of the pectoral fin. Their colour is variable, either a dull grey or pale brown above, turning to a silvery-grey below. They average between 90 and 160 kg in weight and between 2 and 3 metres in length. This is an extremely docile shark when hooked and is easily pulled to the surface on a handline.

DISTRIBUTION: Queensland, Western Australia, Victoria, South Australia and New South Wales, where they are fully protected as an endangered species.

Blue whaler, *Prionace glauca*: An uncommon variety also known as the blue shark, seldom caught by game fishermen. They grow to at least 3 metres in Australian waters and are closely related to a European species that reach 4 metres. They are a wide-ranging, oceanic shark with the first dorsal fin set well back towards the centre of the body. They sometimes appear in the nets of Tasmanian and Victorian professional fishermen.

FEATURES: Easily recognised by their unusually long, floppy, scythe-like pectoral fins and the manner in which they swim with the dorsal fin and tail-tip out of the water. They have elongate blue bodies.

DISTRIBUTION: New South Wales, Victoria, Tasmania, South Australia and Western Australia, but very rarely in Queensland.

Porbeagle shark, *Lamna nasus*: A fast, streamlined shark similar in appearance to the mako but not rated highly by game fishermen because it lacks the mako's superb fighting qualities. Also known as Beaumaris shark and mackerel shark, and one of the most common New Zealand sharks. Porbeagle sharks feed on schooling fish. Their name is of Cornish origin.

FEATURES: Porbeagles are stouter in the body than the mako. They are slaty grey on top and sides and yellowish or silver beneath. The teeth are their main identifying feature as they are much smaller than the mako's and far broader, with two small cusps at the base. The eyes are deep green while those of the mako are dark, almost black.

DISTRIBUTION: Porbeagle sharks are found in Western Australia, Tasmania, Victoria, and New South Wales.

Tiger shark, *Galeocerdo cuvier*: A large dangerous shark recorded up to 5.7 metres in length in Australian waters. They are, with the white shark and the whaler, one of Australia's proven man-eaters, rated by game fishermen as a formidable opponent not easily conquered. They are known to have straightened hooks to escape. They

Porbeagle shark, *Lamna nasus*

Tiger shark, *Galeocerdo cuvier*

Scalloped hammerhead,
Sphyrna lewini

are often caught at 450 to 600 kg in weight and from 4.5 to 6 metres in length. Examination of their stomach has revealed whole dogs, tin cans, turtles, car tyres, dolphin, lobsters, birds and even parts of crocodiles.

FEATURES: Tiger sharks take their name from the dark bars that cross their greyish-green bodies vertically, with a creamy underbelly. The bars disappear with age but return for a few moments when tiger sharks are killed. They have distinctive teeth with saw-like edges that lean sideways and are dark grey in colour with a tinge of brown. They have five gill openings, the last two above the junction of the pectoral fin. The eyes are fixed and staring and cannot be closed.

DISTRIBUTION: Northern Australia and all around the southern States. Many of the largest specimens have been taken off Sydney Heads.

Hammerhead sharks: Curious sharks with heads that form a hammer into the ends of which the eyes are set. They belong to

the family *Sphyrnidae*, nine of which are distributed around the world, four of them in Australia. They are generally sighted in offshore coastal regions but will enter bays and harbours. They are proven man-killers elsewhere in the world but there is no record of them being involved in a fatal Australian attack. They reach 5 metres in length and have been reported with hammers almost 2 metres wide. Australian hammerheads include the scalloped hammerhead, *Sphyrna lewini*, which has an unusually high first dorsal fin and by the five depressions, one of them in the centre, on the rounded leading edge of the hammer; the narrow-headed hammerhead, *Eusphyrna blochii*, which takes its name from the narrow hammer that curves towards the centre, a variety found in Australia's warmer waters; the smooth-headed hammerhead, *Sphyrna zygaena*, which lacks any notch or identification on the hammer and is found in our colder seas; and the great hammerhead, *Sphyrna mokarran*, the largest of the hammerheads with a world-wide distribution which has been implicated in several attacks on man.

FEATURES: The four Australian hammer-heads can be separated by differences in their heads such as variations in the nasal groove, the shape and number of teeth. They feed on fish, stingrays, and small sharks, and they are one of the few sharks that will take a lure or a trolled bait. They are viviparous, with an umbilical attachment between the mother and young in the uterus.

DISTRIBUTION: All the hammerheads found in Australia prefer the warmer waters of northern Western Australia, the Northern Territory, but have been recorded well down the east and west coasts in summer.

White shark, *Carcharodon carcharius*: The largest of the man-eating sharks, credited with being the most ferocious monster in the sea. They grow to 6 metres in length and have been caught up to 1207 kg in weight. But larger specimens estimated to have weighed more than 2000 kg have escaped capture after being hooked. They appear to live most of their lives in the same area, eating almost anything from seals to dogs and other sharks. The great shark fisherman, Alf Dean, lost one off Ceduna, South Australia, in 1958 and in 1960 landed the same shark, still with his hook and trace in its jaws. Dean calculated the two encounters with this shark were only about two kilometres apart. Museums throughout the world display specimens of the white shark's jaws and one in London's

British Museum shows a man sitting inside the jaws. The threat they present to anybody in the water is underlined by a lightening-fast swimming speed and a highly developed sense of smell.

FEATURES: Usually greyish above and white below, but variable from blue-grey to black and according to water temperatures. Their large, regular, triangular teeth with their serrated edges are characteristic.

DISTRIBUTION: Southern Queensland, New South Wales, Victoria, South Australia, Western Australia and Tasmania. The heaviest taken so far occurred in Streaky Bay, South Australia, and scientists head there when they want to study the great whites in their "home" environment.

Thresher shark, *Alopias superciliosus*: Easiest of all sharks to recognise because its tail is longer than the head and body together. The mouth of the thresher is small and the stomach has been found to contain rather small fish. Apparently the thresher uses its tail to beat the water and frighten small fish into a more compact mass or it stuns a particular fish before devouring it. There appear to be two groups in the world and many variations of these. One form has small eyes, the other large eyes. Both are found in Australian waters. They are a particularly active group in the north island of New Zealand where most of the world records for this species have been set. They are also known as fox shark or by the Maori

White shark,
Carcharodon carcharius

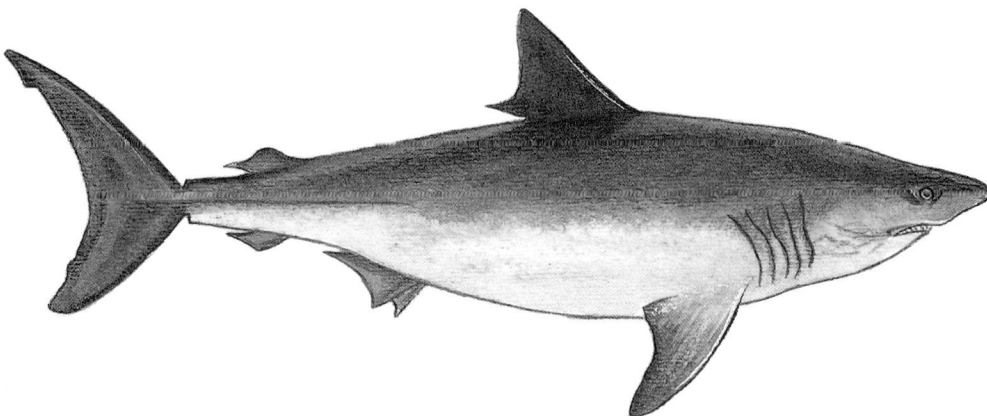

Thresher shark, *Alopias superciliousus*

Gummy shark, *Mustelus antarcticus*

name mango-ripi. There have been frequent scientific discussions on whether thresher sharks attack whales with a whip-like movement of their tails.

FEATURES: Apart from their long upper caudal lobe (tail), the thresher is characterised by its remarkably small and harmless teeth, all of them pointed, with rooted bases. The second dorsal and anal fins are very small in comparison with the first dorsal and ventral fins. They have no value to Australians as table fare but their fins are sold commercially in Japan, Taiwan and Uruguay.

DISTRIBUTION: The small-eyed *Alopias vulpinus* is more common in Australia and ranges from Queensland to New South Wales, Victoria, Tasmania, South Australia and Western Australia. The big-eyed thresher, *Alopias superciliosus*, is a deepwater variety less frequently seen.

Gummy shark, *Mustelus antarcticus*: Harmless members of the shark family *Carcharhinidae*, also known as sweet William, and in the markets as flake. They are taken in large numbers by commercial boats using nets or long lines and their flesh is sold as "boneless fillets". They live on sea bottoms, feeding on crabs and shellfish which they crush with their smooth, flattened teeth and are a mainstay of the fish and chips trade in southern Australia. They are closely related to the whiskery shark, *Furgaleus macki*, which is found in South Australia, Western Australia, Tasmania and Victoria.

FEATURES: The teeth are not erect or pointed but are arranged in a pavement, with each tooth flattened. The dorsal fin originates above the inner angle of the pectoral fin. The first to third gill slits are longer than the fourth and fifth. Ash-grey in colour with some lighter patches, they average about a metre in length.

DISTRIBUTION: South Queensland, New South Wales, Victoria, Tasmania, South Australia, and Western Australia. They are most abundant in the Great Australian Bight.

Mako shark, *Isurus oxyrinchus*: The fastest of all sharks, a streamlined speedster with a bullet-shaped snout and a highly developed lateral keel merging into the tail. They have tremendous fighting qualities and are the only shark the Americans rate a game fish. They were known for many years in Australia as blue pointer but from the start of game fishing in Australia in the early 1930s, the name mako was adapted, a Maori word used throughout the world. The teeth of the mako were highly prized by Maori warriors who wore them in their ears. They are sharks of the open seas, preferring colder water to tropical seas. They are gun-barrel blue on top changing to white below. They grow to a length of 4 metres and a weight of 450 kg.

FEATURES: Five moderately large gill slits are present, a large first dorsal fin and a very small second dorsal. The teeth are larger, slender and awl-like, similar to those in the grey nurse shark but lacking the two cusps on either side of the base. They are known to attack boats and even snap at rotating propellors, and are among the few sharks who jump clear of the water in an effort to escape capture. They readily take trolled baits and feed on fish and squid, which they swallow whole.

DISTRIBUTION: Southern Queensland, New South Wales, Victoria, Tasmania, South Australia and Western Australia, mainly well offshore in deep water but occasionally near the coast.

School shark, *Galeorhinus galeus*: Also known as tope or snapper shark. They are small, harmless, gummy sharks usually caught at around one metre in length. They are a pest to game fishermen because of their habit of rushing snapper being pulled in on a line, severing them just behind the head. They are named as the young of almost every shark, but they are easily identified by their tails, which are large on one side of the fork and short on the other, giving the appearance of a tail and a half. They are extremely fertile and bear up to 35 young at a time. Tagging records indicate they live for 40 years. They are an important commercial fish in Tasmania.

FEATURES: The long snout is equal to the width of the mouth. The teeth are coarsely serrated and depressed. The gill slits are very small. The first dorsal fin is equidistant from the pectoral and ventral fins. The ventral originates well behind the

Mako shark, *Isurus oxyrinchus*

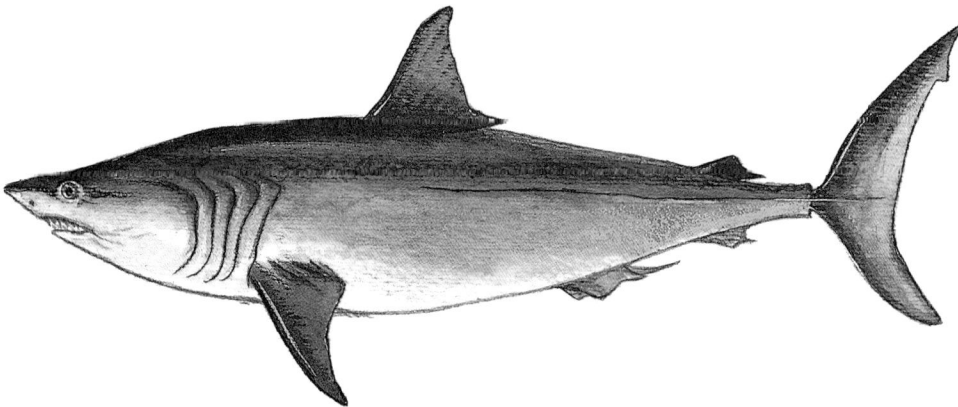

School shark,
Galeorhinus galeus

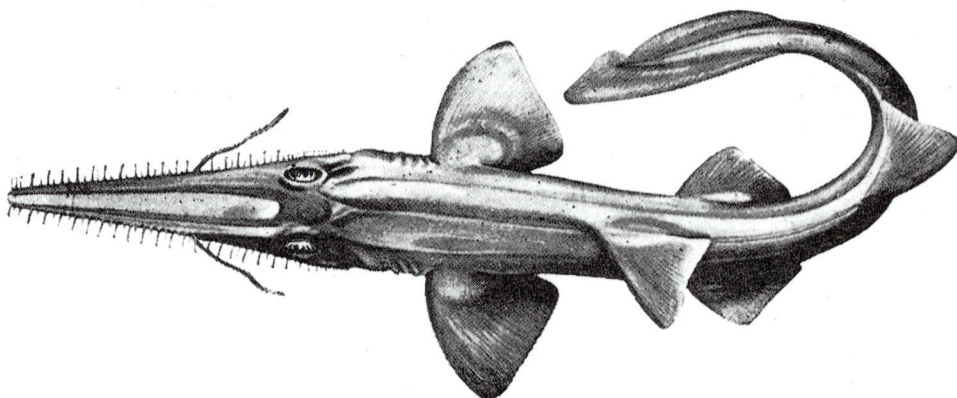

Saw shark, *Pristiophorus nudipinnis*

middle of the body. They are slate-blue or bluish-grey on top, lighter below and none of the fins carry dark marks.

DISTRIBUTION: Queensland, New South Wales, Victoria, Tasmania, South Australia and Western Australia.

Saw shark, *Pristiophorus cirratus* and *Pristiophorus nudipinnis*: Members of the shark family *Pristiophoridae*, saw sharks are fairly common in deep water and are frequently taken by Australian trawlers when their blade-like snouts become entangled in nets. The snout has teeth along its edges and acts like a saw. Saw fishes possess similar snouts but are separated from saw sharks by their two fleshy barbels in the middle of the snout. Saw sharks feed on crustaceans and some fish and use their snout to lash from side to side, cutting to pieces any fish in the way. Despite this they are of no threat to man. When their heads

are cut off, they can be filleted to provide excellent food sometimes sold as flake or fish fillets.

FEATURES: Saw sharks have gill slits along the side of the body as do all sharks, whereas saw fishes have the gill slits underneath and are classified as rays. Saw sharks lack an anal fin and the tail has a much reduced lower lobe. Baby saw fish are born with their saws folded back so that they do not cause damage to the mother.

DISTRIBUTION: New South Wales, Queensland, from Caloundra southwards, Victoria, Tasmania, South Australia, and Western Australia.

Seven-gilled shark, *Notorynchus cepedianus*: A sandy-grey shark with seven gill slits from which it takes its name. Known in New Zealand, where it is considered harmless, by the Maori name tuatini. In Tasmania it is marketed commercially as Tasmanian tiger shark, and in South Australia it is known as seven-gilled or ground shark. South Australians rate them dangerous to man. They have wide heads with a broadly rounded snout and a single dorsal fin. Their teeth are remarkably dissimilar in the two jaws; jagged and cusped in the upper and comb-like in the lower. There is a single median tooth in the upper jaw. They grow to 3 metres but average around 2 metres and their smooth skin often is strikingly spotted in red and yellow. Seven-gilled sharks range around Tasmania, Victoria and New South Wales and are abundant around Kangaroo Island, basking along the bottom in shallow waters.

Great blue shark, *Prionace glauca*: A striking blue whaler that is easily identified by its exceptionally long, scythe-like pectoral fin. They resemble the mako but their teeth are small serrated triangles in both jaws, whereas those of the mako are like sharply-pointed daggers and can be seen even when the mako's mouth is closed. The great blue shark is vividly blue above, white below and the junction of these colours is well marked. The first dorsal is nearer the ventrals than the pectorals. They have been recorded up to 3.8 metres in length but some biologists claim they reach 6 metres. They are viviparous, one female producing 46 young. They are seldom seen in Queensland but are frequently reported by game fishermen, swimming on the surface with their dorsal fin and tail clear of the water, in New South Wales, Victoria, Tasmania, South Australia, and Western Australia.

Draughtboard shark, *Cephaloscyllium nascione*: A small, prettily-marked shark easily spotted by the draughtboard-like pattern of irregular dark bars across their greyish-brown backs. They prefer deep waters and are rarely taken by anglers but frequently appear in trawlers' nets. They have a close relative in New Zealand where fishermen claim they bark like a dog. Cray fishermen call this shark sleepy Joe because of its reluctance to move when tipped out of crayfish pots. They defend themselves by gulping down mouthfuls of water which inflates the stomach and leads to their other name, swell sharks. They are closely related to the spotted swell shark, *Cephaloscyllium laticep*, which has many dark-brown spots across the back, and the western swell shark, *Cephaloscyllium fasciatum*, which has rich brown bands on a much paler body.

They grow to two metres but generally are smaller. Found in all States.

Tawny shark, *Nebrius concolor*: A tropical variety that grows to three metres in length and is known for its great curiosity. Some skindivers in Australia's northern waters rate them a pest. They cough and spurt water when brought to a boat and their stomachs often reveal vast quantities of tiny blue sprats. The tawny shark took a long time to be identified because no specimens were forwarded to museums in the south for classification. The famous professional shark fisherman Norman Caldwell referred to it as "Madam X", a name which stuck, although anglers thought spitting shark more appropriate. Females carry up to 300 eggs in onion-shaped cases, which are all laid at one time. The skin is covered in coarse denticles, sandy-brown in colour. They grow to three metres but are mostly spotted resting on sandy bottoms at around two metres. They range through Queensland Barrier Reef waters, north to Torres Strait and New Guinea and on to north-western Australia.

Epaulette shark, *Hemiscyllium ocellatum*: An elongate shark with a skin of polished denticles and a characteristic black spot above each pectoral fin. This provides the shark with badges or epaulettes. The slim, snake-like brownish body is studded by black spots, but the mouth is too small to take a hook. They are oviparous and harmless and by day when they grope about the bottom of coral reefs with their eyes half-shut they appear blind and can be taken by the tail. At night they are far more active, foraging about reef flats for shrimps, crabs and other shellfish. They grow to one metre in length and are abundant on the reef flats of Queensland, north and north-west Australia.

Brown-banded catshark, *Chilocyllium punctatum*: Elongate little sharks with a ridge of hard tissue along the back behind the first dorsal fin in which the fourth and fifth gill slits are unusually close together. The pupils of their eyes contract to a vertical, cat-like look under bright light. Their rusty, brownish bodies are marked with heavy dark bands in the young but the bands fade with age and mature species are uniformly pale brown. They grow to just over one metre and are harmless to humans. Juveniles are popular in aquariums. The eggs are laid in tiny shell

Seven-gilled shark,
Notorynchus cepedianus

Great blue shark,
Prionace glauca

cases which carry tufts of string-like membranes that anchor them to rocks and crevices while they hatch. Brown-banded catshark range through northern Australia from the Gulf of Carpentaria down the Barrier Reef coastline as far south as Moreton Bay and are common in Western Australia's warmer seas.

Sharp-toothed shark, *Negaprion acutidens*: A tropical species taken along the inshore coastline of northern Australia this shark has become notorious for wrecking crabbing pots and taking baits intended for small game fish. Their second dorsal fin is almost as large as the first, and the teeth are slender, erect and smooth-edged—ideal for cutting through nets. The young are pale brown above, white below, but they acquire

a yellowish tinge with maturity. They range from north Western Australia, across the Northern Territory and down the Queensland coast as far south as Moreton Bay, where they are commonly caught near jetties and docks. They grow to just short of three metres.

FISHING TECHNIQUE: Australians do more fishing for sharks than any other people. Perhaps because the sharks found here are bigger and more aggressive than those found elsewhere, our fishermen have learned to respect sharks. Game fishermen usually drift for sharks or drop anchor over a known reef to try for them. Hammerhead and mako sharks are taken while trolling because both will take moving baits. Berleying for sharks often involves days of preparation and some of the brews dropped overboard after calls at butcher shops and fish shops are as foul as they are lovingly prepared. The best bait is undoubtedly small fish, with one side filleted, hooked through the tail with a 16/0 Mustad hook with the hook sewn or tied to the baitfish. A trace of about nine metres on a line with a 100 kg breaking strain is common, with the bait carried out from the boat by a football bladder, balloon or cork. Some prefer to drop the bait directly below the boat. Generally two rods are used, one bait to float out around 50 metres from the boat, the other fed down near the bottom as a deep bait. Although the Australian Game Fishing Association bans the use of mammals for berley, there can be really no check on what is used. The ban has, however, largely stopped the use of porpoises for bait. When one bait is taken, the other line should be retrieved to prevent snags. No attempt should be made to turn the shark until it has made a long run, as they often spit it out after a short swim. They invariably return and often it takes several strikes to set the hook. Otherwise the bait is picked up in a net for future use. Fights with sharks can take several hours and do not include the thrill of sighting the quarry leap clear of the water as marlin do. The idea is to tire the shark by playing it away from the boat and bring it to the surface well away from the boat's propellors. When the shark is brought along side, the trace is taken as it is hauled in and the slack portion dropped into the water so that nobody on board will be endangered by the trace if the shark attempts a sudden getaway. The man on the gaff has to place it carefully, and immediately after gaffing some sharks will roll on their backs and thrash about. A second gaff should then be used until a tailrope can be put on the shark and tied to a bollard. The shark can then be towed to home base. Smaller sharks can be lifted on board large boats but they should always be beaten on the tip of the snout with a baseball bat or heavy waddy. Otherwise they may thrash about the boat and cause havoc. Mako sharks should never be taken on board. Sometimes catching the shark and preparing it for towing is only the start of the battle as other sharks will often attack and mutilate sharks tied along side game boats. Shooting or lancing the catch will disqualify it in club competitions.

BIG SHARK TROPHIES: To secure a gleaming white trophy to commemorate capture of a large shark, game fishermen use a special curing technique. They start by removing the shark's mouth and lowering it into deep water so that sea lice can eat off the meat. Then they cut the jaws from the head, holding the mouth open with sticks, and drop the jaws into a solution of one part formalin and 10 parts water, adding 568 millilitres (a pint) of peroxide for bleaching. After a week they remove the jaws from the solution, dry them in the shade, and apply lacquer to produce the finished trophy.

SILVERBELLY *Gerreidae*

Small, shallow water fishes ideal for bait-fishing that inhabit Australia's tropical seas, and are easily identified by their bright silvery colour. They grow to only 26 cm in length and have distinctly weak, protruding jaws. Professional fishermen consider them nuisance fishes because they often appear in their nets when they are after mullet, bream, snapper, tarwhine or other commercially viable species. Their flesh has a sweet taste, and their large, soft scales come off in handling. Fisheries inspectors investigating reports of destruction of undersized bream and snapper often find they are dealing with 'silver biddies'. Among the varieties so far identified in Australia are the Darnley Island silverbelly, *Gerres darnleynse*, which appears to occur only in north Queensland waters and has four or five dark bars along the flanks; the common silverbelly, *Gerres subfasciatus*, which has a dark blotch on the leading edge of the dorsal fin; and the lowfin silverbelly, *Parequula melbournesis*, a loner frequently

Darnley Island silverbelly, *Gerres darnleynse*

found in the shallow waters of Victoria, South Australia and Western Australia.

FEATURES: They are mostly silvery-blue in colour, with forked tails and extensible mouths. Mature common silverbelly turn a silvery-bronze colour along the sides and their tails become almost transparent.

FISHING TECHNIQUE: Silverbelly are netted, pecking away at weed beds and inshore reefs, by estuarine prawn boats, crews of which know them as silver biddy, soapy, pip and roach. Like their relatives the pony fish, they form splendid bait for whiting and flathead, snapper, emperor, and school mackerel. Sportsfishermen sometimes scoop up what they need for bait simply by using hand nets.

DISTRIBUTION: Predominately a tropical species, they have been found in all States when the water is warm.

SILVER PERCH *Terapontidae*

Silver perch, *Bidyanus bidyanus*

An appealing native perch which ranks as Australia's third most important native freshwater species after Murray cod and golden cod. Their flesh is firmer, whiter and drier than Murray cod or golden perch and is ideal for smoking but for some reason there is a prejudice against accepting them as a top-class table fish. Vast numbers of silver perch are caught every year and many acclimatisation societies breed them to restock dams and lakes. They have a notable tolerance to high water temperatures and always provide good sport. Silver perch, *Bidyanus bidyanus*, are also known as bream, black bream, Murray bream, bidyan, grunter and bidyan grunter, the grunter labels arising because of the noise they often make on capture by rotating their bladders. In South Australia, some anglers continue to refer to silver perch as tcheri, an Aboriginal name.

FEATURES: Silver perch grow to a weight of 8 kg or 17 lb, but are not often caught over 3 kg. Their body colour is dull-black over olive-brown, silvery below and the upper surface sometimes has what Whitley called dotted worm-like markings. They spawn in September-October and a silver perch of 1.7 kg can produce half a million eggs. These are largely buoyant and will float downstream until the juveniles hatch and start to swim. Their fertility makes them ideal for cultivation in dams and fish farms.

FISHING TECHNIQUE: They bite avidly on worms, shrimps and grasshoppers and despite their small mouths will tenaciously attack large trolled lures. At first they seem likely to dodge the hooks but once a hook is set they fight hard and with surprising speed.

DISTRIBUTION: Queensland, New South Wales, Victoria, South Australia and Western Australia, abundant in the Murray River system. Bidyan was the aboriginal name for silver perch noted by explorer Thomas Mitchell.

Skates   *Rajidae*

Flat, blunt-tailed fish very simlar to rays that lack spines or stings. Their discs are more angular in shape than in rays, with a definite, pointed snout, and they swim by undulating their disc flaps. These flaps are excellent eating in more than 30 species found in Australia but have never won the popularity they enjoy in Europe. Main Australian varieties are the common skate, *Raja australis*, also known as Pommy skate because of their resemblance to English skate, have thorns on their olive-brown discs and light spots near the base of the fins; thornback skate, *Raja lemprieri*, also known as Lempriere's skate, has a pronounced snout, blackish-grey disc, with minute spines on the head, the anterior margins of the pectorals and the tail; peacock skate, *Pavoraja nitida*, known by their so-called peacock eyes, scattered dark patches studded with small yellow or white spots; white-spotted skate, *Raja cerva*, which have distinctive white spots sprinkled over their diamond-shaped dusky brown discs and small fins set in their short, sharp tails; and Melbourne skate, *Raja whitleyi*, which always has a series of three or four spines on each side of the back, short, narrow tails armed with three series of strong spines, and grow to a weight of 50 kg which makes them the largest of our skates.

FEATURES: Skates usually have long, pronounced snouts with their vents nearer the snout than the end of their tails. Their spines are never as dangerous as in rays, their skins are smoother than rays' and they have two posterior dorsal fins well back towards the tail. All skates are oviparous, laying quadrangular-shaped egg cases. Oldtime sailors made intriguing little figures known as Jenny Havers from dried skates, twisting or cutting the figures into grotesque shapes.

DISTRIBUTION: Skates are found in temperate, southern Australian coastal waters.

Peacock skate, *Pavoraja nitida*

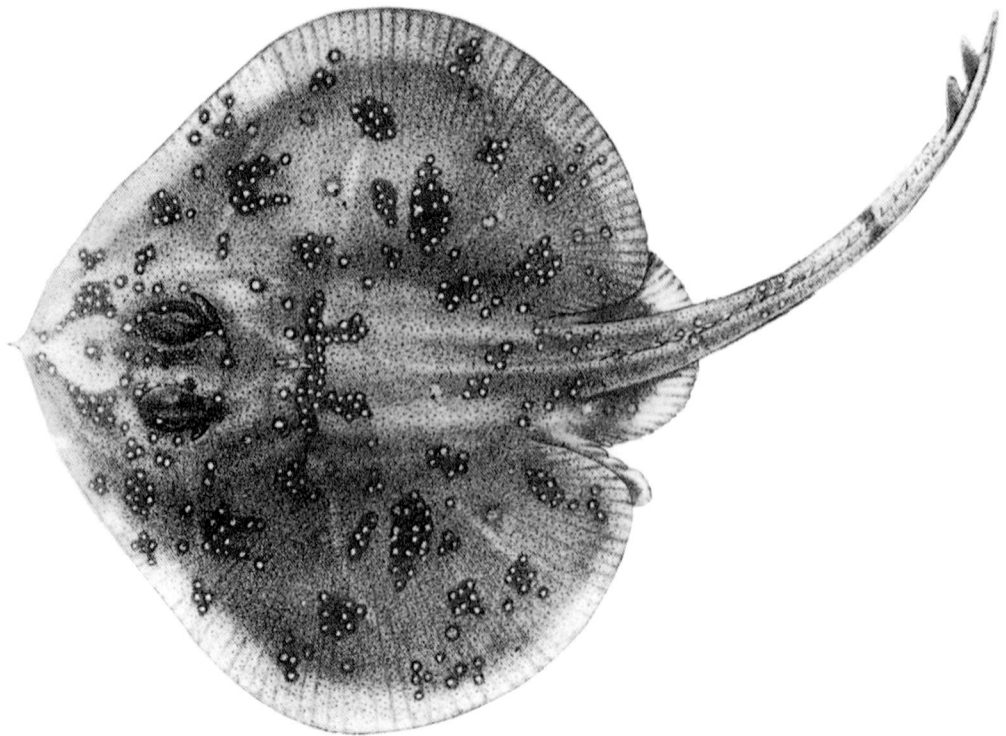

Smelts   *Retropinnidae*

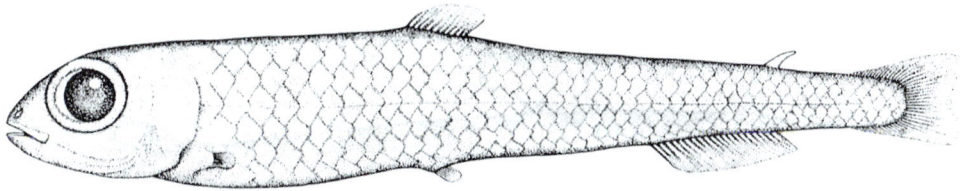

A family of small, but extremely active school fishes that are preyed on by most of the larger fishes. They are transparent and rarely grow beyond 6 cm and all the details of the brains, gills, viscera and bones are visible. They swim near the surface in shoals of a thousand fish or more. They are such good foodfish for bigger fish they were at one time introduced into Tasmania to provide food for captive trout. They prosper in both saltwater and freshwater. Australia's significant freshwater species are the Australian smelt, *Retropinna semoni*, which is so transparent it is difficult to see against a sandy bottom, and the Tasmanian smelt, *Retropinna tasmanica*, which is more slender-bodied and elongate and is said to smell like cucumber when it is caught. Australia also boasts a family of Bathylagidae, deepsea smelts which include the Antarctic big-eyed smelt, *Bathylagus antarcticus*, and silver big-eyed smelt, *Bathylagus argyrogaster*.

FEATURES: When they spawn in the spring, Australian smelt take on a reddish colour and the large black blotch on the tail becomes more prominent. There is an adipose fin behind the true dorsal fin, which is well back, and a membrane stretches from near the ventral fins to the vent. They are too small to have any angling interest but survive in aquariums on dry food, and worms.

DISTRIBUTION: Australian smelt are found in the coastal streams of southern Queensland and throughout the Murray-Darling system in New South Wales and South Australia. Tasmanian smelt are restricted to Tasmania. Distribution of deep sea smelts is little known but they are widespread in the Southern Ocean at depths below 800 metres.

Antarctic big-eyed smelt, *Bathylagus antarcticus*

COOKING YOUR TROUT: Trout should be killed and gutted as soon as possible after capture to preserve their edible qualities. Remove the strip of dark red kidney that stretches along the backbone, wash and dry the trout thoroughly—but don't scale or skin it—and cook the fish whole, head and tail intact. Wrap the fish in well-buttered foil and bake at 190 degrees for 15 minutes, serving hot with lemon. Cooked on the bank like this straight after they are caught trout taste better than in any big city restaurant.

SMILER *Opistognathidae*

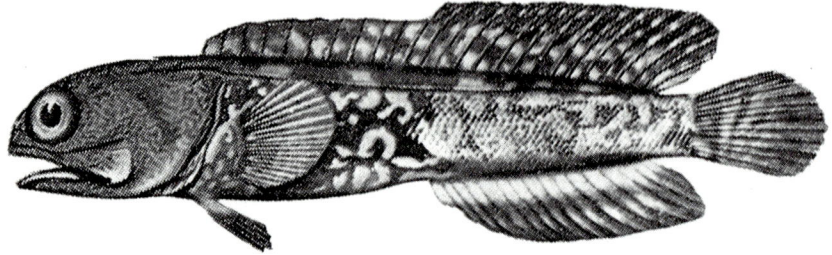

Southern smiler,
Opistognathus
jacksoniensis

Ornate, marbled, streaked or spotted fish also known as harlequins, missing links, pugs, jawfish, grinners, and monkey fish which burrow in sub-tropical sands. They bite out burrows at the bottom near rocky or coral shores, entering tail first. Studies in the Bahamas proved that the males incubate eggs in their mouths. Australia has about five varieties, ranging from the southern smiler, *Opistognathus jacksoniensis*, a bright yellow fish heavily blotched in army-style brown camouflage that extends from tail to the throat and big black eyes tinted in blue, to the harlequin smiler, *Opistognathus eximius*, which has a glittering light blue body, big yellow blotches and spots across the body, and a yellow bar that runs along the top, merging with the dull golden head. The southern smilers grow to 25 cm and harlequin smilers to 40 cm.

FEATURES: The smiler has an unusually large mouth that enables it to steal baits put down for snapper and sweetlip over inshore reefs. They frequently turn up in the nets of trawlers who scrape sandy bottoms. They have no appeal as table fish.

DISTRIBUTION: From the New South Wales central coast north across the tip of Australia to Western Australia.

CONTEST CHEATS BEWARE: Since fishing contests began in Australia, organisers have banned the use of dynamite, nets, spears and boomerangs. They are also wise to attempts to increase the weight of fish by filling them up with lead or sand. Judges at weighing stations are alert for traces of sand around the mouth and examine the scales of so-called 'freshly-caught' fish for traces of newspaper or ice from freezers. Scales heavy with beach sand are a sure sign of fish that have been buried beforehand and dug up on the day of competition.

SNAPPER   *Sparidae*

An outstanding food fish found in all Australian States except the Northern Territory, usually around reefs. The snapper is one of our oldest fishes and the remains of their bones found in Victoria have been dated by hydro-carbons as 4,700 years old, which means they were present before the "little ice age" and are probably of Eocene origin. Their erratic feeding habits can make them difficult to catch and have built up a cult of devoted snapper fishermen, with techniques varying in each State. Their popularity stems from their eagerness to bite on light game tackle, their determination to fight when hooked, their handsome appearance, and a table quality that appeals to even the most fastidious palates. They are in no way related to queen snapper, *Nemadactylus valenciennesi*, which belongs to the morwong family.

Snapper have had name problems since the time of the First Fleet. Our early settlers always intended that it should be called by the English word snapper because of its habit of snapping at its prey but somehow the unwanted German variant "schnapper" found its way into the *Sydney Gazette* of 1836. The Australian snapper, a member of the family *Sparidae* found in tropical and sub-tropical waters throughout the world, has been labelled *Chrysophrys guttulatus*, *C. unicolor* or *C. auratus*, but a Japanese authority has suggested that both be classified as *Pagrus auratus*. To conform with the scientific label used in other Australian books the name *Chrysophrys auratus* is used in this book.

Australian snapper are closely related to the Japanese sea bream, *Chrysophyrs major*, and a similar fish found in African waters.

Snapper. *Chrysophrys guttulatus*

Snapper, showing the hump that develops on the head after their third year

Its closest relatives in Australian waters are the various forms of bream, pikey, yellow-fin, black bream and tarwhine, which are all members of the *Sparidae* family. They are known as cockney bream until they are 12.5 cm long, less than half a kilo and under a year old. They become red bream at about a year old and 0.75 kg and at this stage spawn for the first time. They are known as squire at about two years old by which time they weigh around 1.4 kg. At three they become school snapper and thereafter, as the hump develops on the head, they become old man snapper or knocky. Early settlers sometimes called them Light Horsemen when they had matured to the bulging head size and weighed around 3.5 kg. Some authorities recognise two separate species of snapper, the western and eastern snapper. There is no anatomical reason for this and they are simply eastern and western stock of the same species.

FEATURES: Lumpy heads, colour rosy pink, often with scattered blue spots along the back and sides. When freshly caught they sparkle but the colours quickly fade to a lightish brown on top, silvery underneath. The young have darker vertical bars.

Snapper taken at night lose some of their pink colouration and become silvery and in their night-time garb are often mistaken for bream. Deepwater snapper are usually red rather than pink. They grow to a metre and a half in length and and weigh 20 kg although the current Australian Anglers' Association record is 16 kg for a snapper taken at Semaphore, South Australia, in 1971 by D. Luckman.

FISHING TECHNIQUE: Snappering is one of the most popular forms of fishing in Australia and New Zealand, where boat owners often rise before dawn to travel out to their favourite snapper reefs by daylight. Others hire skiffs and motor boats to fish for snapper on the reefs and deep holes of big harbours and bays. Still others go to the rocks and cast for snapper in the deep. One group of Australian fishermen has developed a technique of casting garfish from the tops of cliffs as dawn arrives and waiting for snapper or tailor to grab the garfish as it floats to the surface.

Modern echo sounders are of immense help to boat skippers in locating offshore snapper reefs. The mature snapper prefer to live around these reefs but often move inshore around August when they are caught from the rocks or on isolated harbour reefs. Sportsfishermen will argue for hours about the best times to catch snapper, but they appear to bite best between dawn and 9 am. On offshore reefs snapper experts fish by allowing their boats to drift over the reef or by anchoring over it. Anchors have a tendency to get caught in the reefs so drifting is more popular. Most use lines from 9.07 kg (20 lb) to 16.33 kg (36 lb) breaking strain on plastic or wooden spools. In strong currents or heavy winds they use large sinkers to keep lines on the bottom but the larger the sinker the more difficult it becomes to detect the bite.

Snapper take a very wide range of baits, including nannygai, morwong, jackass fish, teraglin, sergeant baker, cowanyoung, leatherjacket, gurnard, red rock cod, latchet, parrot perch, flathead, kingfish and mulloway, but their favourites seem to be king prawn, crabs, octopus and squid. Hook sizes vary from 2/0 to 8/0. Some snapper experts use a 6/0 hook on the top cast and a 2/0 on the bottom which will pick up the smaller bait fish. The wisest course in settling on a bait is to gut the first snapper caught and assess the stomach contents.

The mouth of a mature snapper is hard and bony and can blunt, crush or break weak hooks. For big fish of the species French and beak hooks are recommended and sometimes the O'Shaughnessy. The strong, recurved hooks used by the Japanese on their commercial long lines are very effective for medium-sized snapper. Snapper specialists use 4.5 to 9 kg monofilament nylon or slightly heavier if the bottom is rough. A rod and reel provides a "feel" that a handline cannot match. Even with a trace, handling a big snapper involves a lot of skill.

DISTRIBUTION: Snapper are caught by anglers in southern Australia and northern New Zealand from Geraldton on the Western Australian coast to Bowen on the Queensland coast and Cook Strait in New Zealand. They can stray north of these limits but generally the biggest catches are taken in the north during winter and in the south during summer. Successful snapper anglers get to know the annual movements and habits of snapper in their own region. They tend to move inshore in the spring before they spawn. The big ones appear around ocean rocks along the centre of the New South Wales coast in August and remain plentiful until the end of October. The best snapper runs in Port Phillip Bay are from August to October, but there is a second run in December. Good catches of snapper are made for most of the year in Cockburn Sound, the natural harbour south of Fremantle, with the snapper moving inshore to places like Robb Jetty and Palm Beach during the wild winter storms. Snapper fishing in Shark Bay, Western Australia, was big business in the 1950s but lately commercial boats seldom find it worthwhile.

SNAPPER TANDOORI STYLE

INGREDIENTS

4-6 Cutlets
2 cartons natural yoghurt, 200 g
3 cloves garlic, crushed
2 tablespoons tomato sauce
1 tablespoon chopped ginger
2 teaspoons curry powder
1 teaspoon turmeric
1 teaspoon paprika
½ teaspoon chilli powder

METHOD

Combine yoghurt, garlic, sauce, ginger, curry powder, turmeric, paprika and chilli powder. Mix until well combined.

Add cutlets. Marinate 2-4 hours, or overnight. Drain. Place onto a well greased BBQ plate or grill. Cook approximately 3-4 minutes each side, basting frequently with marinade.

SOLE   *Soleidae and Cynoglossidae*

Large numbers of sole occur in Australian waters, but few species are abundant enough to reach the markets in profitable quantities. They remain the gourmet's treat, repeatedly confused with flounder, with whom they share a common lifestyle. Sole have the same flattened bodies and both eyes come together on the left or right-hand side of their heads soon after birth. In soles, the preopercular margin is not free, the sides of their cheeks being covered with scales. The lower jaw is never prominent as it is in flounder. Apart from the group known as tongue soles, which have eyes on the left side of the body, all Australian soles are right-eyed. The underside of the head has whorls or rows of whisker-like feelers for finding food at night by touch and taste. The pectoral fins of some soles are reduced or even absent. The dorsal and anal fins are frequently merged with the tail. They are invariably plain colour on the bottom side, but on the topside, may be beautifully marked with stripes, speckles or flecked in vivid colours. Soles are present in most Australian coastal waters and one or two permanently inhabit freshwater. Indeed most soles go through the period in which they travel up-river, some kilometres away from the influence of saltwater, maintaining their maturity in safety

Many-banded sole,
Zebrias fasciatus

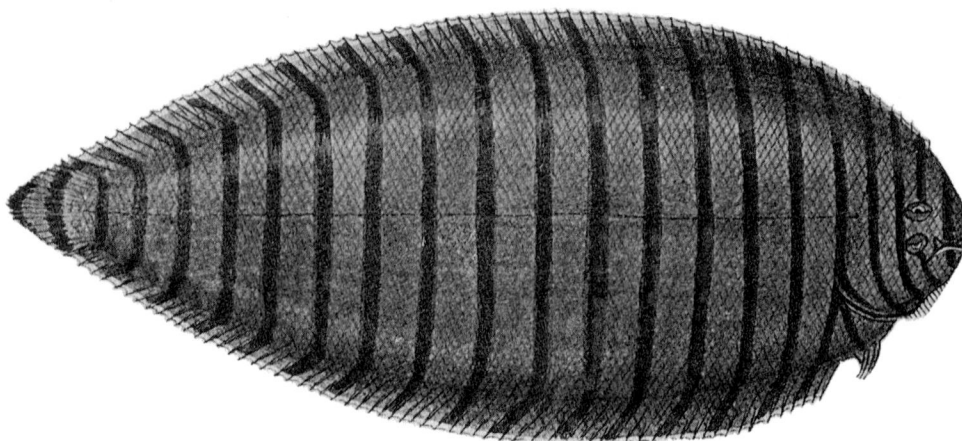

and only returning to the sea when they are fully grown adults and ready to reproduce. Australia's best known soles are:

Peacock sole, *Achirus pavoniniu*: A north Queensland variety that grows to 20 cm with an array of big black dots scattered across a reddish-brown upper body. The tail fin is rounded and clearly separated from the side fins. They are outstanding table fare, the fins being easily removed with a fork when in the pan.

Many-banded sole, *Zebrias fasciatus*: The only true sole found in Tasmania. They are a rare variety known by the few that have been dredged from Bass Strait. The blind side is whitish, the top side brownish with 22 to 24 dark transverse bars extending from in front of the eyes to the base of the tail. There is a continuous longitudinal stripe along the central region of the anal, dorsal and tail fins. They reach at least 220 mm in length and have been known to stray into Victoria and New South Wales.

Black sole, *Achlyopa nigra*: A culinary favourite, dull-green in colour as juveniles and dusky black in maturity. They are a heavily bodied species that grows to 40 cm in which the tail fins merge with the side

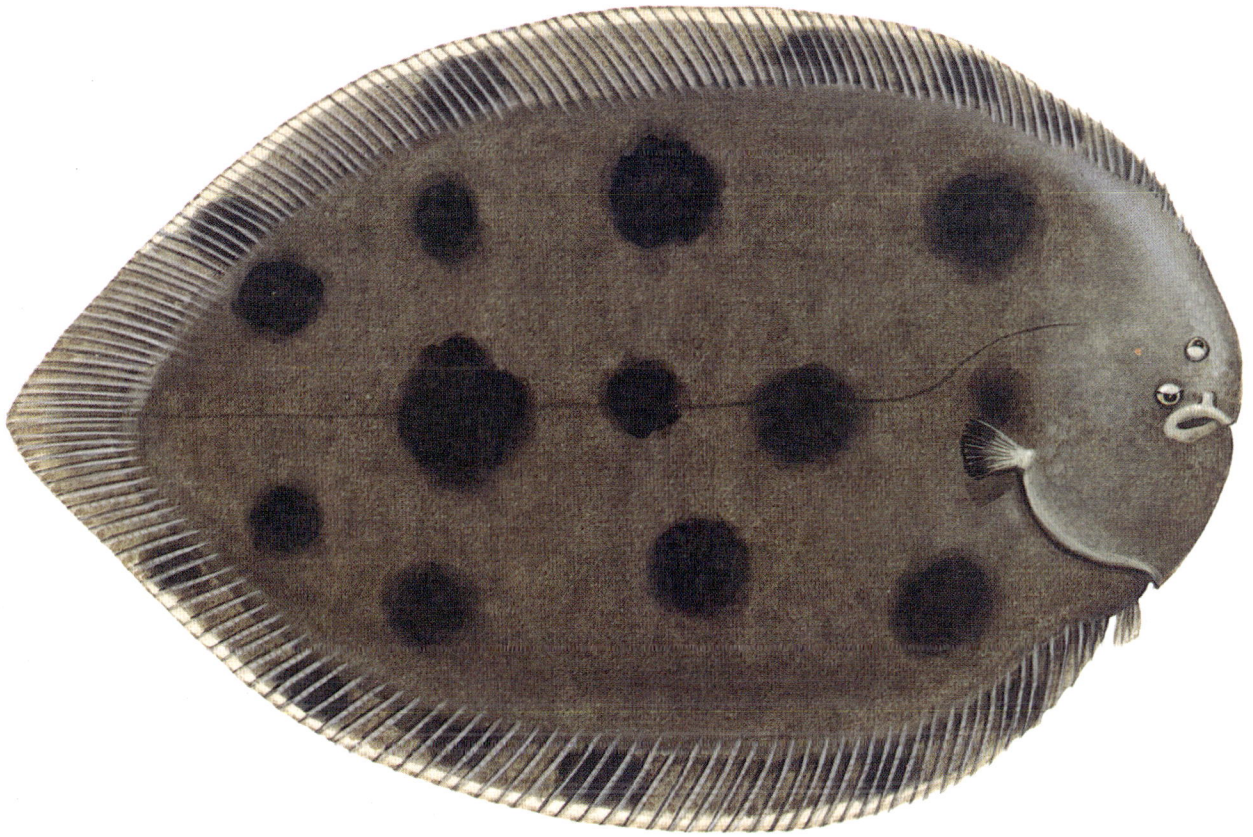

Black sole, *Achlyopa nigra*

Two-lined tongue sole, *Cynoglossus bilineatus*

fins. There are numerous dusky blotches or thumb-prints on the upper side. They remain common in the coastal shallows of New South Wales, Queensland and northern Australia.

Narrow-banded sole, *Aseraggodes macleayanus*: A notable burrower able to bury itself beneath mounds of sand, swimming forward and downward with what Grant describes as a movement reminiscent of a carpet being shaken. They have pale brown bodies with at least 28 dark brown cross bars, each of them wider than the intervening space. Their rounded tails are separated from the long side fins. Grows to a third of a metre in length and is a memorable eating fish. They occur in southern Queensland and New South Wales.

Two-lined tongue sole, *Cynoglossus bilineatus*: One of the best examples of Australia's tongue soles or tongue fishes, a group of left-eyed soles easily distinguished from oval-shaped soles belonging to the family *Cynoglossidae*. Some tongue soles have a fleshy snout shaped like a hook. They are all shaped like an animal's tongue. Silvery white on the blind side, they range in colour from light brown to pale yellow. Rarely sighted at the markets, they are outstanding panfish, growing to a third of a metre in length. They take their name from the two lines running down both sides of the body.

Lemon tongue sole, *Paraplagusia unicolor*: An elongate, gently tapered sole, cinnamon-brown in body colour on top and plain below, with pointed tails and unbroken fins along the eyeless right-hand side. They are mostly caught by prawn trawlers working along the New South Wales and Queensland coasts, as well as Western Australia. They grow to a third of a metre.

FISH WITH PEANUT SAUCE

INGREDIENTS

4 fillets fish
2 tablespoons vegetable oil
1 tablespoon coriander

PEANUT SAUCE
6 tablespoons crunchy peanut butter
1 clove garlic, crushed
¾ cup water
¼ cup coconut milk
1 teaspoon raw sugar
1 tablespoon lemon juice
2 tablespoons soy sauce
1 teaspoon fish sauce

METHOD

Fish sauce is available in Chinatown grocery stores and from most Asian specialty shops. The fresh coriander adds a wonderful flavour to this Indonesian dish.

For peanut sauce put all ingredients in a saucepan and stir over a low heat until thoroughly mixed (add more water if you want a thinner consistency).

Heat oil in a frying pan and fry on both sides until cooked through. Drain any excess oil out of pan and spoon peanut sauce over fish. Add coriander, cover and simmer 2-3 minutes.

Serves 4

Reprinted with permission, Carolyn Dunne, *The Semi-Vegetarian Cookbook*, Bantam, 1989

SOOTY GRUNTER *Terapontidae*

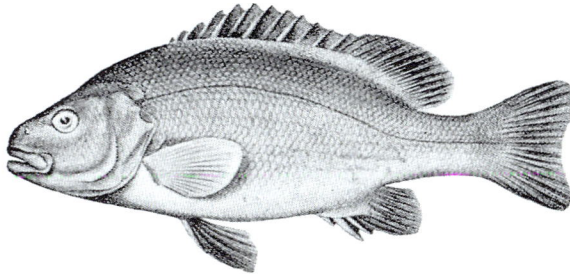

Australia's northern coastal and inland waters support big populations of small fish which local people refer to as black bream but which are really grunters. Best known of these is the Sooty grunter, *Hephaestus fuliginosus*, a freshwater fish of flowing streams that prefer clear water and are first-class eating. They range up to 1.5 kg but at that size are hard to land in small, rocky streams; stocky fish just shy enough to provide an angling challenge. Advanced anglers from Mt. Isa and Atherton have enjoyed fly rod fishing for grunter for years and have found that despite their small mouths and natural suspicion, sooty grunter can be enticed on to a carefully presented bait when they fight with ability on a par with southern bass or genuine black bream.

FEATURES: Sooty grunters are uniformly brownish-black in colour, with eight or nine rays on the anal fin, and a band of villiform teeth in each jaw. Their cheeks carry eight rows of scales. They are also known as purple grunter.

FISHING TECHNIQUE. Grunters offer wonderful sport for fly rod devotees. Worms or shrimps on a Kendall Kirby No. 6 hook will do the job, but they have been taken on everything from kangaroo meat to buffalo steak. Noted top end angler Vic McCristal favours large insects and crickets and allows the bait to wash into deeper pools from the set of rapids above them, without a sinker. A bubble float helps. For those who neglect to take fly rods north, spinning tackle will suffice, generally with smaller lures, float-diving poppers, midget bellbrooks and wobblers of similar size. Weighted stream flies or bass poppers, worked from under the shelter of trees, have also succeeded, but all lures directed at grunters need to be presented as carefully as they would be for bass or trout in the south.

DISTRIBUTION: From Cooper's Creek and the Eyre drainage system of South Australia, through the Barkly Basin, Lommen Bight, and tropical Queensland into the Northern Territory.

Sooty grunter,
Hephaestus fuliginosus

BALLOON FISHING: Ordinary party balloons make ideal floats for anglers drifting live or dead baits. Rock and beach fishermen often use them to get their baits well out, in offshore winds. They are also handy for large, active baits that would pull conventional bobby corks under water. The balloon should be attached to the main line by a short length of nylon or thread so that the balloon leaves the main line when big fish strike.

SPINECHEEKS *Nemipteridae*

A family of warmwater fishes with a prominent spine just under their eyes, generally with a row of spines below it. They have to be handled cautiously as these spines can inflict nasty cuts. All the family are vividly coloured little fishes, ideal for aquariums and bring gasps of admiration from holidaymakers on reef excursions. They include the large-eyed spinecheek, *Scolopsis affinis*, which has a large black eye, a throat and under-belly of lilac and a pale green top; the bridled spinecheek, *Scolopsis bilineatus*, a gleaming silvery-white fish, on which the upper part of the head and sides have alternating black and golden yellow stripes that resemble a bridle; and the bar-faced spinecheek *Scolopsis monogramma*, which have three bright blue bars across the face, trailing upper and lower filaments, bright greenish bodies, and deeply crescentic tails.

FEATURES: Spinecheeks are noted for their graceful swimming and the agility with which they flit about coral pools and tidal bays. They are all too small for the pan, averaging around 200 mm. Only the barred-faced spinecheek, which grows to more than 460 mm and will take a 5/0 hook has any angling potential, but it is disappointing on the table.

DISTRIBUTION: Northern New South Wales, into Queensland and the Northern Territory and into tropical Western Australia. Some species have been identified in Fiji, Japan and Sri Lanka.

Bridled spinecheek,
Scolopsis bilineatus

SPOOKFISH   *Chimaeridae*

Compressed, cartilaginous fishes with only four gill openings that are covered with a soft gill cover or operculum without bony plates. They are small and harmless, silvery in colour, closely related to sharks and rays so ancient in their lineage that it is virtually impossible to trace their evolution. Australia's spookfishes or ghost sharks are currently under review but appear to include nine species. They are also known as ratfishes, chaemeras and elephant fish and are split into the *Chimaeridae*, found along the shelves and slopes of our oceans; the bottom-dwelling *Callorhinchidae*, a plow-nose variety; and the long-nose deepsea *Rhinochimaeridae*, which are found at depths down to 2600 metres. Spookfish or ghost sharks were once quite rare, but are appearing more frequently in deepsea trawlers' nets. They differ from sharks in a number of ways: their upper jaws are fused to the braincase; the jaws are not supported by the hyoid arch; they have largely naked skins without denticles; and their rodent teeth consist simply of three pairs of ever-growing tooth plates.

FEATURES: Ghost sharks have large googly eyes, faintly luminescent bodies and tapering tails that together provide them with a ghoulish appearance. Their beak-like jaws are more fish-like than shark-like. The male has a little curved spine horn on his forehead and leg-like claspers near their ventral fins. The female is adorned with all these fripperies and sometimes carries, hanging from her body, long, leathery eggs of marvellous design, each with an embryo ghost shark wrapped inside. The illustrated Olgiby's ghost shark, *Hydrolagus ogilbyi*, has a curious boot-like mark on its snout similar to the trunk of an elephant and has been known as the elephant fish. They have large pectorals, large pointed ventral fins (but no anal fin) tapering to a long pointed and filamentous tail. They are a vivid silver on the body, yellowish below. Membranes of the fins are bluish-black, and the bases of the pectorals and ventrals are a tawny colour. They have black-tipped snouts, yellow eyes, and streaks of brown on the head and anterior part of the body.

FISHING TECHNIQUE: Ghost sharks have little interest to Australian sport-fishermen but Norwegians eat both their eggs and flesh.

DISTRIBUTION: Southern New South Wales, Bass Strait, Tasmanian coast, Great Australian Bight, and Victoria.

Olgiby's ghost shark,
Hydrolagus ogilbyi

SQUIRRELFISH   *Holocentridae*

Pugnacious, carnivorous fish that mostly spend their lives in the shallow waters of Australia's coral reefs. Most have a sword-like operculum spine that demands careful handling with gloves. They are predominantly red in colour and extremely active at night. Even on the Barrier Reef their vivid colouring attracts admiration. Australia's squirrelfish include the red squirrelfish, *Sargocentron rubrum*, a striking variety instantly identified by the alternating silvery and crimson stripes that run from head to tail. Two of these red stripes continue on to the upper and lower tips of the forked tail. They grow to a third of a metre and are frequently taken by line fishermen right across Australia's northern coastline. Another brilliantly coloured variety is the crowned squirrelfish, *Sargocentron diadema*, a vivid crimson over-all with seven or eight white, black-edged stripes running the length of the body. Their jet black eyes are circled in silver and there is an oblique silvery stripe across the cheeks. Perhaps our largest specimen is the spiny squirrelfish, *Sargocentron spiniferum*, which grows to 45 cm and has a brilliantly red spinous dorsal fin and a tail washed with bright red. They are common in Western Australia, the Northern Territory and down the Queensland coast to the rocky inshore reefs of northern New South Wales.

FEATURES: Apart from their striking coloring, squirrelfish invariably have 10 to 13 dorsal spines and four anal spines, the third of which is dagger-like. They have tough body scales and gill covers protected by sharp spines.

FISHING TECHNIQUE: Hooks become firmly set in the strong jaws of squirrel-fish and this, plus all the cutting edges on their bodies, make them a bigger headache in a boat than out of it. They should always be handled with gloves or an old towel or blanket.

DISTRIBUTION: Coral reefs of tropical Australia.

Red squirrelfish,
Sargocentron rubrum

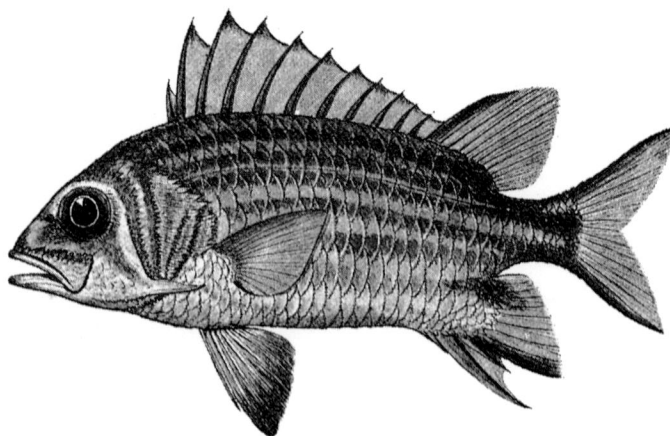

STARGAZERS *Uranoscopidae*

An ugly family of ocean fishes with large, cube-like bony heads, upward staring eyes that look to be gawking at the stars, and a highly developed facility for snagging anglers' lines. Most of the Australian varieties have very large mouths, paddle-style pectorals, and a prominent fringed flap behind each shoulder. They are bottom-dwelling carnivores who virtually disappear when they burrow into the sand, leaving only the mouth and the rim of the eyes showing. Australian specimens include the illustrated common or spotted stargazer, *Ichthyscopus lebecksannio*, one of the biggest of the group which grows to a weight of 7.5 kg and two thirds of a metre in length; the deepwater stargazer, *Kathetostoma nigrofasciatum*, found in waters 150 fathoms deep; the fringed stargazer, *Ichthyscopus barbatus*, which have two barbels below the chin; and the southern stargazer, *Kathetostoma laeve*, which dwarfs other members of the group by reaching 12 kg. Stargazers are also known as stone-lifters, mud gurnard, dogfish, Winston Churchills, and by the Maori name kourepoua.

FEATURES: All stargazers are adept at shovelling sand over their bodies with their large pectoral fins. They pull hard on anglers' hooks, giving the impression the line is badly snagged. Some can shock their prey with an electric discharge. They have fringed lips and their nostrils communicate with the inside of the mouth, a remarkable feature in fishes. Some can inflate their bellies.

FISHING TECHNIQUE: Occasionally taken on handlines by fishermen seeking bream, flathead or other species. They are poor swimmers and despite their hideous appearance provide delicious flesh. Grant has a record of a stargazer whose stomach contained a 454 g (1 lb) luderick.

DISTRIBUTION: Fifteen species are found around the southern half of Australia and well up the Western Australian coast. Also found in both islands of New Zealand.

Common stargazer, *Ichthyscopus lebecksannio*

STONEFISH *Scorpaenidae*

Stonefish belong to the group known as scorpionfishes, a family that includes waspfish, firefish, stingfish, demon fish, rogue fish, demon stinger and ghoul, all of them among the world's most venomous fishes. A sting from a stonefish, the most poisonous fish known, will cause immediate pain and the victim can become so demented he will fall into the water and drown. The other effect, swelling of the body, caused by the sting, can result in suffocation unless medical treatment is quickly given. Fortunately the Commonwealth Serum Laboratories have developed an effective stonefish antivenene. Two species of stonefish are found in Australian waters, the illustrated estuarine stonefish, *Synanceia horrida*, which is found along the mainland foreshores amid areas of mud, rubble, rock and reef clinker, and the reef stonefish, *Synanceia verrucosa*, which is encountered over coral reef tidal sands. Both are efficient burrowers, using their scoop-like pectoral fins to dig holes into which stonefish swim and cover themselves with sand and silt.

FEATURES: The colours of stonefish are extremely variable. Generally brownish or greenish, mottled or marbled, the fish can change in chameleon fashion. Australia's stonefishes are separable by the sculpturing of the heads around their tiny eyes, and by the pectoral fin count. The estuarine stonefish's eyes are set on a taller bony base, and it has 16 rays to the pectoral fin, while the reef stonefish has 18 or 19. The venom in both stonefishes is released only after a certain pressure is exceeded, as when the weight of a foot clumps down on them. Stonefish spines penetrate sand-shoes with ease. Estuarine stonefish grow to 470 mm, reef stonefish 350 mm.

DISTRIBUTION: Estuarine stonefish are found throughout tropical Australia and as far south as Moreton Bay, Queensland; reef stonefish in all coral reef areas within that range.

Estuarine stonefish,
Synanceia horrida

STRIPEY   *Lutjanidae*

There are two fish in Australian waters that go under the name of stripey, the outstanding food fish *Lutjanus carponotatus*, which is a member of the snapper family, and *Chaetodon trifascialus*, a butterflyfish mainly of interest to aquarians. The snapper stripey are the variety of most appeal to anglers, roamers admired as panfish but also frequently used as bait for larger fish. They grow to only 400 mm in length and often live in water just 50 mm deep, lying on their sides while they await the incoming tide. This stripey belongs to the same family as the hussar, red emperor, red bass, and Moses perch. These fish are well-known among Barrier Reef experts for their habit of darting in and out of coral ledges, scattering little prey fish.

FEATURES: The illustrated stripey varies in colour from red to reddish-brown to bright yellow, with eight or more parallel broad bars running the length of their sides. There is a prominent black blotch at the base of the pectoral fin. All fins are yellow. Their colour varies little in the three States in which they are abundant, Western Australia, Northern Territory and Queensland, only the number of stripes changing.

FISHING TECHNIQUE: Generally line-fished around the shallow reef waters of tropical Australia, where it will rise hungrily to a trolled bait or lure, bottom baits of cut fish, hardyheads, pilchards, and crustaceans. Because of its size, small hooks are advisable.

DISTRIBUTION: Northern Western Australia, Northern Territory, and Queensland down to Moreton Bay. Not to be confused with striped trumpeter or striped butterflyfish.

Stripey, *Lutjanus carponotatus*

SUCKER FISH *Echeneididae*

Short sucker fish,
Remora remora

Very old fishes that are the hitch-hikers of the world's oceans, with a history dating back more than one million years, according to scientific examination of fossils. They catch rides on other fishes by using the suction pads attached to their spiny dorsal fins. They are excellent swimmers but they prefer to attach themselves to groper, shark, marlin, turtles, rays and boats until they feel the need for food. They then detach themselves and feed on passing fragments or on parasites stuck to their hosts. They are splendid table fish provided they are skinned before they are cooked. The illustrated short sucker fish, *Remora remora*, is a small variety that grows to only 45 cm, dark brown to grey in colour, although some are jet black. Even these small sucker fish can be pulled apart from their sucker pads without the pad separating from the host. The slender sucker fish, *Echineus naucrates*, have pointed pectorals and a thick black band from the mouth to the tail.

FEATURES: Sucker fish push the rim of their suction discs against their intended hosts and create suction by a muscular action, turning up two rows of plates that attach themselves to their targets by creating a vacuum. They never harm fish to which they are joined. Each ridge inside the sucker pad has its own muscular action.

FISHING TECHNIQUE: Nobody deliberately goes fishing for sucker fish but they fight pugnaciously when they seize baits intended for other fish, and provide excellent sport. Most anglers who hook one, either on the side of a big shark or on the bottom of their boat, simply take the chance to study one of the oldest, most remarkable fish in the sea.

DISTRIBUTION: All Australian coastal waters, off Lord Howe Island and in New Zealand. Australia's seven varieties are widely distributed. There is no evidence to support the old fishermen's tale that when sucker fish are present sharks will be nearby.

Sunfish *Molidae*

Drifters that amble through the sea like old-time swaggies in the outback. They are remarkable for their size and for their breeding pattern. Gilbert Whitley, a lifetime researcher into the habits of fish, got quite excited explaining that sunfish increased their birth size 60 million times. Female sunfish carry millions of eggs and their young are spiny toado-like creatures, with finrays in the tail, gobbled up by surface fishes. Adults grow to 3.3 metres in length with a fin span of at least 3.6 metres and a weight of 970 kg. Australia's best known sunfish are the short or ocean sunfish, *Mola ramsayi*, that grow three metres in length and are sometimes found washed up on beaches, and the oblong or short sunfish, *Ranzania laevis*, which is illustrated. Sunfish should not be confused with freshwater sunfishes of the family *Melanotaeniidae*, which includes rainbow fish, jewel fish and small sunfish. The big ocean sunfish has a bluntly-rounded tail called the clavus or rudder and is grey to brown in colour. The short sunfish is a swift swimmer, travelling in schools over vast areas, and growing to around one metre in length and a weight of 8.6 kg.

FEATURES: The torso of the ocean-going sunfish is that of a fish cut in half. Bumps are often present above and below the eyes. The tail is bluntly rounded, and scalloped into lobes unlike other fishes. Ocean sunfish are grey to brownish and turn white after death. Short sunfish are dark blue, silvery beneath, with some oblique cross bars under the eyes.

FISHING TECHNIQUE: No true sportsman would want to kill one of these unique creatures, though some spearmen have done so. They offer a challenge to underwater cameramen anxious to secure an unusual shot. The speed of short sunfish often defies photographers.

DISTRIBUTION: Fish of the open sea which seldom penetrate harbours or bays. Ocean sunfish occur in Western Australia, South Australia, New South Wales and Tasmania, short sunfish in New South Wales and Queensland.

Short sunfish, *Ranzania laevis*

SURGEONFISH   *Acanthuridae*

A group of slab-sided fishes also known as tangs, doctorfish and spinefish, most of them vividly colourful and living in coral reefs. Most of them have lance-like spines on each side of the butt of the tail, which can inflict nasty cuts and which give them their name. They exist on a vegetarian diet of marine algae that makes them virtually inedible. The family includes the zebra surgeonfish, *Acanthurus lineatus*, which has black-edged, bright blue lines running from head to tail across the top half of a shimmering yellow body and is plain silvery-blue beneath; the ring-tailed surgeonfish, *Acanthurus xanthopterus*, whose olive-green body is covered in brown dots, with the glittering blue tail carrying a white base; the convict surgeonfish, *Acanthurus triostegus*, whose greyish body displays five or six vertical black bars similar to old-time convict uniforms; the orange-spot surgeonfish, *Acanthurus olivaceus*, which can be readily identified by the orange blotch on its olive-brown body; and the yellow-banded surgeonfish, *Acanthurus glauco-pareius*, which has short white bars beneath the eyes and the rear of its mouth, yellow bands running along the base of the dorsal and anal fins, and bright yellow bars across its white tail.

FEATURES: Surgeon fishes grow to around 45 cm and 1 kg but the ring-tailed surgeonfish reach 60 cm and 2 kg. They have velvety skins. Their mouths are too small for them to take hooks or lines and very few are seen by amateur fishermen. They are an easy target for spear fishermen, who soon learn the danger of handling them.

DISTRIBUTION: Mostly Indo-Pacific, from Queensland through the Northern Territory to northern Western Australia. Occasionally in New South Wales as larvae.

Ring-tailed surgeonfish, *Acanthurus xanthopterus*

SWEEP *Scorpididae*

Deep-bodied fishes of outstanding pan quality that seldom reach more than a kilogram in weight but remain a worthwhile target for anglers because of their delicious taste. They are not easy to hook because of their small mouths, although they are plentiful near wharves, rocks, and breakwaters. They seldom move far from cover and appear to have an inbuilt awareness of their lack of size. Only mature, larger fish venture into deep water. Of the sweep in Australian waters, the most plentiful are sea sweep, *Scorpis aequipinnis*; blue sweep, *Scorpis lineolatus*; and banded sweep, *Scorpis georgianus*; mado sweep, *Atypichthys strigatus*, known in New Zealand as mado, are silvery fishes with six or seven browny-black stripes running the length of their bodies, with deeply-forked tails and vivid yellow fins, popular with children and aquarium owners. Sea sweep are the largest members of the group and one of 2.71 kg or 6¼ lb has been taken. They are brownish in colour on top, silvery below, and lack the bars sometimes found in other sweep. The blue sweep is the children's favourite, green when young and living in rock pools. Later they turn a bluish colour, with prominent dark brown to yellow fins.

FEATURES: The vertical bars on banded sweep are pronounced. All sweep are symmetrical fishes with streamlined ventral and dorsal fins and they are subject to minimum legal length laws in South Australia (21 cm) and Western Australia (23 cm).

FISHING TECHNIQUE: In most states, sweep are unpopular with anglers because of their habit of stealing baits intended for bream. They bite on cut fish baits, crustaceans, molluscs, squid, octopus, and prawns. No floats or rigs are needed. They are ideal fish for introducing beginners to fishing for they will always give them plenty of nibbles. They require little preparation for cooking and will provide quick, easy meals.

DISTRIBUTION: There are varieties of sweep in all States but they seldom get into tropical waters, preferring temperate, colder water.

Sea sweep, *Scorpis aequipinnis*

TAILOR *Pomatomidae*

Tailor, *Pomatomus saltator*

A fast-moving saltwater pelagic of cooler coastal waters that schools in large numbers and provides sport unmatched by any other small game fish. They bite powerfully and fight vigorously when hooked and have a habit of gorging themselves in their feeding frenzies, moving in to chop through schools of pilchard and sea mullet, yellowtail and garfish with a zest no other Australian fish can muster. They offer outstanding beach fishing and will continue to fight vigorously after they have been lifted from the water. Australian tailor are identical with the fish known as bluefish in America, where it has the same habits. Their name comes from the manner in which they shear through prey like a tailor's scissors. A Western Australian tailor weighed 13.9 kg and measured 1.5 metres. If they are bled and chilled on capture they are splendid table fare, but some anglers who have allowed them to lie neglected in their boats have a poor opinion of them as food fish.

FEATURES: The sharp teeth and strong, undershot jaws of tailor should be carefully handled as they can inflict nasty cuts in anglers' hands. They are pale green to bluish above, silvery below and are built for speed, their olive-grey to white fins and forked tails combining to increase their swimming ability. No fish in the sea will over-eat like tailor; they have to vomit bits of their prey out before they resume their attack. Their annual appearances along our beaches are so unpredictable it is rare to go through a year without complaints from amateur tailor anglers somewhere in Australia about professionals fishing them out.

FISHING TECHNIQUE: Despite their vicious bite, tailor have soft mouths. They should be played firmly without tearing the mouth and brought in before they have a chance to chop at the line. They will take spinners and are caught in numbers from beaches, boats, rocks and out to sea. From the beach heavy sinkers are advisable to keep the bait down on the sand. Gangs of two or three hooks with a treble at the end provide a popular tailor rig. Wire traces and nylon strand casts are essential. Best tailor baits are garfish, yellowtail, mackerel, and bonito.

DISTRIBUTION: The biggest tailor appear off Australia's eastern and south-west coasts in late autumn and early winter and move north along the New South Wales and Western Australia coasts. Those that escape commercial fishermen reach as far as Rockhampton on the east coast and Carnarvon on the west coast.

TENCH *Cyprinidae*

A member of the English carp family introduced to the waters of Tasmania in the 1870s and later into streams of southern Victoria. They were first distributed in Victoria in 1876 by the Geelong and Western Districts Acclimatisation Society and the following year further distributions were made by the Ballarat Acclimatisation Society. They are abundant in Victoria and South Australia in lakes, swamps and sluggish sections of the Murray River. They are not widely sought by anglers who are suspicious of their edible qualities, but in fact are good to eat and, with redfin perch, form the basis of Victoria's commercial freshwater fishing industry. The unpopularity of Tench, *Tinca tinca*, with Australian anglers is in direct contrast to their status in Britain, where they are the most eagerly sought target when the coarse fishing season opens each June.

FEATURES: Tench up to 7.7 kg and 70 cm in length have been recorded in Australian waters, but they are most frequently caught at weights between 1 and 1.5 kg. The Australian Anglers' Association record is a surprisingly low 2.6 kg in the Torrens River, South Australia, by G. Hume in January 1965. Tench can be distinguished from European carp by the lack of barbels at the corners of their mouths. Scales in carp are very large, but small in tench. The lateral line in tench exceeds 90 scales. They have a solid body shape, with a bright orange iris in the eye. Their scales are a golden yellow, and the body colour is darker above and lighter below, with a slight greenish tinge. Tench spend a lot of time each year in Europe buried in bottom mud, but in Australia where the winter is less severe they are active for most of the year, continually scavenging and turning over dead and decayed matter that would otherwise foul up the pool. Biologists believe they are helpful to other fish because of this cleaning role. Tench have the typical carp ability to withstand waters with a low oxygen content, which eventually may allow them to extend their present southern distribution.

FISHING TECHNIQUE: Recommended baits for tench are bread pieces, worms, mussels, shrimps, insects of all varieties, larvae and small yabbies. They have a preference for quiet pools with a muddy bed where they can grope about for molluscs and worms. The slimy exterior probably explains our anglers' opposition to tench, but in England they are known as doctor fish and the slimy skin exudes a fluid that is said to cure any sick fish that rubs against their sides.

Tench, *Tinca tinca*

TERAGLIN *Sciaenidae*

Common teraglin,
Atractoscion aequidens

Small members of the *Sciaenidae* family easily distinguished from their close relatives, the mulloway, by the shape of their tails. Teraglin tails are always curved inwards, whereas mulloway tails are curved outwards. Teraglin are restricted to the coastal waters of southern Queensland and to the open coastal waters of New South Wales. Mulloway, the largest of Australian jewfish, are found in all States except Tasmania and are known as kingfish in Western Australia and Victoria. The teraglin does not enter harbours or estuaries like the mulloway, remaining offshore.

FEATURES: The common teraglin, *Atractoscion aequidens*, is found at depths between 25 and 100 metres right along the Queensland and New South Wales coasts, particularly around reefs where the bottom is a gravel bed. They stay around the same reefs for extended periods. Snapper fishermen catch a few in daylight but the big teraglin hauls usually are made at night. The famous saltwater angler Wal Hardy

was a great teraglin fan and described how hungry specimens followed hooked fish to the surface, where the action became spectacular. Teraglin can be berleyed to the surface when hungry. The silver teraglin, *Otolithes ruber*, alias wire tooth or yankee whiting, mainly is taken along the Queensland coast north off Fraser Island, and at times has been abundant at Alligator Creek, just south of Townsville, Queensland. It grows to 80 cm, an impressive silvery fish that displays iridescent blue and pink shades when first lifted from the sea. There is a distinctive dark, blotchy area behind the eyes and on the gill covers. Like its southern relative it is an excellent food fish.

FISHING TECHNIQUE: Suitable baits are prawns, blue mackerel, bonito, yellowtail, mullet, garfish, squid and salmon. They feed about nine metres from the bottom, and the baits must be held there. At night they move from the bottom, so the challenge is to assess the depth at which they are feeding.

THREADFIN SALMON   *Polynemidae*

A group of highly edible food fish found in warm Australian waters in which the elongate lower rays of the pectoral fins are used as feelers to find and taste food. Their eyes are usually covered by fat which has led to the alternative name of blind salmon. Other aliases include tasselfish, puttynoses, mango fish and salmon kingfish. They are unrelated to the salmonids but apparently have been called salmon because of the pinkish tinge on the bodies of larger specimens. The best known varieties are king threadfin, *Polydactylus macrochir*, seven-fingers threadfin, *Polydactylus multiradiatus*, the striped threadfin or puttynose perch, *Polydactylus plebeius*, and the illustrated blue threadfin, *Eleutheronema tetradactylum*, which is also known as Cooktown salmon. Although not in the same class as pearl perch, barramundi or Atlantic salmon, both

King threadfin,
Polydactylus macrochir

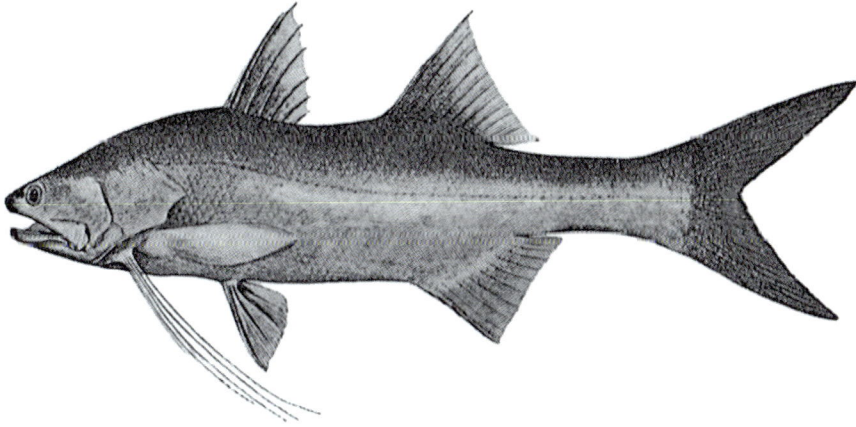

Blue threadfin,
Eleutheronema tetradactylum

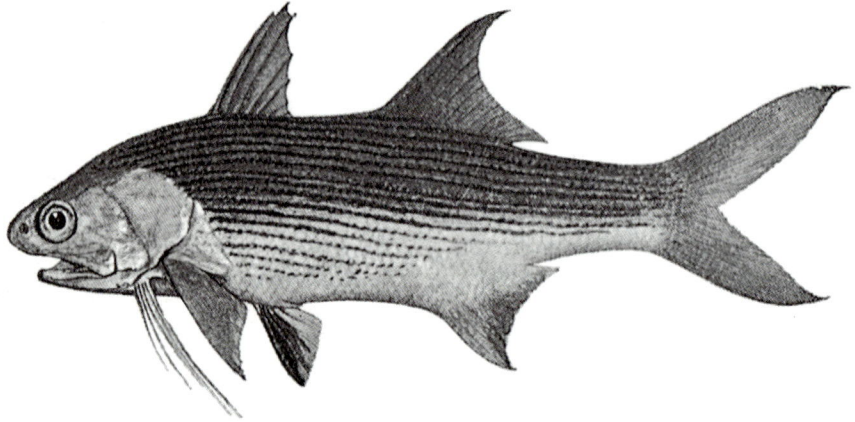

Striped threadfin,
Polydactylus plebeius

the king threadfin and blue threadfin are outstanding table fish eagerly sought by sportsfishermen. King threadfin grow to 30 kg, blue threadfin to just under 20 kg, but are more easily filleted in smaller sizes because of the bony nodules they develop with age along the backbone.

FEATURES: Contrary to widespread belief, threadfin salmon are not almost blind. They are bottom-feeders that scratch along coastal bays and inside muddy rivers, using their feelers to find food, but their eyes do not cloud over or become opaque until after death. Blue threadfin are a dull bluish-green above, with silvery-white bellies, deeply forked darkish tails and yellow pectoral fins.

FISHING TECHNIQUE: Most threadfins rise to take small fish like mullet, yellowtail or garfish and they will just as readily take trolled lures or plugs. They feed at full tide and just on dusk and when hooked will provide exciting sport by flinging themselves into the air to escape the hook.

DISTRIBUTION: Northern coastal waters, ranging from Western Australia, the Northern Territory, into the Gulf of Carpentaria, and along the tropical Queensland coast. Common in tidal rivers. Grant says he has taken king threadfin as far south as the Noosa River, where they fed on prawns that migrated from Lake Cootharaba into the John's River.

MARINATED THREADFIN

INGREDIENTS

4-6 cutlets
¹/₃ cup vermouth
¹/₃ cup lime or lemon juice
¹/₄ cup oil
I tablespoon chopped parsley
I teaspoon grated lime or lemon rind
¹/₄ teaspoon pepper

METHOD

Combine vermouth, lime or lemon juice, oil, parsley, rind and pepper. Mix until well combined.

Add cutlets. Marinate 2-4 hours, or overnight. Drain. Place onto a well greased BBQ plate or grill. Cook approximately 3-4 minutes each side, basting frequently with marinade.

TOADFISH *Tetraodontidae*

Common toadfish,
Tetractenos hamiltoni

A group of lethal fishes that include puffers which are known for their ability to swallow vast quantities of water or air to enlarge their soft-skinned bellies to grotesque proportions. They have been responsible for the death of humans and domestic animals and should under no circumstances be eaten. The family includes the giant toadfish, *Lagocephalus sceleratus*, which grows to 960 mm and is also known as the silver-cheeked toadfish or silver-stripe pufferfish, the prickly toadfish, *Contusus brevicaudus*, which has prickly spines across their bodies, the weeping toadfish, *Torquigener pleurogramma*, which take their name from the black bars that cross their eyes, the stars and stripes toadfish, *Arothron hispidus*, which produces a gruff, coughing noise when hooked; the golden toadfish, *Lagocephalus lunaris*, which can bite through wire traces as easily as a monofilament line; the diagonal-banded toadfish, *Arothron aerostaticus*, which have wide black bands over their yellow bodies, and the illustrated common toadfish, *Tetractenos hamiltoni*, which can not only vary their body shape but also change colour at will. Their teeth are fused to form beak-like mouths.

FEATURES: Most of the toadfishes cause nausea or dizziness within ten minutes of consumption. This is followed by respiratory failure, paralysis and a tingling feeling in the feet and fingers. They are scavengers that take baits intended for bream from jetty fishermen and inflate like balloons when stamped on. Like the stonefish they often allow themselves to be stranded as the tide recedes from coastal flats, content to feed on soldier crabs until they are freed by the tides. They have been found in freshwater as well as in open seas and will prosper in aquariums. They are seldom taken on lines and are mostly captured in nets. All are accomplished bait-stealers. They are feeble swimmers.

DISTRIBUTION: The common toadfish is abundant in Queensland bays and estuaries and ranges south to New South Wales, Victoria, South Australia and south-western Australia, but there are 130 species around the world.

267

TOMMY RUFF   *Arripidae*

Unlike its near relative Australian salmon (not to be confused with Atlantic Salmon), Tommy ruff are good table fish. They are perches, also known as ruff and sea herring. Tommy ruff, *Arripis georgianus*, also should not be confused with the roughy, *Trachichthys australis*, a relative of the nannygai. Tommy ruff grows to an average of 25 cm and is an important fish in winter for sportsmen in South Australia and Western Australia. They are known to spawn off Rottnest Island in numbers that turn the sea black. In World War II Australian servicemen found them a regular part of their diet under the alias Perth herring. They are oily, soft-fleshed fish ideal for barbecuing and provide good sport for jetty anglers.

FEATURES: Tommy ruff feed on rotting weed banks around Australia's cooler coastline. They school in large numbers and when news arrives that they are on hand, fishing communities turn out in their hundreds along beaches, wharves and rocky shorelines to be part of the action. They are predominantly blue in colour on top, silvery beneath, and have forked tails. Tommy ruff addicts pursue them with the intensity trout specialists show towards their prey.

FISHING TECHNIQUE: Tommy ruff are taken in buckets when there are huge schools, otherwise on handlines and with rod and reel, offering fine sport despite their small size. They appear at varying depths, feeding on all types of fish life. They are particularly responsive to berley flavoured with whale oil and such baits as crayfish, sardine, peeled prawns and whitebait. Western Australian anglers cultivate home-grown maggots and insects to use all the year on Tommy ruff, and even load their floats with whale oil or pollard to tempt them. The common rig is a light line below a free-running float with two or three hooks baited with wriggling worms.

DISTRIBUTION: Scarce in southern New South Wales and Victoria but abundant in South Australia and Western Australia.

Tommy ruff, *Arripis georgianus*

TREVALLA *Centrolophidae*

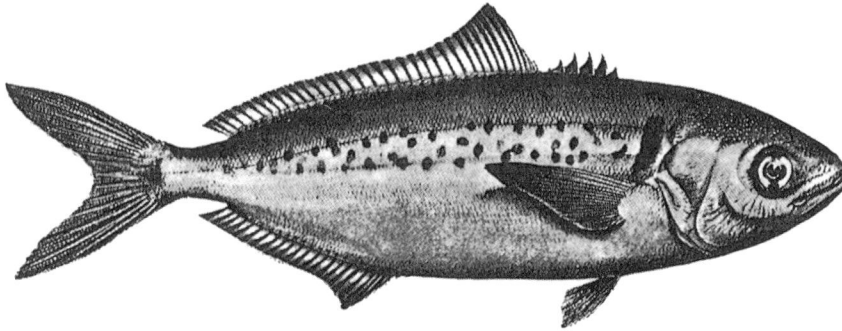

A deepsea fish, seldom encountered by amateur anglers, but a reliable catch for commercial fishermen. They belong to a small group of fishes with toothy gullets, pelagics that have a close association with jellyfish. They undergo big changes in body form with growth, losing body depth, becoming more forked in the tail, and altering their fin positions. Mature trevallas have easily-damaged fin rays and loose scales which makes identification of Australian species difficult. Their flesh is firm, moist and flavoursome but they are seldom caught at depths less than 100 metres and more often around 500 metres. Trevalla prefer cold water and grow to 36 kg in weight and are related to mackerels and tunas. The family includes the rudderfish, *Centrolophus niger*, a large fish trawled near the bottom at depths between 200 and 600 metres; deepsea trevalla, *Hyperoglyphe antarctica*, one of the best-eating scale fish in Australian waters; New Zealand ruffe, *Schedophilus huttoni*, an elongate, compressed coldwater variety that grows

to 3.5 kg in weight; mackerel trevalla, *Seriolella maculata*, a highly edible variety common near the continental shelf off Tasmania at depths between 500 and 800 metres; spotted trevalla, *Seriolella punctata*, which starts life under jellyfish but later is trawled on the continental slope at depths around 500 metres.

FEATURES: Trevalla are perplexing to taxonomists because of their dramatic changes with age, but they are all delicious eating fish of steel-blue colouring. They are pelagics as juveniles, only found in deep water when they mature, but never lose their perch-like profile.

FISHING TECHNIQUE: Trevalla fall to net and line in our large bays, and anglers need to be rigged to get down to the depths where they feed. They take cut fish baits, crustaceans and marine worms.

DISTRIBUTION: New South Wales, Victoria, Tasmania, and South Australia.

Mackerel trevalla,
Seriolella maculata

TREVALLY *Carangidae*

Yellowtail kingfish,
Seriola lalandi

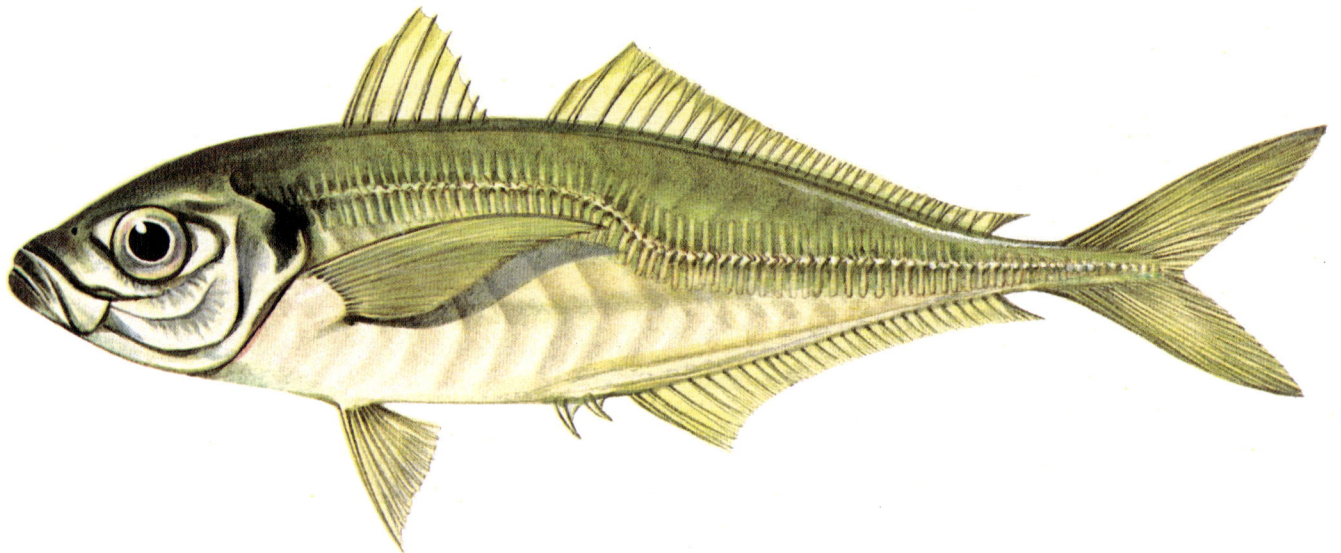

Yellowtail, *Trachurus
nouaezelandiae*

Fast, compressed fishes immediately recognised by their deeply-forked tails, their extended gill covers, and the ridge of hard, spiny scales extending forwards along each side of the tail butt. Around the world there are an estimated 140 species of this formidable family *Carangidae*, with more than 60 species recorded from temperate and tropical waters of Australia. The family has no connection with trevalla, a deep sea group of the family *Centrolophidae*, but are close relatives of dart, samsom fish, and turrum, which have separate entries in this book. Trevally suffer from a confusion of names and are known

overseas as pompano, Cuban jacks, cobble-fish and pennantfish. They are of variable table quality but all are highly rated as sportsfish. Young trevally forage in large schools but the older members of the family are loners.

Yellowtail kingfish, *Seriola lalandi*: A powerful, fast-swimming fish, admired by anglers for their fighting qualities. They are generally called kingfish but they should not be confused with black kingfish or cobia of the family *Rachycentridae*. They were known at one time as yellowtail but because of the presence of the small related yellowtail, *Trachurus nouaezelandiae*, the States decided on the name yellowtail kingfish. Unlike the smaller fish, yellowtail kingfish has no scutes and no easily discernible lateral line. They grow to 68 kg and 2.4 metres, but in large schools, common off our coasts are far smaller, with fish of 15 kg considered good catches. They include yellowtail in their diet, along with pilchards, mullet, octopus, herring and garfish. Schools up to 10 kilometres long have been reported off Australia. They are most plentiful from October to December when other fish are in short supply at the markets and thus they sell well despite a toughness in the flesh of mature fish. Scientists believe they have a big future as a cannery fish. They are dark blue above, silvery white below, with a yellowish-green stripe down the midline. The spinous dorsal and pectoral fins are light blue, with the remaining fins yellowish. The tail is a vivid yellow.

FISHING TECHNIQUE: Yellowtail kingfish are best caught just after dawn or just before dusk and will bite on bait or artificial lures. A few are caught from the surf but mostly they are taken at sea. They succumb easily to fast retrieval, often swimming to within a metre or two of baits or lures before they strike. The best so far taken in California weighed 32.65 kg, the best in New Zealand 52 kg. The Australian record is 47.25 kg for a fish of 168 cm in length.

DISTRIBUTION: Southern sector of the Great Barrier Reef, New South Wales, Victoria, sometimes in Tasmania, and across the South Australian coast to the sub-tropical waters of Western Australia.

Golden trevally, *Gnathanodon speciosus*: One of the most attractive of the family *Carangidae*, particularly when they are young and at their golden best. They are probably the best eating of all trevallies and they further enhance their reputation among anglers with their willingness to fight when hooked. The juvenile golden trevally are a brilliant gold with ten or more well defined vertical stripes across the shoulders and back, one of them through the eye. As they mature, the glow in their colour fades and the dark bars become indistinct. The fins retain their golden hue but the body colour takes on a silvery-green

Golden trevally,
Gnathanodon speciosus

tinge. They reach 1.2 metres in length and 37 kg or 86 lb in weight and specimens caught anywhere near that size appear to have lost their stripes. However, the stripes reappear as they lie dying on the boat. Golden trevally have no teeth and are topclass eating.

Diamond trevally, *Alectis indicus*: A bright-silvery bodied fish that is almost transparent, sometimes known as mirror fish. They have a big hump on the head above the eyes, and particularly long trailing filaments to the dorsal and anal fins. The body gives off a range of sparkling diamond colours, pink, pale green, deep blue, or rich red when waved in front of the viewer. Juvenile diamond trevally have at least six faint dark bands over their silvery torsos. Mature specimens, which reach 12.5 kg lie on their sides to fight the line, showing up as silvery blue. They are disappointing table fare.

FISHING TECHNIQUE: Most diamond trevally are taken by fishing the sea bottom with cut fish baits and not by trolling. They fight tenaciously and their protruding lower jaws often disgorge the hook.

Diamond trevally, *Alectis indicus*

DISTRIBUTION: Australia's warmer coastal waters, and particularly in the water between the Barrier Reef and the Queensland mainland. A few stragglers in New South Wales but the main populations is in the Northern Territory, the Gulf of Carpentaria and northern Western Australia.

Great trevally, *Caranx sexfasciatus*: They are very similar to turrum. The best method of separating them is by a count of the soft dorsal fin, which has 21 rays in the great trevally and 29 to 31 in the turrum. There is a second round black spot on the great trevally's gill cover. There are strong moves in Queensland to have the great trevally renamed big-eye trevally in recognition of its unusually large eyes. They are silvery-grey on top with a dusky lobe on the soft dorsal fin, which is white-edged. There are small lateral keels set on either side of the tail base and the belly is scaleless.

FISHING TECHNIQUE: Taken with strip fish bait, squid, crustaceans and plugs and lures. They fight savagely for life when hooked. Best time for them is at night when they feed in shallow water on damselfish and blennies, drifting with live baits.

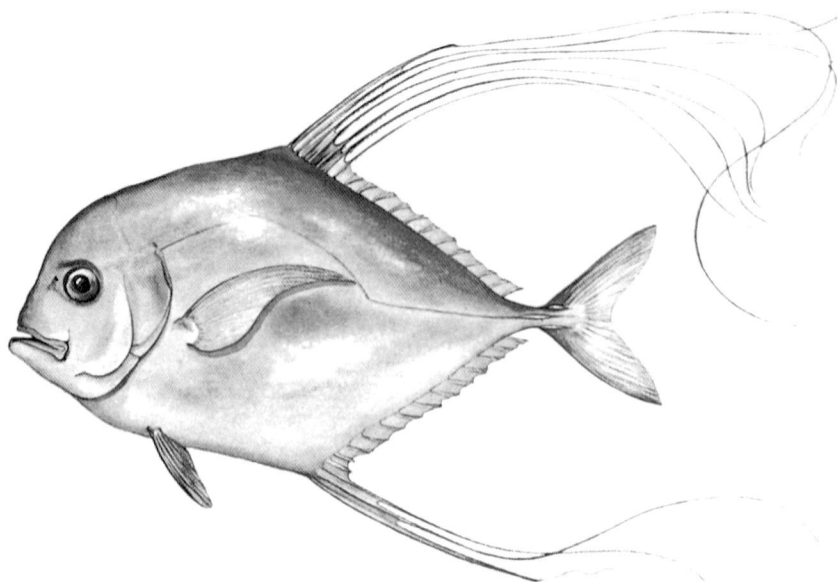

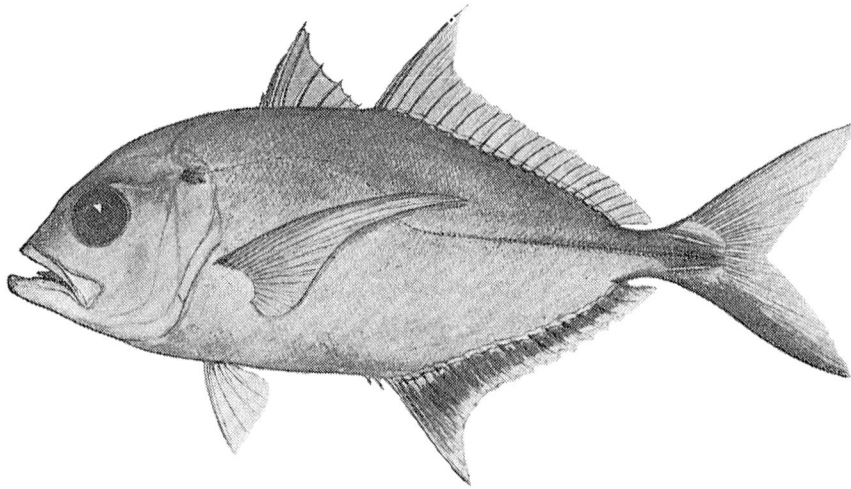

DISTRIBUTION: North coast of Western Australia and across northern Australia to the Barrier Reef, and south to northern New South Wales.

Black-cheeked trevally, *Carangoides plagiotaenia*: An elongated variety identified by their protruding lower jaw and the large black margin immediately behind the eye to the preoperculum. There is a curious curve in the leading part of the lateral line, the rear part of which carries flimsy scutes. The belly is heavily covered in scales. One of the finest food fish in the trevally family, growing to a length of 400 mm.

FISHING TECHNIQUE: By rod and reel or with handlines, usually with no more than a 7 kg or 15 lb breaking strain. Best baits fish strips, prawns or crustaceans.

DISTRIBUTION: Common in shallow water on the northern section of the Barrier Reef.

White trevally, *Pseudocaranx dentex*: A wide-ranging variety known in Tasmania and Victoria as silver trevally. Juveniles are also known as silver bream. In some parts of Western Australia, they are called skipjack trevally. Whatever the name preferred, they are excellent food fish, bright-bluish silver on top, paler below, with a pale yellow wash along the lateral line. The silver of the belly runs along to the chin and lower cheeks. There is a large black blotch on the rear edge of the gillcover. The ventral fin is white, the other fins yellow. They reach 10 kg in weight.

FISHING TECHNIQUE: Bait fished with handlines or rods on the bottom of inshore reefs.

DISTRIBUTION: All Australian States, including South Australia, where they are often caught in shark nets. The larger adults are found over deeper areas of the continental shelf.

Bludger trevally, *Carangoides gymnostethus*: A northern Australian variety which anglers use almost exclusively for bait. The flesh is dark and soft and oily. They are green on top, silvery white beneath with dark smudges on the gill covers. They average around 85 cm in length. Grant says they take their name from Queensland mackerel fishermen who detest the way they continually grab baits intended for larger, more marketable fish. The fishermen have to make do with them as bait or chop them up for berley. Bludgers are highly regarded as food fish in Japan where their oily flesh is rated a delicacy.

Great trevally, *Caranx sexfasciatus*

273

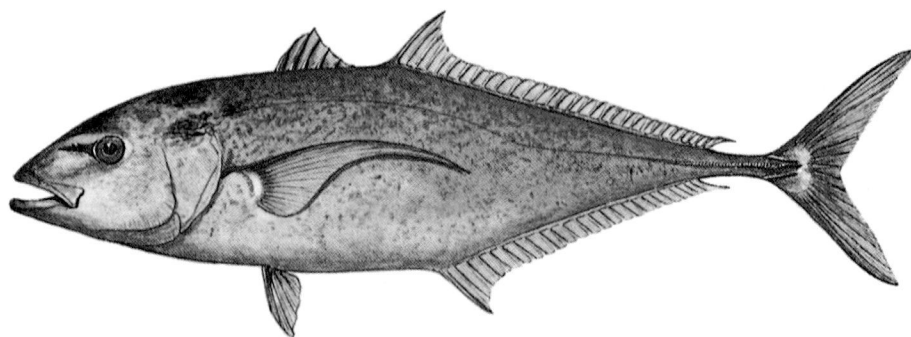

Bludger trevally,
*Carangoides
gymnostethus*

Pilot fish, *Naucrates
ductor*

FISHING TECHNIQUE: By handlines with squid, prawn and crustaceans for bait. Their oily flesh makes them ideal bait for large game fish.

DISTRIBUTION: Warm waters, inside the Barrier Reef and from Western Australia to the Gulf of Carpentaria with another closely related species.

Pilot fish, *Naucrates ductor*: A nomadic little fish that ranges over vast areas of the ocean, usually swimming on the surface in the company of sharks or other large marine creatures, such as whales, turtles and even boats. They feed off the scraps that sharks and others leave. In ancient times, they were said to lead ships to safety. They are plump-bodied with small scales and a keel on either side of the butt of the tail. They are a dark, iridescent blue on top, paler below, with five dark transverse bands extending on to the dorsal and anal fins. Young pilotfish have spines on the head and are found under floating objects such as bluebottles, jellyfish and weed.

FISHING TECHNIQUE: By handline, for use as baitfish or berley.

DISTRIBUTION: Queensland to Tasmania and Western Australia. Travels huge distances in the open sea.

Yellowtail or **scad**, *Trachurus novaezelandiae*: Also known as bung. A small fish found around jetties and piers in bays, estuaries, harbour mouths and boatsheds. They provide great entertainment for school children and are highly prized as baitfish. The schools are often so dense they can be taken with scoop nets, with anglers taking a bucketful of live yellowtail as they head for chosen fishing grounds. Greenish-yellow about the body, they are recognised by the row of hard scutes along the lateral line, golden around the tail, which is deeply forked. Classified as horse mackerel in South Australia. Yellowtail are closely related and almost identical in appearance to cowanyoung, *Trachurus declivis*.

Pennant-fish, *Alectis ciliaris*: A fascinating trevally which is restricted in size in Australia to around a third of a metre but grows to almost 13 kg and 103 cm overseas. They have diamond-shaped silvery-grey torsos, white or light blue fins and extremely long, delicate, trailing filaments

on both the anal and dorsal fins. They develop more elongate bodies as they mature and with age the filaments disappear or shorten. Pennant-fish are also known as old maids or mirror fish. Juveniles look like jellyfishes and are probably avoided on that account.

FISHING TECHNIQUE: Mature pennant-fish are good eating and put up a strong fight on prawn or fish bait.

DISTRIBUTION: Queensland and northern New South Wales and in warmer seas of Western Australia and the top end.

Brassy trevally, *Caranx papuensis*: A heavily-bodied variety whose silver torso carries a brassy tint and scattered small black spots across the upper sides and back. They are also known as Papuan trevally. Apart from a small patch on the head, there are no scales. The yellow in the fins becomes a dusky brown on death.

FISHING TECHNIQUE: The trick is to try for the smaller ones, which are splendid eating. The older fish, up around a metre in length, lack flavour. They take most baits in their inshore habitat.

DISTRIBUTION: The Indian and Pacific Oceans, New Guinea, and north Queensland.

Pennant-fish, *Alectis ciliaris*

TRIGGERFISH *Balistidae*

Big-spotted triggerfish,
Balistoides conspicillum

A family of erratically-shaped fish, closely related to leatherjackets, with furry or prickly skins. These fish can produce sounds like gunshot when captured. Some of them do this by vibrating the swim bladder, others by grinding their teeth. They are distinguished from leatherjackets by their three dorsal spines—leatherjackets have only two—and their well-developed scales. Leatherjackets have small scales with tiny spines, creating a furry skin. The group includes some captivating varieties such as the big-spotted trigger- or clownfish, *Balistoides conspicillum*, a vividly marked fish covered with large oval-shaped white spots and a large greenish-yellow area beneath the dorsal spine that glows or darkens at will; the wedge-tailed triggerfish, *Rhinecanthus rectangulus*, which has a greenish-orange body strikingly marked with black, yellow and bluish-white bands and a black wedge near the tail; the blue-throated triggerfish, *Sufflamen chrysopterus*, whose throat lights up in a glittering purple-blue when it is disturbed; the white-barred triggerfish, *Rhinecanthus aculeatus*, which has a greenish-yellow body with a silvery belly and a blue-edged black stripe running through the eyes; the black-spotted triggerfish, *Pseudobalistes flavimarginatus*, which has dark spots on each scale of its brown to green body; red-line triggerfish, *Balistapus undulatus*, whose green body carries 14 or more reddish-orange lines that run over the head and cheeks.

FEATURES: Renowned for their brilliant colouring, most triggerfish have mouths too small to take baited hooks. An exception is the starry triggerfish, *Abalistes stellaris*, which grows to two-thirds of a metre and takes hooks, and is partial to peeled prawns. The rest are bait-stealers.

DISTRIBUTION: The Northern Territory, northern Western Australia, Queensland, the Great Barrier Reef south to Heron Island.

TRIPLETAIL   *Lobotidae*

A cagey, energetic fish of Australia's tropical and temperate waters highly sought-after by anglers because of their high table quality and pugnacious fighting ability. They take their name from their extended anal and soft dorsal fins that almost match the length of their large, rounded tails. They use their tail structure and their deep, compressed bodies to fight all the way when hooked and will even jump out of the boat after capture. Another trick is to lie tilted to one side, feigning exhaustion. They are of such delicious flavour many Queenslanders prefer them to barramundi. The common tripletail of Australia's north, *Lobotes surinamensis*, is also known as jumping cod, black perch, flash, and dusky perch. They inhabit coastal and brackish waters close to rocky reefs, mooring buoys and floating logs, feeding on small fishes. Young specimens mimic floating leaves to escape notice. They grow to 1.2 metres in length and up to 3 kg in weight in Australia but a 14.2 kg specimen was taken in Florida.

FEATURES: The body is uniformly black to brownish in colour, with some yellow near the gills. Their steep profiles are slightly concave over the eyes. Both sides have a mottled appearance.

FISHING TECHNIQUE: Tripletails bite eagerly on pilchards, cut fish pieces, and will take most lures and plugs. They often congregate around jetties and disused wharves. The larger specimens are popular light game fish in America.

DISTRIBUTION: The Northern Territory, south down the Queensland coast to northern New South Wales and down much of the northern Western Australian coast, always preferring warmer waters.

Common tripletail,
Lobotes surinamensis

BARBECUED TRIPLETAIL

INGREDIENTS

4-6 cutlets
¹/₂ cup chopped basil
¹/₂ cup oil
¹/₂ cup chopped pine nuts
¹/₃ cup grated parmesan cheese
¹/₄ cup olive oil
3 cloves garlic, crushed
¹/₄ cup lemon juice
2 teaspoons grated lemon rind

METHOD

Combine basil, oil, pine nuts, cheese, olive oil, garlic, lemon juice and lemon rind. Mix until well combined.

Add cutlets. Marinate 2-4 hours, or overnight. Drain. Place onto a well greased BBQ plate or grill. Cook approximately 3-4 minutes each side, basting frequently with marinade.

TROUT *Salmonidae*

Brook trout, *Salvelinus fontinalis*

Brown trout, *Salmo trutta*

Prized sporting fish introduced into cooler Australian freshwater dams, streams and lakes from Europe and America by enthusiasts hoping to enliven our inland fishing. Australian trout differ from those in other countries; they cannot reach the sea and have to feed entirely on freshwater yabbies, worms, insects, snails and crustaceans. Overseas trout experts are amazed at the size our trout reach considering the limited amount of suitable cold-water trout territory available in Australia, and the severe restrictions on their diet. Several members of the *Salmonidae* family have, in fact, failed to prosper in Australian waters, including salmon trout, Loch Leven trout, quinnat salmon, sockeye salmon and migratory salmon. Those that have shown they can reproduce here, the brook trout, *Salvelinus fontinalis*, brown trout, *Salmo trutta*, and rainbow trout, *Oncorhyncluis mykiss*, have all had to be carefully nurtured in government hatcheries and by expensive studies of the environment. They have done so well, the practice of re-stocking has been stopped in some areas. Fish farms specialising in breeding trout for restaurants are flourishing.

The French naturalist De Quatrefages pioneered the artificial fertilisation of fish ova in 1848. The idea was treated sceptically until Joseph Remy, a fisherman from Bresse, demonstrated the technique of stripping eggs from trout, to the French Academy of Sciences. By 1852 the idea had gained sufficient support for an attempt to be made to introduce salmon ova to Tasmania, but none of the first shipment survived. Similar attempts to ship ova alive in an ice house failed in 1860 and 1862, despite a continuous flow of water over the eggs. The fourth attempt in 1864 was successful, with 100,000 Atlantic salmon ova and 3000 brown trout ova landed alive in Melbourne after a 74-day voyage from England. On 4 May, 1864, at the Plenty hatchery in Tasmania the first trout in the southern hemisphere were hatched, and the next day the first salmon. Six pairs of brown trout reached maturity in the Plenty ponds and the progeny of these became the progenitors of brown trout in the whole of Australasia. The turning point had come when James Youl, the Tasmanian Agent in London, had the idea of packing the ova with moss and ice, a procedure that is still followed.

New Zealand received trout from the Plenty hatchery in 1867, brown trout from that original shipment from England. New Zealand's first rainbow trout were introduced into Lake Taupo in 1903. From the start New Zealand's fast-running streams with gravel bottoms and a temperature between 14 and 19.5 degrees C proved ideal for the propagation of trout. But in Australia, the amount of cover on trout streams became crucial, with landlocked fish dependent on insects from over-hanging trees, logs, and water-edge brush. All three Australian trout varieties have their supporters as table fare. Brook trout are the most edible and although brown and rainbow trout lose flavour and become coarse if transported for long distances, they remain a superb meal if thrown on the bank and barbecued immediately after capture.

Brook trout: One of Australia's most appealing freshwater sportfish, both for their fighting prowess and pan quality. They are delicious eating, bite more freely than brown or rainbow trout, and grow faster. Brook trout are chars, members of the genus *Salvelinus*. They were originally native to north eastern America but were introduced to most waters of America and Europe, reaching England in 1865, Continental Europe in 1884, and New Zealand in 1890. From New Zealand they popped up temporarily in New South Wales. They proved to be hardy customers that did well in the wild but in streams

HOOK ARRANGEMENTS FOR TROUT

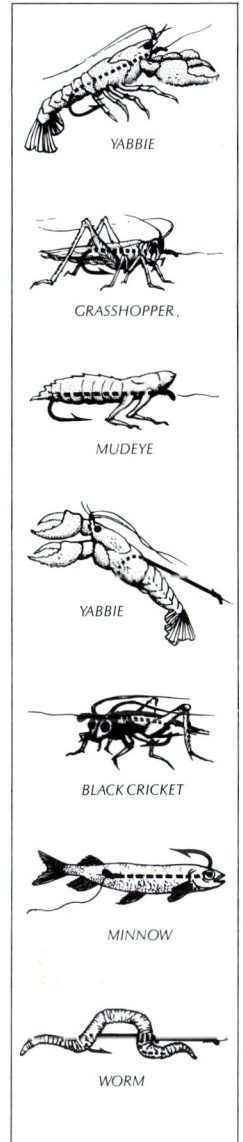

YABBIE

GRASSHOPPER.

MUDEYE

YABBIE

BLACK CRICKET

MINNOW

WORM

Rainbow trout,
Oncorhyncluis mykiss

TYING A FLY

MAKING BODY

Trim

Tying the whisks or setae to hook

2

3

4

5

Body finished note taper both ends

HACKLE TYING

1

Trim

2 *Wind hackle around hook shank in front of body*

3

Tie hackle ends and trim unwanted ends

FINISHED WINGLESS FLY

Whip finish head

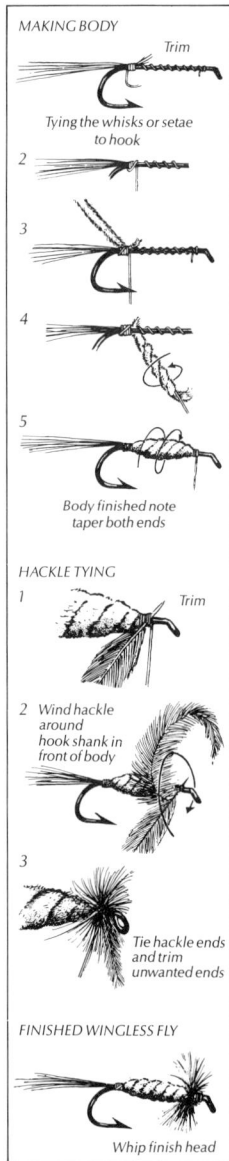

where brown or rainbow trout were present they quickly disappeared. Since 1963 they have been introduced to specially chosen Tasmanian waters free of other trout, where large specimens are now regularly caught. Brook trout can be separated from other trout by their smaller scales and more rounded body. The tail is only slightly forked. They have a heavy, whitish, maze-like pattern on the back, dark wavy lines on the dorsal fin, and white margins on the leading edges of the pectoral, ventral and anal fins. There are distinctive red spots along the sides and down the belly, and the lower fins are a salmon-pink colour. They grow to a weight just short of 1 kg and 28 cm in length.

FISHING TECHNIQUE: Brook trout are caught with live bait, spinning lures and by plug casting and trolling, methods that are considered blasphemy by dedicated fly fishermen. The world record brook trout, 6.6 kg for an 80 cm fish, was taken on a spoon.

DISTRIBUTION: Clarence Lagoon, Little Pine Lagoon, and Little Waterhouse Lagoon in Tasmania.

Brown trout: The most difficult to catch of our three trouts. Some fly fishermen release them after capture as a tribute to their rare fighting qualities. They are natives of Europe, first introduced into Australia in 1888, and more cautious feeders than rainbow or brook trout. They also have an ability to survive in warmer waters than the other trout. Their wariness has enabled them to survive the encroachment of cities and towns into trout terrain. Brown trout vary from brown to blackish-brown with numerous x-shaped red and black spots on the side and dorsal area. These markings are bigger than on the rainbow trout. There is often a yellowish margin on the front of the dorsal, and anal and outer edge of the ventral fins. They have been caught up to 10 kg in Tasmania but brown trout over 2 kg are exceptional. Most mature specimens are around 1 kg. The males develop a hooked underjaw in areas where the fish tend to be cannibals and feed on other fish species.

FISHING TECHNIQUE: Trout will take a wide variety of worms, small fish pieces, grasshoppers, freshwater mussels and just as large a selection of artificial lures from wobblers to spoons, from chrome spinners to plastic wrigglers. To experts, however, trout fishing requires a special fly rod, fly reel, floating or sinking line to match, tapered leaders, and a range of wet or dry flies. Wet flies are those that descend below the water and need to be free of grease or oil. Dry flies have to be treated with oil to make them buoyant on the surface. Fly casting requires a lot of practice but experts can present flies to the trout in a life-like fashion. To catch brown trout regularly, anglers need a variety of flies from which to choose. Flies that work well on one outing often disappoint later.

DISTRIBUTION: Colder waters of New South Wales, Tasmania, Victoria and at Pemberton, Western Australia.

Rainbow trout: Outstanding sporting fish, native to America where they are known as steelheads and a range of local names. They do best in Australian streams with no access to the sea and quickly disappear from waters that are too warm. Australia has large stocks of rainbow and brown trout in a network of government hatcheries. All of these hatcheries have found the fish have a better survival rate if introduced as yearlings rather than fingerlings. Hatchery-reared trout probably account for most of the fishing that tempts thousands of tourists each year. Rainbow do better in fast-flowing streams than in big open waterways like Lake Eucumbene. Their upper bodies are greenish, sometimes purple, and their sides are silver with small black spots, which are fairly dense above the lateral line. The head, dorsal fin, adipose fins, and tail are studded with black spots. The broad crimson band along the flanks that brightens in the breeding season gave them their rainbow appearance. Rainbow trout can reach 10 kg in weight but catches above 2 kg are uncommon.

FISHING TECHNIQUE: Same as for brown trout, with perhaps a variation in the selected flies.

DISTRIBUTION: High country regions of New South Wales, Victoria and Tasmania, in restricted areas of South Australia and at Pemberton in Western Australia. They have been tried at Spring Creek near Warwick in southern Queensland without success.

TROUT COD *Percichthyidae*

Only recently confirmed as a species separate from the Murray cod. Both fish have similar diets and are the same excellent table quality. Both respond to similar angling methods, but trout cod prefer colder water to Murray cod. For many years biologists considered that trout cod, now classified as *Maccullochella macquariensis*, was the cold water Murray cod, but studies by the American biologist Dr. Tim Berra confirmed trout cod as a separate species. Dr. Berra showed that trout cod can be clearly distinguished from Murray cod by the shape of the heads and by the overhanging lower jaw in trout cod. Murray cod appear almost elongate by comparison with the blunter snout, and the dapper rounded bodies of trout cod. Achieving their own identity has not benefitted the trout cod, which is regarded as a threatened species.

FEATURES: The back and sides of trout cod are generally blue-grey, with small grey to black spots or dashes, the spots extending to lower surfaces and into the fin bases. The spots are few on the head. The belly is a light greyish-white, and the tail, soft dorsal, anal, pelvic and pectoral fins are broadly edged in white. A dark stripe extends from the preoperculum through the eyes and nostrils.

FISHING TECHNIQUE: Trout cod grow to 800 mm in length and 16 kg in weight and respond to similar angling methods for catching the Murray cod. They are caught commercially in some States. Like Murray cod, they bite consistently at aeroplane spinners, and most natural baits, including yabbies, worms, molluscs and cut fish.

DISTRIBUTION: Restricted to the cooler reaches of the Murray River and its southern tributaries, as well as the Glenbawn Dam, Lake Sambell, Seven Creeks near Euroa, and the Murrumbidgee near Tharwa, ACT.

Trout cod,
Maccullochella macquariensis

TRUMPETER *Latrididae*

Striped Tasmanian
trumpeter, *Latris lineata*

Large, deeply-bronzed fishes confined to southern Australia and New Zealand, much sought by gourmets because of the superb flavour. They should not be confused with the smaller, striped fishes of the *Terapontidae* family also called trumpeters. The *Latrididae* family of trumpeters is known in shallow coastal waters where the terapons can be reached by children fishing from jetties and piers just for the fun of hearing their grunts, but mostly get down to depths up to 70 fathoms. The best known Australian trumpeters include the illustrated striped Tasmanian trumpeter, *Latris lineata*, which Roughley said reached a weight of 26 kg or 60 lb and a length of 1.21 metres or 4 ft. The bastard trumpeter, *Latridopsis forsteri*, lacks the stripes of the Tasmanian trumpeter but has similar distribution and feeding habits. The real bastard trumpeter, *Mendosoma allporti*, is found in large schools around deep reefs along our southern coasts and has the unusual habit of feeding vertically in the water. All three are prized food fish that have not been properly exploited commercially.

FEATURES: Our two bastard trumpeters are said to have earned their names because of the difficulty in hooking them. More bastard trumpeter are caught in nets than on lines. The tails are deeply forked in all species. Bastard trumpeter are not as brown as Tasmanian trumpeter and are dark olive-green in colour. There is a growing suspicion among biologists that some trumpeters are hybrids.

FISHING TECHNIQUE: A challenging adversary which feeds mainly at night and generally avoids handlines. They mainly feed on crustaceans. They are taken mostly by spearfishermen or in nets but a few succumb to anglers using long shanked hooks on light lines. They bite on barracouta, squid, octopus, lobster tails and molluscs. When caught in numbers, it is usually on snapper rigs offshore. They are fast swimmers that will fight impressively, using rough ground swell as they try to escape.

DISTRIBUTION: From Sydney, New South Wales, south into Victorian and Tasmanian waters and around to south Western Australia. Most plentiful in Tasmania. Also caught in New Zealand under the Maori name moki.

Tuna   *Scombridae*

A group of spirited, voracious fish that provide outstanding sport all around the Australian coast and form an important part of our commercial fishing industry. All 11 species found in Australian coastal waters are streamlined for speed. These fish sustain their lavish expenditure of energy through their ability to eat and digest food quickly, always keeping their body temperature several degrees higher than the seas in which they swim. Whitley credited tuna with swimming speeds up to 64 km/h. Large members of the mackerel family, the tunas include albacore, wahoo, and bonito, which are dealt with separately in this book. They differ from mackerels in having a keel on each side of the butt of their well-forked tail, which, with an impressive set of finlets, helps their speed and stability. They are incessant predators, fearless in their quest for food.

Australian tunas were originally known as tunny. The name was changed on discovery of a potentially huge export market to America, where tuna are considered a luxury. New Zealanders still use the name tunny. Only a small part of Australia's export goals with tuna have been realised, but world demand has dramatically improved through the discovery that eaters of deepsea fish are less likely to have heart attacks than those who do not enjoy tuna and similar species.

Tuna are characteristically blue on top and able to tuck their fins into sheaths or grooves to improve their swimming speed. The various species are separated by their stripes, fin colours and arrangement of spots. Often when they are hooked, their first run will cover close to 100 metres, and they will fight just as tenaciously to escape as marlin or swordfish.

Strangely, the commercial value of tuna was not recognised until 1936 when an aerial survey of New South Wales and Tasmanian waters by Stanley Fowler of the CSIRO disclosed enormous tuna schools. This led to the establishment of canneries at Narooma in New South Wales, and at Port Lincoln in South Australia. The various species of tuna in Australian waters were separated in 1941 by Dr. Serventy in another CSIRO report. In 1950 the Federal government chartered an American tuna clipper, *Senibua*, to demonstrate live bait pole fishing in Australian waters. The *Senibua* caught 117 tonnes of tuna in 70 days fishing, and this, together with a visit to

Yellowfin tuna, *Thunnus albacares*

South Australia in 1956 of two American skippers of pole fishing boats, led to the introduction of the new method in New South Wales and South Australia.

Today's commercial tuna boats are assisted in locating the big schools by spotter aircraft. Catches that had been depleted by the Japanese and Korean longline fishing boats are expected to improve now that new laws have pushed the Japanese boats further away from the Australian coast. Sportsmen operating without the support of aircraft do not appear to have suffered any decline in their catches because of the activities of commercial boats, which is a tribute to the tunas' high fertility rate. Schools with up to 50,000 tuna in them may even reappear.

Skipjack tuna, *Katsuwonus pelamis*: Also known as triped tuna, this is smaller than other tunas, seldom reaching 9 kg in weight, and it is highly rated for the delicacy of its flesh. They have been caught throughout the world and in every Australian State, but have been exploited commercially only in Victoria. Boats based at Lakes Entrance took them in gill nets until 1964 when they transferred their attentions to edible sharks. Skipjack are easily identified by the four dark stripes on the belly that run from the pectoral fin to the tail. There are no markings on the steely-blue back. The ventral and pectoral fins are exceptionally small. The world record for this tuna is 19 kg for a fish caught off Mauritius. The Australian record is 6.57 kg for a fish caught by Dawn Everett off Sydney in 1963, and equalled by Moira Jeffrey off Sydney in 1982. Skipjack tuna takes almost any lure and on light tackle is a splendid sports fish.

Yellowfin tuna, *Thunnus albacares*: A superb fighting fish with sweeping sickle-shaped pectoral fins that reach back to the origin of the second dorsal fin. The anal fin is also longer, matching the second dorsal. The prominence of these fins becomes more apparent in adults than in juveniles and at one time some scientists believed the adults were a separate species, which they called longfin yellowfin tuna. The name is misleading as bluefin tunas also have yellow fins or finlets. They are a rich dark blue on top, yellowy in the middle, and silvery beneath and are mainly identified by their long pectoral fin, which is considerably longer than in bluefin tunas and extended beyond the level of the second dorsal to the anal fin. The second dorsal and anal fins are far taller than the first dorsal and grow larger as the fish matures. In large fish they extend back to the level of the tail flukes. Yellowfin tuna are caught on trolled bait at brisk speeds or on whole live fish while drifting. They attract a large number of sporting boats

Northern bluefin tuna,
Thunnus tonggol

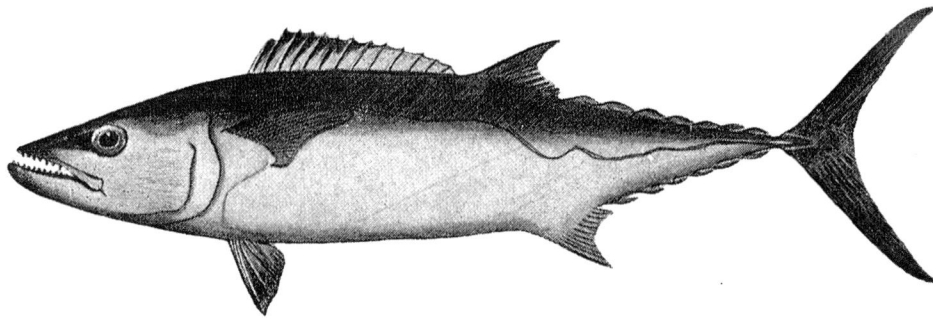

between Port Stephens and Bermagui on the New South Wales coast and are caught regularly off Sydney. The Australian record is 102 kg by Harvey Howe off Bermagui in 1982, but the world record stands at 176.4 kg. They are highly rated table fish, ideal for sashimi.

Northern bluefin tuna, *Thunnus tonggol*: A slightly-built, elongate tuna found for most of the year in tropical waters which moves into cooler seas in summer. They have been reported in huge shoals off both north-eastern and north-western Australia and Grant recorded dense concentrations of them in Moreton Bay in autumn. They are dark-bluish fish with drab daubs over the lower sides and belly between the anal and pectoral fins. Their grey-tipped finlets and the edges of the dorsal and anal fins are yellow. They grow to 35 kg in weight but most of those caught are half that size. They are highly responsive to berleying, but Grant recommends that anglers stick to one type—hardyheads, and their fillets are satisfying to eat if they are blanched by dipping them into hot water before they are deepfried.

Dog-toothed tuna, *Gymnosarda unicolor*: A much-admired variety which fights pugnaciously when hooked, swimming in deep circles or seeking out coral ledges that may cut the line. They are immediately recognised by their dog-like conical teeth. The body lacks scales except over the thorax. They are suspicious, wary predators that swim in small groups and will circle skindivers several times, showing their

quite large teeth. They can be trolled successfully on smaller tunas, squid and mackerel. Dogtooth tuna, which are confined to the warmer waters of northern Australia, are violet-blue above, paler blue across the body, and silvery beneath. Their fins and finlets are a dull golden hue, and the second dorsal and anal fins are trimmed in white.

Southern bluefin tuna, *Thunnus maccoyii*: The largest marine game fish taken in southern Australia, where fish over 100 kg in weight cause no surprise when landed. They are high quality fish that attract high prices in Asian markets and are one of the prime targets of Japanese long-line boats. Their flesh, canned by locals, is eagerly sought as 'sashimi'. In the day of imperial measurements a tradition was established off the Tasmanian coast whereby the skipper of any boat that landed a bluefin over 100 lb received a bottle of spirits. Fish over 200 lb were "two bottlers", those over 300 lb "three bottlers" etc. Every year dozens of one bottler and a few two bottlers between 200 lb and 300 lb were landed, and the fact that four bottlers were sighted but not taken brought fishermen back to the Tasmanian Peninsula year after year. Even when George Park landed an incredible 625 pounder (282.59 kg) bluefin off The Peak near Maroubra, New South Wales, Tasmanian waters lost none of their attraction because visitors spotted so many bluefin over 400 lb. Some were hooked but lost, as was one reputed to have weighed 800 lb (364 kg). Experiments have shown that southern bluefin spawn in the Indian

Dog-toothed tuna, *Gymnosarda unicolor*

DEEP-DIVING PARAVANE

When trolled, paravanes dive deep, taking the lures with them, with the keel stabilising the line.

285

Southern bluefin tuna,
Thunnus maccoyii

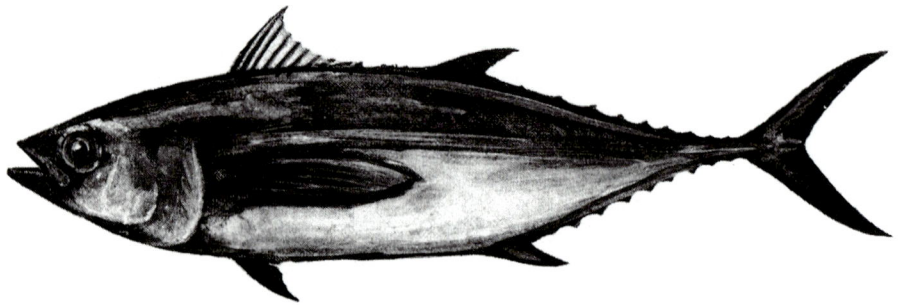

Big-eyed tuna, *Thunnus
obesus*

Ocean and appear as two-year-old fish off Western Australia in summer. Older fish migrate to South Australian, Victorian and Tasmanian waters in summer and up the New South Wales coast in winter. They are believed to live for 20 years and a bluefin tagged in Australia turned up 13.5 years later in the Atlantic off South Africa. Southern bluefin are cobalt blue on top, silvery below, with the tail base and lateral keels golden in juveniles and black in adults. The second dorsal fin and the tail are yellowish, other fins grey. They are the major quarry for game fish boats in Tasmania and New South Wales which troll for them with live baits such as nannygai, whiting, yellow-tail and squid. The best lures are small to medium pink and purple squid on Christmas tree rigs.

Big-eyed tuna, *Thunnus obesus*: A warm-water variety, rich blue above and silvery below with dull yellow finlets edged in black. They are more heavily built than yellowfin and are distinguished from other tunas by their big eyes. They are a white meat fish that attract high prices from Japanese canneries but few of them have been taken by Australian game anglers. The Australian record is 120 kg for a fish caught by Neville Ivill off Bermagui in 1985. Far bigger specimens have been taken by Japanese long-liners. They are distributed through Western Australia, the Northern Territory and Queensland, with some movement into New South Wales and South Australia in warm weather. An identifying feature is that on either side of the tail base there is a large powerful keel

Mackerel tuna, *Euthynnus affinis*

between two smaller keels. Big-eye tuna have the admiration of game fishermen for their fighting qualities when they succumb to baits of small mackerel, squid, tuna sardines and crustaceans.

Mackerel tuna, *Euthynnus affinis*: A captivating fish easily recognised by the patch of wavy, mackerel-like markings on the upper back, which extend from the dorsal fin to the tail. There are four rounded spots on the belly between the pectoral and ventral fins. Some have spots level with the pectoral fin and these are considered to be an Atlantic variation of the species. Those with spots below the pectoral fin belong to the Indian and Pacific Oceans. Mackerel tuna are robust, tapering fish which shoal in inshore waters, where they feed on pilchards, blue sprats and herring. They are common on mackerel grounds where they are a nuisance to professional mackerel-trolling boats. They are a glittery blue above and silvery below, and grow to a weight of 14 kg. They are distributed in northern Western Australia, the Northern Territory, Queensland and northern New South Wales. Their flesh is dark but suitable for steaming if it is blanched before cooking by dunking it in boiling water.

Frigate mackerel, *Auxis thazard*: The smallest of Australia's tunas, a blue water variety seldom seen in estuaries and harbours. They grow to 4.5 kg but are more often seen at 1.5 kg. Their main value is as a baitfish. Scientists have for years given their range as the tropical warm waters in Australia's north but there are increasing reports of frigate mackerel off southern Western Australia, southern New South Wales around Eden and occasionally even in the Great Australian Bight. They have rounder, deeper bodies than common mackerel and usually have eight small finlets between the second dorsal fin and the tail, and seven underneath between the anal fin and the tail. The upper body is dark blue, shading to silvery white on the belly, with broad, wavy lines forming mackerel-like markings on the back. These markings are not as distinct as in mackerel tuna and there are no spots below the pectorals as in mackerel tuna.

FISHING TECHNIQUE: Tunas are migratory, surface fish which only swim at any depth in the later stages of life. They have a marked preference for live fish baits, but will take feathered lures and spinners. They are generally taken by trolling from boats but a few are caught from the shore. Wire traces are essential when fishing for the bigger species, as is a swivel that will prevent tangles. Recommended hooks are 6/0 to 12/0 with line strength anything from 5 kg to 15 kg.

TURRUM *Carangidae*

Turrum, *Carangoides fulvoguttatus*

Important game fish of remarkable endurance that contributed largely to the reputation of Cairns and other north Queensland fishing centres, and promise to do the same for the prestige of the Abrolhos Islands. Turrum are members of the great trevally family *Carangidae* which includes superb game fish like yellowtail, samson fish, dark queenfish, scad, pomfret, runner, pilot fish, leatherskin, jack mackerel and bludger. They have earned the respect of game fishermen, for they are among the most tenacious and crafty fighters in a family whose sixty-odd Australian members are all built for a scrap. They have powerful, compressed bodies and deeply forked tails, milky-blue on top, silvery beneath. There are at least six indistinct dark vertical bands across the body. The pectoral fin has a dark smudge at the base. Golden spots are speckled across the top of the body. Turrum also known as gold-spotted trevally, grow to around 40 kg overseas but the biggest so far caught in Australia weighed 11.6 kg. They are frequently confused with their relatives, giant trevally, *Caranx ignobilis*.

FEATURES: Turrum, *Carangoides fulvoguttatus*, lack the giant trevally's scales at the base of the pectoral fin. The second dorsal fin in turrum has 25 to 30 rays, giant trevally only 18 to 21. The bony scutes on the lateral line towards the tail number 15 to 21 in turrum and 26 to 38 in giant trevally. In turrum there is a broken line of bronze marks running along the base of the anal fin.

FISHING TECHNIQUE: Trolling from game boats. Turrum will take cut fish baits, live garfish, octopus, squid, prawns and molluscs, and also bite on spoons and drones. A brisk boat speed is important if they are to take artificial lures. A turrum usually strikes without being seen by anglers, fighting in a sequence of deep lunges, jolting its head back to turn on its side and take advantage of its deep torso. They tire slowly, testing the patience of the angler with rare stamina. Linked hooks and wire traces are advisable on these reef-dwellers, which demand at least breaking strain lines of 27.21 kg (60 lb) and 6/0 to 8/0 XXX hooks. Half-hour battles with turrum are common.

DISTRIBUTION: Tropical and sub-tropical waters of the Barrier Reef and northern Australia and down to the Albrolhos Islands in Western Australia. Rarely seen below the Tropic of Capricorn.

Unicornfish   *Acanthuridae*

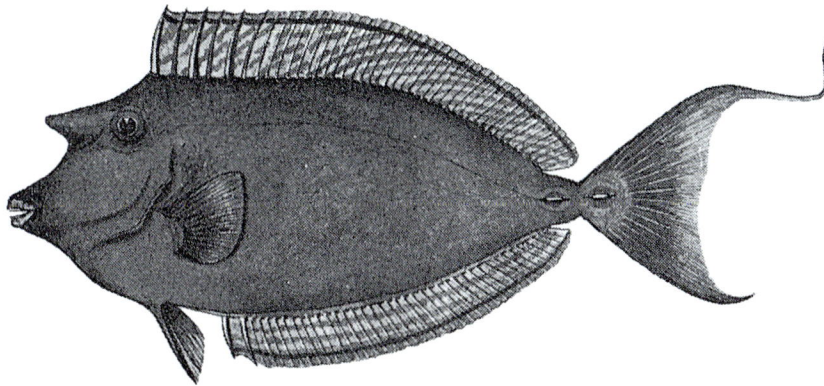

Warm sea fishes with a distinctive horn in front of the eyes which appear to become more prominent in mature specimens, and two knife-sharp blades on each side of the tail which can inflict painful cuts. They resemble leatherjacket but are more closely related to tangs and surgeonfishes. The main Australian varieties are the short-horned unicornfish, *Naso brevirostris*, which has only a short hump in front of the eyes; the black-finned unicornfish, *Naso lituratus*, the only member of the family that does not grow a horn or lump on the forehead; the brown unicornfish, *Naso unicornis*, whose dark brown body is mottled with a darker brown; and the ring-tailed unicornfish, *Naso annulatus*, which has a broad white band around the base of the tail.

FEATURES: All unicornfish have sharp keels at the base of the tail and extended dorsal fins. They are oily and mainly poor foodfish. The black-finned unicornfish has been implicated in ciguatera poisoning. Most have five or six dorsal spines and three ventral rays. Brown unicornfish have a prominent filament trailing back from the upper edge. They have small mouths and concentrate on a vegetable diet at depths that make them unseen by anglers.

DISTRIBUTION: Western Australia, Northern Territory, and Queensland. Some of them treat shallow water as territorial, retreating to their special crevices when harrassed. Difficult to approach, they are more often speared than photographed.

Brown unicornfish, *Naso unicornis*

CIGUATERA POISONING: The most common source of illness caused by toxins in fish eaten by Australians. The name came from Spaniards who settled in the Caribbean. At various times some 300 species of fish have been blamed for causing this form of poisoning. The problem can be blamed more on geographical boundaries rather than on species. However, Australia's north-east coast, the islands of the central and south Pacific, the West Indies, Japan and the southern American coast provide the unsafe fish. Fish known to have caused ciguatera have turned up in the Brisbane fishmarkets but originated from the Gladstone area, at the southern end of the Barrier Reef. Only a few reef fish are affected, and usually the trouble has been traced to very large fish from which families have had several meals.

WAHOO *Scombridae*

Wahoo, *Acanthocybium solandri*

A noted game fish of exceptional speed and stubborn fighting qualities whose willingness to jump from the sea in an effort to free themselves has thrilled many fishermen. Wahoo, *Acanthocybium solandri*, are faster than Spanish mackerel or barracuda, the finest sport fish of all the mackerel family, and their tapered bodies give them an edge in speed on dolphin fish and queenfish. They strike lures at great speed and their first run is a regular line-stripper. They are loners, often intercepting baits intended for marlin. They are highly regarded table fish, with finely-grained sweet flesh.

FEATURES: The teeth of the wahoo slash with speed and power, biting baits in half with a barely perceptible underwater movement. There are 50 or more teeth on each side of their jaws and because of this, they need to be treated with caution when removing hooks. They are navy blue above to aluminium on the sides, light grey below. The fins are mostly silvery or grey, the eyes yellow or grey, the first dorsal and part of the ventral blue. Wahoo grow to around 1.8 metres in length and are generally caught at weights between 14 and 18 kg. The Australian record was a wahoo of 46.15 kg taken by Clifford Egar in Botany Bay, Sydney, in April, 1981. They are particularly plentiful in the waters off Narooma on the New South Wales south coast, where Tom Scott caught a 42 kg specimen on a 24 kg line in April, 1978. One of the best wahoo catches was Tim Simpson's 35 kg fish on a 6 kg line in Broken Bay, NSW, in January, 1980. Overseas wahoo appear to grow to larger sizes, and there is a record of a 67.7 kg catch in the Bahamas. International sport fishermen call them Jack mackerel.

FISHING TECHNIQUE: Wahoo will take high speed drones and similar lures, usually weighted for additional trolling depth. Trolled baits include large pilchards, whole mullet, large garfish, and bonito strips. The hooks need to be very sharp and set well back in the bait. They are especially partial to flying fish, small tuna and squid, but when hooked will take out several hundred metres of line in their first run.

DISTRIBUTION: North-western Australia, coastal waters of northern New South Wales and Queensland, Lord Howe Island, New Guinea and a wide range of tropical seas. Marlin fishermen operating from the northern tip of the Great Barrier Reef know them well.

WESTRALIAN JEWFISH   *Glaucosomatidae*

The most sought after fish in Western Australian waters and largest member of its family available in the west. They are not impressive in their colouring and show inconsistent fighting qualities, but they have won more respect from western anglers than any other fish. Like their east coast ally, the pearl perch or epaulette fish, *Glaucosoma scapulare*, the Westralian jewfish, *Glaucosoma herbraicum*, is a fish of outstanding table quality. Roughley said the pearl perch was the most delicious eating fish in Australian waters and its western relative is not far behind it. Many a fishing outing has become a triumph through the capture of a big Westralian jewfish. They are unrelated to eastern jewfish or mulloway of the *Sciaenidae* family, which are also plentiful in the west. Westralian jewfish have one or more dorsal produced rays, and a shoulder blade bone that grows to a round lobe and darkens in older fish.

FEATURES: Silvery to greyish in colour with dark transverse bars on the head and body. Sometimes there is a dark oblique bar from the eye to the interopercle. They have big heads and very powerful mouths and have been caught up to 25 kg in weight. The Western Australian Department of Fisheries and Wildlife enforces a daily bag limit of ten Westralian jewfish and the minimum legal length at which they may be retained when caught is 50 cm or 20 inches.

FISHING TECHNIQUE: By handlines or rod and reel from the rocks or boats. Best baits are squid, prawns, octopus, small live fish, cut pieces of whiting or parrotfish. They fight hard inshore but are unpredictable in deep water, where the big ones are generally taken. They are inclined to pick at the bait and anglers have learned to give them more line when this occurs. They use every ounce of their weight to exert pressure on the line as they are lifted and come on board like a sack of coal. Recommended rigs for Westralian jewfish are similar to those for snapper with a fixed sinker at the end of the line to keep the rig well down. Hooks should be attached to swivels about a metre up the line and spaced around a metre apart further up the line.

DISTRIBUTION: Only in Western Australia. From Cape Naturaliste in the south to Shark Bay in the north. They are most plentiful off Rottnest Island, the Albrolhos Islands, Port Moore, Lucky Bay and Port Gregory. They are the main species caught by game boats around Fremantle, Busselton and Bunbury.

Westralian jewfish, *Glaucosoma herbraicum*

WHITE EAR   *Pomacentridae*

White ear scalyfin, *Parma microlepis*

A family of around 320 tropical marine fishes known as damselfishes, three of which, the common scalyfin, *Parma victoriae*, the white ear scalyfin, *Parma microlepis*, and the one-spot puller, *Chromis hypsilepis*, venture into cool Australian temperate waters. White ear are brownish-grey to black along the body and are immediately known by the white blotch set at the ear. These carnivores pull hard when hooked, which is why they are sometimes known as puller. There is a marked difference between juvenile and adult white ears, with the mature specimens scarcely recognisable. Juveniles have the same white markings on the ears but are brilliantly coloured on the body, whereas mature white ears are plain and drab. They generally have only a single nostril on either side of the head. The anal fin has two spines, and the dorsal fin is continuous with 9 to 14 spines. The jaw is toothless. White ear grow to 170 mm in length. The common scalyfin is the largest representative of the family, reaching 1.3 kg or 3 lb. Their flesh is edible but lacks flavour.

FEATURES: Grown white ears have much smaller eyes and a deeper body than the young, although both retain the characteristic white spot on the ears. The eye is relatively low on their heads. The body is moderately elongated and moderately depressed, and the opercle is generally silvery-white.

FISHING TECHNIQUE: White ear are fearless fishes and will attack skindivers to protect their territory. They are only occasionally taken by line but their true place in the scheme of things is in aquariums where their colouring and energy is a source of awe.

DISTRIBUTION: *Parma microlepis* are found in New South Wales, Victoria, and in Bass Strait as far south as Port Arthur; *Parma victoriae* in South Australia, Western Australia, Victoria and Tasmania.

WHITING   *Sillaginidae*

Fast, alert little fish of delicious table quality despite many fine bones. There are eleven species of *Sillaginid* whiting in Australian waters, many of them exclusive to Australia. They are not related to the English whiting, which is a member of the cod family, and are also distinct from Australia's rock whitings, which are related to parrot-fishes. They all have long soft noses, well-rounded mouths, and small teeth, and are probably the only marine fish Australian anglers should snatch at, as soon as they start to nip at the bait. All eleven species are slightly compressed, elongate, with tapering tails and longish snouts. Although they average about 30 cm in length and the biggest rarely exceed 45 cm, they provide splendid sport.

Australian whiting prefer to swim in sandy shallows, which they resemble in colour, and sometimes bury in the sand. They are olive-brown or sandy above, white below. Some species have rusty or brown spots on the body, or a dark black or blue patch at the base of the pectoral fin. They are very selective over what they take into their small, horseshoe-shaped mouths, and have small teeth. Their two dorsal fins are generally only slightly separated.

Whiting are sought from beaches, sand-pits, jetties, seawalls, rivers, tidal lakes, estuaries and bays, mostly by boat. Whatever the rig used, it is essential that the slightest touch be immediately transmitted to the angler and for this, a light, stiff spinning rod is ideal. Hook sizes are debatable but should be long-shanked because of the whiting's soft, small mouth. Successful whiting anglers generally use two lines, one to drag along with the drift of the boat, and another to keep a bait bobbing up and down just above the bottom. The alternative is to anchor the boat on a sand flat and berley the area with chopped-up prawns or pipis. In estuaries use handlines on cork winders or plastic casting spools. Long rods usually are taboo because it is impossible to cast accurately with them in a boatload of other fishermen.

On ocean beaches the whiting are found mostly in active white water in the shallower sections of the surf, demanding a heavier type of surf tackle. In the surf, whiting often bite better on the ebb than they do on the rise and they can crowd the potholes and gutters of the surf at low tide. It is easy to relax in these conditions while wading in the shallows but success comes to those who remain alert for the whiting's nip at the bait followed by their dash for cover.

School whiting, *Sillago bassensis*: School whiting, also known as Bass Strait whiting or silver whiting, are excellent eating but are less in demand than other whiting because of their small size. They occur in large schools in the deeper regions of large bays but frequently venture into shallow water at night. They are sometimes caught by anglers fishing for flathead. They grow to around 30 cm and the body colours are reddish-brown, shading to silver on the belly, with a silvery longitudinal stripe and a brown longitudinal stripe above it. The dorsal, pectoral and tail fins are greyish-brown. The tapered head and orange-brown spots along the body make them easily identifiable.

DISTRIBUTION: Tasmania, Victoria, New South Wales, South Australia, Queensland, and Western Australia, where they are plentiful off the south coast.

WHITING DRIFTING RIG

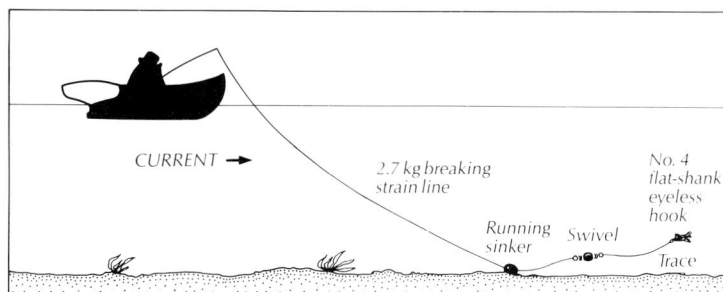

CURRENT →

2.7 kg breaking strain line

Running sinker

Swivel

Trace

No. 4 flat-shank eyeless hook

Golden-lined whiting, *Sillago analis*: A delicious whiting which shoals in such numbers that catches of 100 from an outing are not uncommon. They are also known as rough-skinned whiting and "Tin Can Bay" whiting because of their prevalence in that area. Their overall body colour is more uniformly silver than in sand whiting and the anal and ventral fins are bright yellow. Another factor that distinguishes them from sand whiting is their smaller size—they grow to a maximum of only 30 cm, whereas sand whiting reach 50 cm. They feed voraciously on yabbies and often use their conical snouts to stir up soft, sandy bottoms in the search for marine worms.

DISTRIBUTION: Golden-lined whiting are the most commonly taken whiting around Fraser Island in the Piabla-Scarness region and in Hervey Bay. They are found in Moreton Bay all the way up the Queensland coast into the Northern Territory, and are common in Shark Bay, Western Australia.

Sand whiting, *Sillago ciliata*: The most commonly caught Australian whiting, abundant all the year in the eastern states but more restricted in the south and west. When sand whiting are biting, they attract hordes of anglers in Maroochydore, Tweed Heads, Brunswick Heads, Ballina and Iluka-Yamba. They are olive-green along the

Golden-lined whiting, *Sillago analis*

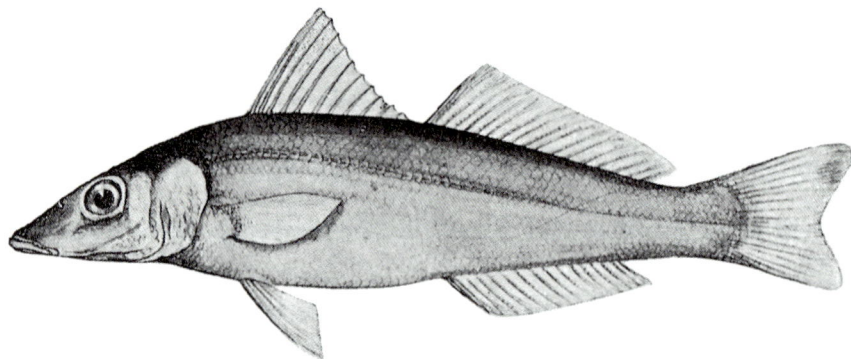

Sand whiting, *Sillago ciliata*

back, merging to silvery-green, silver and then white below. The lower fins show strong yellow tinges, and the dorsal fins are studded with small dark spots. They live mainly on the sandflats and along the shallow channels in estuaries, on ocean sandbars, and in the surf along ocean beaches. They are adept at burying into the sand and throw up puffs of silt as they drive into the sand, propelled, it seems, by their tails, to escape from seine nets and lines. Whiting specialists learn to clomp about sandbanks or smack the bottom with a paddle to bring up buried sand whiting. They take light tackle baits like live worms, yabbies, peeled prawns and soldier crabs and bite best at night on rising tides. They bite so freely when feeding that once-a-year holiday anglers who use two or three hooks often land a fish on each hook. Only in strong surf should the breaking strain of lines used for sand whiting be increased above 3 kg, for they are basically a light tackle fish on which small hooks and a small sinker half a metre above the hook suffice.

DISTRIBUTION: Right along the eastern coastline from Cape York to Tasmania. Most plentiful in southern Queensland and on the New South Wales north coast. Occasionally in eastern Victoria.

King George or **spotted whiting,** *Sillaginodes punctata*: Largest and most notable of Australia's whiting and a particularly important commercial fish in South

Australia. They provide superb sport and are a gourmet's delight, unmistakable in their colouration of scattered black spots spread over a golden-brownish upper body and a silvery belly. The dorsal fins are decorated with a liberal number of somewhat larger spots. Young King George whiting venture into shallow bays but mature specimens prefer water to 10 fathoms in depth. They have been recorded to lengths of 70 cm and 4.8 kg but average around 1 kg. The biggest specimens are solitary fish, providing an additional challenge for sportsmen. The big ones require No. 1 to 4 hooks and are highly selective in their feeding, limiting the range of baits to which they will respond. Sand shrimps and pink nippers taken with yabby pumps from estuary flats are soft bait but the big whiting relish them.

DISTRIBUTION: Southern Western Australia—they take their name from King George Sound through South Australia into Victoria. A few stragglers enter New South Wales waters. They are at their best in Spencer Gulf and the Gulf of St. Vincent in South Australia.

Northern whiting, *Sillago sihama*: A warm water variety prevalent in northern Australia. They show up in nets cast for mullet and herring along coastal flats, a small fish that grows to only 30 cm and is easily distinguished from sand whiting by the absence of a black bar in front of

Trumpeter whiting,
Sillago maculata

the pectoral fins. The pectoral fins and tail are strongly tinted in yellow, but the rest of the fish is uniformly silver. A vague golden stripe runs along the lateral line.

DISTRIBUTION: Throughout tropical Australia.

Stout whiting, *Sillago robusta*: An offshore variety seldom caught by anglers. They are pale yellow above, silvery below and have a bright silvery band running along the body that separates these colours. The cheeks have a vivid golden patch and there are no dark markings on the pectoral fin. They are almost exclusively captured by trawlers.

DISTRIBUTION: The entire Western Australian coast across to the Northern Territory into Queensland and New South Wales. There appears to be both an eastern and western population of them.

Trumpeter whiting, *Sillago maculata*: A smaller member of the whiting family which does not rate as highly as King George whiting and sand whiting. They shoal densely and will bite on almost any bait, but rarely penetrate the big harbours and bays. Found further out from shore than sand whiting. Trumpeter whiting are also known as winter whiting and diver whiting. Trawlers take large numbers of them from the deeper waters that anglers cannot reach and there is often a glut of them in the markets but their flesh lacks the firmness and flavour of other whiting. They are seldom seen in lengths beyond 20 cm. They shoal in such vast numbers that anglers who go out two or three kilometres from shore frequently catch 70 or 80 in a session. Trumpeter whiting vary in colour from the silvery-green hue of the Queensland specimens to the dark golden brown of those caught in the south. They are ideal for steaming.

DISTRIBUTION: Plentiful in all States except Victoria, South Australia and Tasmania, where their appearance is unpredictable.

WIRRAH   *Serranidae*

Shallow-water cod immediately recognised by their large, ocellated spots. The spots completely cover the head and body. They are also known as pepper or peppermint cod, mother-in-law fish, and old boots because their flesh is so coarse, tough and bland. Whitley told how humourists suggested the best way to cook wirrah was to boil it with an axehead, when the axehead softened, eat it and throw away the wirrah. Australia's two main varieties of wirrah are known as the eastern wirrah, *Acanthistius ocellatus*, and the western wirrah, *Acanthistius serratus*, which are separated largely by colour. Both grow to around 500 mm or 20 inches, and are equally despised as food fish. Their young are common in rock pools.

FEATURES: The eastern wirrah is identified by its brown body, tinged with green above and white to bluish-white below. Their dark fins are smudged in dull blue-grey towards the edges. The western wirrah has two broad black bars immediately below and behind the eye. In the eastern wirrah the body spots are bluish, in the western wirrah the spots are small and black. Both have 13 dorsal spines and 14 to 16 rays, and the scales on the head and body are very small.

FISHING TECHNIQUE: Nobody would deliberately seek to catch wirrah but they are frequently hooked by rock fishermen seeking luderick. In some fishing clubs, the angler who catches the largest wirrah collects a booby prize.

DISTRIBUTION: Eastern wirrah from the rocky reefs of eastern Victoria, New South Wales, southern Queensland and Lord Howe Island; western wirrah from the coastal waters of South Australia and Western Australia.

Western wirrah, *Acanthistius serratus*

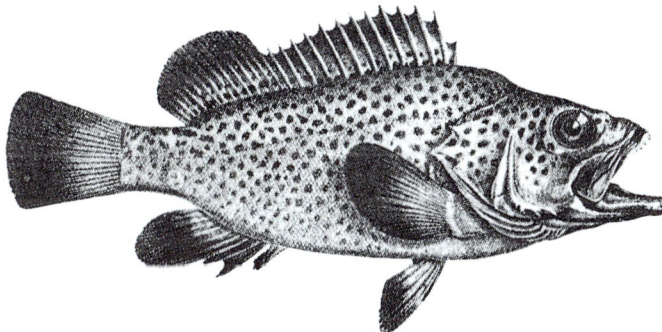

BAG LIMITS: Apart from imposing fines on amateur fishermen who catch certain species below minimum legal lengths, most States have the right to restrict bag limits. In Western Australia, for instance, only five Westralian jewfish may be taken in a day. Trout are restricted to 10 per day, blue groper to one per day, greenlip abalone and brownlip abalone to 10 per day. In South Australia, abalone are restricted to five a day but the bag limit on King George whiting is a generous 30 fish per day. New South Wales had a complete ban on catching groper when that species seemed an endangered fish, but now allows two groper per day provided they are taken on rods or handlines. Queensland now has a closed season for barramundi. Tasmania has a bag limit of 12 trout per day. Lists of all these bag limits are available at state government tourist offices.

Wrasses *Labridae*

Highly-coloured reef-dwellers of the family that includes tusk fishes, jaw slingers, thicklips, combfish, pigfish and rainbow, but not parrotfish, which belong to the family *Scaridae*. The teeth of parrotfish are fused together, whereas in wrasses they are separate, peg-like crushing stems. There are more than 400 wrasses around the world and Australia has a large percentage of them, chiefly in Queensland. They present a spectacular, if bewildering array of colours and most are eagerly sought for aquariums. They are usually carnivorous, feeding on shellfish, crabs, shrimps and small fish. They include the elongate quaker or cigar wrasses (*Chelio*); the spotty (*Psuedolabrus*); pretty polly (*Dotalabrus*); the remarkable jaw slinger, *Epibulus insidiator*, a restless fish that sometimes swims upside down and has an extensible tube-like mouth; the comb fish, *Coris picta*, with its jagged comb-like lateral line; and the black-eyed thick-lipped wrasse, *Hemigymnus melapterus*, with its highly-developed protruding upper and lower lips. Most wrasses are protogynous hermaphrodites, starting life as females and changing to become males. In most, the change of sex is accompanied by a change of colour. Some of the juvenile members of the family act as cleaner fish, removing parasites from the bodies, fins and gills of other fish. They range in size from 45 cm in length and 1.3 kg in weight to 2.1 metres in length and weighing 170 kg, the size attained by the giant Maori wrasse or Napoleon, *Cheilinus undulatus*. They are sometimes difficult to clean and fillet and require careful handling because of the sharp, protruding tusks, but they are generally good eating.

Venus tusk-fish, *Choerodon venustus*: Big, pugnacious fish that have to be turned quickly before they reach the safety of reef rocks or crevices. They are greenish-grey on top but become bright pink along the sides, which is why they are known as cockies in some areas. The head and cheek

Venus tusk-fish,
Choerodon venustus

are pink and the body is studded with blue and white spots. The young have slightly curved tails but this becomes square-cut in adults. All the fins are edged in light blue but the tail is predominantly blue.

FISHING TECHNIQUE: Venus tusk-fish average 900 grams but have been rod-fished weighing 4.54 kg (10 lb) on Cape Moreton reefs in southern Queensland. They are generally taken on lures or cut fish baits. Their flesh is white and well textured.

DISTRIBUTION: All of the Queensland coast and especially on southern sections of the Barrier Reef. Occasional stragglers in northern New South Wales.

Harlequin tusk-fish, *Choerodon fasciatus,* a gorgeous coral fish whose colouring rivals the most brilliant parrots. Even the teeth are an unusual bright blue. Their heads are pink, the body silvery-grey to greenish, fading to dark blue and purple towards the tail. There are six to nine crimson or scarlet crossbars, one of them crossing the eye from nape to throat. The first dorsal, soft dorsal and anal fins have blue near the base, and the pectoral fin is golden yellow.

FISHING TECHNIQUE: Few would consider eating such a beautiful fish and they are mostly taken alive for aquariums, a suitable fate as they are hardy and easy to look after. Whitley wrote of one who became so popular in 18 months of activity in the Noumea aquarium that it was widely mourned when it died and later figured on a New Caledonian stamp.

DISTRIBUTION: They are not as common today as they once were on the Barrier Reef, but are found in northern Queensland and in Caledonia to the Riu Kui islands.

Hump-headed Maori wrasse, *Cheilinus undulatus*: The largest member of the group found in the southern hemisphere. They develop a large fleshy hump on the nape of the neck as they mature, a tricorn hat effect that brought the fish the nickname Napoleon. They are not uncommon at weights of 23.4 kg or 100 lb and there is a record of one caught at Hayman Island that weighed 182.60 kg or 420 lb. They do not form large shoals but generally move about the bays or coral reefs in groups of six or eight, grinding chunks of coral in their powerful teeth to extract mussels and

Hump-headed Maori wrasse, *Cheilinus undulatus*

worms. The cheeks carry a pattern of wavy cream lines that extend back over the body beyond the pectoral fins. The body is brown, with green on top, and the brown fins are studded in yellow. Two prominent black lines run back from the eye and two other lines slant down from the eyes to the upper lip. The hump that develops with age rises directly between the eyes.

FISHING TECHNIQUE: This is a very difficult fish to land. Blessed with outstanding bulk the Maori wrasse offers a stubborn, sustained fight that makes the task of bringing it into a boat hard work. Heavy lines of at least 22.68 kg (50 lb) breaking strain, with a strong wire trace are essential. They take most cut fish, molluscs, shellfish, cunjevoi, crabs, crayfish, and can crack triton shells in their teeth, but are adept in dragging lines on which they are hooked over coral.

DISTRIBUTION: All around northern Australia, down to Carnarvon on the west coast and as far as Fraser Island on the east coast. Common on the Barrier Reef.

Black-spot tusk-fish, *Choerodon schoenleinii*: A stubborn warm-water variety, highly rated as a table fish, that takes its name from the black spot set high on the back, at the start of the dorsal rays. Mature specimens make every bit of their 15 kg count when they are hooked. Fishermen looking down at them feeding through the clear waters of a reef cannot but admire the manner in which they remove slabs of coral and then burrow through the sand to crush the crabs uncovered. They are so popular, a group of anglers in Moreton Bay fish for nothing else. Their head is bright blue to purple, usually with a light blue bar behind the eye. There is a pattern of short vertical blue stripes over the greenish-blue body. The stripes carry on into the tail, which is vivid purple, and edged in brown.

FISHING TECHNIQUE: Grant highly recommends blue swimmer crabs as bait for this challenging fish. Remove the shell and use half the crab for each bait. Take the same safeguards as for other sharp-toothed, heavily-built fish, by turning it before it finds a hole or crevice amid the coral. A wire trace that can be detached with a ring or swivel makes the fish easier to boat and will save the line when snags occur.

DISTRIBUTION: Right along the New South Wales coastline north into southern Queensland and the Barrier Reef, on into Torres Strait and the Gulf of Carpentaria.

Graphic tusk-fish, *Choerodon graphicus*: An easily recognised reef-dweller with a drab tan body over which a series of heavy dark green bands stretch from top to belly. Heavy green fins, a striking blue eye, and the characteristic peg teeth combine to produce a dramatic overall effect. The fish itself attracts further attention through its habit of digging holes which they occupy for a time before backing off to watch for crabs and molluscs it may have stirred up.

FISHING TECHNIQUE: A fish for cameramen rather than anglers. It grows to around 45 cm.

DISTRIBUTION: Queensland coral reefs.

Ringed wrasse, *Hologymnosus annulatus*: One of the smaller more elongate wrasses, which, unlike others in the family, prefers small fish to crabs and shellfish and does not make such a habit of nibbling on coral. Identification is difficult because of their variations in colour, but the body generally is bright green, shading to light blue over the mouth and throat. There are 17 to 19 dark vertical bars running across the body. There is a small black spot at the back of the gill covers. The black eyes are surrounded in orange or red, but they change colour so readily, the extremely long pectoral fins are a much better means of identification.

FISHING TECHNIQUE: Another fish for cameramen, not anglers, with big appeal in aquariums. They grow to 56 cm.

DISTRIBUTION: The Indian and Pacific Oceans, from Victoria to the Barrier Reef and across to Western Australia.

Bird wrasse, *Gomphosus varius*: A warm-water variety with an amazing beak-like snout which swims around with a sculling action that makes it resemble an underwater bird, using the pectoral fins like wings. The males closely resemble the females but are much larger, with a blue beak and head, a yellow-green smudge on the pectorals, and a greenish body merging into a blue tail.

FISHING TECHNIQUE: An aquarium variety of little angling or food value.

DISTRIBUTION: The top half of Australia in shallow coral areas, with a few stragglers reaching into New South Wales and Victoria in the east and as far as Perth in the west.

Baldchin groper, *Choerodon rubescens*: This is a tusk fish so often referred to as a groper that authorities have gone along with public opinion. They have the tell-tale protruding tusks of the wrasse family, and the characteristic peg-like teeth, but retain the name groper simply because of public usage. They grow to 25 kg and unlike most other wrasses are unknown on the Barrier Reef. They are generally blue-green on the body with tinges of pink and a head that dominates their profile. The clear white of the chin and lower lip give it its name, contrasting as it does with the glowing green of the lower cheeks. The pectoral fins are a prominent blue-white at the base, and all other fins are a vivid blue.

FISHING TECHNIQUE: One of the fish most sought by Western Australian anglers, who bait with cut fish and crabs and recognise a tenacious adversary. They mainly congregate at a depth of 20 fathoms.

DISTRIBUTION: Restricted to the reefs of Western Australia from Shark Bay to Geographe Bay and generally thought to live among the sand areas between rocky outcrops.

Moon wrasse, *Thalassoma lunare*: A flavoursome little wrasse of brilliant colouring which takes its name from the new moon crescent formed by the upper and lower edges of the tail. Their vivid green bodies are striped with red bars. Every scale is streaked in pink. Around the head there is a pattern of wavy red-mauve lines. The pectoral fin is boldly splashed with red and blue. Grant has found on various fishing excursions that Queensland anglers often return the moon wrasse to the water on capture, believing that such a lovely fish deserves to survive.

FISHING TECHNIQUE: Despite their small mouths moon wrasses are often taken by fishermen on the southern Queensland snapper grounds. They grow to about a third of a metre and prefer shallow water, where their inquisitive nature makes them easy prey for well presented baits of crustaceans and cut fish.

DISTRIBUTION: Moon wrasse have been identified from Rottnest Island in Western Australia right up the Western Australian coast to the Northern Territory and the Gulf of Carpentaria and down the Queensland coast into northern New South Wales.

Blue-throated wrasse, *Pseudolabrus tetricus*: Also known as southern purple wrasse and banded parrotfish. A series of yellow vertical bars cover their green-to-purple

Moon wrasse,
Thalassoma lunare

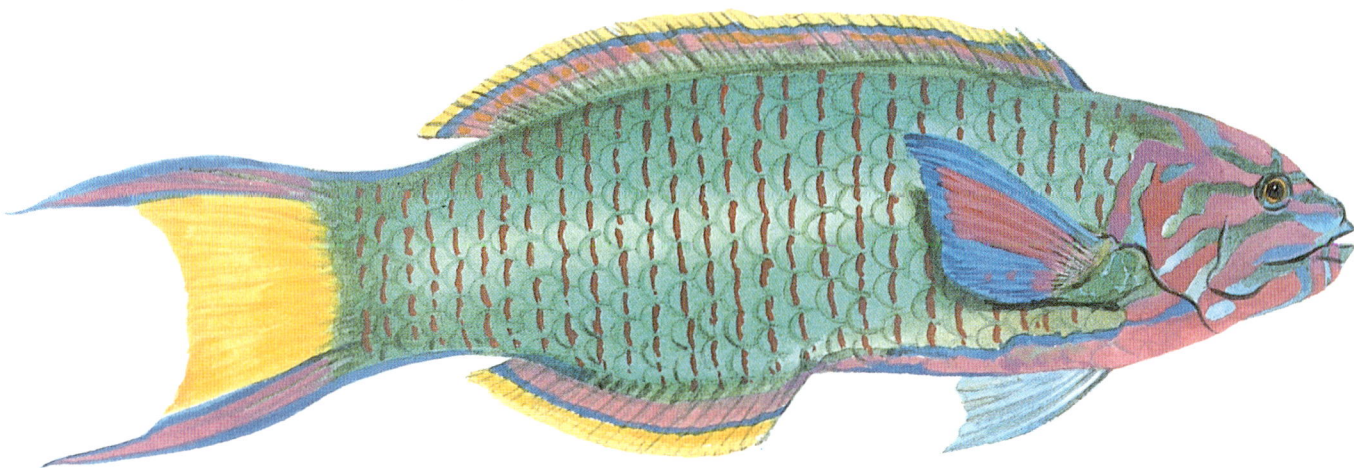

Rock whiting, *Haletta
semifasciata*

Blue-throated wrasse,
Pseudolabrus tetricus

bodies and their head is heavily tinted in a superb light blue that stretches back to the gill covers. Some Queensland fishermen refer to them as winter bream and they grow to the same size as bream, 2 kg or 4.5 lb.

FISHING TECHNIQUE: The white flesh of this wrasse is so well-known to be highly palatable (provided the fish is bled soon after capture), they have become targets for net fishermen. Orthodox anglers find they respond well to small baits of prawns and crabs and do not require traces or heavy lines.

DISTRIBUTION: The Blue-throated wrasse is plentiful in Australia's southern waters, and is often spotted on shallow reefs in Tasmania, South Australia, Victoria and New South Wales.

Rock whiting, *Haletta semifasciata*: A member of the wrasse family, also known as grass whiting and stranger, which prefers Australia's temperate waters. They have the lengthy dorsal fin, characteristic of the wrasse family, and non-protractile mouth in which the teeth are fused to form a parrot-like beak. They are bright blue on the back, shading to light greenish-blue below. Their bodies are covered by a network of thin golden lines and there are ten or more indefinite dark, blotchy vertical lines on the sides. There is a large dark spot behind the mid-point of the dorsal fin.

FISHING TECHNIQUE: Commercial fishermen take small numbers in gill nets for markets in South Australia, Tasmania and Victoria, but they have a fluctuating commercial value. Amateur anglers take them from inshore rocks but their largest catches are out over coastal reefs with weedy bottoms. They grow to 40 cm in length and 800 grams in weight and will bite on cabbage, fresh weed and crustaceans.

DISTRIBUTION: Found from New South Wales around to Western Australia, with the biggest quantities taken in Victoria, South Australia and Tasmania. They are present at the southern end of the Barrier Reef but are overshadowed there by the marvellous array of more appetising and challenging sporting fish.

SUSPECT FISH: Fish known to have caused ciguatera poisoning, now barred from sale in the Brisbane fish market, are: red bass, *Lutjanus bohar*, chinaman fish, *Symphorus nematophorus*, and the paddle-tail, *Lutjanus gibbus*. A number of others are rated as dangerous but not regarded with the same degree of suspicion. These include coral trout, reef cod, surgeon fish, yankee whiting, and Maori wrasse. Not every fish in schools made up of these species is affected. Usually only the very large specimens who live close to reefs for long periods are contaminated.

MAKING YOUR OWN BOBBY CORK: Bobby corks are easy to make from pieces of polystyrene foam. The first step is to roughly shape the bobby cork with a sharp knife, and then pierce the foam at each end with a metal knitting needle, taking care to avoid pushing out chunks of foam with the needle point. A standard power drill will complete the hole through the foam and can be used for sanding the cork to the required shape. Cut a piece of bushing from PVC tubing and glue this bushing into the bore of the bobby cork with Araldite. Load the float with lead wire until it sits vertically in the water. Paint the finished bobby cork in red or orange, using oil-based paints, and finish the job with a coat of clear varnish.

Scientific Index

Page numbers in **bold type** refer to paintings. Page numbers in *italics* refer to photographs.

General Index

Page numbers in **bold type** refer to paintings. Page numbers in *italics* refer to photographs.